THE OFFICIAL

2006

PRICE GUIDE TO
UNITED STATES
POSTAGE
STAMPS

EIGHTH EDITION

BY MARC HUDGEONS, N.L.G.
TOM HUDGEONS JR.,
AND TOM HUDGEONS SR.

"The Scott Catalogue Numbers are used herein
under license from Scott Publishing Co., the
copyright owner. All rights thereto are reserved
under the Pan American and Universal Copyright Conventions."

HOUSE OF COLLECTIBLES
Random House Reference • New York

Copyright © 2005 by Random House, Inc.

This book is available for special discounts for bulk purchases for sales promotions or premiums. Special editions, including personalized covers, excerpts of existing books, and corporate imprints, can be created in large quantities for special needs. For more information, write to Special Markets/Premium Sales, 1745 Broadway, MD 6–2, New York, NY 10019 or e-mail specialmarkets@randomhouse.com

House of Collectibles and colophon are trademarks of Random House, Inc.

Published by: House of Collectibles
Random House Reference
New York, New York

Distributed by Random House Reference, an imprint of Random House, Inc., New York, and simultaneously in Canada by Random House of Canada Limited, Toronto.

www.randomhouse.com

Stamp designs © United States Postal Service

Printed in the United States of America

Buy It • Use It • Become an Expert is a trademark of Random House, Inc.

ISSN: 0195-3559

ISBN: 1-4000-4846-X

10 9 8 7 6 5 4 3 2 1

Twenty-eighth Edition: June 2005

TABLE OF CONTENTS

OFFICIAL BOARD OF CONTRIBUTORS

The author would like to express a special thank-you to:

Robert Lamb, Executive Director, Kim Kowalczyk, Education Director, and Judy Johnson, Membership Director at THE AMERICAN PHILATELIC SOCIETY, State College, PA, 16803, for directory listings,

Michael Laurence and Donna Houseman at LINN'S STAMP NEWS, Sidney, OH 45365, for their article,

Donald Sundman at Mystic Stamp Company, Camden, NY 13316 for their article and pricing information,

Daisy Ridgway, Public Affairs Manager at THE NATIONAL POSTAL MUSEUM, Smithsonian Institution, Washington, D.C, 20560, for articles,

Alex Bereson at UNITED NATIONS PHILATELIST, San Francisco, CA 94131, for his pricing information,

Peter Martin of THE AMERICAN FIRST DAY COVER SOCIETY, P.O. Box 791, State College PA 16804 for his pricing information,

Robert Dumaine of DUCK STAMP COLLECTORS SOCIETY, Houston, TX 77282,

Kelly L. Spinks at THE UNITED STATES POSTAL SERVICE, Washington, D.C., 20260, for permission to reproduce the photography of U.S. stamps. *The designs for the stamps issued from 1978 to date are copyrighted by THE U.S. POSTAL SERVICE and are used with the permission of the U.S. Postal Service.*

NOTE TO READERS

All advertisements appearing in this book have been accepted in good faith, but the publisher assumes no responsibility in any transactions that occur between readers and advertisers.

THE OFFICIAL®

2006
BLACKBOOK
PRICE GUIDE TO
UNITED STATES
POSTAGE
STAMPS

LINN'S LOOK AT THE NEW STAMP ISSUES

by George Amick

In 2004, stamp collectors savored a second consecutive year in which the United States Postal Service held its output of collectible new varieties of stamps and postal stationery to a manageable level. It was manageable, at least, in comparison to some of the excesses of the recent past, such as the record 242 stamps issued in 2002. The total count for 2004 is 145 stamps and postal stationery items, up from the 121 of the year before. The difference is accounted for in part by the unusually high number of postal cards, of which 31 were issued in 2004.

Among the year's 109 stamps are 65 commemoratives. These include a se-tenant pair bearing portraits of explorers Meriwether Lewis and William Clark, in two 10-stamp panes bound in a souvenir booklet celebrating the 200th anniversary of their 1804–06 expedition across the American West.

The Lewis and Clark booklet is the Postal Service's third souvenir booklet, and the first to sell at more than face value.

Collectors and stamp writers complained that they had to spend $8.95 to obtain $7.40 worth of stamps, but postal officials replied that the premium was justified by the value added in the booklet and its illustrated text.

The Postal Service also issued a single 37¢ commemorative in a pane of 20 for the Lewis and Clark expedition—with no price markup. The single sold out at Stamp Fulfillment Services, but the souvenir booklet still is available as of late November.

The designs of all three Lewis and Clark stamps imitate the look of 1920s commemorative stamps, and their frames are printed by intaglio, a recess-printing method that appeals to stamp-collecting traditionalists.

The first of three planned Art of Disney blocks of four stamps depict Mickey Mouse, Donald Duck, and other familiar animated cartoon characters from the Walt Disney Studios.

Each block is to have a specific theme—that of the 2004 stamps is friendship.

1

Although many small stamp-issuing countries have issued Disney-inspired stamps over the years, the company's executives previously had been cold to the idea of allowing Mickey Mouse and his pals to grace U.S. stamps.

The Postal Service's Looney Tunes series, however, helped change Disney's attitude, postal officials said.

The Looney Tunes stamps ran from 1997 to 2001 and promoted Bugs Bunny and other members of the Warner Bros. cartoon ensemble.

The Postal Service accompanied the Disney stamps with a matching set of 23¢ picture postal cards, which happens with many U.S. issues, and with a set of 37¢ letter sheets bearing the imprinted images of the stamps. The letter sheets are new.

The letter sheets sell in packs of 12 for $14.95, more than triple their $4.44 face value, and the protests that followed from collectors and others were even more intense than for the surcharge on the Lewis and Clark souvenir booklet.

Postal advocate Douglas F. Carlson filed a formal complaint with the Postal Rate Commission, charging that the letter sheets are excessively priced. He asked the commission to set a maximum price for them, just as it does for other forms of postal stationery.

In its answer, the Postal Service argued that a Disney letter sheet is "a philatelic and mailing product" of the kind the commission has not regulated in the past and that offers much more quality in terms of paper stock and graphic arts than "the utilitarian stamped envelope." The commission still has not ruled as of late November.

Quality notwithstanding, the Disney letter sheets tend to suffer more damage than ordinary stamped envelopes from processing by automated postal equipment. Linn's Stamp News published photographs of postally used sheets that had been scraped and torn on their way to their recipients. The heavy paper stock apparently is the culprit, causing a sheet to bow out at the middle when folded and sealed, instead of lying flat.

Other highlights among the year's commemorative stamps are a 15-stamp Cloudscapes pane depicting different cloud formations, a 10-stamp Art of the American Indian pane featuring artwork of various Indian tribes, and five black-and-white stamps in a pane of 20 reproducing the sculpture of Isamu Noguchi.

Several ongoing series continued in 2004.

The sixth entry in the Nature of America series, and the first to feature an underwater biome, is the 10-stamp mural-type pane illustrating flora and fauna of a Pacific coral reef.

The stamp, in a double-sided, foldable pane of 20 (what the Postal Service calls a convertible booklet), is part of the American Treasures series. It reproduces Martin Johnson Heade's painting *Giant Magnolias on a Blue Velvet Cloth*.

Black Heritage, the longest-running commemorative series in U.S. history, got its 28th entry with a stamp depicting singer-actor–civil rights activist Paul Robeson, a highly controversial figure because of his outspoken pro-Stalinist views.

Robeson's admirers had lobbied for a stamp marking his 100th birth anniversary in 1998, but their request was vetoed by Postmaster General Marvin Runyon.

The 12th and final Happy New Year stamp commemorated the Year of the Monkey.

John Wayne, who had been waiting in the wings to be on a Legends of Hollywood stamp, finally got his due when Spencer Tracy was bumped from the 2004 schedule because Tracy's estate proved too difficult for the Postal Service to deal with.

The Literary Arts series entry for 2004 is a stamp for author James Baldwin.

A block of four commemoratives depict noted American choreographers. Single-design stamps honor other prominent figures in popular culture: playwright and director Moss Hart, children's author Dr. Seuss and film composer Henry Mancini.

A stamp for R. Buckminster Fuller reproduces a famous 1964 *Time* magazine cover that depicts the innovator's head in the pattern of his signature invention, the geodesic dome.

The Postal Service continued its tradition of public-health message stamps with a single 37¢ stamp urging early detection of sickle cell anemia.

Other single-design stamps mark the 50th anniversary of the U.S. Air Force Academy and the opening of the National World War II Memorial on the Mall in Washington, D.C.

The sesquicentennial of *USS Constellation,* the U.S. Navy's last all-sail warship, was marked with an all-intaglio, monochrome commemorative.

Differences between the Postal Service and the International Olympic Committee over stamp designs and other issues that led to a U.S. stamp boycott of the 2000 Summer Olympic Games were laid to rest, and a U.S. commemorative was issued for the 2004 Summer Games in Athens.

Among the year's 22 special stamps are a 37¢ stamp and a 60¢ stamp that the Postal Service intends for use on wedding invitations (the 60¢ stamp) and on accompanying reply envelopes (the 37¢ stamp).

In the past, couples have used Love stamps for the 1-ounce and 2-ounce denominations to mail invitations, but brides and their mothers have been dissatisfied with some of the designs, particularly the 37¢ and 60¢ Stylized Love stamps of 2002 with their extremely graphic looks. As a result, the Citizens' Stamp Advisory Committee recommended a special set of stamps for wedding invitations, with the designs changing every other year.

The garden flowers depicted on the 2004 wedding set "remind us of the traditional bouquet toss that's a treasured part of many wedding ceremonies," the Postal Service said.

The issuance of Hanukkah and Kwanzaa stamps in new designs represent a change of heart for the Postal Service, which had announced in 2001 that the 34¢ We Give Thanks stamp of that year would be the last new design in the Holiday Celebrations series.

The original Hanukkah and Kwanzaa designs appeared in 1996 and 1997, respectively, and they were recycled three times with new denominations to cover increases in the first-class rate.

The number of definitive (regular-issue) stamps, 23, is low in 2004 because there was no rate change, an event that causes new stamps featuring flags and other patriotic icons to pour off the presses of the Postal Service's contract printers.

Most of the year's definitives are repeats of previously used designs, including the new water-activated nondenominated (25¢) American Eagle service-inscribed coil stamps in 10 color variations.

Only three new designs appeared: new low-denomination stamps in the American Design series that depict a Chippendale chair (4¢ stamp) and a Navajo necklace (2¢), and two 23¢ Distinguished Americans stamps honoring track star Wilma Rudolph. There is only one Rudolph design, but the three formats result in two stamps.

In 2004, the Postal Service again offered collectors selected commemorative stamps as uncut press sheets. Four issues were made available in that form: Pacific Coral Reef, John Wayne, Isamu Noguchi, and the Lewis and Clark sheet stamp.

Two stamps, 37¢ U.S. Air Force Academy and 37¢ National World War II Memorial, incorporate a hidden image of the kind that can be seen only with a special acrylic decoder lens sold by the Postal Service's Stamp Fulfillment Services office.

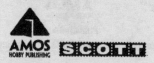

MARKET REVIEW

by Donald Sundman

The U.S. stamp market has been consistent for several years. Overall, there was modest growth in 2004. However, demand for classic, older stamps—especially in premium conditions—has continued to rise steadily. Nineteenth-century U.S. stamps remain difficult to acquire. This is especially true of rare, very high quality, and famous stamps.

The market for old and rare stamps is becoming more competitive for several reasons. There's been an influx of newly wealthy collectors to the hobby. Additionally, many Baby Boomers now have more disposable income. Although these folks are not necessarily wealthy, they're experiencing new levels of financial security and are able to indulge their interests like never before.

As prices are driven higher at the top of the stamp market, all stamp prices have a tendency to rise. So I see this as a positive trend. Our hobby can only benefit from the increased attention brought about from an active high-end market. That said, there are a lot of bargains to be had in the low- to mid-priced sectors of the market. Many U.S. stamps many currently be undervalued. Supplies of many modern U.S. commemoratives are surprisingly low. If you're building a collection of U.S. stamps, now is a great time to be buying.

One of the biggest stories of 2004 was the prestigious Royal Philatelic Society of London's ruling that the legendary Grinnell Missionaries are indeed counterfeits. However, in providing its explanation the Royal actually disproved many of the reasons previously cited for declaring the stamps forgeries. The owners of the remaining Grinnell Missionaries maintain that their evidence proves the stamps are genuine and have vowed to use this new information from the Royal to further investigate the origins of the stamps.

In the beginning of 2004, the National Postal Museum announced its plans to sell a portion of its large holding of 20th Century U.S. Revenue stamps and destroy the remainder. Many collectors were upset by the idea of a museum destroying stamps. As a result, the museum decided to sell many more of the revenue stamps than originally planned.

In 2004, one of our hobby's oldest publications, *Stamp Collector*, ceased publication. Overall, subscriptions to philatelic publications have been declining for years. More and more collectors are receiving their information from the Internet. And with the growth of the World Wide Web, this trend will surely continue.

The Universal Postal Union, or UPU, is continuing its fight against illegal stamps. More and more, stamp-like labels, sometimes called "Cinderellas," are appearing on the stamp market. These labels often have no tie to the nations whose names they bear. The UPU has created lists of illegal stamps, which can easily be found on the Internet.

In 2004, the USPS issued the Lewis and Clark souvenir booklet and Art of Disney letter sheets for more than face value. In the case of the Lewis and Clark souvenir booklet, the USPS justified the additional charge by claiming the text and pictures in the booklet added substantial value. However, the USPS claimed the additional charge for the Disney letter sheets were directly related to production costs.

In summary, the U.S. stamp market is in good shape. Demand for scarce, old U.S. stamps, especially those of high quality, continues to grow. Rarities are fetching high prices. And new philatelic research, such as that conducted by the Royal Philatelic Society of London on the Grinnell Missionaries, is attracting a great deal of attention to our hobby.

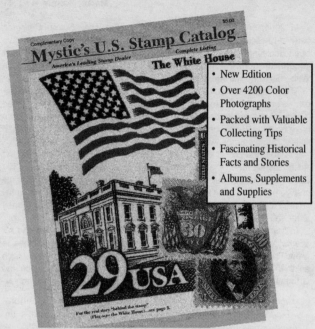

Yours Free – Mystic's New U.S. Stamp Catalog

A free copy of America's best U.S. stamp catalog is waiting for you. Enjoy 128 pages of color photographs, valuable collecting tips, fascinating history and more. Collectors agree, a catalog like this is worth its weight in gold, but we'll send yours Free!

Send today for Mystic's Free 128-page catalog and also receive other stamp offers on approval.

Mail your name and address to:

Mystic Stamp Company, Dept. SC215
9700 Mill Street, Camden, New York 13316-6109

Or call toll free 1-800-433-7811 and give Customer Service the department number listed above.

250 Mint Mexico Stamps
For Just $5 – SAVE $10.00!

Get this collection of 250 mint Mexico stamps for just $5 – you SAVE over 65% off the retail price.

With these 250 mint Mexico stamps you'll gain an insider's perspective of Mexican history and culture. Discover revolutionary leaders, cultural events and more. For just $5, here's an affordable way to start a new collection.

Send today and also receive special collector's information along with other interesting offers on approval. Your satisfaction is guaranteed. Limit one at this special price, please.

HOW TO USE THIS BOOK

The main section of this book lists U.S. postage stamps with the exception of special issues such as airmail, revenues, etc. Special issues are grouped separately in sections of their own. Please refer to the Table of Contents.

Identification. Illustrations appear together with stamps. In some cases, two or more stamp issues are similar in appearance, but differ only in minor details, such a watermark or gauge of perforation. They are known as face-identical stamps. Listings of face-identical stamps subsequent to the first variety are cross-referenced to the initial listing and its illustration by use of a tilde and the initial catalogue number in parentheses, e.g. Scott number 18 (~5), which indicates that stamp No. 18 possesses the same design as No. 5.

The denomination and a description are given for each stamp. Denominations for non-denominated stamps are given in parentheses, e.g. (15¢) "A" & Eagle.

The type of gum (water activated or self-adhesive) is given only where necessary to distinguish two similar issues.

Prices. Prices are given in columns for unused and used examples, in the median grade of fine to very fine (F-VF). Those of higher quality sell for more; those of lesser quality sell for less. Stamps with faults or defects are worth only a small fraction of catalogue value.

Prices shown are intended to be actual retail selling prices, however, be aware that prices vary with the market and from dealer to dealer. A dash (—) in place of a price indicates that the item is either seldom available or that it does not exist in the form indicated. It should not be assumed, however, that such items are invariably more valuable than those for which prices are shown.

Prices for unused stamps issued before 1935 are for hinged examples Never hinged examples sell for more. The never hinged premium appears in parentheses where applicable, e.g. (NH add 50%). Prices for unused stamps issued after 1935 are for never-hinged (NH) examples. Stated values are a general guide and do not reflect the price of the occasional superb example, such as an early imperforate with four wide margins.

A minimum price of 14¢ has been assigned to the most common stamps, such as those that you might receive on everyday mail. The minimum price reflects the labor incurred by a stamp dealer when filling an order for an individual example, should one be requested. Common stamps can be obtained in packets and bulk mixtures for much less than the listed minimum price.

No prices are given from multiples of used self-adhesive se-tenants, because once the stamps have been removed from their backing paper they cannot be reattached to form a multiple.

A box is provided to the left of each listing for keeping a record of the stamps in your collection.

Plate Blocks. Prices for plate blocks appear in the column headed "Plate Block." Prices for plate blocks of se-tenant issues appear on the line describing the se-tenant multiple under the heading "Plate Block." Plate blocks are assumed to be blocks of four unless otherwise indicated. When the number of stamps is greater than four, it is shown in parentheses following the price of the plate block.

Line Pairs and Plate Number Coil (PNC) Strips. Prices for line pairs are given in the column headed "Line Pair." Prices for plate number coil strips are given in the column headed "PNC Strip (5)". The numeral "5" in parentheses indicates that the price is for a strip of 5 stamps with the plate number located on the center stamp. The standard length for collecting PNC strips is five stamps, although both longer and shorter strips are sometimes collected. In many cases, prices for longer or shorter strips vary only slightly from those for strips of 5; however, some shorter strips (especially early PNCs) are significantly less valuable than strips of five. Check with a dealer active with PNCs for up-to-the-minute prices.

Mint Sheets. Mints sheets are priced in a separate section following the section for stamps.

Se-tenant Stamps. Listings indicate the minimum number of stamps necessary in each instance for a complete se-tenant multiple (block or strip). It is often possible to obtain blocks or strips containing all the designs necessary for a complete multiple but in an order or sequence other than that listed. Only in those cases where the listed sequence is necessary to form a larger design (e.g. No. 1331-32, the Space Twins issue), is the exact order crucial. In all other cases, it is okay to collect se-tenants in whatever order the individual stamps may occur. Some se-tenants can be collected either as blocks or strips; they are indicated in the listings.

HOW TO GRADE STAMPS

A person need not be an expert to judge the quality or grade of a stamp. All he needs is a discerning eye, possibly a small linear measuring device, and the grading instructions listed below.

The major catalogs traditionally list stamps simply as "Unused" or "Used." Auction houses, however, will describe the stamps for sale in a more informative manner. The greater the value of the stamp, the more thoroughly it is described.

There is no officially accepted system of grading stamps. What we have done in this book is essentially to set up a system of grading stamps using the suggestions and practices of stamp dealers from all over the country. Total agreement was made to the following categories and grades of stamps that are most frequently traded.

CATEGORIES

Mint—The perfect stamp with superb centering, no faults, and usually with original gum (if issued with gum).

Unused—Although unused, this stamp may have a hinge mark or may have suffered some change in its gum since it was issued.

Used—Basically this will be the normal stamp that passed through the government postal system and will bear an appropriate cancellation.

Cancelled to Order—These are stamps that have not passed through the postal system but have been carefully cancelled by the government usually for a commemoration. These are generally considered undesirable by collectors.

GRADE—STAMP CENTERING

Average—The perforations cut slightly into the design.

Fine—The perforations do not touch the design at all, but the design will be off center by 50 percent or more of a superb centered stamp.

Very Fine—The design will be off center by less than 50 percent of a superb stamp. The off-centered design will be visibly noticeable.

Extra Fine—The design will be almost perfectly centered. The margin will be off by less than 25 percent of a superb stamp.

Superb—This design will be perfectly centered with all four margins exactly the same. On early imperforate issues, superb specimens will have four clear margins that do not touch the design at any point.

GRADE—STAMP GUM

Original Gum—This stamp will have the same gum on it that it had the day it was issued.

Regummed—This stamp will have new gum applied to it as compared to an original gummed stamp. Regummed stamps are worth no more than those with gum missing.

No Gum—This stamp will have had its gum removed or it may have not been issued with gum.

Never Hinged—This stamp has never been hinged so the gum should not have been disturbed in any way.

Lightly Hinged—This stamp has had a hinge applied. A lightly wetted or peelable hinge would do very little damage to the gum when removed.

Heavily Hinged—This stamp has had a hinge applied in such a manner as to secure it to the stamp extremely well. Removal of this hinge usually proves to be disastrous, in most cases, since either part of the hinge remains on the stamp or part of the stamp comes off on the hinge, causing thin spots on the stamp.

GRADE—STAMP FAULTS

Any fault in a stamp such as thin paper, bad perforations, creases, tears, stains, ink marks, pin holes, etc., and depending upon the seriousness of the fault, usually results in grading the stamp to a lower condition.

OTHER STAMP CONSIDERATIONS

CANCELLATIONS

Light Cancel—This stamp has been postally cancelled but the wording and lines are very light and almost unreadable.

Normal Cancel—This stamp has been postally cancelled with just the right amount of pressure. Usually the wording and lines are not distorted and can be made out.

Heavy Cancel—This stamp has been postally cancelled. In the process excessive pressure was used, and the wording and lines are extremely dark and sometimes smeared and in most cases unreadable.

PERFORATIONS

Not to be overlooked in the appearance of a stamp are its perforations. The philatelist might examine these "tear apart" holes with a magnifying glass or microscope to determine the cleanliness of the separations. One must also consider that the different types of paper, upon which the stamp was printed, will sometimes make a difference in the cleanliness of the separations. The term "pulled perf" is used to denote a badly separated stamp in which the perforations are torn or ragged.

COLOR

Other important factors such as color affect the appearance and value of stamps. An expert will have a chart of stamp colors. Chemical changes often occur in inks. Modern printing sometimes uses metallic inks. These "printings" will oxidize upon contact with the natural secretions from human skin.

In some cases, the color of a stamp is deliberately altered by chemicals to produce a rare shade. Overprints can be eliminated. Postmarks may be eradicated. Replacing gum is a simple process. Some stamps have been found to bear forged watermarks. The back of the paper was cut away and then the stamps rebacked with appropriately watermarked paper.

There are stamp experts who earn a living in the business of stamp repairing. They are craftsmen of the first order. A thin spot on a stamp can be repaired by gluing it on a new layer of paper. Missing perforations can be added. Torn stamps can be put back together. Pieces of stamps may be joined.

In some countries it is accepted practice for an expert, upon examination of a stamp, to certify the authenticity by affixing his signature to the back of the stamp. If the stamp is not genuine, it is his right and duty to so designate on the stamp, but these signatures can also be faked.

FACTORS THAT DETERMINE STAMP VALUES

The collector value (or "market value") of any stamp rests with a variety of factors. Philately becomes a bit less mysterious when one understands the forces at work in the stamp marketplace.

A beginner often assumes that expensive stamps are expensive because of rarity. Certainly there is a great deal of talk about stamp rarities within the hobby, and so it is natural enough to ascribe high prices to the phenomenon of rarity. In fact, rarity is only one of several factors that influence stamp prices, and the influence it carries is not particularly clear-cut.

In this book you will note some stamps (mostly among the early regular issues) with values of $1,000, $2,000, and even higher. Obviously these stamps are rarer than those selling for $10 or $15. But having said that, we have virtually summed up our useful knowledge of rarity and its effect on prices. A comparison of prices, between stamps in roughly similar ranges of value, does not indicate which is the rarer. A stamp selling for $1,000 is not necessarily rarer than one selling for $500. A $10,000 stamp may actually be more abundant than one which commands $5,000. This hard-to-comprehend fact of philatelic life prevails because of the other factors involved in determining a stamp's price. If rarity were the only factor, one could, of course, easily see which stamps are the rarest by the prices they fetch.

The word "rare" is an elixir to many collectors, not only of stamps but other collectors' items. Sellers are well aware of this, and seldom fail to sprinkle the word liberally in their sales literature. There is no law against calling a stamp rare, as this represents a personal opinion more than anything else and opinions are allowable in advertising. Unfortunately, there is no standard definition for rarity. Does "rare" mean just a handful of specimens in existence, with one reaching the sales portals once in five years? Does it mean 100 in existence, or 1,000, or some other number? Since stamps are—today, at any rate—printed in the multimillions, a thousand surviving specimens might seem a very tiny total to some people. Further complicating this situation is the fact that the specific rarity of most stamps cannot be determined, or even estimated, with any hope of accuracy. The quantities printed are recorded for most of our stamps, going back even into the nineteenth century, but the quantity surviving of any particular stamp is anyone's guess. It is obvious that a stamp that goes through the auction rooms once a year is fairly rare, but this provides no sound basis for guessing the number of specimens in existence. That could only be accomplished if some sort of grand census could be taken, and all specimens tallied. This, of course, is nothing but a pipe dream. Some collectors would not participate in such a census; some might be unaware that it was being conducted. Then, too, there are many scarce or rare stamps in hands other than those of collectors, such as dealers and museums. Additionally, there could be (and probably are) existing specimens of rare stamps yet to be discovered, as fresh discoveries are made periodically in the hobby through attic cleaning and the like.

In terms of influence on price, rarity is outdistanced somewhat by popularity. Some stamps, for one reason or other, are simply more popular than others. They have a sort of innate appeal for hobbyists, either through reputation, exquisite designing, circumstances of issue, oddity, or various other potential reasons. These stamps sell out rapidly from the stocks of dealers, while some stamps that are supposedly scarcer will linger in stock albums for ages and ages waiting to tempt a customer. It is no wonder, then, that the prices of popular stamps rise more quickly than those that are scarce but not in brisk demand. The Columbian series typifies the effect of popularity on stamp values. If stamp prices were fixed by scarcity alone, none of the Columbians would be selling for nearly as much. Much of their value derives from their overwhelming popularity with collectors of U.S. stamps. It would be safe to say, in fact, that all of the Columbians from the lowest face value to the $5, are more plentiful than other U.S. stamps selling for precisely the same sums. Every dealer has Columbians in stock, and quite a few dealers have the high value of the set, too. They are not "hard to get." But they are very costly.

Popularity, of course, does not remain constant forever. There are shifts in philatelic popularity, usually slight but occasionally extreme. The popularity of commemoratives as a whole versus regular issues as a whole can change from time to time. Then, too, there are swings of popularity for airmails, first-day covers, blocks, coil pairs, mint sheets, and all other philatelic material. A climb or decline in the price of any philatelic item is often an indication of the forces of popularity at work. Then there are activities of investors to consider, whose buying habits seldom reflect those of the pure collector. A great deal of buying by investors in any short period of time (such as occurred during 1979 and 1980, and to less extent in 1981) can make prices seem well out of balance.

Also on the subject of prices, it is important for the beginner to realize that arithmetic is usually futile when dealing with stamp values. You cannot determine the price of one philatelic item by knowing the value of a similar one. This can best be shown by the relative values of singles and blocks of four. A block of four is, as one would expect, worth more than four times as much as single specimens of that stamp. It is not just four specimens of the stamp, but four of them attached, which lends added scarcity and appeal. The difficulty lies in trying to use mathematics to determine a block's value. Some blocks are worth five times as much as the single stamp; some six times; some ten times as much or even more. Almost all blocks—except very common ones—will vary somewhat in value, in relation to the value of the individual stamp. There is no satisfactory explanation for this, other than the presumption that some blocks are scarcer than others or just in greater demand than others.

In the case of common philatelic items, the value hinges greatly on the method of sale. If you want to buy one specimen of a common cover, you may have to pay $1.50. But if you were willing to buy a hundred common first-day covers of the dealer's choice, you could very likely get them for $75, or 75¢ each. Buying in quantity, and allowing the dealer to make the selections, can save a great deal of money. Of course one may then ask: What is the real value of those covers? Is it $1.50 or 75¢? The only answer is that it depends on how you buy!

If this article seems to raise a great many questions without supplying many answers, it will, hopefully, serve to show that stamp collecting is not bound to rigid formulas. What happens in the stamp market is largely beyond prediction, or precise explanation. This, indeed, is one of the exciting aspects of the hobby.

REPAIRS, FAKES, AND OTHER UNDESIRABLES

Philately, like most hobbies, is not without its pitfalls. The collector who buys from reputable dealers runs very little risk, as today's stamp pros have high principles and are hard to fool. Buying from auction sales and small dealers, who may not have expert knowledge, is another matter. Here the collector must call into play his own expertise and learn to distinguish the bad from the good.

In the early years of philately, stamps provided a playground for fakers and swindlers. They took advantage of the public's gullibility and the general lack of published information about stamps. Copies were printed of rare stamps, as well as of stamps that never existed in the first place. Cancels were bleached from used specimens to make them appear unused. Fake margins were added to imperforates, to allow ordinary copies to be sold as "superb with jumbo margins." Perforated stamps were reperforated to make them better centered. Thin spots in the paper were filled in, tears closed, missing portions of paper replaced. Stamps were doctored and manipulated in more ways than could be imagined, all in the hope of fooling collectors and making anywhere from a few extra cents to thousands of dollars on them. One of the favorite tricks of fakers was to apply bogus overprints or surcharges. By merely using a rubber handstamp and a pad of ink, they could stamp out a hundred or more "rarities" in a few minutes, turning ordinary British or other issues into varieties not found in any catalog. It was all a great game and proved very profitable, until collectors and the philatelic public at large became wary of such practices. Even though most of these fakes from the hobby's pioneer years have disappeared out of circulation, a few still turn up and must be guarded against.

U.S. stamps have not been faked nearly so extensively as those of many other nations, notably South America and Japan. Still, the collector should learn to watch for fakes and also for repaired specimens.

Total Fake. The counterfeit stamp always varies somewhat from a genuine specimen, though the difference may be very slight. Detection can usually be made if the suspect stamp is examined alongside one known to be genuine. By using a magnifier, the lines of engraving and paper quality can be compared. The ink on a fake is likely to have a fresher appearance and will lie on the surface as a result of being printed at a later date and on less sophisticated equipment; however, this is not always the case. Experts say that when a stamp appears to be a fake, or a reprint, the odds are very good that it is. Some experience is necessary before anyone can get a first-glance reaction to a stamp. The presence or absence of a cancel has no bearing on the likelihood of a stamp being a fake, as cancels can be faked, too.

Faked Cancel. Faked cancels are very rare on U.S. stamps, as nearly all are worth more unused than used. One notable exception is the 90¢, 1857–1861. These are applied either with a fake hand stamp or simply drawn with pen and ink. Skillfully drawn faked cancels can be very deceptive. Faked cancels are much more numerous on covers than loose stamps.

Removed Cancels. So-called cleaned copies of used stamps, sold as unused, were once very plentiful and are still encountered from time to time. The faker, of course, chooses lightly cancelled specimens from which the obliteration can be removed without leaving telltale evidence. In the case of imperforates he may trim down the margins to remove part of the cancel. Rarely will he attempt to clean a stamp whose cancel falls across the face or any important portion of the stamp. Holding the stamp to a strong light may reveal the cancel lines. X-ray examination provides positive proof.

Added Margin(s). When margins have been added to an imperforate stamp, the paper fibers are woven together (after moistening) along the back and at the front where the margin extends beyond the stamp's design. They can usually be detected by looking closely for a seam or joint at the point where the design ends and the margin begins. A magnifying glass will be necessary for this. When held against a light, the reverse side will probably show evidence of the weaving operation. Sometimes the added margins are of a slightly different grade of paper.

Reperforated. A stamp that has been reperforated to improve its centering will usually be slightly smaller than a normal specimen, and this can be revealed by placing it atop an untampered copy.

Filled Thin Spots. If held to a light and examined with a good magnifier, filled-in thin spots will normally appear darker than the remainder of the stamp. Such spots are often mistaken for discoloration by beginners. Thin spots are filled in by making a paste of paper pulp and glue and applying it gradually to the injured area. After drying, the stamp is placed in a vise so that no telltale hills or valleys are left. This is not really considered forgery but honest repair work; it becomes forgery only if done with the intent of selling the stamp as undamaged.

Closed Tears. These are almost always visible against a light with a magnifier, even if small. A routine examination of any rare stamp should include a check of its margins for possible closed or open tears.

Type Identifier

Types of the 1¢ Franklin 1851–1860.

Type I   Type Ia

Type I. The scrollwork on all sides is complete. The curved lines at top and bottom are complete and unbroken. The curls at the bottom scrollwork are complete.

Type Ia. Similar to Type I at bottom, but the line at the top of the inscription is cut away as are the tops of the ornaments.

Type Ib. Similar to Type I at top, but at bottom the curved line below the denomination is partly cut away and the scrollwork is not as complete. (Not illustrated.)

Type II   Type III

Type II. The curls and plumes of the bottom ornaments are incomplete. The curved line below the denomination is complete, as are the side ornaments.

Type III. The center portions of the curved lines at both top and bottom are incomplete. Side ornaments are intact.

Type IIIa. Similar to Type III, but only one of the curved lines, either top or bottom, has been cut away. (Not illustrated.)

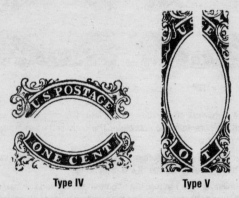

Type IV   Type V

Type IV. Similar to Type II, but the curved lines at either top or bottom (or both) are complete and more pronounced, having been reworked.

Type V. Similar to Type III, but the side ornaments are partially cut away.

Types of the 3¢ Washington of 1851–1860 (Scott Nos. 10, 11, 26, 26a, and 41).

Type I. The frame line is complete all around the design.

Type II. No horizontal frame lines along the top and bottom of stamps. Vertical frames at sides, however, are unbroken and continuous.

Type IIa. Similar to Type II except vertical frame lines break between stamps.

Types the 5¢ Jefferson of 1851–1860 (Scott Nos. 12, 27, 28, 28A, 29, 30, 30A and 42).

Type I. The projections at top, bottom and sides are complete.

Type II. The projections at top and bottom are cut away.

Types of the 10¢ Washington of 1851–1860 (Scott Nos. 13, 14, 15, 16, 31, 32, 33, 34, 35 and 43).

Type I. The shells at the lower corners are almost complete. The outer line below the inscription "Ten Cents" is nearly complete. The outer lines at top above "U.S. Postage" and letters "X" at each corner are not complete.

Type II. The outer lines at top above "U.S. Postage" and letters "X" at each corner are complete. The outer line below the inscription "Ten Cents" is broken. The shells at the lower corners are partially cut away.

Type III. The outer lines of the inscriptions at both top and bottom are broken. The outer lines above the letters "X" at top are broken and the shells at the lower corners are partially cut away.

Type IV. The outer lines of the inscriptions at both top and bottom have been recut and appear more pronounced.

Type V. One or two of the three small "pearls" that appear at the sides on the lower part of the design have been cut away. The outer line atop the letter "X" at top right has been cut away.

Secret Marks on the Banknote Issues.

1¢. The secret mark is contained in the ball just to the left of the top of the numeral "1."

2¢. The secret mark is a small diagonal line beneath the scroll above and to left of the letters "U.S."

3¢. The secret mark is additional heavy shading in the ribbon below the letters "R.E."

6¢. The secret mark is additional heavy shading of the four vertical lines in the lower left ribbon.

7¢. The secret mark is two semicircles added to the ball ornament at lower right.

10¢. The secret mark is a small semicircle added to the pendant ball at the right end of the denomination tablet.

12¢. The secret mark is the addition of two balls to the numeral "2."

15¢. The secret mark is the strengthening of lines at the "v" at the top left triangle.

Types of the 2¢ Washington of 1894–1898 (Scott Nos. 249, 250, 251, 252, 265, 266 and 267).

| Type I | Type II | Type III |

Type I. Horizontal lines across the triangles at top are of the same thickness throughout.

Type II. Horizontal lines are thin inside the triangles.

Type III. The double frame of the triangles do not contain any lines.

Types of the $1 Perry of 1894–1895 (Scott Nos. 261, 261A, 276 and 276A).

| Type I | Type II |

Type I. Circles around the numeral in the lower corners are broken.

Type II. Circles around the numeral in the lower corners are complete.

Types of the 10¢ Webster of 1898 (Scott Nos. 282C and 283).

Type I   Type II

Type I. Circles around the numerals in the lower corners are complete.

Type II. Circles around the numerals in the lower corners are broken.

Types of the 2¢ Washington of 1912–1920.

Type I   Type II

Type I. The tip of the left ribbon contains a single vertical mark. The second curve in the right ribbon contains a single vertical mark. The top line of the toga is faint. Shading lines on the face that terminate at the ear are not joined. Type I occurs on both flat plate and rotary press printings.

Type Ia. Similar to Type I except that the lines atop the toga and toga button are heavy. (Not illustrated).

Type II. Vertical marks in the ribbons are the same as Type I. The line atop the toga and toga button are heavy. A pronounced vertical line joins the shading lines on the face that terminate at the ear. Type II occurs only on rotary press printings.

Type III

Type IV

Type III. Similar to Type II except that the ribbons contain two vertical marks instead of one. Type III occurs only on rotary press printings.

Type IV. The top line of the toga is broken. The lines inside the button for the letters "Ɔ I D."

Type V

Type Va

Type V. The toga button contains five vertical lines. The top line of the toga is complete. The nose is shaded as illustrated. Type V occurs only on offset printings.

Type Va. Similar to Type V except that the third row of dots from the bottom on the nose contains only four dots rather than six dots. Type Va occurs only on offset printings.

Type VI   **Type VII**

Type VI. Similar to Type V except that the line of shading in the numeral "2" at left is extremely pronounced. Type VI occurs only on offset printings.

Type VII. Contains three vertical rows of dots below the nose. Additional dots of shading have been added to the hair at the top of Washington's head. Type VII occurs only on offset printings.

Types of the 3¢ Washington of 1912–1920.

Type I   **Type II**

Type I. The top of the toga line is weak. The fifth shading line of the toga is partly cut away. The line between the lips is thin. Type I occurs on both flat plate and rotary press printings.

Type II. The top line of the toga is complete and heavy as are the shading lines that join it. Type II occurs on both flat plate and rotary press printings.

Type III   **Type IV**

Type III. Similar to Type II except that the fifth shading line from the left is missing. The letters "P" and "O" in the inscription "Postage" are separated. Type III occurs only on offset printings.

Type IV. Similar to Type III except that the vertical line in the center of the button is a single unbroken vertical line. The letters "P" and "O" in the inscription "Postage" are joined. Type IV occurs only on offset printings.

Types of the 2¢ Washington of 1922 (Scott Nos. 599 and 599A).

Type III   **Type IV**

Type I. Contains thin hair lines atop the head.

Type II. Contains heavy hair lines atop the head.

Watermarks.

USPS

Double Line Watermark

USPS

Single Line Watermark

GENERAL ISSUE

Pricing Note: Prices for unused stamps issued before 1890 are for examples without original gum. Examples with original gum command a premium, which can amount to as much as 50 percent or more. Beware regummed examples. Prices are for sound stamps. Those with faults or defects sell for much less.

1
(3)

2
(4)

Scott No.			Unused	Used
1847.				
❑ 1	5¢	Red Brown	2400.00	500.00
❑ 2	10¢	Black	—	710.00

1875. Reproductions of the 1847 Issue, Issued without Gum.

❑ 3	5¢	Red Brown (~1)	700.00	—
❑ 4	10¢	Black (~2)	900.00	—

NOTE: On originals of the 5¢, the white shirt frill falls well below the top of the numeral "5." On reproductions, the top white shirt frill is even with the top of numeral "5." On originals of the 10¢, the left vertical line of Washington's collar falls below the top of the letter "X." On reproductions, it falls above the top of the "X."

5
(5A, 6, 7, 8, 8A, 9, 18, 19, 20, 21, 22, 23, 24, 40)

1851–1856. Imperforate.

❑ 5	1¢	Blue (~5) (type I)		
❑ 5A	1¢	Blue (~5) (type Ib)	5000.00	3800.00
❑ 6	1¢	Blue (~5) (type Ia)	8200.00	5000.00

10	**12**	**13**	**17**
(11, 25, 26, 26a, 41)	(27, 28, 28A, 29, 30, 30A, 42)	(14, 15, 16, 31, 32, 33, 34, 35, 43)	(36, 36b, 44)

Scott No.			Unused	Used
❏ 7	1¢	Blue (~5) (type II)	600.00	160.00
❏ 8	1¢	Blue (~5) (type III)	3000.00	1800.00
❏ 8A	1¢	Blue (~5) (type IIIa)	2500.00	740.00
❏ 9	1¢	Blue (~5) (type IV)	350.00	100.00
❏ 10	3¢	Orange Brown (type I)	1400.00	87.00
❏ 11	3¢	Dull Red (~10) (type I)	100.00	9.50
❏ 12	5¢	Red Brown (type I)	1000.00	700.00
❏ 13	10¢	Green (type I)	800.00	400.00
❏ 14	10¢	Green (~13) (type II)	1600.00	230.00
❏ 15	10¢	Green (~13) (type III)	1800.00	200.00
❏ 16	10¢	Green (~13) (type IV)	1200.00	900.00
❏ 17	12¢	Black	2000.00	310.00

1857–1861. Same Designs as the 1851–1856 Issue, Perforated 15.

❏ 18	1¢	Blue (~5) (type I)	800.00	510.00
❏ 19	1¢	Blue (~5) (type Ia)	6000.00	450.00
❏ 20	1¢	Blue (~5) (type II)	500.00	225.00
❏ 21	1¢	Blue (~5) (type III)	1600.00	1200.00
❏ 22	1¢	Blue (~5) (type IIIa)	900.00	410.00
❏ 23	1¢	Blue (~5) (type IV)	4000.00	600.00
❏ 24	1¢	Blue (~5) (type V)	95.00	40.00
❏ 25	3¢	Rose (~10) (type I)	1150.00	90.00
❏ 26	3¢	Dull Red (~10) (type II)	50.00	7.10
❏ 26a	3¢	Dull Red (~10) (type IIa)	125.00	60.00
❏ 27	5¢	Brick Red (~10) (type I)	11100.00	1210.00

NOTE: Refer to the Type Identifier for information on types.

37	**38**	**39**
(45)	(46)	(47)

Scott No.			Unused	Used
❏ 28	5¢	Red Brown (~12) (type I)	2100.00	740.00
❏ 28A	5¢	Indian Red (~12) (type I)	2600.00	1600.00
❏ 29	5¢	Brown (~12) (type I)	1100.00	300.00
❏ 30	5¢	Orange Brown (~12) (type II)	900.00	800.00
❏ 30A	5¢	Brown (~12) (type II)	600.00	280.00
❏ 31	10¢	Green (~13) (type I)	7400.00	800.00
❏ 32	10¢	Green (~13) (type II)	2100.00	260.00
❏ 33	10¢	Green (~13) (type III)	2200.00	210.00
❏ 34	10¢	Green (~13) (type IV)	1600.00	900.00
❏ 35	10¢	Green (~13) (type IV)	150.00	75.00
❏ 36	12¢	Black (~17) (type I)	600.00	250.00
❏ 36b	12¢	Black (~17) (type II)	400.00	160.00
❏ 37	24¢	Gray Lilac	600.00	200.00
❏ 38	30¢	Orange	750.00	340.00
❏ 39	90¢	Blue	1600.00	—

1875. Reprints of the 1857–1861 Issue, Perforated 12, Issued without Gum.

❏ 40	1¢	Bright Blue (~5)	550.00	—
❏ 41	3¢	Scarlet (~10)	2700.00	—
❏ 42	5¢	Orange Brown (~12)	1100.00	—
❏ 43	10¢	Blue Green (~13)	2400.00	—
❏ 44	12¢	Greenish Black (~17)	2700.00	—
❏ 45	24¢	Blackish Violet (~37)	1900.00	—
❏ 46	30¢	Yellow Orange (~38)	3100.00	—
❏ 47	90¢	Deep Blue (~39)	4200.00	—

NOTE: Refer to the Type Identifier for information on types.

63
(63b, 86,
92, 102)

64
(64b, 65, 66, 79, 83,
85, 85C, 88, 94, 104)

67
(75, 76,
95, 105)

68
(62B, 89, 96,
106)

69
(85E, 90,
97, 107)

70
(70b, 70c, 78,
99, 109)

71
(100, 110)

72
(101, 111)

Scott No.			Unused	Used
1861. Perforated 12.				
❑ 62B	10¢	Dark Green (~68)	2800.00	900.00
1861–1862.				
❑ 63	1¢	Blue	160.00	28.00
❑ 63B	1¢	Dark Blue	250.00	90.00
❑ 64	3¢	Pink	3800.00	680.00
❑ 64B	3¢	Rose Pink	260.00	110.00
❑ 65	3¢	Rose	75.00	2.80
❑ 66	3¢	Lake	—	—
❑ 67	5¢	Buff	800.00	630.00
❑ 68	10¢	Yellow Green	350.00	45.00
❑ 69	12¢	Black	610.00	82.00
❑ 70	24¢	Red Lilac	900.00	165.00
❑ 70b	24¢	Steel Blue	3600.00	690.00
❑ 70c	24¢	Violet	5000.00	1000.00
❑ 71	30¢	Orange	710.00	150.00
❑ 72	90¢	Blue	1275.00	360.00

73
(84, 85B, 87, 93, 103)

77
(91, 98, 108)

Scott No.			Unused	Used
1861–1866. New Values or New Colors.				
❑ 73	2¢	Black	160.00	50.00
❑ 75	5¢	Red Brown (~67)	1900.00	385.00
❑ 76	5¢	Brown (~67)	700.00	110.00
❑ 77	15¢	Black	875.00	130.00
❑ 78	24¢	Lilac (~70)	600.00	110.00

1867. Same Designs as the 1861–1866 Issue, Grill with Points Up.

A Grill. Grill Covers Entire Stamp.

❑ 79	3¢	Rose (~64)	2400.00	1100.00

C Grill. Grill Measures About 13 x 16 mm.

❑ 83	3¢	Rose (~64)	2400.00	840.00

1867. Same Designs as the 1861–66 Issue, Grill with Points Down.

D Grill. Grill Measures About 12 x 14 mm.

❑ 84	2¢	Black (~73)	7400.00	2800.00
❑ 85	3¢	Rose (~64)	2400.00	890.00

Z Grill. Grill Measures About 11 x 14 mm.

❑ 85B	2¢	Black (~73)	3400.00	950.00
❑ 85C	3¢	Rose (~64)	5100.00	2600.00
❑ 85E	12¢	Black (~69)	5200.00	1250.00

E Grill. Grill Measures About 11 x 13 mm.

❑ 86	1¢	Blue (~63)	1300.00	390.00
❑ 87	2¢	Black (~73)	600.00	100.00
❑ 88	3¢	Rose (~64)	320.00	21.00
❑ 89	10¢	Green (~68)	1800.00	255.00
❑ 90	12¢	Black (~69)	1850.00	285.00
❑ 91	15¢	Black (~77)	3500.00	480.00

Scott No.			Unused	Used
F Grill. Grill Measures About 9 x 13 mm.				
❑ 92	1¢	Blue (~63)	450.00	200.00
❑ 93	2¢	Black (~73)	200.00	45.00
❑ 94	3¢	Red (~64)	165.00	7.00
❑ 95	5¢	Brown (~67)	1400.00	610.00
❑ 96	10¢	Yellow Green (~68)	1100.00	175.00
❑ 97	12¢	Black (~69)	1200.00	200.00
❑ 98	15¢	Black (~77)	1400.00	250.00
❑ 99	24¢	Gray Lilac (~70)	2000.00	750.00
❑ 100	30¢	Orange (~71)	2400.00	600.00
❑ 101	90¢	Blue (~72)	4100.00	1200.00

1875. Re-issue of 1861–1866 Issues, without Grill, Perforated 12, Hard White Paper.

❑ 102	1¢	Blue (~63)	410.00	210.00
❑ 103	2¢	Black (~73)	1500.00	1000.00
❑ 104	3¢	Brown Red (~64)	1650.00	1100.00
❑ 105	5¢	Light Brown (67)	1400.00	1000.00
❑ 106	10¢	Green (~68)	1800.00	1100.00
❑ 107	12¢	Black (~69)	2000.00	1400.00
❑ 108	15¢	Black (~77)	2200.00	1500.00
❑ 109	24¢	Deep Violet (~70)	2700.00	1800.00
❑ 110	30¢	Brownish Orange (~71)	2500.00	190.00
❑ 111	90¢	Blue (~72)	3200.00	2200.00

112	**113**	**114**	**115**
(123, 133)	(124)	(125)	(126)

1869. Pictorial Issue, with Grill.

❑ 112	1¢	Buff	310.00	140.00
❑ 113	2¢	Brown	260.00	50.00
❑ 114	3¢	Ultramarine	160.00	15.00
❑ 115	6¢	Ultramarine	1300.00	170.00

116
(127)

117
(128)

118
(119, 129)

120
(130)

121
(131)

122
(132)

Scott No.			Unused	Used
❏ 116	10¢	Yellow	875.00	130.00
❏ 117	12¢	Green	900.00	140.00
❏ 118	15¢	Brown & Blue (type I)	3200.00	500.00
❏ 119	15¢	Brown & Blue (~118) (type II)	1400.00	210.00
❏ 120	24¢	Green & Violet	275.00	500.00
❏ 121	30¢	Blue & Carmine	2650.00	460.00
❏ 122	90¢	Carmine & Black	4100.00	175.00

NOTE: Type II (No. 119) contains a small diamond-shaped ornament at center just above the central picture. Type I (No. 118) does not contain the diamond-shaped ornament.

1875. Re-issue of the 1869 Pictorial Issue, Hard White Paper, without Grill.

❏ 123	1¢	Buff (~112)	300.00	250.00
❏ 124	2¢	Brown (~113)	370.00	410.00
❏ 125	3¢	Blue (~114)	2750.00	1700.00
❏ 126	6¢	Blue (~115)	910.00	600.00
❏ 127	10¢	Yellow (~116)	1150.00	800.00
❏ 128	12¢	Green (~117)	1400.00	900.00
❏ 129	15¢	Brown & Blue (~118) (type III)	1150.00	710.00
❏ 130	24¢	Green & Violet (~120)	1200.00	750.00
❏ 131	30¢	Blue & Carmine (~121)	1500.00	900.00
❏ 132	90¢	Carmine & Black (~122)	2600.00	1700.00

NOTE: Type III (No. 129) is similar to Type I (No. 118) above except that it does not contain the fringe of brown shading lines around the central picture as does Type I.

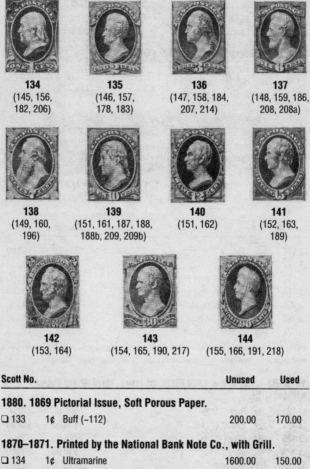

134
(145, 156, 182, 206)

135
(146, 157, 178, 183)

136
(147, 158, 184, 207, 214)

137
(148, 159, 186, 208, 208a)

138
(149, 160, 196)

139
(151, 161, 187, 188, 188b, 209, 209b)

140
(151, 162)

141
(152, 163, 189)

142
(153, 164)

143
(154, 165, 190, 217)

144
(155, 166, 191, 218)

Scott No.			Unused	Used
1880. 1869 Pictorial Issue, Soft Porous Paper.				
❑ 133	1¢	Buff (~112)	200.00	170.00
1870–1871. Printed by the National Bank Note Co., with Grill.				
❑ 134	1¢	Ultramarine	1600.00	150.00
❑ 135	2¢	Red Brown	1000.00	60.00
❑ 136	3¢	Green	550.00	20.00
❑ 137	6¢	Carmine	3000.00	410.00
❑ 138	7¢	Vermilion	2600.00	350.00
❑ 139	10¢	Brown	3800.00	560.00
❑ 140	12¢	Light Violet	—	2400.00
❑ 141	15¢	Orange	4500.00	1000.00
❑ 142	24¢	Purple	—	5000.00

Scott No.			Unused	Used
❏ 143	30¢	Black	1200.00	2000.00
❏ 144	90¢	Carmine	11000.00	1400.00

1870–1871. Same Designs, without Grill.

❏ 145	1¢	Ultramarine (~134)	400.00	12.00
❏ 146	2¢	Red Brown (~135)	260.00	8.10
❏ 147	3¢	Green (~136)	240.00	1.50
❏ 148	6¢	Carmine (~137)	650.00	20.00
❏ 149	7¢	Vermilion (~138)	750.00	78.00
❏ 150	10¢	Brown (~139)	800.00	21.00
❏ 151	12¢	Dull Violet (~140)	1600.00	120.00
❏ 152	15¢	Bright Orange (~141)	1600.00	125.00
❏ 153	24¢	Purple (~142)	1300.00	100.00
❏ 154	30¢	Black (~143)	4000.00	175.00
❏ 155	90¢	Carmine (~144)	3000.00	260.00

1873. Same Designs as the 1870–1871 Issue, Printed by the Continental Bank Note Co., with Secret Marks, Thin Hard Grayish-White Paper.

❏ 156	1¢	Ultramarine (~134)	215.00	4.00
❏ 157	2¢	Brown (~135)	310.00	15.00
❏ 158	3¢	Green (~136)	100.00	.65
❏ 159	6¢	Dull Pink (~137)	300.00	17.00
❏ 160	7¢	Orange Vermilion (~138)	1150.00	78.00
❏ 161	10¢	Brown (~139)	700.00	18.00
❏ 162	12¢	Black Violet (~140)	1600.00	82.00
❏ 163	15¢	Yellow Orange (141)	1500.00	95.00
❏ 164	24¢	Purple (~142)	—	—
❏ 165	30¢	Gray Black (~143)	2200.00	90.00
❏ 166	90¢	Rose Carmine (~144)	2400.00	200.00

NOTE: Refer to the Type Identifier for information on secret marks.

179
(185)

1875.

❏ 178	2¢	Vermilion (~135)	300.00	9.50
❏ 179	5¢	Blue, Zachary Taylor	3000.00	17.00

Scott No.			Unused	Used

1879. Same Designs as the 1870–1875 Issue, Printed by the American Bank Note Co., Soft Porous Yellowish-White Paper.

❏ 182	1¢	Dark Ultramarine (~134)	250.00	2.50
❏ 183	2¢	Vermilion (~135)	100.00	2.10
❏ 184	3¢	Green (~136)	90.00	.60
❏ 185	5¢	Blue (~179)	400.00	11.00
❏ 186	6¢	Pink (~137)	800.00	17.00
❏ 187	10¢	Brown (~139), without secret mark	2400.00	20.00
❏ 188	10¢	Brown (~139), with secret mark	150.00	20.00
❏ 188b	10¢	Black Brown (~139)	850.00	80.00
❏ 189	15¢	Red Orange (~141)	275.00	19.00
❏ 190	30¢	Full Black (~143)	920.00	50.00
❏ 191	90¢	Carmine (~144)	1850.00	210.00

NOTE: Refer to the Type Identifier for information on secret marks.

205
(216)

1882.

❏ 205	5¢	Yellow Brown, James Garfield	300.00	8.50

1881–1882. Designs of the 1873 Issue, Re-engraved.

❏ 206	1¢	Gray Blue (~134)	150.00	1.00
❏ 207	3¢	Blue Green (~136)	140.00	.60
❏ 208	6¢	Rose (~137)	150.00	64.00
❏ 208a	6¢	Brown Red (~137)	140.00	81.00
❏ 209	10¢	Brown (~139)	300.00	5.00
❏ 209b	10¢	Black Brown (~139)	250.00	43.00

NOTE: Re-engraved types can be distinguished as follows: The 1¢ is a milky gray blue and lines of shading have been added to the ornament balls in the upper corners. The 3¢ contains a short horizontal line engraved below the "ts" of "cents." The 6¢ contains three vertical lines at the left of the design instead of four. The 10¢ contains four vertical lines between the outer border and portrait oval instead of five.

| | 210
(213) | 211
(215) | 212 |

Scott No.			Unused	Used

1883.

❑ 210	2¢	Red Brown	47.00	.60
❑ 211	4¢	Blue Green	140.00	15.00

1887.

❑ 212	1¢	Ultramarine	90.00	1.50
❑ 213	2¢	Green (~210)	40.00	.45
❑ 214	3¢	Vermilion (~136)	62.00	48.00

1888.

❑ 215	4¢	Carmine (~211)	190.00	19.00
❑ 216	5¢	Indigo (~205)	190.00	14.00
❑ 217	30¢	Orange Brown (~143)	375.00	92.00
❑ 218	90¢	Purple (~144)	700.00	200.00

PRICING NOTE: From this point forward, prices for unused stamps are for examples with original gum.

| | 219 | 219D
(220, 220a, 220c) |

1890–1893. (NH Add 100%)

❑ 219	1¢	Dull Blue	38.00	.40
❑ 219D	2¢	Lake	300.00	1.00
❑ 220	2¢	Carmine (~219D)	30.00	.30
❑ 220a	2¢	Carmine (Cap on left 2)	120.00	6.00
❑ 220c	2¢	Carmine (Cap both 2s)	480.00	16.00

221	222	223	224	225

226	227	228	229

Scott No.			Unused	Used
❏ 221	3¢	Purple	100.00	6.50
❏ 222	4¢	Dark Brown	90.00	2.10
❏ 223	5¢	Chocolate	80.00	2.75
❏ 224	6¢	Brown Red	80.00	17.00
❏ 225	8¢	Lilac	60.00	9.00
❏ 226	10¢	Green	210.00	2.50
❏ 227	15¢	Indigo	215.00	17.50
❏ 228	30¢	Black	350.00	24.00
❏ 229	90¢	Orange	510.00	95.00

230	231	232

1893. Columbian Exposition Issue. (NH Add 100–200%)

❏ 230	1¢	Blue	22.00	.46
❏ 231	2¢	Violet	24.00	.29
❏ 231c	2¢	"Broken Hat" variety (~231)	81.00	.85
❏ 232	3¢	Green	75.00	14.00

NOTE: A notch appears at the top of Columbus's hat on the broken hat variety.

Scott No.			Unused	Used
❏ 233	4¢	Ultramarine	75.00	6.00
❏ 234	5¢	Chocolate	100.00	7.10
❏ 235	6¢	Purple	105.00	19.00
❏ 236	8¢	Magenta	70.00	10.00
❏ 237	10¢	Black Brown	120.00	8.00
❏ 238	15¢	Dark Green	250.00	60.00
❏ 239	30¢	Orange Brown	300.00	76.00
❏ 240	50¢	Slate Blue	610.00	140.00
❏ 241	$1	Salmon	1000.00	500.00
❏ 242	$2	Brown Red	1400.00	500.00

NOTE: Refer to the Type Identifier for information on types.

| **243** | **244** | **245** |

Scott No.			Unused	Used
❏ 243	$3	Yellow Green	2400.00	100.00
❏ 244	$4	Crimson Lake	2600.00	1000.00
❏ 245	$5	Black	3000.00	200.00

246
(247, 264, 279)

248
(249, 250, 251, 252, 265,
266, 267, 279B, 279C, 279D)

253
(268)

254
(269, 280)

255
(270, 281)

1894. Similar to the Series of 1890–1893 but with Triangles added in Upper Corners, Unwatermarked. (NH Add 100%)

❏ 246	1¢	Ultramarine	26.00	4.60
❏ 247	1¢	Blue (~246)	60.00	2.10
❏ 248	2¢	Pink (type I)	24.00	4.00
❏ 249	2¢	Carmine Lake (~248) (type I)	140.00	4.00
❏ 250	2¢	Carmine (~248) (type I)	26.00	.70
❏ 251	2¢	Carmine (~248) (type II)	250.00	6.00
❏ 252	2¢	Carmine (~248) (type III)	110.00	7.00
❏ 253	3¢	Purple	95.00	8.00
❏ 254	4¢	Dark Brown	125.00	4.00
❏ 255	5¢	Chocolate	100.00	5.00

NOTE: Refer to the Type Identifier for information on types.

| **256** | **257** | **258** | **259** |
| (271, 282, 282a) | (272) | (273, 282C, 283) | (274, 284) |

| **260** | **261** | **262** | **263** |
| (275) | (261A, 276, 276A) | (277) | (278) |

Scott No.			Unused	Used
❏ 256	6¢	Dull Brown	150.00	20.00
❏ 257	8¢	Violet Brown	125.00	12.50
❏ 258	10¢	Dark Green	250.00	10.00
❏ 259	15¢	Dark Blue	240.00	45.00
❏ 260	50¢	Orange	500.00	95.00
❏ 261	$1	Black (type I)	800.00	240.00
❏ 261A	$1	Black (~261) (type II)	1600.00	500.00
❏ 262	$2	Blue	2600.00	800.00
❏ 263	$5	Dark Green	4000.00	1500.00

1895. Same Designs as the 1894 Issue, Double Line Watermark.
(NH Add 100%)

❏ 264	1¢	Blue (~246)	6.00	.41
❏ 265	2¢	Carmine (~248) (type I)	26.00	2.00
❏ 266	2¢	Carmine (~248) (type II)	25.00	3.50
❏ 267	2¢	Carmine (~248) (type III)	6.00	.28
❏ 268	3¢	Purple (~253)	31.00	1.40
❏ 269	4¢	Dark Brown (~254)	48.00	1.50
❏ 270	5¢	Chocolate (~255)	35.00	2.00
❏ 271	6¢	Dull Brown (~256)	85.00	5.00
❏ 272	8¢	Violet Brown (~257)	60.00	2.00
❏ 273	10¢	Dark Green (~258)	78.00	1.40
❏ 274	15¢	Dark Blue (~259)	200.00	10.00

NOTE: Refer to the Type Identifier for information on types.

Scott No.			Unused	Used
❏ 275	50¢	Dull Orange (~260)	250.00	20.00
❏ 276	$1	Black (~261) (type I)	500.00	65.00
❏ 276A	$1	Black (~261) (type II)	1200.00	140.00
❏ 277	$2	Blue (~262)	900.00	260.00
❏ 278	$5	Dark Green (~263)	2000.00	375.00

1898. Same Designs as the 1894 Issue but with Changed Colors, Double Line Watermark. (NH Add 100%)

❏ 279	1¢	Deep Green (~246)	9.00	.35
❏ 279B	2¢	Red (~248)	9.00	.30
❏ 279C	2¢	Rose Carmine (~248)	340.00	65.00
❏ 279D	2¢	Orange Red (~248)	20.00	.60
❏ 280	4¢	Rose Brown (~254)	30.00	1.00
❏ 281	5¢	Dark Blue (~255)	36.00	.80
❏ 282	6¢	Lake (~256)	40.00	3.00
❏ 282a	6¢	Purplish Lake (~256)	60.00	3.60
❏ 282C	10¢	Brown (~258) (type I)	160.00	3.00
❏ 283	10¢	Orange Brown (~258) (type II)	110.00	3.00
❏ 284	15¢	Olive Green (~259)	130.00	7.00

285 286 287

288 289

1898. Trans-Mississippi Exposition Issue. (NH Add 100%)

❏ 285	1¢	Yellow Green	28.00	5.00
❏ 286	2¢	Copper Red	30.00	1.35
❏ 287	4¢	Orange	145.00	18.00
❏ 288	5¢	Dull Blue	145.00	17.00
❏ 289	8¢	Violet Brown	170.00	32.00

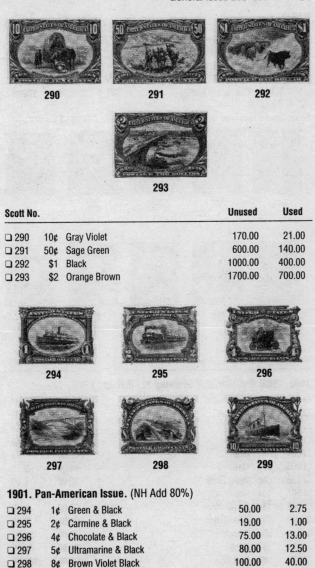

290

291

292

293

Scott No.			Unused	Used
❏ 290	10¢	Gray Violet	170.00	21.00
❏ 291	50¢	Sage Green	600.00	140.00
❏ 292	$1	Black	1000.00	400.00
❏ 293	$2	Orange Brown	1700.00	700.00

294

295

296

297

298

299

1901. Pan-American Issue. (NH Add 80%)

❏ 294	1¢	Green & Black	50.00	2.75
❏ 295	2¢	Carmine & Black	19.00	1.00
❏ 296	4¢	Chocolate & Black	75.00	13.00
❏ 297	5¢	Ultramarine & Black	80.00	12.50
❏ 298	8¢	Brown Violet Black	100.00	40.00
❏ 299	10¢	Yellow Brown Black	160.00	22.00

300
(314, 316, 318)   **301**   **302**   **303**

304
(315, 317)   **305**   **306**   **307**   **308**

309   **310**   **311**   **312**
(479)   **313**
(480)

Scott No.			Unused	Used
1902–1903. Definitives, Perforated 12. (NH Add 100%)				
❑ 300	1¢	Blue Green	10.00	.24
❑ 301	2¢	Carmine	13.00	.22
❑ 302	3¢	Violet	50.00	2.50
❑ 303	4¢	Brown	50.00	1.50
❑ 304	5¢	Blue	60.00	1.25
❑ 305	6¢	Claret	65.00	2.50
❑ 306	8¢	Violet Black	40.00	2.00
❑ 307	10¢	Red Brown	60.00	1.50
❑ 308	13¢	Purple Black	55.00	6.75
❑ 309	15¢	Olive Green	160.00	5.00
❑ 310	50¢	Orange	500.00	23.00
❑ 311	$1	Black	800.00	60.00
❑ 312	$2	Dark Blue	1000.00	140.00
❑ 313	$5	Dark Green	2400.00	500.00

Scott No.			Unused	Used

1906–1908. Designs of the 1902–1903 Issue, Imperforate.
(NH Add 80%)

| ❑ 314 | 1¢ | Blue Green (~300) | 21.00 | 16.00 |
| ❑ 315 | 5¢ | Blue (~304) | 3100.00 | 500.00 |

1908. Coil Stamps, Perforated 12 Horizontally.

| ❑ 316 | 1¢ | Blue Green (~300) | 4600.00 | — |
| ❑ 317 | 5¢ | Blue (~304) | 4200.00 | — |

1908. Coil Stamp, Perforated 12 Vertically.

| ❑ 318 | 1¢ | Blue Green (~300) | 4800.00 | 3000.00 |

319
(319a, 320, 320a)

1903. Perforated 12. (NH Add 85%)

| ❑ 319 | 2¢ | Carmine | 6.50 | .28 |
| ❑ 319a | 2¢ | Lake (~319) | — | — |

1906. Imperforate. (NH Add 85%)

| ❑ 320 | 2¢ | Carmine (~319) | 26.00 | 16.00 |
| ❑ 320a | 2¢ | Lake (~319) | 56.00 | 35.00 |

323   **324**   **325**

1904. Louisiana Purchase Issue. (NH Add 90%)

❑ 323	1¢	Green	28.00	4.00
❑ 324	2¢	Carmine	24.00	1.90
❑ 325	3¢	Violet	94.00	25.00

326 **327**

Scott No.			Unused	Used
❑ 326	5¢	Dark Blue	120.00	20.00
❑ 327	10¢	Red Brown	210.00	26.00

328 **329** **330**

1907. Jamestown Exposition Issue. (NH Add 90%)

❑ 328	1¢	Green	30.00	3.00
❑ 329	2¢	Carmine	28.00	3.00
❑ 330	5¢	Blue	110.00	24.00

331 **332** **333** **334**

(343, 348, 352, 357, 374, 383, 385, 387, 390, 392)	(344, 349, 353, 358, 375, 384, 386, 388, 391, 393, 519)	(345, 359, 376, 394, 426, 445, 456, 464, 483, 484, 489, 493, 494, 501, 502, 529, 530, 535, 541)	(346, 350, 354, 360, 377, 395, 427, 446, 457, 465, 495, 503)

1908–1909. Washington-Franklin Series, Perforated 12, Double Line Watermark. (NH Add 90%)

❑ 331	1¢	Green	6.50	.20
❑ 332	2¢	Carmine	6.00	.20
❑ 333	3¢	Violet	30.00	2.60
❑ 334	4¢	Orange Brown	36.00	1.00

335
(347, 355, 351, 361,
378, 396, 428, 447,
458, 466, 467, 496,
504, 505)

336
(362, 379,
429, 468,
506)

337
(363, 380)

338
(356, 364,
381)

339
(365)

340
(366, 382)

341

342

Scott No.			Line Pair	Unused	Used
❑ 335	5¢	Blue		46.00	1.90
❑ 336	6¢	Red Orange		51.00	5.00
❑ 337	8¢	Olive Green		42.00	3.15
❑ 338	10¢	Yellow		60.00	1.40
❑ 339	13¢	Blue Green		40.00	14.00
❑ 340	15¢	Pale Ultramarine		75.00	6.00
❑ 341	50¢	Violet		300.00	18.00
❑ 342	$1	Violet Black		415.00	72.00

1908–1909. Imperforate, Double Line Watermark. (NH Add 90%)

❑ 343	1¢	Green (~331)		6.50	4.50
❑ 344	2¢	Carmine (~332)		9.00	3.75
❑ 345	3¢	Deep Violet (~333)		20.00	20.00
❑ 346	4¢	Orange Brown (~334)		28.00	21.00
❑ 347	5¢	Blue (~335)		46.00	31.00

1908–1910. Coil Stamps, Perforated 12 Horizontally. (NH Add 90%)

❑ 348	1¢	Green (~331)	220.00	31.00	18.00
❑ 349	2¢	Carmine (~332)	370.00	90.00	10.00
❑ 350	4¢	Orange Brown (~334)	850.00	160.00	92.00
❑ 351	5¢	Blue (~335)	850.00	160.00	120.00

Scott No.			Line Pair	Unused	Used

1909. Coil Stamps, Perforated 12 Vertically. (NH Add 90%)

❑ 352	1¢	Green (~331)	650.00	75.00	39.00
❑ 353	2¢	Carmine (~332)	600.00	85.00	9.00
❑ 354	4¢	Orange Brown (~334)	800.00	200.00	61.00
❑ 355	5¢	Blue (~335)	810.00	220.00	92.00
❑ 356	10¢	Yellow (~338)	—	2100.00	930.00

1909. Washington-Franklin Series, Printed on Bluish Gray Paper. (NH Add 90%)

				Unused	Used
❑ 357	1¢	Green (~331)		120.00	84.00
❑ 358	2¢	Carmine (~332)		90.00	90.00
❑ 359	3¢	Violet (~333)		2000.00	1800.00
❑ 360	4¢	Orange Brown (~334)		20000.00	—
❑ 361	5¢	Blue (~335)		7800.00	3200.00
❑ 362	6¢	Orange (~336)		1200.00	3200.00
❑ 363	8¢	Olive Green (~337)		20000.00	—
❑ 364	10¢	Yellow (~338)		2100.00	3400.00
❑ 365	13¢	Blue Green (~339)		2900.00	3100.00
❑ 366	15¢	Pale Ultramarine (~340)		1500.00	7800.00

367
(368, 369)

1909. Lincoln Memorial Issue. (NH Add 85%)

			Unused	Used
❑ 367	2¢	Carmine, perforated 12	6.00	1.65
❑ 368	2¢	Carmine (~367), imperforate	21.00	19.00
❑ 369	2¢	Carmine (~367), perforated 12, on bluish gray paper	180.00	190.00

370
(371)

372
(373)

Scott No.			Line Pair	Unused	Used
1909. Alaska–Yukon Issue. (NH Add 80%)					
❑ 370	2¢	Carmine, perforated 12		9.00	1.75
❑ 371	2¢	Carmine (~370), imperforate		35.00	19.00
1909. Hudson–Fulton Issue. (NH Add 80%)					
❑ 372	2¢	Carmine, perforated 12		12.00	3.40
❑ 373	2¢	Carmine (~372), imperforate		36.00	20.00

1910–1911. Washington-Franklin Series, Perforated 12, Single Line Watermark. (NH Add 90%)

❑ 374	1¢	Green (~331)		7.00	.26
❑ 375	2¢	Carmine (~332)		7.10	.25
❑ 376	3¢	Deep Violet (~333)		24.00	1.80
❑ 377	4¢	Brown (~334)		37.00	1.00
❑ 378	5¢	Blue (~335)		36.00	.70
❑ 379	6¢	Red Orange (~336)		41.00	.85
❑ 380	8¢	Olive Green (~337)		115.00	11.00
❑ 381	10¢	Yellow (~338)		120.00	4.50
❑ 382	15¢	Ultramarine (~340)		260.00	14.00

1910. Washington-Franklin Series, Imperforate, Single Line Watermark. (NH Add 80%)

❑ 383	1¢	Green (~331)		4.00	3.00
❑ 384	2¢	Carmine (~332)		7.00	2.90

1910. Coil Stamps, Perforated 12 Horizontally, Single Line Watermark. (NH Add 90%)

❑ 385	1¢	Green (~331)	410.00	40.00	12.00
❑ 386	2¢	Carmine (~332)	780.00	70.00	16.00

Scott No.			Line Pair	Unused	Used

1910–1911. Coil Stamps, Perforated 12 Vertically, Single Line Watermark. (NH Add 90%)

| ❏ 387 | 1¢ | Green (~331) | 900.00 | 210.00 | 42.00 |
| ❏ 388 | 2¢ | Carmine (~332) | 3800.00 | 870.00 | 30.00 |

1910. Coil Stamps, Perforated $8\frac{1}{2}$ Horizontally, Single Line Watermark. (NH Add 90%)

| ❏ 390 | 1¢ | Green (~331) | 36.00 | 6.50 | 4.00 |
| ❏ 391 | 2¢ | Carmine (~332) | 240.00 | 38.00 | 10.00 |

1910–1913. Coil Stamps, Perforated $8\frac{1}{2}$ Vertically, Single Line Watermark. (NH Add 90%)

❏ 392	1¢	Green (~331)	165.00	26.00	21.00
❏ 393	2¢	Carmine (~332)	310.00	50.00	12.00
❏ 394	3¢	Violet (~333)	340.00	62.00	50.00
❏ 395	4¢	Brown (~334)	420.00	60.00	46.00
❏ 396	5¢	Blue (~335)	400.00	62.00	46.00

397
(401)

398
(402)

399
(403)

400
(400A, 404)

1913. Panama–Pacific Issue, Perforated 12. (NH Add 90%)

❏ 397	1¢	Green	20.00	1.50
❏ 398	2¢	Carmine	22.00	.70
❏ 399	5¢	Blue	82.00	9.00
❏ 400	10¢	Orange Yellow	150.00	19.00
❏ 400A	10¢	Orange	280.00	16.00

Scott No.			Line Pair	Unused	Used

1914–1915. Panama-Pacific Issue, Perforated 10. (NH Add 90%)

❑ 401	1¢	Green (~397)		27.00	6.50
❑ 402	2¢	Carmine (~398)		80.00	1.70
❑ 403	5¢	Blue (~399)		210.00	15.00
❑ 404	10¢	Orange (~400)		120.00	60.00

405
(408, 410, 412, 424, 441, 443, 448, 452, 462, 481, 486, 490, 498, 525, 531, 536, 538, 542, 543, 544, 545)

406
(409, 411, 413, 425, 442, 444, 449, 450, 453, 454, 455, 459, 461, 463, 482, 487, 488, 491, 492, 499, 500, 526, 527, 528, 528A, 528B, 532, 533, 534, 534A, 534B, 539, 540, 546)

407
(430, 469, 507)

1912–1914. Washington-Franklin Series, Perforated 12, Single Line Watermark. (NH Add 90%)

❑ 405	1¢	Green		7.25	.20
❑ 406	2¢	Carmine		7.25	.20
❑ 407	7¢	Black		85.00	9.00

1912. Washington-Franklin Series, Imperforate, Single Line Watermark. (NH Add 90%)

❑ 408	1¢	Green (~405)		1.50	.62
❑ 409	2¢	Carmine (~406)		1.50	.67

1912. Coil Stamps, Perforated 8½ Horizontally, Single Line Watermark. (NH Add 90%)

❑ 410	1¢	Green (~405)	42.00	8.00	3.80
❑ 411	2¢	Carmine (~406)	64.00	11.00	3.60

1912. Coil Stamps, Perforated 8½ Vertically, Single Line Watermark. (NH Add 90%)

❑ 412	1¢	Green (~405)	130.00	29.00	6.00
❑ 413	2¢	Carmine (~406)	285.00	50.00	1.70

414
(431, 470, 508)

415
(432, 471, 509)

416
(433, 472, 497, 510)

417
(435, 435a, 474, 512)

418
(437, 475, 514)

419
(438, 476, 515)

420
(439, 476A, 516)

421
(422, 440, 477, 517)

423
(460, 478, 518, 518b)

Scott No.			Unused	Used

1912–1914. Washington-Franklin Series, Perforated 12, Single Line Watermark. (NH Add 90%)

			Unused	Used
❑ 414	8¢	Olive Green	48.00	1.35
❑ 415	9¢	Salmon Red	58.00	10.50
❑ 416	10¢	Orange Yellow	46.00	.50
❑ 417	12¢	Claret Brown	50.00	4.00
❑ 418	15¢	Gray	96.00	3.60
❑ 419	20¢	Ultramarine	220.00	15.00
❑ 420	30¢	Orange Red	140.00	16.00
❑ 421	50¢	Violet	450.00	17.00

1912. Franklin Types, Perforated 12, Double Line Watermark. (NH Add 90%)

			Unused	Used
❑ 422	50¢	Violet (~421)	280.00	17.50
❑ 423	$1	Violet Black	550.00	61.00

434
(473, 511)

Scott No.			Line Pair	Unused	Used

1914–1915. Washington-Franklin Series, Perforated 10, Single Line Watermark. (NH Add 90%)

Scott No.			Line Pair	Unused	Used
❏ 424	1¢	Green (~405)		2.60	.21
❏ 425	2¢	Carmine (~406)		2.70	.21
❏ 426	3¢	Deep Violet (~333)		18.00	1.30
❏ 427	4¢	Brown (~334)		41.00	.64
❏ 428	5¢	Blue (~335)		44.00	.64
❏ 429	6¢	Orange (~336)		60.00	1.65
❏ 430	7¢	Black (~407)		88.00	4.80
❏ 431	8¢	Olive Green (~414)		45.00	2.00
❏ 432	9¢	Salmon Red (~415)		67.00	11.00
❏ 433	10¢	Orange Yellow (~416)		58.00	.64
❏ 434	11¢	Dark Green		31.00	7.00
❏ 435	12¢	Claret Brown (~417)		31.00	6.00
❏ 435a	12¢	Copper Red (~417)		33.00	6.50
❏ 437	15¢	Gray (~418)		150.00	7.40
❏ 438	20¢	Ultramarine (~419)		240.00	5.00
❏ 439	30¢	Orange Red (~420)		320.00	16.00
❏ 440	50¢	Violet (~421)		675.00	18.00

1914. Coil Stamps, Perforated 10 Horizontally, Single Line Watermark. (NH Add 90%)

Scott No.			Line Pair	Unused	Used
❏ 441	1¢	Green (~405)	11.00	2.00	1.10
❏ 442	2¢	Carmine (~406)	76.00	11.00	6.40

1914. Coil Stamps, Perforated 10 Vertically, Single Line Watermark. (NH Add 90%)

Scott No.			Line Pair	Unused	Used
❏ 443	1¢	Green (~405)	174.00	28.00	6.00
❏ 444	2¢	Carmine (~406)	310.00	42.00	1.60
❏ 445	3¢	Violet (~333)	725.00	300.00	110.00
❏ 446	4¢	Brown (~334)	750.00	135.00	42.00
❏ 447	5¢	Blue (~335)	280.00	63.00	36.00

Scott No.			Line Pair	Unused	Used

1914–1916. Rotary Press Coil Stamps, Perforated 10 Horizontally, Single Line Watermark. (NH Add 90%)

❏ 448	1¢	Green (~405)		10.00	4.00
❏ 449	2¢	Red (~406) (type I)		2500.00	410.00
❏ 450	2¢	Carmine (~406) (type III)		12.00	3.75

1914–1916. Rotary Press Coils, Perforated 10 Vertically, Single Line Watermark. (NH Add 90%)

❏ 452	1¢	Green (~405)	95.00	16.00	2.25
❏ 453	2¢	Red (~406) (type I)	720.00	142.00	3.60
❏ 454	2¢	Carmine (~406) (type II)	500.00	120.00	9.70
❏ 455	2¢	Carmine (~406) (type III)	70.00	12.00	1.50
❏ 456	3¢	Violet (~333)	1200.00	300.00	91.00
❏ 457	4¢	Brown (~334)	190.00	31.00	19.00
❏ 458	5¢	Blue (~335)	200.00	36.00	19.00

1914. Imperforate, Single Line Watermark. (NH Add 60%)

❏ 459	2¢	Carmine (~406)		510.00	880.00

1915. Franklin Type, Perforated 10, Double Line Watermark. (NH Add 90%)

❏ 460	$1	Violet Black (~423)		1100.00	92.00

1915. Washington Type, Flat Plate Printing, Perforated 11, Single Line Watermark, Design Measures 18½–19 x 22 mm. (NH Add 90%)

❏ 461	2¢	Pale Carmine Red (~406)		215.00	190.00

1916–1917. Washington-Franklin Series, Perforated 10, Unwatermarked. (NH Add 90%)

❏ 462	1¢	Green (~405)		10.00	.40
❏ 463	2¢	Carmine (~406)		6.00	.30
❏ 464	3¢	Violet (~333)		86.00	13.00
❏ 465	4¢	Orange Brown (~334)		64.00	1.90
❏ 466	5¢	Blue (~335)		86.00	2.10
❏ 467	5¢	Carmine (error) (~335)		715.00	62.00
❏ 468	6¢	Red Orange (~336)		110.00	7.50
❏ 469	7¢	Black (~407)		150.00	10.50
❏ 470	8¢	Olive Green (~414)		75.00	7.00

NOTE: Refer to the Type Identifier for information on types.

Scott No.			Line Pair	Unused	Used
❏ 471	9¢	Salmon Red (~415)		74.00	15.00
❏ 472	10¢	Orange Yellow (~416)		126.00	1.80
❏ 473	11¢	Dark Green (~434)		50.00	16.00
❏ 474	12¢	Claret Brown (~417)		7.00	6.50
❏ 475	15¢	Gray (~418)		310.00	13.00
❏ 476	20¢	Ultramarine (~419)		310.00	13.00
❏ 476A	30¢	Orange Red (~420)		4500.00	—
❏ 477	50¢	Light Violet (~421)		1200.00	62.00
❏ 478	$1	Violet Black (~423)		900.00	20.00

1916–1917. Designs of 1902–1903, Perforated 10, Unwatermarked. (NH Add 80%)

❏ 479	$2	Dark Blue (~312)		440.00	43.00
❏ 480	$5	Light Green (~313)		300.00	41.00

1916–1917. Washington-Franklin Series, Imperforate, Unwatermarked. (NH Add 90%)

❏ 481	1¢	Green (~405)		1.20	.90
❏ 482	2¢	Carmine (~406)		2.10	1.20
❏ 483	3¢	Violet (~333) (type I)		16.00	8.00
❏ 484	3¢	Violet (~333) (type II)		12.10	4.60

1916–1922. Rotary Press Coil Stamps, Perforated 10 Horizontally, Unwatermarked. (NH Add 85%)

❏ 486	1¢	Green (~405)	6.00	1.30	.24
❏ 487	2¢	Carmine (~406) (type II)	120.00	18.00	4.50
❏ 488	2¢	Carmine (~406) (type III)	25.00	3.00	1.70
❏ 489	3¢	Violet (~333)	40.00	6.50	1.70

1916–1922. Rotary Press Coil Stamps, Perforated 10 Vertically, Unwatermarked. (NH Add 90%)

❏ 490	1¢	Green (~405)	6.50	.80	.25
❏ 491	2¢	Carmine (~406) (type II)	1200.00	2400.00	55.00
❏ 492	2¢	Carmine (~406) (type III)	70.00	12.00	.30
❏ 493	3¢	Violet (~333) (type I)	130.00	20.00	3.10
❏ 494	3¢	Violet (~333) (type II)	80.00	12.00	1.10
❏ 495	4¢	Orange Brown (~334)	90.00	12.00	3.50
❏ 496	5¢	Blue (~335)	40.00	5.00	1.00
❏ 497	10¢	Orange Yellow (~416)	150.00	270.00	11.00

513

Scott No.			Unused	Used

1917–1919. Washington-Franklin Series, Flat Plate Printing, Perforated 11, Unwatermarked. (NH Add 90%)

❑ 498	1¢	Green (~405)	.50	.26
❑ 499	2¢	Rose (~406) (type I)	.50	.26
❑ 500	2¢	Deep Rose (~406) (type Ia)	350.00	180.00
❑ 501	3¢	Violet (~333) (type I)	16.00	.25
❑ 502	3¢	Violet (~333) (type II)	18.00	.65
❑ 503	4¢	Brown (~334)	15.00	.30
❑ 504	5¢	Blue (~335)	12.00	.30
❑ 505	5¢	Rose (error) (~335)	500.00	380.00
❑ 506	6¢	Red Orange (~336)	15.00	.50
❑ 507	7¢	Black (~407)	30.00	1.15
❑ 508	8¢	Olive Bistre (~414)	15.00	.90
❑ 509	9¢	Salmon Red (~415)	15.00	2.00
❑ 510	10¢	Orange Yellow (~416)	19.00	.34
❑ 511	11¢	Light Green (~434)	11.00	3.00
❑ 512	12¢	Claret Brown (~417)	11.00	.55
❑ 513	13¢	Apple Green	15.00	6.50
❑ 514	15¢	Gray (~418)	40.00	1.00
❑ 515	20¢	Ultramarine (~419)	50.00	.50
❑ 516	30¢	Orange Red (~420)	42.00	1.00
❑ 517	50¢	Red Violet (~421)	90.00	.70
❑ 518	$1	Violet Brown (~423)	74.00	1.60
❑ 518b	$1	Deep Brown (~423)	1900.00	910.00

1917. Washington Type, Perforated 11, Double Line Watermark. (NH Add 80%)

❑ 519	2¢	Carmine (~332)	650.00	700.00

NOTE: Refer to the Type Identifier for information on types.

523
(547)

524

Scott No.			Unused	Used

1918. Washington-Franklin Series, Perforated 11, Unwatermarked. (NH Add 90%)

❑ 523	$2	Orange Red & Black	800.00	220.00
❑ 524	$5	Deep Green & Black	260.00	31.00

1918–1920. Washington-Franklin Series, Offset Printing, Perforated 11, Unwatermarked. (NH Add 90%)

❑ 525	1¢	Gray Green (~405)	2.50	1.00
❑ 526	2¢	Carmine (~406) (type IV)	31.00	4.00
❑ 527	2¢	Carmine (~406) (type V)	26.00	1.25
❑ 528	2¢	Carmine (~406) (type Va)	10.00	.70
❑ 528A	2¢	Carmine (~406) (type VI)	60.00	1.50
❑ 528B	2¢	Carmine (~406) (type VII)	32.00	.60
❑ 529	3¢	Violet (333) (type III)	4.50	.40
❑ 530	3¢	Purple (~333) (type IV)	2.50	.40

1918–1920. Washington-Franklin Series, Offset Printing, Imperforate, Unwatermarked. (NH Add 90%)

❑ 531	1¢	Gray Green (~405)	11.00	9.00
❑ 532	2¢	Carmine (~406) (type IV)	45.00	28.00
❑ 533	2¢	Carmine (~406) (type V)	200.00	80.00
❑ 534	2¢	Carmine (~406) (type Va)	140.00	9.00
❑ 534A	2¢	Carmine (~406) (type VI)	41.00	28.00
❑ 534B	2¢	Carmine (~406) (type VII)	2100.00	850.00
❑ 535	3¢	Violet (~333)	10.00	7.00

1918–1920. Washington Type, Offset Printing, Perforated 12½, Unwatermarked. (NH Add 90%)

❑ 536	1¢	Gray Green (~405)	31.00	20.00

PLEASE NOTE: Unless otherwise noted, plate blocks are assumed to be blocks of 4. Where the number is more than 4, it appears in parentheses immediately following the price for the plate block. Blocks containing fewer than the appropriate number of stamps are not considered to be plate blocks and sell for much less.

537

Scott No.			Plate Block	Unused	Used

1919. (NH Add 90%)

| ❏ 537 | 3¢ | Victory | 110.00 (6) | 7.50 | 3.10 |

1919–1921. Washington-Franklin Series, Rotary Press Printing, Perforated 11 x 10. (NH Add 90%)

❏ 538	1¢	Green (~405)	125.00	16.00	8.50
❏ 539	2¢	Carmine Rose (~406) (type II)	—	2850.00	4100.00
❏ 540	2¢	Carmine Rose (~406) (type III)	125.00	17.00	10.00
❏ 541	3¢	Violet (~333)	430.00	50.00	29.00

1920. Washington-Franklin Series, Rotary Press Printing, Perforated 10 x 11, Design Measures 19 x 22½–22½ mm. (NH Add 90%)

| ❏ 542 | 1¢ | Green (~405) | 200.00 | 16.00 | 1.40 |

1921. Washington-Franklin Series, Rotary Press Printing, Perforated 10 x 10, Design Measures 19 x 22½ mm. (NH Add 90%)

| ❏ 543 | 1¢ | Green (~405) | 20.00 | 1.25 | .34 |

1922. Washington-Franklin Series, Rotary Press Printing, Perforated 11 x 11, Design Measures 19 x 22½ mm. (NH Add 90%)

| ❏ 544 | 1¢ | Green (~405) | — | 16000.00 | 3000.00 |

1921. Washington-Franklin Series, Rotary Press Printing, Perforated 11 x 11, Design Measures 19½–20 x 22 mm. (NH Add 90%)

| ❏ 545 | 1¢ | Green (~405) | 1000.00 | 1900.00 | 135.00 |
| ❏ 546 | 2¢ | Carmine Rose (~406) | 650.00 | 150.00 | 125.00 |

1920. Washington-Franklin Series, Flat Press Printing, Perforated 11 x 11. (NH Add 90%)

| ❏ 547 | $2 | Carmine & Black (~523) | 3100.00 | 210.00 | 40.00 |

| 548 | 549 | 550 |

Scott No.			Plate Block	Unused	Used

1920. Pilgrim Issue. (NH Add 80%)

❏ 548	1¢	Green	49.00 (6)	5.50	2.50
❏ 549	2¢	Carmine Rose	70.00 (6)	7.00	1.50
❏ 550	5¢	Deep Blue	500.00 (6)	52.00	15.00

| 551 | 552 | 553 | 554 |
| (653) | (575, 578, 581, 597, 604, 532) | (557, 582, 598, 605, 631, 633) | (577, 579, 583, 595, 599, 599A, 606, 634, 634A) |

| 555 | 556 | 557 | 558 |
| (584, 600, 635) | (585, 601, 636) | (586, 602, 637) | (587, 638, 723) |

1922–1925. Definitives, Flat Press Printing, Perforated 11.
(NH Add 80%)

❏ 551	½¢	Olive Brown	6.00 (6)	.40	.24
❏ 552	1¢	Deep Green	24.00 (6)	1.80	.24
❏ 553	1½¢	Yellow Brown	40.00 (6)	3.00	.25
❏ 554	2¢	Carmine	22.00 (6)	2.40	.24
❏ 555	3¢	Violet	190.00 (6)	20.00	1.30
❏ 556	4¢	Yellow Brown	190.00 (6)	20.00	.40
❏ 557	5¢	Dark Blue	180.00 (6)	21.00	.25
❏ 558	6¢	Red Orange	420.00 (6)	40.00	.90

559
(588, 639)

560
(589, 640)

561
(590, 641)

562
(591, 603, 642)

563
(692)

564
(693)

565
(695)

566
(696)

567
(698)

568
(699)

569
(700)

570
(701)

Scott No.			Plate Block	Unused	Used
❏ 559	7¢	Black	70.00 (6)	12.00	.80
❏ 560	8¢	Olive Green	600.00 (6)	52.00	.90
❏ 561	9¢	Rose	165.00 (6)	18.00	1.35
❏ 562	10¢	Orange	240.00 (6)	24.00	.30
❏ 563	11¢	Blue Green	35.00 (6)	3.00	.45
❏ 564	12¢	Brown Violet	85.00 (6)	8.00	.30
❏ 565	14¢	Dark Blue	65.00 (6)	6.00	.90
❏ 566	15¢	Gray	270.00 (6)	25.00	.30
❏ 567	20¢	Carmine Rose	250.00 (6)	25.00	.25
❏ 568	25¢	Green	250.00 (6)	25.00	.60
❏ 569	30¢	Olive Brown	250.00 (6)	42.00	.55
❏ 570	50¢	Lilac	675.00 (6)	60.00	.35

571

572

573

Scott No.			Plate Block	Unused	Used
❏ 571	$1	Violet Black	475.00 (6)	55.00	.60
❏ 572	$2	Deep Blue	850.00 (6)	92.00	8.00
❏ 573	$5	Carmine & Blue	230.00 (8)	200.00	13.00

Series of 1922–1925, Imperforate. (NH Add 60%)

❏ 575	1¢	Green (~552)	85.00 (6)	8.00	5.00
❏ 576	1½¢	Yellow Brown (~553)	30.00 (6)	2.20	1.60
❏ 577	2¢	Carmine (~554)	32.00 (6)	2.20	1.50

1923–1926. Definitives, Rotary Press Printing, Perforated 11 x 10, Designs Measure 19½ x 22½ mm. (NH Add 60%)

❏ 578	1¢	Green (~552)	875.00	95.00	130.00
❏ 579	2¢	Carmine (~554)	750.00	95.00	110.00

1923–1926. Series of 1922–1925, Rotary Press, Perforated 10. (NH Add 60%)

❏ 581	1¢	Green (~552)	125.00	10.00	1.25
❏ 582	1½¢	Brown (~553)	42.00	7.00	1.00
❏ 583	2¢	Carmine (~554)	36.00	4.00	.26
❏ 584	3¢	Violet (~555)	300.00	34.00	2.40
❏ 585	4¢	Yellow Brown(~556)	250.00	20.00	.72
❏ 586	5¢	Blue (~557)	250.00	19.00	.40
❏ 587	6¢	Red Orange (~558)	115.00	11.00	.78
❏ 588	7¢	Black (~559)	120.00	15.00	6.00
❏ 589	8¢	Olive Green (~560)	240.00	35.00	5.00
❏ 590	9¢	Rose (~561)	60.00	6.50	2.50
❏ 591	10¢	Orange (~562)	550.00	75.00	.74

Scott No.			Line Pair	Unused	Used

1923–1926. Series of 1922–1925, Rotary Press Coil Stamps, Perforated 11. (NH Add 60%)

❑ 595	2¢	Carmine (~554)	2000.00	320.00	270.00

NOTE: No. 595 is a sheet stamp made from coil waste. Its design measures 19½ x 22½ mm.

1923–1929. Series of 1922–1925, Rotary Press Coil Stamps, Perforated 10 Vertically. (NH Add 60%)

❑ 597	1¢	Green (~552)	2.30	.50	.24
❑ 598	1½¢	Deep Brown (~553)	6.00	1.00	.20
❑ 599	2¢	Carmine (~554) (type I)	2.50	.50	.24
❑ 599A	2¢	Carmine (~554) (type II)	700.00	150.00	11.00
❑ 600	3¢	Deep Violet (~555)	36.00	7.00	.30
❑ 601	4¢	Yellow Brown (~556)	33.00	5.00	.40
❑ 602	5¢	Dark Blue (~557)	12.00	2.10	.25
❑ 603	10¢	Orange (~562)	32.00	4.00	.25

NOTE: Refer to the Type Identifier for information on types.

1924–1925. Series of 1922–1925, Coil Stamps, Perforated 10 Horizontally. (NH Add 70%)

❑ 604	1¢	Green (~552)	4.50	.42	.24
❑ 605	1½¢	Yellow Brown (~553)	4.10	.42	.25
❑ 606	2¢	Carmine (~554)	3.00	.42	.24

610
(611, 612)

Scott No.			Plate Block	Unused	Used

1923. Harding Memorial Issue. (NH Add 80%)

❑ 610	2¢	Black, perforated 11	26.00 (6)	.75	.25
❑ 611	2¢	Black (~610), imperforate	100.00 (6)	7.25	4.25
❑ 612	2¢	Black (~610), perforated 10	300.00	22.00	2.40

| 614 | 615 | 616 |

Scott No.			Plate Block	Unused	Used
1924. Huguenot–Walloon Issue. (NH Add 80%)					
❑ 614	1¢	Green	40.00 (6)	4.00	3.50
❑ 615	2¢	Carmine Rose	65.00 (6)	6.00	2.50
❑ 616	5¢	Dark Blue	350.00 (6)	30.00	16.00

| 617 | 618 | 619 |

1925. Lexington–Concord Sesquicentennial. (NH Add 60%)					
❑ 617	1¢	Green	45.00 (6)	3.75	2.50
❑ 618	2¢	Carmine Rose	75.00 (6)	6.00	4.00
❑ 619	5¢	Dark Blue	310.00 (6)	30.00	15.00

| 620 | 621 |

1925. Norse-American Issue. (NH Add 80%)					
❑ 620	2¢	Carmine & Black	215.00 (8)	4.00	3.00
❑ 621	5¢	Dark Blue & Black	700.00 (8)	18.00	11.00

622
(694)

623
(697)

Scott No.			Plate Block	Unused	Used

1925–1926. 1922–1925 Series New Values, Perforated 11.
(NH Add 80%)

| ☐ 622 | 13¢ | Green | 160.00 (6) | 17.00 | .65 |
| ☐ 623 | 17¢ | Black | 22.00 (6) | 20.00 | .50 |

627

628

629
(630)

1926. (NH Add 60%)

☐ 627	2¢	Sesquicentennial Exposition	40.00 (6)	3.00	.60
☐ 628	5¢	Ericsson Memorial	90.00 (6)	7.00	3.25
☐ 629	2¢	Battle of White Plains	41.00 (6)	2.50	2.00
☐ 630	2¢	White Plains souvenir sheet (~629)	—	525.00	480.00

1926. Series of 1922–1925, Rotary Press Printing, Imperforate. (NH Add 60%)

| ☐ 631 | 1½¢ | Brown (~553) | 72.00 | 2.10 | 1.75 |

1926–1928. Series of 1922–1925, Perforated 11 x 10½.
(NH Add 60%)

☐ 632	1¢	Green (~552)	34.00	.30	.20
☐ 633	1½¢	Yellow Brown (~553)	40.00	2.00	.21
☐ 634	2¢	Carmine (~554) (type I)	10.00	.30	.21
☐ 634A	2¢	Carmine (~554) (type II)	600.00	260.00	13.00

Scott No.			Plate Block	Unused	Used
❏ 635	3¢	Violet (~555)	13.00	1.50	.20
❏ 636	4¢	Yellow Brown (~556)	80.00	3.00	.20
❏ 637	5¢	Dark Blue (~557)	18.00	3.00	.20
❏ 638	6¢	Red Orange (~558)	18.00	2.75	.20
❏ 639	7¢	Black (~559)	18.00	2.75	.20
❏ 640	8¢	Olive Green (~560)	18.00	2.75	.20
❏ 641	9¢	Orange Red (~561)	18.00	2.75	.20
❏ 642	10¢	Orange (~562)	24.00	3.00	.20

643

644

1927. (NH Add 60%)

❏ 643	2¢	Vermont Sesquicentennial	40.00 (6)	1.45	1.00
❏ 644	2¢	Oriskany - Saratoga	40.00 (6)	4.00	2.15

645

646

647

648

649

650

1928. (NH Add 50–60%)

❏ 645	2¢	Valley Forge	30.00 (6)	1.10	.60
❏ 646	2¢	Molly Pitcher	39.00	1.50	1.25
❏ 647	2¢	Hawaii	130.00	5.00	4.20
❏ 648	5¢	Hawaii	300.00	16.00	12.00
❏ 649	2¢	Aeronautics Conference	16.00 (6)	1.50	.90
❏ 650	5¢	Aeronautics Conference	60.00 (6)	5.00	3.50

651

654
(655, 556)

Scott No.			Plate Block	Unused	Used
1929. (NH Add 50%)					
❏ 651	2¢	George Rogers Clark	13.00 (6)	.75	.52
❏ 652		**need info**			

1929. Series of 1922–1925, Rotary Press Printing, 11 x 10½.
(NH Add 10–35%)

❏ 653	½¢	Olive Brown (~551)	2.00	.30	.20
❏ 654	2¢	Edison - Light Bulb, perforated 11	32.00 (6)	.95	.70
❏ 655	2¢	Edison (~654), perforated 11 x 10½	45.00	.80	.25

Scott No.			Line Pair	Unused	Used
1929. Coil Stamp.					
❏ 656	2¢	Edison – Light Bulb (~654)	75.00	15.00	2.00

657

Scott No.			Plate Block	Unused	Used
1929.					
❏ 657	2¢	Sullivan Expedition	28.00 (6)	.90	.70

658

669

Scott No.			Plate Block	Unused	Used

1929. Series of 1922–1925, Perforated 11 x 10½, Overprinted "Kans." (NH Add 50%)

			Plate Block	Unused	Used
❑ 658	1¢	Green	40.00	3.50	2.20
❑ 659	1½¢	Brown	50.00	5.00	2.60
❑ 660	2¢	Carmine	50.00	5.00	1.20
❑ 661	3¢	Violet	220.00	26.00	12.00
❑ 662	4¢	Yellow Brown	200.00	26.00	9.10
❑ 663	5¢	Deep Blue	165.00	17.00	9.10
❑ 664	6¢	Red Orange	450.00	40.00	16.00
❑ 665	7¢	Black	500.00	36.00	21.00
❑ 666	8¢	Olive Green	950.00	125.00	60.00
❑ 667	9¢	Light Rose	225.00	20.00	11.00
❑ 668	10¢	Orange Yellow	350.00	30.00	11.00

1929. Series of 1922–1925, Perforated 11 x 10½, Overprinted "Nebr." (NH Add 50%)

			Plate Block	Unused	Used
❑ 669	1¢	Green	52.00	5.00	2.10
❑ 670	1½¢	Brown	52.00	5.00	2.10
❑ 671	2¢	Carmine	45.00	4.50	1.40
❑ 672	3¢	Violet	200.00	21.00	10.00
❑ 673	4¢	Brown	250.00	25.00	13.00
❑ 674	5¢	Blue	310.00	24.00	13.00
❑ 675	6¢	Orange	500.00	50.00	22.00
❑ 676	7¢	Black	300.00	32.00	17.00
❑ 677	8¢	Olive Green	410.00	42.00	23.00
❑ 678	9¢	Rose	510.00	50.00	23.00
❑ 679	10¢	Orange Yellow	900.00	140.00	21.00

NOTE: Fakes abound, especially on used stamps.

| **680** | **681** | **682** | **683** |

Scott No.			Plate Block	Unused	Used
1929. (NH Add 35%)					
❑ 680	2¢	Battle of Fallen Timbers	26.00 (6)	1.00	.80
❑ 681	2¢	Ohio River Canalization	21.00 (6)	.68	.75
1930. (NH Add 35%)					
❑ 682	2¢	Massachusetts Bay Colony	29.00 (6)	.70	.60
❑ 683	2¢	Charleston, SC	45.00 (6)	1.25	.95

| **684** | **685** |
| (686) | (687) |

1930. Series of 1922–1925, Rotary Press Printing, Perforated 11 x 10½. (NH Add 35%)

❑ 684	1½¢	Warren G. Harding (full face)	2.50	.40	.16
❑ 685	4¢	William Howard Taft	12.50	1.00	.16

Scott No.			Line Pair	Unused	Used

1930. Series of 1922–1925, Rotary Press Coil Stamps, Perforated 10 Vertically. (NH Add 40%)

❑ 686	1½¢	Harding (~684)	5.00	2.00	.22
❑ 687	4¢	Taft (~685)	8.50	3.60	.60

| 688 | 689 | 690 |

Scott No.			Plate Block	Unused	Used

1930. (NH Add 35%)

❑ 688	2¢	Battle of Braddock's Field	36.00 (6)	1.10	.84
❑ 689	2¢	Von Steuben	25.00 (6)	.60	.40
❑ 690	2¢	Pulaski	11.00 (6)	.35	.25

1931. Series of 1922–1925, Rotary Press Printing, Perforated 11 x 10½ or 10½ x 11. (NH Add 40%)

❑ 692	11¢	Light Blue (~563)	15.00	3.00	.25
❑ 693	12¢	Brown Violet (~564)	26.00	6.00	.25
❑ 694	13¢	Yellow Green (~622)	16.00	2.10	.25
❑ 695	14¢	Dark Blue (~565)	26.00	3.50	.45
❑ 696	15¢	Gray (~566)	36.00	7.50	.25
❑ 697	17¢	Black (~623)	33.00	5.00	.29
❑ 698	20¢	Carmine Rose (~567)	40.00	11.00	.25
❑ 699	25¢	Blue Green (~568)	45.00	11.00	.25
❑ 700	30¢	Brown (~569)	75.00	17.00	.25
❑ 701	50¢	Lilac (~570)	185.00	40.00	.25

| 702 | 703 |

1931. (NH Add 25%)

| ❑ 702 | 2¢ | Red Cross | 1.80 | .28 | .20 |
| ❑ 703 | 2¢ | Surrender at Yorktown | 2.10 | .40 | .25 |

PLEASE NOTE: Unless otherwise noted, plate blocks are assumed to be blocks of 4. Where the number is more than 4, it appears in parentheses immediately following the price for the plate block. Blocks containing fewer than the appropriate number of stamps are not considered to be plate blocks and sell for much less.

704   705   706   707

708   709   710   711

712   713   714   715

Scott No.			Plate Block	Unused	Used
1932. Washington Bicentennial Set. (NH Add 40%)					
❏ 704	½¢	Olive Brown	4.75	.30	.16
❏ 705	1¢	Green	5.00	.30	.16
❏ 706	1½¢	Brown	20.00	.45	.20
❏ 707	2¢	Carmine	2.50	.25	.16
❏ 708	3¢	Purple	17.00	.62	.20
❏ 709	4¢	Light Brown	8.00	.36	.20
❏ 710	5¢	Blue	20.00	1.50	.20
❏ 711	6¢	Orange	8.00	3.50	.20
❏ 712	7¢	Black	9.00	.40	.21
❏ 713	8¢	Olive Bistre	60.00	3.50	.50
❏ 714	9¢	Pale Red	48.00	3.75	.22
❏ 715	10¢	Orange Yellow	100.00	12.00	.22
		Set of 12 (704–715)	—	26.00	6.00

716	717	718	719	720
				(721, 722)

Scott No.			Plate Block	Unused	Used

1932. (NH Add 30%)

Scott No.			Plate Block	Unused	Used
❑ 716	2¢	Olympics - Lake Placid	11.00 (6)	.50	.22
❑ 717	2¢	Arbor Day	9.00	.40	.20
❑ 718	3¢	Olympics - Runner	15.00	1.60	.24
❑ 719	5¢	Olympics - Discus Thrower	25.00	2.50	.28
❑ 720	3¢	George Washington	2.00	.25	.16

Scott No.			Line Pair	Unused	Used

1932. Coil Stamps. (NH Add 30%)

Scott No.			Line Pair	Unused	Used
❑ 721	3¢	Washington (~720) perf 10 vertically	6.50	3.00	.25
❑ 722	3¢	Washington (~720) perf 10 horizontally	6.00	1.90	.50
❑ 723	6¢	Garfield (~558) perf 10 vertically	54.00	12.00	.30

724	725

Scott No.			Plate Block	Unused	Used

1932. (NH Add 30%)

Scott No.			Plate Block	Unused	Used
❑ 724	3¢	William Penn	12.00 (6)	.45	.25
❑ 725	3¢	Daniel Webster	21.00 (6)	.60	.30

726	727	728	729
	(752)	(730, 766)	(731, 767)

Scott No.			Plate Block	Unused	Used

1933. (NH Add 30%)

☐ 726	3¢	General Oglethorpe	14.00 (6)	.50	.22
☐ 727	3¢	Washington at Newburgh	5.00	.28	.20
☐ 728	1¢	Century of Progress - Fort Dearborn	2.40	.26	.20
☐ 729	3¢	Century of Progress - Skyscrapers	3.00	.26	.20

730	731

1933. A.P.S. Convention Souvenir Sheets, Imperforate, Ungummed.

☐ 730	1¢	Sheet of 25 (~728)	—	32.00	28.00
☐ 730a	1¢	Single stamp	—	.75	.60
☐ 731	3¢	Sheet of 25 (~729)	—	31.00	29.00
☐ 731a	3¢	Single stamp	—	.70	.55

732   **733**   **734**
        (735, 753, 768)

Scott No.			Plate Block	Unused	Used
1933. (NH Add 20%)					
❑ 732	3¢	National Recovery Act (NRA)	1.80	.30	.15
❑ 733	3¢	Byrd Antarctic Expedition	14.00 (6)	.60	.50
❑ 734	5¢	Kosciuszko	36.00 (6)	.60	.30

735

1934. National Philatelic Exhibition Souvenir Sheet, Imperforate, Ungummed .

❑ 735	3¢	Sheet of 6 (~733)	—	14.00	9.00
❑ 735a	3¢	Single stamp	—	3.50	3.00

736

737
(738, 754)

739
(755)

Scott No.			Plate Block	Unused	Used
1934. (NH Add 20%)					
❑ 736	3¢	Maryland Tercentenary	9.00 (6)	.25	.20
❑ 737	3¢	Mother's Day, perf 11 x 10½	2.00	.25	.20
❑ 738	3¢	Mother's Day (~737), perf 11	5.00 (6)	.35	.25
❑ 739	3¢	Wisconsin Tercentenary	4.50 (6)	.30	.20

741
(757)

742
(750, 758, 770)

740
(751, 756, 769)

743
(759)

744
(760)

1934. National Parks Issue, Perforated. (NH Add 25%)

❑ 740	1¢	Yosemite	1.60 (6)	.24	.20
❑ 741	2¢	Grand Canyon	2.00 (6)	.50	.20
❑ 742	3¢	Mt. Rainier	2.40 (6)	.50	.20
❑ 743	4¢	Mesa Verde	10.00 (6)	.65	.45
❑ 744	5¢	Yellowstone	10.00 (6)	1.25	.65

745
(761)

746
(762)

747
(763)

748
(764)

749
(765, 797)

Scott No.			Plate Block	Unused	Used
❑ 745	6¢	Crater Lake	21.00 (6)	1.50	.90
❑ 746	7¢	Acadia	13.00 (6)	.95	.80
❑ 747	8¢	Zion	21.00 (6)	2.20	1.75
❑ 748	9¢	Glacier	21.00 (6)	2.40	.75
❑ 749	10¢	Smoky Mountains, gray black	30.00 (6)	3.50	1.00
		Set of 10 (740–749)	—	9.00	4.50

750

1934. A.P.S. Convention Souvenir Sheet, Imperforate, Gummed.
(NH Add 25%)

❑ 750	3¢	Sheet of 6 (~742)	—	41.00	35.00
❑ 750a	3¢	Single stamp	—	4.50	3.00

751

Scott No.			Plate Block	Unused	Used

1934. Trans-Mississippi Philatelic Exposition Souvenir Sheet, Imperforate, Gummed. (NH Add 25%)

| ❏ 751 | 1¢ | Sheet of 6 (~740) | — | 15.00 | 13.00 |
| ❏ 751a | 1¢ | Single stamp | — | 2.00 | 1.40 |

1935. Farley Special Printing, Perforated, Ungummed.

| ❏ 752 | 3¢ | Washington at Newburgh (~727) | 21.00 | .20 | .24 |
| ❏ 753 | 3¢ | Byrd Antarctic Expedition (~733) | 15.00 (6) | 1.00 | .50 |

1935. Farley Special Printing, Imperforate, Ungummed.

| ❏ 754 | 3¢ | Mother's Day (~737) | 18.00 (6) | .80 | .60 |
| ❏ 755 | 3¢ | Wisconsin Tercentenary (~739) | 16.50 (6) | .80 | .60 |

1935. Farley Special Printing, National Parks Set, Imperforate, Ungummed.

❏ 756	1¢	Yosemite (~740)	4.50 (6)	.45	.24
❏ 757	2¢	Grand Canyon (~741)	7.00 (6)	.45	.25
❏ 758	3¢	Mt. Rainier (~742)	16.00 (6)	.60	.35
❏ 759	4¢	Mesa Verde (~743)	20.00 (6)	1.10	1.00
❏ 760	5¢	Yellowstone (~744)	24.00 (6)	1.40	1.10
❏ 761	6¢	Crater Lake (~745)	36.00 (6)	2.00	1.60
❏ 762	7¢	Acadia (~746)	32.00 (6)	1.50	1.20
❏ 763	8¢	Zion (~747)	41.00 (6)	2.00	1.50
❏ 764	9¢	Glacier (~748)	42.00 (6)	1.75	1.75
❏ 765	10¢	Smoky Mountains (~749), gray black	55.00 (6)	4.50	3.00
		Set of 10 (756–765)	—	10.00	8.00

771

Scott No.			Plate Block	Unused	Used

1935. Farley Special Printing, Imperforate, Ungummed.

			Plate Block	Unused	Used
❑ 766	1¢	Souvenir sheet of 25 (~730)	—	23.00	19.00
❑ 767	3¢	Souvenir sheet of 25 (~731)	—	22.00	17.00
❑ 768	3¢	Souvenir sheet of 6 (~735)	—	18.00	15.00
❑ 769	1¢	Souvenir sheet of 6 (~751)	—	15.00	10.00
❑ 770	3¢	Souvenir sheet of 6 (~750)	—	24.00	20.00
❑ 771	16¢	Airmail Special Delivery	75.00 (6)	4.00	2.25

NOTE: Farley Special Printing items (752–771) were issued in uncut press sheets. Position pairs and blocks that include guide lines or interpane gutters help distinguish Farley items from their regularly issued counterparts.

NOTE: Prices for stamps from 1935 forward are for never-hinged (NH) examples.

772
(778a)

773
(778b)

774

775
(778c)

1935.

❑ 772	3¢	Connecticut Tercentenary	2.00	.31	.25
❑ 773	3¢	California Pacific Exposition	1.80	.30	.25
❑ 774	3¢	Boulder Dam	2.00 (6)	.30	.25
❑ 775	3¢	Michigan Centenary	1.90	.30	.25

776
(778d)

777

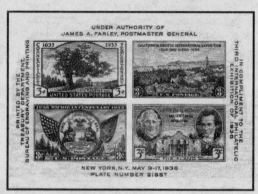

778

Scott No.			Plate Block	Unused	Used
1936.					
❑ 776	3¢	Texas Centennial	1.50	.30	.25
❑ 777	3¢	Rhode Island Tercentenary	1.50	.30	.20
❑ 778	3¢	TIPEX souvenir sheet	—	3.00	2.00
❑ 778a	3¢	Single Stamp (~772), imperforate	—	.82	.45
❑ 778b	3¢	Single Stamp (~773), imperforate	—	.80	.65
❑ 778c	3¢	Single Stamp (~775), imperforate	—	.80	.60
❑ 778d	3¢	Single Stamp (~776), imperforate	—	.82	.65

NOTE: Prices for stamps from 1935 forward are for never-hinged (NH) examples.

782   **783**   **784**

Scott No.			Plate Block	Unused	Used
❑ 782	3¢	Arkansas Centennial	2.00	.44	.17
❑ 783	3¢	Oregon Territory Centennial	1.80	.30	.16
❑ 784	3¢	Susan B. Anthony	1.25	.48	.16

785   **786**

787   **788**

789   **790**

1936–1937. Army and Navy Issue.

❑ 785	1¢	Washington & Greene	1.20	.35	.24
❑ 786	2¢	Jackson & Scott	1.25	.35	.24
❑ 787	3¢	Sherman, Grant & Sheridan	2.00	.40	.24
❑ 788	4¢	Lee & Stonewall Jackson	10.00	.50	.30
❑ 789	5¢	West Point	11.00	.75	.30
❑ 790	1¢	Jones & Barry	1.25	.30	.24

791   792

793   794

Scott No.			Plate Block	Unused	Used
❏ 791	2¢	Decatur & McDonough	1.10	.32	.21
❏ 792	3¢	Farragut & Porter	1.50	.32	.18
❏ 793	4¢	Sampson, Dewey & Schley	11.00	.52	.20
❏ 794	5¢	Annapolis	10.00	.70	.28
		Set of 10 (785–779)	—	1.50	1.00

795   796   797

1937.

❏ 795	3¢	Ordinance of 1787	1.50	.35	.25
❏ 796	5¢	Virginia Dare	8.50 (6)	.35	.25
❏ 797	10¢	SPA souvenir sheet (~749), blue green	—	1.00	.70

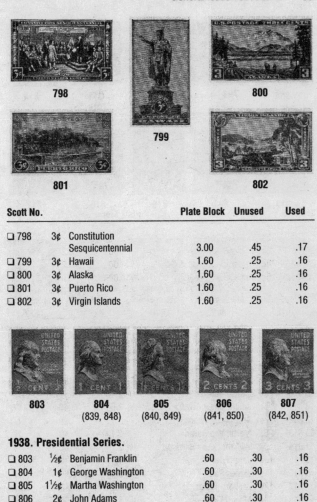

798

799

800

801

802

Scott No.			Plate Block	Unused	Used
❑ 798	3¢	Constitution Sesquicentennial	3.00	.45	.17
❑ 799	3¢	Hawaii	1.60	.25	.16
❑ 800	3¢	Alaska	1.60	.25	.16
❑ 801	3¢	Puerto Rico	1.60	.25	.16
❑ 802	3¢	Virgin Islands	1.60	.25	.16

803

804
(839, 848)

805
(840, 849)

806
(841, 850)

807
(842, 851)

1938. Presidential Series.

❑ 803	½¢	Benjamin Franklin	.60	.30	.16
❑ 804	1¢	George Washington	.60	.30	.16
❑ 805	1½¢	Martha Washington	.60	.30	.16
❑ 806	2¢	John Adams	.60	.30	.16
❑ 807	3¢	Thomas Jefferson	.60	.30	.16

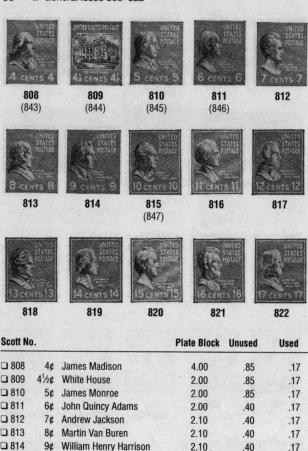

808
(843)

809
(844)

810
(845)

811
(846)

812

813

814

815
(847)

816

817

818

819

820

821

822

Scott No.			Plate Block	Unused	Used
❏ 808	4¢	James Madison	4.00	.85	.17
❏ 809	4½¢	White House	2.00	.85	.17
❏ 810	5¢	James Monroe	2.00	.85	.17
❏ 811	6¢	John Quincy Adams	2.00	.40	.17
❏ 812	7¢	Andrew Jackson	2.10	.40	.17
❏ 813	8¢	Martin Van Buren	2.10	.40	.17
❏ 814	9¢	William Henry Harrison	2.10	.40	.17
❏ 815	10¢	John Tyler	1.60	.40	.17
❏ 816	11¢	James Polk	3.50	.65	.17
❏ 817	12¢	Zachary Taylor	6.50	1.10	.21
❏ 818	13¢	Millard Fillmore	8.00	1.50	.21
❏ 819	14¢	Franklin Pierce	7.50	1.10	.21
❏ 820	15¢	James Buchanan	2.10	.50	.16
❏ 821	16¢	Abraham Lincoln	6.50	1.25	.50
❏ 822	17¢	Andrew Johnson	6.50	1.00	.21

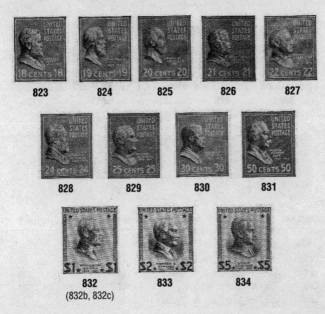

823   824   825   826   827

828   829   830   831

832
(832b, 832c)
    833   834

Scott No.			Plate Block	Unused	Used
☐ 823	18¢	Ulysses S. Grant	10.00	2.00	.17
☐ 824	19¢	Rutherford B. Hayes	7.00	1.50	.50
☐ 825	20¢	James A Garfield	5.00	1.00	.17
☐ 826	21¢	Chester A. Arthur	10.00	1.50	.24
☐ 827	22¢	Grover Cleveland	11.00	1.50	.60
☐ 828	24¢	Benjamin Harrison	20.00	4.50	.35
☐ 829	25¢	William McKinley	4.50	.90	.16
☐ 830	30¢	Theodore Roosevelt	20.00	4.00	.16
☐ 831	50¢	William Howard Taft	30.00	7.25	.24
☐ 832	$1	Woodrow Wilson, dark violet & black	40.00	10.00	.24
☐ 832b	$1	Wilson (~832), watermarked "USIR"	—	260.00	65.00
☐ 832c	$1	Wilson, (~832), red violet & black	37.00	8.00	.24
☐ 833	$2	Warren G. Harding	140.00	25.00	5.00
☐ 834	$5	Calvin Coolidge	450.00	120.00	4.50

835 836

837 838

Scott No.			Plate Block	Unused	Used
1938.					
❏ 835	3¢	Constitution Ratification	4.00	.48	.21
❏ 836	3¢	Swede-Finn Tercentenary	3.00 (6)	.27	.21
❏ 837	3¢	Northwest Territory	11.00	.27	.21
❏ 838	3¢	Iowa Territory Centennial	7.00	.28	.21

Scott No.			Line Pair	Unused	Used
1939. Presidential Series Coil Stamps, Perforated 10 Vertically.					
❏ 839	1¢	G. Washington (~804)	1.30	.26	.16
❏ 840	1½¢	M. Washington (~805)	1.40	.26	.16
❏ 841	2¢	Adams (~806)	1.25	.26	.16
❏ 842	3¢	Jefferson (~807)	1.65	.45	.20
❏ 843	4¢	Madison (~808)	29.00	6.00	.55
❏ 844	4½¢	White House (~809)	4.80	.60	.45
❏ 845	5¢	Monroe (~810)	26.00	4.00	.42
❏ 846	6¢	J. Q. Adams (~811)	6.70	1.30	.20
❏ 847	10¢	Tyler (~815)	43.00	10.00	.78
1939. Presidential Series Coil Stamps, Perforated 10 Horizontally.					
❏ 848	1¢	G. Washington (~804)	2.50	.82	.26
❏ 849	1½¢	M. Washington (~805)	3.60	1.30	.40
❏ 850	2¢	Adams (~806)	6.00	2.15	.56
❏ 851	3¢	Jefferson (~807)	6.10	2.20	.62

852   853   854

855   856

857

858

Scott No.			Plate Block	Unused	Used
1939.					
☐ 852	3¢	Golden Gate Exposition	1.60	.24	.16
☐ 853	3¢	New York World's Fair	2.00	.25	.16
☐ 854	3¢	Washington's Inaugural	7.50 (6)	.84	.16
☐ 855	3¢	Baseball Centennial	10.00	2.00	.25
☐ 856	3¢	Panama Canal	4.00 (6)	.36	.21
☐ 857	3¢	Colonial Printing	1.60	.21	.16
☐ 858	3¢	Washington, Montana & the Dakotas	1.65	.24	.16

NOTE: Prices for stamps from 1935 forward are for never-hinged (NH) examples.

859 860 861 862

863 864 865 866

867 868 869 870

Scott No.			Plate Block	Unused	Used

1940. Famous Americans Series.

Scott No.			Plate Block	Unused	Used
❑ 859	1¢	Washington Irving	1.30	.25	.16
❑ 860	2¢	James Fenimore Cooper	1.40	.25	.16
❑ 861	3¢	Ralph Waldo Emerson	1.60	.25	.16
❑ 862	5¢	Louisa May Alcott	10.00	.40	.30
❑ 863	10¢	Samuel Clemens	42.00	2.10	1.50
❑ 864	1¢	Henry Wadsworth Longfellow	2.50	.30	.12
❑ 865	2¢	John Greenleaf Whittier	2.10	.23	.12
❑ 866	3¢	James Russell Lowell	2.50	.21	.12
❑ 867	5¢	Walt Whitman	12.00	.52	.12
❑ 868	10¢	James Whitcomb Riley	42.00	2.25	2.00
❑ 869	1¢	Horace Mann	2.60	.22	.16
❑ 870	2¢	Mark Hopkins	1.60	.22	.16

Scott No.			Plate Block	Unused	Used
❏ 871	3¢	Charles W. Elliot	3.00	.24	.18
❏ 872	5¢	Frances W. Willard	14.00	.50	.30
❏ 873	10¢	Booker T. Washington	32.00	2.15	1.80
❏ 874	1¢	John James Audubon	1.30	.25	.17
❏ 875	2¢	Crawford W. Long	1.35	.25	.17
❏ 876	3¢	Luther Burbank	1.35	.25	.17
❏ 877	5¢	Walter Reed	7.50	.32	.30
❏ 878	10¢	James Adams	26.00	1.40	1.25
❏ 879	1¢	Stephen Collins Foster	1.50	.26	.17
❏ 880	2¢	John Philip Sousa	1.50	.23	.17
❏ 881	3¢	Victor Herbert	1.60	.25	.17
❏ 882	5¢	Edward A. McDowell	12.00	.52	.30

NOTE: Prices for stamps from 1935 forward are for never-hinged (NH) examples.

883   884   885   886

887   888   889   890

891   892   893

Scott No.			Plate Block	Unused	Used
❏ 883	10¢	Ethelbert Nevin	40.00	4.00	1.60
❏ 884	1¢	Gilbert Charles Stuart	1.50	.28	.16
❏ 885	2¢	James A. McNeill Whistler	1.25	.22	.17
❏ 886	3¢	Augustus Saint-Gaudens	1.60	.35	.16
❏ 887	5¢	Daniel Chester French	9.00	.65	.30
❏ 888	10¢	Frederic Remington	32.00	2.10	1.15
❏ 889	1¢	Eli Whitney	2.60	.35	.16
❏ 890	2¢	Samuel F. B. Morse	1.40	.25	.16
❏ 891	3¢	Cyrus McCormick	2.00	.40	.16
❏ 892	5¢	Elias Howe	14.00	1.25	.40
❏ 893	10¢	Alexander Graham Bell	80.00	12.00	3.25
		Set of 35 (859–893)	—	21.00	6.00

NOTE: Prices for stamps from 1935 forward are for never-hinged (NH) examples.

894

895

896

897

898

899

900

901

902

Scott No.			Plate Block	Unused	Used
1940.					
☐ 894	3¢	Pony Express	4.00	.45	.20
☐ 895	3¢	Pan American Union	3.75	.35	.17
☐ 896	3¢	Idaho Statehood	2.10	.25	.17
☐ 897	3¢	Wyoming Statehood	1.75	.25	.17
☐ 898	3¢	Coronado Expedition	1.50	.25	.17
☐ 899	1¢	Defense – Statue of Liberty	.55	.22	.17
☐ 900	2¢	Defense – Artillery	.55	.22	.17
☐ 901	3¢	Defense – Torch of Liberty	.80	.22	.17
☐ 902	3¢	13th Amendment	4.00	.30	.24

903

Scott No.			Plate Block	Unused	Used
1941.					
☐ 903	3¢	Vermont Statehood	2.00	.37	.18

904

905

906

1942.					
☐ 904	3¢	Kentucky	1.50	.25	.17
☐ 905	3¢	Win the War	.84	.22	.17
☐ 906	5¢	China	13.00	.30	.25

907

908

1943.					
☐ 907	2¢	Allied Nations	.78	.20	.17
☐ 908	1¢	Four Freedoms	.78	.20	.17

NOTE: Prices for stamps from 1935 forward are for never-hinged (NH) examples.

909

910

911

912

913

914

915

916

Scott No.			Plate Block	Unused	Used
1943–1944. Overrun Countries Issue.					
❑ 909	5¢	Poland	7.00	.30	.22
❑ 910	5¢	Czechoslovakia	3.50	.30	.22
❑ 911	5¢	Norway	2.10	.30	.22
❑ 912	5¢	Luxembourg	1.60	.30	.22
❑ 913	5¢	Netherlands	1.60	.30	.22
❑ 914	5¢	Belgium	1.60	.30	.22
❑ 915	5¢	France	1.60	.30	.22
❑ 916	5¢	Greece	14.00	.72	.35

917   918

919   920

921

Scott No.			Plate Block	Unused	Used
❏ 917	5¢	Yugoslavia	7.00	.42	.21
❏ 918	5¢	Albania	7.00	.42	.21
❏ 919	5¢	Austria	6.00	.30	.21
❏ 920	5¢	Denmark	6.00	.40	.21
❏ 921	5¢	Korea	6.00	.36	.21
		Set of 13 (909–921)	—	4.00	3.00

NOTE: Plate blocks of the Overrun Nations Issue are inscribed with the name of country instead of a plate number.

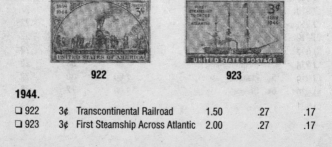

922   923

1944.

❏ 922	3¢	Transcontinental Railroad	1.50	.27	.17
❏ 923	3¢	First Steamship Across Atlantic	2.00	.27	.17

924

925

926

Scott No.			Plate Block	Unused	Used
❏ 924	3¢	Telegraph Centenary	1.25	.26	.18
❏ 925	3¢	Corregidor	1.20	.26	.18
❏ 926	3¢	Motion Pictures	1.10	.26	.18

927

928

929

930

931

1945.

❏ 927	3¢	Florida	1.10	.25	.16
❏ 928	5¢	Toward United Nations	.66	.20	.16
❏ 929	3¢	Iwo Jima	2.10	.32	.16
❏ 930	1¢	Roosevelt – Hyde Park	2.50	.78	.40
❏ 931	2¢	Roosevelt – Warm Springs	.52	.21	.16

932

933

934

935

936

937

938

Scott No.			Plate Block	Unused	Used
❏ 932	3¢	Roosevelt – White House	.75	.21	.17
❏ 933	5¢	Roosevelt – Four Freedoms	1.10	.21	.17
❏ 934	3¢	Army – Victory March	1.10	.21	.17
❏ 935	3¢	Navy – Sailors	1.10	.21	.17
❏ 936	3¢	Coast Guard – Landing Craft	.90	.21	.17
❏ 937	3¢	Alfred E. Smith	.90	.21	.17
❏ 938	3¢	Texas Centennial	1.12	.21	.17

NOTE: Prices for stamps from 1935 forward are for never-hinged (NH) examples.

939 940 941

942 943 944

Scott No.			Plate Block	Unused	Used
1946.					
❏ 939	3¢	Merchant Marine	.75	.26	.16
❏ 940	3¢	Discharge Emblem	.95	.26	.16
❏ 941	3¢	Tennessee Statehood	1.10	.26	.16
❏ 942	3¢	Iowa Statehood	1.00	.25	.16
❏ 943	3¢	Smithsonian Institution	1.00	.26	.16
❏ 944	3¢	Kearny Expedition	.90	.26	.16

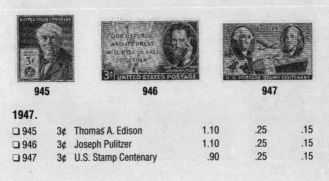

945 946 947

1947.					
❏ 945	3¢	Thomas A. Edison	1.10	.25	.15
❏ 946	3¢	Joseph Pulitzer	1.10	.25	.15
❏ 947	3¢	U.S. Stamp Centenary	.90	.25	.15

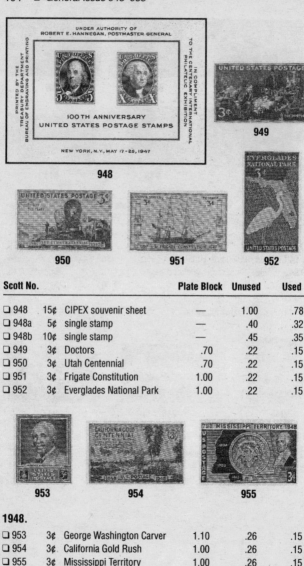

948

949

950

951

952

Scott No.			Plate Block	Unused	Used
❏ 948	15¢	CIPEX souvenir sheet	—	1.00	.78
❏ 948a	5¢	single stamp	—	.40	.32
❏ 948b	10¢	single stamp	—	.45	.35
❏ 949	3¢	Doctors	.70	.22	.15
❏ 950	3¢	Utah Centennial	.70	.22	.15
❏ 951	3¢	Frigate Constitution	1.00	.22	.15
❏ 952	3¢	Everglades National Park	1.00	.22	.15

953

954

955

1948.

❏ 953	3¢	George Washington Carver	1.10	.26	.15
❏ 954	3¢	California Gold Rush	1.00	.26	.15
❏ 955	3¢	Mississippi Territory	1.00	.26	.15

956 957 958

959 960 961

962 963 964

965 966 967

Scott No.			Plate Block	Unused	Used
❑ 956	3¢	Immortal Chaplains	1.00	.25	.15
❑ 957	3¢	Wisconsin Centennial	1.00	.25	.15
❑ 958	5¢	Swedish Pioneers	.75	.22	.15
❑ 959	3¢	Progress of Women	1.00	.25	.15
❑ 960	3¢	William Allen White	.75	.24	.15
❑ 961	3¢	U.S. Canada Friendship	.75	.21	.15
❑ 962	3¢	Francis Scott Key	1.10	.25	.15
❑ 963	3¢	Youth Month	.70	.21	.15
❑ 964	3¢	Oregon Territory	.70	.21	.15
❑ 965	3¢	Harlan Fiske Stone	1.00	.20	.15
❑ 966	3¢	Mount Palomar	1.00	.20	.15
❑ 967	3¢	Clara Barton	.70	.20	.15

968   969   970

Scott No.			Plate Block	Unused	Used
❑ 968	3¢	Poultry Industry	1.00	.25	.17
❑ 969	3¢	Gold Star Mothers	.75	.22	.17
❑ 970	3¢	Fort Kearny	.90	.21	.17

971   972   973

974   975   976

1948.

❑ 971	3¢	Volunteer Firemen	1.50	.25	.15
❑ 972	3¢	Indian Centennial	.90	.20	.15
❑ 973	3¢	Rough Riders	.75	.20	.15
❑ 974	3¢	Juliette Low	1.00	.30	.15
❑ 975	3¢	Will Rogers	.90	.21	.15
❑ 976	3¢	Fort Bliss Centennial	1.00	.21	.15

977   978

979

980

Scott No.			Plate Block	Unused	Used
❏ 977	3¢	Moina Michael	1.00	.26	.15
❏ 978	3¢	Gettysburg Address	1.00	.25	.15
❏ 979	3¢	American Turners	.90	.22	.15
❏ 980	3¢	Joel Chandler Harris	1.10	.26	.15

981   982

983   984   985

1949.

❏ 981	3¢	Minnesota Centennia	.50	.21	.15
❏ 982	3¢	Washington & Lee University	.90	.21	.15
❏ 983	3¢	Puerto Rico	.75	.21	.15
❏ 984	3¢	Annapolis Tercentenary	.89	.22	.15
❏ 985	3¢	G.A.R.	.89	.20	.15

Scott No.			Plate Block	Unused	Used
1950.					
❑ 986	3¢	Edgar Allan Poe	1.00	.35	.15
❑ 987	3¢	American Bankers Assn.	1.10	.35	.15
❑ 988	3¢	Samuel Gompers	.75	.22	.15
❑ 989	3¢	Capitol Dome Statue	.70	.22	.15
❑ 990	3¢	White House	.80	.22	.15
❑ 991	3¢	Supreme Court	.92	.25	.15
❑ 992	3¢	Capitol Building	.92	.22	.15
❑ 993	3¢	Casey Jones	1.10	.25	.15
❑ 994	3¢	Kansas City Centennial	1.20	.30	.15
❑ 995	3¢	Boy Scouts	1.10	.25	.15
❑ 996	3¢	Indiana Territory	1.00	.30	.15
❑ 997	3¢	California Statehood	.95	.21	.15

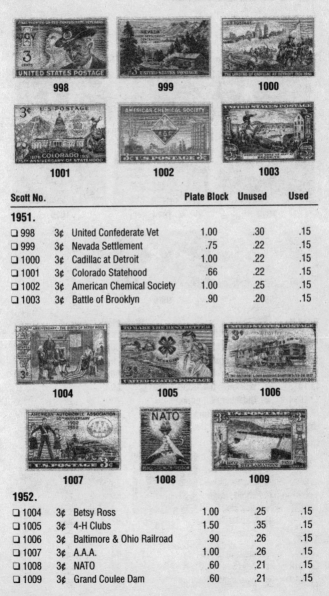

998 999 1000

1001 1002 1003

Scott No.			Plate Block	Unused	Used
1951.					
❑ 998	3¢	United Confederate Vet	1.00	.30	.15
❑ 999	3¢	Nevada Settlement	.75	.22	.15
❑ 1000	3¢	Cadillac at Detroit	1.00	.22	.15
❑ 1001	3¢	Colorado Statehood	.66	.22	.15
❑ 1002	3¢	American Chemical Society	1.00	.25	.15
❑ 1003	3¢	Battle of Brooklyn	.90	.20	.15

1004 1005 1006

1007 1008 1009

1952.					
❑ 1004	3¢	Betsy Ross	1.00	.25	.15
❑ 1005	3¢	4-H Clubs	1.50	.35	.15
❑ 1006	3¢	Baltimore & Ohio Railroad	.90	.26	.15
❑ 1007	3¢	A.A.A.	1.00	.26	.15
❑ 1008	3¢	NATO	.60	.21	.15
❑ 1009	3¢	Grand Coulee Dam	.60	.21	.15

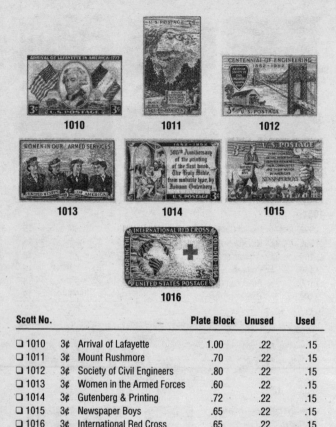

1010

1011

1012

1013

1014

1015

1016

Scott No.			Plate Block	Unused	Used
❏ 1010	3¢	Arrival of Lafayette	1.00	.22	.15
❏ 1011	3¢	Mount Rushmore	.70	.22	.15
❏ 1012	3¢	Society of Civil Engineers	.80	.22	.15
❏ 1013	3¢	Women in the Armed Forces	.60	.22	.15
❏ 1014	3¢	Gutenberg & Printing	.72	.22	.15
❏ 1015	3¢	Newspaper Boys	.65	.22	.15
❏ 1016	3¢	International Red Cross	.65	.22	.15

1017

1018

1019

1953.

❏ 1017	3¢	National Guard	.62	.20	.15
❏ 1018	3¢	Ohio Statehood	.90	.25	.15
❏ 1019	3¢	Washington Territory	.60	.20	.15

Scott No.			Plate Block	Unused	Used
❏ 1020	3¢	Louisiana Purchase	1.00	.25	.15
❏ 1021	5¢	Opening of Japan	1.10	.25	.15
❏ 1022	3¢	American Bar Assn.	.90	.21	.15
❏ 1023	3¢	Sagamore Hill	.90	.21	.15
❏ 1024	3¢	Future Farmers	.62	.21	.15
❏ 1025	3¢	Trucking Industry	.70	.21	.15
❏ 1026	3¢	George S. Patton	.90	.21	.15
❏ 1027	3¢	New York City	.90	.21	.15
❏ 1028	3¢	Gadsden Purchase	.90	.20	.15

1954.

❏ 1029	3¢	Columbia University	.95	.21	.16

1030

1031
(1054)

1031A
(1054A)

1032

1033
(1055)

1034
(1056)

1035
(1057)

1036
(1058)

1037
(1059)

1038

1039

1040

1041

Scott No.			Plate Block	Unused	Used
1954–1961. Liberty Series					
❏ 1030	½¢	Benjamin Franklin	.50	.22	.15
❏ 1031	1¢	George Washington	.50	.22	.15
❏ 1031A	1¼¢	Palace of Governors	.42	.22	.15
❏ 1032	1½¢	Mount Vernon	.90	.25	.15
❏ 1033	2¢	Thomas Jefferson	.60	.22	.15
❏ 1034	2½¢	Bunker Hill	1.10	.21	.15
❏ 1035	3¢	Statue of Liberty	.60	.21	.15
❏ 1036	4¢	Abraham Lincoln	1.00	.25	.15
❏ 1037	4½¢	The Hermitage	.85	.25	.15
❏ 1038	5¢	James Monroe	.82	.26	.15
❏ 1039	6¢	Theodore Roosevelt	1.40	.35	.15
❏ 1040	7¢	Woodrow Wilson	1.00	.30	.15
❏ 1041	8¢	Statue of Liberty	2.25	.30	.15

1042

1042A

1043

1044

1044A

1045

1046

1047

1048
(1059A)

1049

1050

1051

1052

1053

Scott No.			Plate Block	Unused	Used
❑ 1042	8¢	Statue of Liberty (re-engraved)	1.10	.32	.15
❑ 1042A	8¢	John J. Pershing	1.20	.35	.15
❑ 1043	9¢	The Alamo	2.00	.40	.15
❑ 1044	10¢	Independence Hall	2.00	.45	.15
❑ 1044A	11¢	Statue of Liberty	1.50	.36	.15
❑ 1045	12¢	Benjamin Harrison	2.00	.45	.15
❑ 1046	15¢	John Jay	4.00	.85	.15
❑ 1047	20¢	Monticello	2.30	.60	.15
❑ 1048	25¢	Paul Revere	6.00	1.60	.15
❑ 1049	30¢	Robert E. Lee	7.00	1.60	.15
❑ 1050	40¢	John Marshall	11.00	2.10	.15
❑ 1051	50¢	S. B. Anthony	8.50	2.00	.15
❑ 1052	$1	Patrick Henry	28.00	6.10	.26
❑ 1053	$5	Alexander Hamilton	400.00	90.00	8.00

Scott No.			Line Pair	Unused	Used
1954–1973. Coil Stamps.					
❏ 1054	1¢	George Washington (~1031)	1.00	.22	.16
❏ 1054A	1¼¢	Palace of Governors (~1031A)	2.00	.22	.16
❏ 1055	2¢	Thomas Jefferson (~1033)	1.50	.40	.20
❏ 1056	2½¢	Bunker Hill (~1034)	2.10	.26	.26
❏ 1057	3¢	Statue of Liberty (~1035)	.55	.26	.15
❏ 1058	4¢	Abraham Lincoln (~1036)	.90	.26	.15
❏ 1059	4½¢	The Hermitage (~1037)	12.00	1.60	1.25
❏ 1059A	25¢	Paul Revere (~1048)	2.10	.72	.25

1060

1061

1062

1063

1064

1065

1066

Scott No.			Plate Block	Unused	Used
1954.					
❏ 1060	3¢	Nebraska Territory	.55	.22	.15
❏ 1061	3¢	Kansas Territory	.55	.22	.15
❏ 1062	3¢	George Eastman	1.00	.25	.15
❏ 1063	3¢	Lewis & Clark	1.10	.25	.15
1955.					
❏ 1064	3¢	Pennsylvania Academy	1.10	.30	.15
❏ 1065	3¢	Land Grant Colleges	1.00	.26	.15
❏ 1066	8¢	Rotary International	1.50	.35	.15

1067   **1068**   **1069**

1070   **1071**   **1072**

Scott No.			Plate Block	Unused	Used
❑ 1067	3¢	Armed Forces Reserves	.70	.22	.15
❑ 1068	3¢	Old Man of the Mountains	1.00	.30	.15
❑ 1069	3¢	Great Lakes Transportation	.92	.26	.15
❑ 1070	3¢	Atoms for Peace	.92	.22	.15
❑ 1071	3¢	Fort Ticonderoga	1.00	.25	.15
❑ 1072	3¢	Andrew Mellon	.90	.31	.15

1073   **1074**

1956.

❑ 1073	3¢	Benjamin Franklin	1.00	.25	.15
❑ 1074	3¢	Booker T. Washington	1.00	.21	.15

1075

1076

1077

1080

1078

1079

Scott No.			Plate Block	Unused	Used
❑ 1075	12¢	FIPEX Souvenir Sheet	—	2.55	2.00
❑ 1075a	3¢	single stamp	—	.96	.90
❑ 1075b	8¢	single stamp	—	1.10	.95
❑ 1076	3¢	FIPEX	.76	.22	.15
❑ 1077	3¢	Wild Turkey	.76	.22	.15
❑ 1078	3¢	Pronghorn Antelope	.90	.22	.15
❑ 1079	3¢	King Salmon	.90	.25	.15
❑ 1080	3¢	Pure Food & Drug Act	1.00	.25	.15

1081

1082

1083

1084

1085

Scott No.			Plate Block	Unused	Used
❑ 1081	3¢	Wheatland	1.10	.26	.15
❑ 1082	3¢	Labor Day	1.00	.26	.15
❑ 1083	3¢	Nassau Hall	.90	.22	.15
❑ 1084	3¢	Devils Tower	.72	.22	.15
❑ 1085	3¢	Children's Stamp	.72	.22	.15

1086

1087

1088

1089

1957.

❑ 1086	3¢	Alexander Hamilton	.60	.22	.13
❑ 1087	3¢	Fight Against Polio	.60	.22	.13
❑ 1088	3¢	Coast & Geodetic Survey	.60	.22	.13
❑ 1089	3¢	Architects	.60	.22	.13

1090

1091

1092

1093

1094

1095

1096

1097

1098

1099

Scott No.				Plate Block	Unused	Used
❑ 1090	3¢	American Steel Industry		.62	.22	.15
❑ 1091	3¢	International Naval Review		.62	.22	.15
❑ 1092	3¢	Oklahoma Statehood		.62	.22	.15
❑ 1093	3¢	Teachers of America		1.00	.25	.15
❑ 1094	4¢	48-Star U.S. Flag		.74	.22	.15
❑ 1095	3¢	Shipbuilding		1.10	.25	.15
❑ 1096	8¢	Ramon Magsaysay		1.00	.25	.15
❑ 1097	3¢	Lafayette Bicentennial		.90	.25	.15
❑ 1098	3¢	Whooping Cranes		.90	.22	.15
❑ 1099	3¢	Religious Freedom		.90	.22	.15

1100   1104   1105

1106   1107   1108

1109   1110   1111   1112

Scott No.			Plate Block	Unused	Used
1958.					
❏ 1100	3¢	Gardening & Horticulture	.71	.21	.15
❏ 1104	3¢	Brussels Exhibition	.71	.21	.15
❏ 1105	3¢	James Monroe	.71	.21	.15
❏ 1106	3¢	Minnesota Statehood	.71	.22	.15
❏ 1107	3¢	International Geophysical Year	.71	.21	.15
❏ 1108	3¢	Gunston Hall	.71	.21	.15
❏ 1109	3¢	Mackinac Bridge	1.00	.26	.15
❏ 1110	4¢	Simon Bolivar	.74	.21	.15
❏ 1111	8¢	Simon Bolivar	1.10	.27	.15
❏ 1112	4¢	Atlantic Cable Centennial	.70	.22	.15

1113

1114

1115

1116

1117

1118

1119

1120

1121

1122

1123

Scott No.			Plate Block	Unused	Used
❑ 1113	1¢	Youthful Lincoln	.50	.22	.13
❑ 1114	3¢	Bust of Lincoln	1.00	.22	.13
❑ 1115	4¢	Lincoln-Douglas Debates	1.40	.35	.13
❑ 1116	4¢	Statue of Lincoln	1.00	.22	.13
❑ 1117	4¢	Lajos Kossuth	.62	.22	.13
❑ 1118	8¢	Lajos Kossuth	1.20	.25	.13
❑ 1119	4¢	Freedom of the Press	.60	.21	.13
❑ 1120	4¢	Overland Mail	.90	.25	.13
❑ 1121	4¢	Noah Webster	.80	.22	.13
❑ 1122	4¢	Forest Conservation	.64	.22	.13
❑ 1123	4¢	Fort Duquesne	1.00	.25	.13

1124

1125

1126

1127

1128

1129

1130

1131

1132

1133

1134

1135

Scott No.			Plate Block	Unused	Used
1959.					
☐ 1124	4¢	Oregon Statehood	.60	.22	.15
☐ 1125	4¢	Jose de San Martin	.60	.22	.15
☐ 1126	8¢	Jose de San Martin	1.00	.22	.15
☐ 1127	4¢	NATO	.60	.22	.15
☐ 1128	4¢	Arctic Exploration	.50	.22	.15
☐ 1129	8¢	Peace Through Trade	1.00	.25	.15
☐ 1130	4¢	Silver Centennial	.62	.25	.15
☐ 1131	4¢	St. Lawrence Seaway	.90	.25	.15
☐ 1132	4¢	49-Star U.S. Flag	.62	.22	.15
☐ 1133	4¢	Soil Conservation	.70	.22	.15
☐ 1134	4¢	Petroleum Industry	1.00	.25	.15
☐ 1135	4¢	Dental Health	.90	.25	.15

1136   **1137**   **1138**

Scott No.			Plate Block	Unused	Used
❏ 1136	4¢	Ernst Reuter	.60	.21	.15
❏ 1137	8¢	Ernst Reuter	1.10	.21	.15
❏ 1138	4¢	Ephraim McDowell	1.10	.25	.15

1139   **1140**   **1141**

1142   **1143**   **1144**

1145

1960.

❏ 1139	4¢	Credo – Washington	.90	.22	.13
❏ 1140	4¢	Credo – Franklin	.90	.22	.13
❏ 1141	4¢	Credo – Jefferson	.90	.22	.13
❏ 1142	4¢	Credo – Key	1.00	.22	.13
❏ 1143	4¢	Credo – Lincoln	.92	.22	.13
❏ 1144	4¢	Credo – Henry	.92	.22	.13
❏ 1145	4¢	Boy Scouts	1.00	.30	.13

1146 **1147** **1148** **1149**

1150 **1151** **1152**

1153 **1154** **1155** **1156**

Scott No.			Plate Block	Unused	Used
❏ 1146	4¢	Winter Olympics	.60	.23	.15
❏ 1147	4¢	Thomas G. Masaryk	.60	.23	.15
❏ 1148	8¢	Thomas G. Masaryk	.70	.23	.15
❏ 1149	4¢	World Refugee Year	.60	.23	.15
❏ 1150	4¢	Water Conservation	.60	.23	.15
❏ 1151	4¢	SEATO	.60	.23	.15
❏ 1152	4¢	American Women	.60	.23	.15
❏ 1153	4¢	50-Star U.S. Flag	1.00	.32	.15
❏ 1154	4¢	Pony Express	.62	.22	.15
❏ 1155	4¢	Employ the Handicapped	.62	.22	.15
❏ 1156	4¢	World Forestry Congress	.62	.22	.15

1157

1158

1159

1160

1161

1162

1163

1164

1165

1166

1167

Scott No.			Plate Block	Unused	Used
❏ 1157	4¢	Mexican Independence	.62	.22	.15
❏ 1158	4¢	U.S.-Japan Treaty	.62	.22	.15
❏ 1159	4¢	Ignacy Jan Paderewski	1.10	.25	.15
❏ 1160	8¢	Ignacy Jan Paderewski	1.10	.25	.15
❏ 1161	4¢	Robert A. Taft	1.00	.25	.15
❏ 1162	4¢	Wheels of Freedom	.62	.22	.15
❏ 1163	4¢	Boys' Clubs	1.00	.25	.15
❏ 1164	4¢	First Automated P.O.	1.20	.30	.15
❏ 1165	4¢	Gustaf Mannerheim	.90	.22	.15
❏ 1166	8¢	Gustaf Mannerheim	1.10	.22	.15
❏ 1167	4¢	Campfire Girls	1.10	.30	.15

1168

1169

1170

1171

1172

1173

Scott No.			Plate Block	Unused	Used
❑ 1168	4¢	Guiseppe Garibaldi	.60	.22	.15
❑ 1169	8¢	Guiseppe Garibaldi	1.10	.26	.15
❑ 1170	4¢	Walter F. George	1.15	.30	.15
❑ 1171	4¢	Andrew Carnegie	1.00	.26	.15
❑ 1172	4¢	John Foster Dulles	1.00	.26	.15
❑ 1173	4¢	Echo I Satellite	1.10	.30	.15

1174

1175

1176

1961.

❑ 1174	4¢	Mahatma Gandhi	.62	.21	.15
❑ 1175	8¢	Mahatma Gandhi	1.00	.25	.15
❑ 1176	4¢	Range Conservation	.62	.22	.15
❑ 1177	4¢	Horace Greeley	1.00	.25	.15

1177

1178

1179

1180

1181

1182

1183

1184

1186

1185

Scott No.			Plate Block	Unused	Used
❑ 1178	4¢	Fort Sumter	2.00	.40	.15
❑ 1179	4¢	Shiloh	1.25	.31	.15
❑ 1180	5¢	Gettysburg	1.70	.35	.15
❑ 1181	5¢	The Wilderness	1.25	.36	.15
❑ 1182	5¢	Appomattox	2.75	.50	.20
❑ 1183	4¢	Kansas Statehood	1.00	.22	.15
❑ 1184	4¢	George W. Norris	1.00	.30	.15
❑ 1185	4¢	Naval Aviation	.60	.22	.15
❑ 1186	4¢	Workmen's Compensation	.60	.22	.15

| 1187 | 1188 | 1189 | 1190 |

Scott No.			Plate Block	Unused	Used
❏ 1187	4¢	Frederick Remington	1.00	.26	.15
❏ 1188	4¢	Republic of China	1.00	.31	.15
❏ 1189	4¢	Naismith – Basketball	1.10	.31	.15
❏ 1190	4¢	Nursing	1.10	.31	.15

| 1191 | 1192 |

| 1193 | 1194 | 1195 |

1962.

❏ 1191	4¢	New Mexico Statehood	.60	.22	.15
❏ 1192	4¢	Arizona Statehood	.60	.22	.15
❏ 1193	4¢	Project Mercury	.80	.25	.15
❏ 1194	4¢	Malaria Eradication	.60	.22	.15
❏ 1195	4¢	Charles Evans Hughes	.60	.22	.15

1196

1197

1198

1199

1200

1201

1202

1203

1204

Scott No.			Plate Block	Unused	Used
❏ 1196	4¢	Seattle World's Fair	.60	.22	.13
❏ 1197	4¢	Louisiana Statehood	1.00	.30	.13
❏ 1198	4¢	The Homestead Act	.60	.22	.13
❏ 1199	4¢	Girl Scouts	.60	.21	.13
❏ 1200	4¢	Brien McMahon	1.00	.25	.13
❏ 1201	4¢	Apprenticeship Act	.60	.22	.13
❏ 1202	4¢	Sam Rayburn	.90	.25	.13
❏ 1203	4¢	Dag Hammarskjold	.60	.22	.13
❏ 1204	4¢	Hammarskjold, yellow inverted	1.00	.22	.13

1205   **1206**   **1207**

Scott No.			Plate Block	Unused	Used
❏ 1205	4¢	Christmas Wreath	.60	.22	.15
❏ 1206	4¢	Higher Education	.60	.22	.15
❏ 1207	4¢	Winslow Homer	.90	.22	.15

1208   **1209**
(1225)   **1213**
(1229)

1962–1963. Definitives.

❏ 1208	5¢	U.S. Flag	.55	.22	.15
❏ 1209	1¢	Andrew Jackson	.50	.22	.15
❏ 1213	5¢	George Washington	.50	.22	.15

Scott No.			Line Pair	Unused	Used
Coil Stamps.					
❏ 1225	1¢	Andrew Jackson (~1209)	2.00	.26	.15
❏ 1229	5¢	George Washington (~1213)	3.00	1.05	.15

1230

1231

1232

1233

1234

1235

1236

1237

1238

Scott No.			Plate Block	Unused	Used
1963.					
❑ 1230	5¢	Carolina Charter	1.20	.35	.15
❑ 1231	5¢	Food for Peace	.60	.22	.15
❑ 1232	5¢	West Virginia Statehood	.80	.25	.15
❑ 1233	5¢	Emancipation Proclamation	.80	.25	.15
❑ 1234	5¢	Alliance for Progress	.60	.22	.15
❑ 1235	5¢	Cordell Hull	1.10	.30	.15
❑ 1236	5¢	Eleanor Roosevelt	1.00	.25	.15
❑ 1237	5¢	The Sciences	.60	.23	.15
❑ 1238	5¢	City Mail Delivery	.60	.23	.15

1239   **1240**   **1241**

Scott No.			Plate Block	Unused	Used
❏ 1239	5¢	International Red Cross	.60	.22	.15
❏ 1240	5¢	Christmas Tree	.90	.25	.15
❏ 1241	5¢	John James Audubon	1.10	.25	.15

1243   **1244**

1242

1246

1245   **1247**

1964.

❏ 1242	5¢	Sam Houston	.90	.26	.15
❏ 1243	5¢	Charles M. Russell	1.00	.30	.15
❏ 1244	5¢	New York World's Fair	1.00	.26	.15
❏ 1245	5¢	John Muir	.60	.22	.15
❏ 1246	5¢	John F. Kennedy	2.00	.50	.15
❏ 1247	5¢	New Jersey Statehood	1.00	.30	.15

1248   **1249**   **1250**

1251   **1252**   **1253**

1254   **1255**   **1256**   **1257**

Scott No.			Plate Block	Unused	Used
❑ 1248	5¢	Nevada Statehood	.90	.22	.13
❑ 1249	5¢	Register & Vote	.60	.22	.13
❑ 1250	5¢	William Shakespeare	.60	.22	.13
❑ 1251	5¢	The Doctors Mayo	1.00	.25	.13
❑ 1252	5¢	American Music	.50	.22	.13
❑ 1253	5¢	Homemakers	.50	.22	.13
❑ 1254	5¢	Holly	—	.30	.17
❑ 1255	5¢	Mistletoe	—	.30	.17
❑ 1256	5¢	Poinsettia	—	.30	.17
❑ 1257	5¢	Conifer	—	.32	.17
		Block of 4 (1254–1257)	8.00	1.50	1.15

1258   **1259**   **1260**

Scott No.			Plate Block	Unused	Used
❑ 1258	5¢	Verrazano Bridge	1.10	.24	.13
❑ 1259	5¢	Modern Art	.50	.22	.13
❑ 1260	5¢	Amateur Radio	1.00	.30	.13

1261   **1262**   **1263**

1264   **1265**   **1266**

1965.

❑ 1261	5¢	Battle of New Orleans	1.40	.41	.13
❑ 1262	5¢	Fitness – Discus Thrower	.67	.20	.13
❑ 1263	5¢	Crusade Against Cancer	.50	.20	.13
❑ 1264	5¢	Winston Churchill	1.00	.20	.13
❑ 1265	5¢	Magna Carta	.52	.20	.13
❑ 1266	5¢	International Cooperation Year	.60	.20	.13

Scott No.			Plate Block	Unused	Used
❏ 1267	5¢	Salvation Army	.60	.22	.15
❏ 1268	5¢	Dante Alighieri	.60	.22	.15
❏ 1269	5¢	Herbert Hoover	1.00	.25	.15
❏ 1270	5¢	Robert Fulton	.48	.22	.15
❏ 1271	5¢	Florida Settlement	.90	.25	.15
❏ 1272	5¢	Traffic Safety	.62	.22	.15
❏ 1273	5¢	John Singleton Copley	.90	.25	.15
❏ 1274	11¢	I.T.U.	4.00	.46	.20
❏ 1275	5¢	Adlai E. Stevenson	.62	.22	.13
❏ 1276	5¢	Christmas Angel & Trumpet	.60	.22	.13

1278
(1299)

1279

1280

1281
(1297)

1282
(1303)

1283
(1304)

1283B
(1304C)

1284
(1298)

1285

1286

1286A

1287

Scott No.			Plate Block	Unused	Used
1965–1978. Prominent Americans Series.					
❑ 1278	1¢	Thomas Jefferson	.42	.20	.15
❑ 1279	1¼¢	Albert Gallatin	9.00	.20	.15
❑ 1280	2¢	Frank Lloyd Wright	.41	.20	.15
❑ 1281	3¢	Francis Parkman	.50	.20	.15
❑ 1282	4¢	Abraham Lincoln	1.10	.30	.15
❑ 1283	5¢	George Washington	.60	.20	.15
❑ 1283B	5¢	Washington ("clean shaven")	.65	.20	.15
❑ 1284	6¢	Franklin D. Roosevelt	.78	.20	.15
❑ 1285	8¢	Albert Einstein	.90	.40	.15
❑ 1286	10¢	Andrew Jackson	1.25	.40	.15
❑ 1286A	12¢	Henry Ford	1.30	.36	.15
❑ 1287	13¢	John F. Kennedy	1.70	.50	.15

1288
(1288d, 1288B,
1305E)

1289

1290

1291

1292

1293

1294
(1305C)

1295

Scott No.			Plate Block	Unused	Used
❏ 1288	15¢	Oliver Wendell Holmes (type I)	1.80	.40	.15
❏ 1288d	15¢	Holmes (~1288) (type II)	12.00	.90	.15

Type I: The tip of the necktie touches the coat. Type II: The tip of the necktie is well clear of the coat.

Scott No.			Plate Block	Unused	Used
❏ 1288B	15¢	Holmes (~1288), perf 10	7.50	.60	.15
		Booklet pane of 8	—	3.50	2.00
❏ 1289	20¢	George C. Marshall	3.10	.62	.20
❏ 1290	25¢	Frederick Douglass	3.50	1.05	.16
❏ 1291	30¢	John Dewey	4.00	1.05	.17
❏ 1292	40¢	Thomas Paine	3.80	1.05	.17
❏ 1293	50¢	Lucy Stone	6.00	1.25	.16
❏ 1294	$1	Eugene O'Neill	13.00	3.00	.16
❏ 1295	$5	John Bassett Moore	60.00	13.00	2.50

Scott No.			Line Pair	Unused	Used
Coil Stamps. Perforated 10 Horizontally.					
❏ 1297	3¢	Francis Parkman (~1281).	.50	.22	.15
❏ 1298	6¢	Franklin D. Roosevelt (~1284)	1.40	.25	.15

1305

Scott No.			Line Pair	Unused	Used
Coil Stamps. Perforated 10 Vertically.					
❑ 1299	1¢	Thomas Jefferson (~1278)	.35	.22	.15
❑ 1303	4¢	Abraham Lincoln (~1282)	.80	.30	.15
❑ 1304	5¢	George Washington (~1283)	.50	.22	.15
❑ 1304C	5¢	Washington ("clean shaven") (~1283B)	1.75	.21	.15
❑ 1305	6¢	Franklin D. Roosevelt	.73	.25	.15
❑ 1305C	$1	Eugene O'Neill (~1294)	6.50	3.00	.90
❑ 1305E	15¢	Holmes (~1288)	3.00	.76	.32

1306   **1307**

1308   **1309**

Scott No.			Plate Block	Unused	Used
1966.					
❑ 1306	5¢	Migratory Bird Treaty	.65	.22	.15
❑ 1307	5¢	Humane Treatment of Animals	.65	.22	.15
❑ 1308	5¢	Indiana Statehood	1.10	.30	.15
❑ 1309	5¢	Circus Clown	1.00	.25	.15

1310

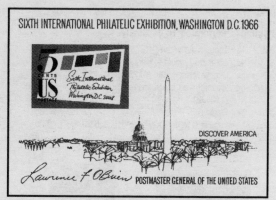

1311

1312

1313

1314

Scott No.			Plate Block	Unused	Used
❑ 1310	5¢	SIPEX	.60	.22	.15
❑ 1311	5¢	SIPEX souvenir sheet	—	.22	.18
❑ 1312	5¢	Bill of Rights	.60	.22	.15
❑ 1313	5¢	Polish Millennium	.60	.22	.15
❑ 1314	5¢	National Park Service	.90	.22	.15

1315 **1316** **1317**

1318 **1319** **1320**

1321 **1322**

Scott No.			Plate Block	Unused	Used
❑ 1315	5¢	Marine Corps Reserve	.62	.22	.15
❑ 1316	5¢	Women's Clubs	.62	.22	.15
❑ 1317	5¢	Johnny Appleseed	1.10	.22	.15
❑ 1318	5¢	Beautification	.50	.22	.15
❑ 1319	5¢	Great River Road	.62	.22	.15
❑ 1320	5¢	Servicemen & Savings Bonds	.62	.22	.15
❑ 1321	5¢	Christmas – Madonna	.65	.22	.15
❑ 1322	5¢	Mary Cassatt	.65	.22	.15

1323

1324

1325

1326

1327

1328

1329

1330

Scott No.			Plate Block	Unused	Used
1967.					
❑ 1323	5¢	Grange Centenary	.90	.22	.15
❑ 1324	5¢	Canada Centennial	.62	.22	.15
❑ 1325	5¢	Erie Canal	1.00	.30	.15
❑ 1326	5¢	Search for Peace	.92	.25	.15
❑ 1327	5¢	Henry David Thoreau	.92	.30	.15
❑ 1328	5¢	Nebraska Statehood	1.10	.31	.15
❑ 1329	5¢	Voice of America	.60	.23	.15
❑ 1330	5¢	Davy Crockett	.90	.30	.15

1331–1332

1333

1334

1335

1336

1337

Scott No.			Plate Block	Unused	Used
❏ 1331	5¢	Astronaut EVA	—	.80	.15
❏ 1332	5¢	Gemini Capsule	—	3.75	.15
		Se-tenant pair (1331–1332)	4.50	2.00	1.20
❏ 1333	5¢	Urban Planning	.62	.22	.15
❏ 1334	5¢	Finland Independence	.62	.22	.15
❏ 1335	5¢	Thomas Eakins	.62	.25	.15
❏ 1336	5¢	Christmas – Madonna	.60	.22	.15
❏ 1337	5¢	Mississippi Statehood	1.10	.35	.15

1338
(1338A, 1338D)

1338F
(1338G)

Scott No.			Plate Block	Unused	Used
1968. Definitive.					
❏ 1338	6¢	U.S. Flag, perf 11	.60	.26	.15

Scott No.			Line Pair	Unused	Used
Coil Stamp.					
❏ 1338A	6¢	U.S. Flag (~1338)	6.00	.25	.15

Scott No.			Plate Block	Unused	Used
1970–1971.					
❏ 1338D	6¢	U.S. Flag (~1338), perf 11x10½	3.50 (20)	.25	.15
❏ 1338F	8¢	U.S. Flag, perf 11 x 10½	4.50	.24	.15

Scott No.			Line Pair	Unused	Used
Coil Stamp.					
❏ 1338G	8¢	U.S. Flag (~1338F)	2.50	.25	.15

1341

1339 **1340**

1342 **1343** **1344**

Scott No.			Plate Block	Unused	Used
1968.					
❑ 1339	6¢	Illinois Statehood	1.50	.36	.15
❑ 1340	6¢	Hemisfair '68	.62	.27	.15
❑ 1341	$1	Airlift	11.00	2.60	2.00
❑ 1342	6¢	Support Our Youth	.62	.27	.17
❑ 1343	6¢	Law & Order	.95	.30	.15
❑ 1344	6¢	Register & Vote	.60	.25	.15

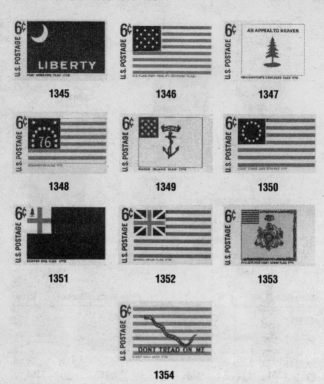

1345   1346   1347

1348   1349   1350

1351   1352   1353

1354

Scott No.			Plate Block	Unused	Used
❏ 1345	6¢	Fort Moultrie Flag	—	.55	.34
❏ 1346	6¢	Fort McHenry Flag	—	.50	.34
❏ 1347	6¢	Washington's Cruisers Flag	—	.45	.34
❏ 1348	6¢	Bennington Flag	—	.45	.34
❏ 1349	6¢	Rhode Island Flag	—	.45	.34
❏ 1350	6¢	First Stars & Stripes	—	.45	.34
❏ 1351	6¢	Bunker Hill Flag	—	.45	.34
❏ 1352	6¢	Grand Union Flag	—	.45	.34
❏ 1353	6¢	Philadelphia Light Horse Flag	—	.45	.34
❏ 1354	6¢	First Navy Jack	—	.45	.34
		Strip of 10 (1345–1354)	8.00 (4)	3.70	3.00

1355
1356
1357
1358
1359
1360
1361
1362
1363
1364

Scott No.			Plate Block	Unused	Used
❑ 1355	6¢	Walt Disney	3.50	.75	.15
❑ 1356	6¢	Father Marquette	1.10	.36	.15
❑ 1357	6¢	Daniel Boone	1.10	.32	.15
❑ 1358	6¢	Arkansas River Navigation	1.20	.35	.15
❑ 1359	6¢	Leif Erikson	1.00	.26	.15
❑ 1360	6¢	Cherokee Strip Land Rush	1.10	.26	.15
❑ 1361	6¢	John Trumball	1.10	.35	.15
❑ 1362	6¢	Waterfowl Conservation	1.00	.26	.15
❑ 1363	6¢	Christmas – Madonna	2.10 (10)	.26	.15
❑ 1364	6¢	Chief Joseph	1.10	.30	.15

1365–1368

1369   1370   1371

1372

Scott No.			Plate Block	Unused	Used
1969.					
❏ 1365	6¢	Beautification – Cities	—	.40	.16
❏ 1366	6¢	Beautification – Parks	—	.40	.16
❏ 1367	6¢	Beautification – Highways	—	.40	.16
❏ 1368	6¢	Beautification – Streets	—	.40	.16
		Block of 4 (1365–1368)	2.10	1.80	1.25
❏ 1369	6¢	American Legion	.60	.24	.16
❏ 1370	6¢	Grandma Moses	.60	.24	.16
❏ 1371	6¢	Apollo 8	.90	.30	.16
❏ 1372	6¢	W. C. Handy	1.00	.35	.16

1373

1374

1375

1376–1379

1380

1381

1382

Scott No.			Plate Block	Unused	Used
❏ 1373	6¢	Settlement of California	1.00	.26	.16
❏ 1374	6¢	John Wesley Powell	1.00	.35	.16
❏ 1375	6¢	Alabama Statehood	1.00	.35	.16
❏ 1376	6¢	Pseudotsuga menziesii	—	.62	.25
❏ 1377	6¢	Cypridedium reginae	—	.62	.25
❏ 1378	6¢	Fouquieria splendens	—	.62	.25
❏ 1379	6¢	Franklinia alatamaha	—	.62	.25
		Block of 4 (1376–1379)	3.10	.62	.25
❏ 1380	6¢	Daniel Webster	1.00	.30	.15
❏ 1381	6¢	Professional Baseball	3.50	.90	.15
❏ 1382	6¢	Intercollegiate Football	2.00	.50	.15

U.S. 6¢ POSTAGE

DWIGHT D.
EISENHOWER

1383

1384

HOPE
FOR THE CRIPPLED

1385

SIX CENTS
AMERICAN PAINTING
UNITED STATES POSTAGE
WILLIAM M. HARNETT

1386

Scott No.			Plate Block	Unused	Used
❑ 1383	6¢	Dwight D. Eisenhower	.70	.22	.15
❑ 1384	6¢	Christmas – Winter Scene	2.60 (10)	.25	.15
❑ 1385	6¢	Hope for the Crippled	.60	.22	.15
❑ 1386	6¢	William Harnett Painting	.60	.22	.15

AMERICAN BALD EAGLE ● AFRICAN ELEPHANT HERD

HAIDA CEREMONIAL CANOE ● THE AGE OF REPTILES

1376–1379

1970.

❑ 1387	6¢	American Bald Eagle	—	.26	.15
❑ 1388	6¢	African Elephant Herd	—	.26	.15
❑ 1389	6¢	Haida Ceremonial Canoe	—	.32	.15
❑ 1390	6¢	The Age of Reptiles	—	.32	.15
		Block of 4 (1387–1390)	1.20	.65	.50

1391

1392

Scott No.			Plate Block	Unused	Used
❏ 1391	6¢	Maine Statehood	1.10	.36	.15
❏ 1392	6¢	Conservation – Bison	1.10	.32	.15

1393
(1401)

1393D

1394
(1395, 1402)

1396

1970–1974. Definitives.

❏ 1393	6¢	Dwight D. Eisenhower	.70	.35	.15
		Booklet pane of 5 + label	—	1.65	.60
		Booklet pane of 8	—	1.80	.60
❏ 1393D	7¢	Benjamin Franklin	.90	.26	.15
❏ 1394	8¢	Eisenhower, red, black & blue	1.00	.25	.15
❏ 1395	8¢	Eisenhower (~1394), claret	—	.35	.15
		Booklet pane of 4 + 2 labels	—	1.72	.70
		Booklet pane of 6	—	1.65	1.10
		Booklet pane of 7 + 1 label	—	2.40	1.30
		Booklet pane of 8	—	2.10	1.50
❏ 1396	8¢	U.S.P.S. Emblem	3.00	.26	.17

1397

1398

1399

1400

Scott No.			Plate Block	Unused	Used
❑ 1397	14¢	Fiorello LaGuardia	1.20	.35	.15
❑ 1398	16¢	Ernie Pyle	2.00	.46	.16
❑ 1399	18¢	Elizabeth Blackwell	1.90	.46	.16
❑ 1400	21¢	Amadeo P. Giannini	2.20	.60	.22

Scott No.			Line Pair	Unused	Used

Coil Stamps. Perforated 10 Vertically.

❑ 1401	6¢	Eisenhower (~1393)	.60	.30	.15
❑ 1402	8¢	Eisenhower (~1394) claret	.65	.26	.15

1405

1406

1407

1408

1409

Scott No.			Plate Block	Unused	Used

1970.

❑ 1405	6¢	Edgar Lee Masters	1.10	.30	.15
❑ 1406	6¢	Women's Suffrage	.90	.23	.15
❑ 1407	6¢	South Carolina	1.10	.35	.15
❑ 1408	6¢	Stone Mountain	—	.35	.15
❑ 1409	6¢	Fort Snelling	1.10	.23	.15

1410–1413

1414

1415–1418

1414a

Scott No.			Plate Block	Unused	Used
❏ 1410	6¢	Save Our Soil	—	.36	.16
❏ 1411	6¢	Save Our Cities	—	.36	.16
❏ 1412	6¢	Save Our Water	—	.36	.16
❏ 1413	6¢	Save Our Air	—	.36	.16
		Block of 4 (1410–1413)	3.00 (10)	1.30	1.00
❏ 1414	6¢	Christmas – Manger Scene	2.10 (8)	.27	.15
❏ 1414a	6¢	Christmas, precanceled	2.40 (8)	.27	.15
❏ 1415	6¢	Locomotive	—	.36	.15
❏ 1416	6¢	Toy Horse	—	.36	.16
❏ 1417	6¢	Tricycle	—	.36	.16
❏ 1418	6¢	Doll Carriage	—	.36	.16
		Block of 4 (1415–1418)	4.50 (8)	3.00	2.50

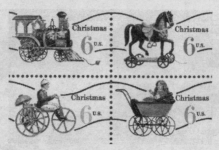

1415a–1418a

1419

1420

1421

1422

Scott No.			Plate Block	Unused	Used
❏ 1415a	6¢	Locomotive, precanceled	—	.92	.19
❏ 1416a	6¢	Toy Horse, precanceled	—	.92	.19
❏ 1417a	6¢	Tricycle, precanceled	—	.92	.19
❏ 1418a	6¢	Doll Carriage, precanceled	—	.92	.19
		Block of 4 (1415a–1418a)	7.00 (8)	3.00	2.60
❏ 1419	6¢	United Nations	.75	.23	.17
❏ 1420	6¢	Landing of the Pilgrims	.75	.23	.17
❏ 1421	6¢	Disabled Veterans	—	.22	.22
❏ 1422	6¢	Honoring U.S. Servicemen	—	.22	.22
		Se-tenant pair (1421–1422)	1.20	.46	.40

1425

AMERICA'S WOOL
1423

DOUGLAS MacARTHUR
1424

1426

1427–1430

Scott No.			Plate Block	Unused	Used
1971.					
❑ 1423	6¢	America's Wool	.62	.25	.15
❑ 1424	6¢	Douglas MacArthur	1.10	.30	.15
❑ 1425	6¢	Giving Blood Saves Lives	.62	.25	.15
❑ 1426	8¢	Missouri Statehood	4.75 (12)	.40	.17
❑ 1427	8¢	Trout	—	.32	.17
❑ 1428	8¢	Alligator	—	.32	.17
❑ 1429	8¢	Polar Bear	—	.32	.17
❑ 1430	8¢	California Condor	—	.32	.17
		Block of 4 (1427–1430)	1.25	.95	.80

1431　　　　1432　　　　1433

1434–1435

1436　　　　1437　　　　1438　　　　1439

Scott No.			Plate Block	Unused	Used
❏ 1431	8¢	Antarctic Treaty	.90	.22	.15
❏ 1432	8¢	Revolution Bicentennial	1.00	.25	.15
❏ 1433	8¢	John Sloan	.92	.25	.15
❏ 1434	8¢	Earth & Lander	—	.25	.15
❏ 1435	8¢	Lunar Rover	—	.24	.15
		Se-tenant pair (1434–1435)	1.00	.50	.45
❏ 1436	8¢	Emily Dickinson	1.10	.30	.15
❏ 1437	8¢	San Juan, Puerto Rico	.92	.25	.15
❏ 1438	8¢	Prevent Drug Abuse	1.40 (6)	.25	.15
❏ 1439	8¢	CARE	1.75 (8)	.25	.15

1440–1443

| 1444 | 1445 | 1446 | 1447 |

Scott No.			Plate Block	Unused	Used
❑ 1440	8¢	Decatur Home	—	.26	.15
❑ 1441	8¢	The Charles W. Morgan	—	.26	.15
❑ 1442	8¢	San Francisco Cable Car	—	.26	.15
❑ 1443	8¢	San Xavier del Bac Mission	—	.26	.15
		Block of 4 (1440–1443)	1.10	.90	.72
❑ 1444	8¢	Christmas – Manger Scene	2.50 (12)	.27	.15
❑ 1445	8¢	Christmas – Partridge	2.50 (12)	.27	.15
1972.					
❑ 1446	8¢	Sidney Lanier	1.10	.36	.15
❑ 1447	8¢	Peace Corps	1.70 (6)	.25	.15

1448–1451

1452

1453

1454

1455

Scott No.			Plate Block	Unused	Used
❑ 1448	2¢	Hatteras – Shipwreck in Surf	—	.27	.15
❑ 1449	2¢	Hatteras – Lighthouse	—	.27	.15
❑ 1450	2¢	Hatteras – 3 Shorebirds	—	.27	.15
❑ 1451	2¢	Hatteras – Shorebirds & Dunes	—	.27	.15
		Block of 4 (1448–1451)	.72	.27	.21
❑ 1452	6¢	Wolf Trap Farm	1.00	.27	.15
❑ 1453	8¢	Old Faithful	.90	.25	.15
❑ 1454	15¢	Mount McKinley	1.50	.25	.15
❑ 1455	8¢	Family Planning	.90	.25	.15

1456–1459

1460   **1461**

1462   **1463**

Scott No.			Plate Block	Unused	Used
❑ 1456	8¢	Craftsmen – Glass Blower	—	.27	.15
❑ 1457	8¢	Craftsmen – Silversmith	—	.27	.15
❑ 1458	8¢	Craftsmen – Wigmaker	—	.27	.15
❑ 1459	8¢	Craftsmen – Hatter	—	.27	.15
		Block of 4 (1456–1459)	1.10	1.00	.90
❑ 1460	6¢	Cycling	2.00 (10)	.25	.15
❑ 1461	8¢	Bobsledding	2.20 (10)	.25	.15
❑ 1462	15¢	Running	3.50 (10)	.42	.15
❑ 1463	8¢	P.T.A.	1.00	.30	.15
❑ 1463a	8¢	P.T.A., reversed plate number	.90	—	—

1464–1467

1468

1469

1470

Scott No.			Plate Block	Unused	Used
❏ 1464	8¢	Fur Seal	—	.27	.15
❏ 1465	8¢	Cardinal	—	.27	.15
❏ 1466	8¢	Brown Pelican	—	.27	.15
❏ 1467	8¢	Bighorn Sheep	—	.27	.15
		Block of 4 (1464–1467)	.90	.60	.40
❏ 1468	8¢	Mail Order	3.00 (12)	.32	.15
❏ 1469	8¢	Osteopathic Medicine	2.00 (6)	.32	.15
❏ 1470	8¢	Tom Sawyer	1.20	.32	.15

1471

1472

1473

1474

Scott No.			Plate Block	Unused	Used
❑ 1471	8¢	Christmas – Angels	2.10 (12)	.24	.15
❑ 1472	8¢	Christmas – Santa	3.00 (12)	.25	.15
❑ 1473	8¢	Pharmacy	1.80	.36	.15
❑ 1474	8¢	Stamp Collecting	.90	.24	.15

1475

1476

1477

1478

1479

1973.

❑ 1475	8¢	LOVE	1.20 (6)	.25	.15
❑ 1476	8¢	Colonial Printing Press	.93	.25	.15
❑ 1477	8¢	Posting a Broadside	.93	.25	.15
❑ 1478	8¢	Post Rider	.93	.25	.15
❑ 1479	8¢	Drummer	.93	.25	.15

1480–1483

1484　　　　1485

1486　　　　1487　　　　1488

Scott No.			Plate Block	Unused	Used
❑ 1480	8¢	Tea Party – Dumping Tea	—	.27	.15
❑ 1481	8¢	Tea Party – Ship at Anchor	—	.27	.15
❑ 1482	8¢	Tea Party – Boats & Lantern	—	.27	.15
❑ 1483	8¢	Tea Party – Bystanders on Pier	—	.27	.15
		Block of 4 (1480–1483)	1.15	.75	.70
❑ 1484	8¢	George Gershwin	2.50 (12)	.26	.15
❑ 1485	8¢	Robinson Jeffers	2.50 (12)	.26	.15
❑ 1486	6¢	Henry O. Tanner	2.50 (12)	.26	.15
❑ 1487	8¢	Willa Cather	3.00 (12)	.26	.15
❑ 1488	8¢	Copernicus	.95	.26	.15

1489–1492

1493–1496

1497–1498

Scott No.			Plate Block	Unused	Used
❏ 1489	8¢	Window Clerk	—	.42	.15
❏ 1490	8¢	Collecting Mail	—	.42	.15
❏ 1491	8¢	Conveyor Belt	—	.42	.15
❏ 1492	8¢	Bagging Parcels	—	.42	.15
❏ 1493	8¢	Mail in Trays	—	.42	.15
❏ 1494	8¢	Sorting to Pigeonholes	—	.42	.15
❏ 1495	8¢	Keypunch Operators	—	.42	.15
❏ 1496	8¢	Loading Mail Truck	—	.42	.15
❏ 1497	8¢	Carrier Walking Route	—	.42	.15
❏ 1498	8¢	Rural Delivery Carrier	—	.42	.15
		Strip of 10 (1489–1498)	3.50 (20)	1.85	1.50

1499

1500

1501

1502

1503

1504

1505

1506

Scott No.			Plate Block	Unused	Used
❑ 1499	8¢	Harry S. Truman	1.25	.40	.15
❑ 1500	6¢	Spark Coil & Spark Gap	.95	.25	.15
❑ 1501	8¢	Transistors	.95	.25	.15
❑ 1502	15¢	Microphone & Speaker	1.60	.25	.15
❑ 1503	8¢	Lyndon B. Johnson	3.50 (12)	.30	.15
❑ 1504	8¢	Angus Cattle	.95	.25	.15
❑ 1505	10¢	Chautauqua	1.10	.25	.15
❑ 1506	10¢	Winter Wheat	1.25	.25	.15

1507

1508

Scott No.			Plate Block	Unused	Used
❏ 1507	8¢	Madonna & Child	2.75 (12)	.25	.15
❏ 1508	8¢	Christmas Tree	2.75 (12)	.25	.15

1509
(1519)   **1510**
(1520)   **1511**

1973–1974. Definitives.

❏ 1509	10¢	Crossed Flags	5.80 (20)	.26	.15
❏ 1510	10¢	Jefferson Memorial	1.25	.26	.15
❏ 1511	10¢	ZIP Code	2.25 (8)	.26	.15

1518

Scott No.			Line Pair	Unused	Used
Coil Stamps.					
❑ 1518	6.3¢	Liberty Bell	.65	.22	.15
❑ 1519	10¢	Crossed Flags (~1509)	—	.30	.15
❑ 1520	10¢	Jefferson Memorial (~1510)	.70	.30	.15

1525	**1526**	**1527**

1528	**1529**

Scott No.			Plate Block	Unused	Used
1974.					
❑ 1525	10¢	V.F.W.	1.25	.26	.15
❑ 1526	10¢	Robert Frost	1.50	.41	.15
❑ 1527	10¢	Expo '74	3.10 (12)	.30	.15
❑ 1528	10¢	Horse Racing	4.50 (12)	.41	.15
❑ 1529	10¢	Skylab	1.10	.26	.15

1530–1437

Scott No.			Plate Block	Unused	Used
❑ 1530	10¢	UPU – Raphael	—	.32	.20
❑ 1531	10¢	UPU – Hokusai	—	.32	.20
❑ 1532	10¢	UPU – Peto	—	.32	.20
❑ 1533	10¢	UPU – Liotard	—	.32	.20
❑ 1534	10¢	UPU – Terborch	—	.32	.20
❑ 1535	10¢	UPU – Chardin	—	.32	.20
❑ 1536	10¢	UPU – Gainsborough	—	.32	.20
❑ 1537	10¢	UPU – Goya	—	.32	.20
		Block of 8 (1530–1537)	3.75 (16)	2.50	2.00

1538–1441

1542

1543–1446

Scott No.			Plate Block	Unused	Used
❑ 1538	10¢	Minerals – Petrified Wood	—	.25	.15
❑ 1539	10¢	Minerals – Tourmaline	—	.25	.15
❑ 1540	10¢	Minerals – Amethyst	—	.25	.15
❑ 1541	10¢	Minerals – Rhodochrosite	—	.25	.15
		Block of 4 (1538–1541)	1.25	1.25	.90
❑ 1542	10¢	Fort Harrod Bicentennial	1.55	.40	.15
❑ 1543	10¢	Carpenters' Hall	—	.32	.15
❑ 1544	10¢	We Ask But For Peace	—	.32	.15
❑ 1545	10¢	Deriving Their Just Powers	—	.30	.15
❑ 1546	10¢	Independence Hall	—	.30	.15
		Block of 4 (1543–1546)	1.75	1.25	1.10

1547

1548

1549

1550

1551

1552

Scott No.			Plate Block	Unused	Used
❏ 1547	10¢	Energy Conservation	1.15	.32	.15
❏ 1548	10¢	Legend of Sleepy Hollow	1.15	.32	.15
❏ 1549	10¢	Retarded Children	1.15	.32	.15
❏ 1550	10¢	Christmas – Angel	2.75 (10)	.32	.15
❏ 1551	10¢	Christmas – Currier & Ives	3.10 (12)	.32	.15
❏ 1552	10¢	Christmas – Weather Vane	6.00 (20)	.32	.15

1553

1554

1555

1556

1557

1558

1559

1560

1561

Scott No.			Plate Block	Unused	Used
1975.					
❏ 1553	10¢	Benjamin West	4.25 (10)	.42	.15
❏ 1554	10¢	Paul Laurence Dunbar	4.25 (10)	.42	.15
❏ 1555	10¢	D. W. Griffith	1.80	.42	.15
❏ 1556	10¢	Pioneer 10	1.20	.30	.15
❏ 1557	10¢	Mariner 10	1.20	.30	.15
❏ 1558	10¢	Collective Bargaining	2.10 (8)	.30	.15
❏ 1559	8¢	Sybil Ludington	2.10 (10)	.29	.15
❏ 1560	10¢	Salem Poor	3.10 (10)	.30	.15
❏ 1561	10¢	Haym Salomon	3.40 (10)	.30	.15

1562

US Bicentennial 10cents

1563

US Bicentennial 10c

1564

1565–1568

1569–1570

Scott No.			Plate Block	Unused	Used
❑ 1562	18¢	Peter Francisco	4.50 (10)	.42	.16
❑ 1563	10¢	Lexington & Concord	4.00 (12)	.35	.16
❑ 1564	10¢	Battle of Bunker Hill	4.00 (12)	.32	.16
❑ 1565	10¢	Continental Army	—	.32	.16
❑ 1566	10¢	Continental Navy	—	.32	.16
❑ 1567	10¢	Continental Marines	—	.32	.16
❑ 1568	10¢	American Militia	—	.32	.16
		Block of 4 (1565–1568)	3.75 (12)	.60	.50
❑ 1569	10¢	Apollo-Soyuz & Earth	—	.32	.15
❑ 1570	10¢	Apollo-Soyuz & Logo	—	.32	.15
		Pair (1569–1570)	3.00 (12)	.60	.46

1571

1572–1575

1576

1577–1578

Scott No.			Plate Block	Unused	Used
❏ 1571	10¢	Int'l Women's Year	1.85 (6)	.32	.15
❏ 1572	10¢	Stagecoach	—	.32	.15
❏ 1573	10¢	Steam Engine	—	.32	.15
❏ 1574	10¢	Biplane	—	.32	.15
❏ 1575	10¢	Satellite	—	.32	.15
		Block of 4 (1572–1575)	2.50 (12)	1.40	.62
❏ 1576	10¢	World Peace Thru Law	1.50	.35	.15
❏ 1577	10¢	Banking	—	.27	.15
❏ 1578	10¢	Commerce	—	.27	.15
		Pair (1577–1578)	2.00	.80	.42

1579

1580
(1580B)

Scott No.			Plate Block	Unused	Used
❏ 1579	10¢	Madonna & Child	4.00 (12)	.32	.15
❏ 1580	10¢	Prang Card, perf 11	4.50 (12)	.35	.16
❏ 1580B	10¢	Prang Card (~1580), perf 10.5 x 11.3	14.00 (12)	.82	.50

1581
(1811)

1582

1584

1585

1590
(1590A, 1591, 1616)

1975–1981. Americana Series.

❏ 1581	1¢	Inkwell	.50	.25	.15
❏ 1582	2¢	Speaker's Lectern	.50	.25	.15
❏ 1584	3¢	Ballot Box	.50	.25	.15
❏ 1585	4¢	Books & Glasses	.60	.25	.15
❏ 1590	9¢	Capitol Dome, white paper, perf 11 x 10½	—	.80	.50
		Pair (1590 & 1623)	—	.80	.45
❏ 1590A	9¢	Capitol Dome, white paper, perf 10	—	.40	.21
		Pair (1590A & 1623A)	—	30.00	15.00
❏ 1591	9¢	Capitol Dome (~1590), gray paper	1.00	.42	.15

1592	**1593**	**1594**
(1617)		(1816)

1595	**1596**	**1597**	**1599**
(1595a–d, 1618)		(1598, 1618C)	(1619)

Scott No.			Plate Block	Unused	Used
❑ 1592	10¢	Justice	1.30	.31	.15
❑ 1593	11¢	Printing Press	1.50	.40	.15
❑ 1594	12¢	Torch of Liberty	1.90	.35	.15
❑ 1595	13¢	Liberty Bell, from booklet pane	—	.37	.15
❑ 1595a	13¢	Booklet pane of 6	—	2.40	1.50
❑ 1595b	13¢	Booklet pane of 7 + label	—	2.10	1.50
❑ 1595c	13¢	Booklet pane of 8	—	2.10	1.10
❑ 1595d	13¢	Booklet pane of 5 + label	—	2.25	2.00
❑ 1596	13¢	Eagle & Shield	4.10 (12)	.22	.15
❑ 1597	15¢	Stars & Stripes	10.00 (20)	.26	.15
❑ 1598	15¢	Stars & Stripes (~1597)	—	.62	.15
		Booklet pane of 8	—	4.50	.78
❑ 1599	16¢	Statue of Liberty	2.50	.50	.15

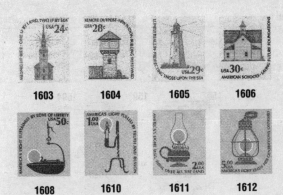

1603	1604	1605	1606

1608	1610	1611	1612

Scott No.			Plate Block	Unused	Used
❏ 1603	24¢	Old North Church	3.00	.62	.16
❏ 1604	28¢	Fort Nisqually	3.50	.70	.16
❏ 1605	29¢	Sandy Hook Lighthouse	4.00	.92	.16
❏ 1606	30¢	School House	4.00	.86	.15
❏ 1608	50¢	Iron Betty Lamp	5.00	1.10	.20
❏ 1610	$1	Rush Lamp	12.00	2.50	.25
❏ 1611	$2	Kerosene Lamp	21.00	5.00	.74
❏ 1612	$5	Railroad Lantern	50.00	12.00	2.00

1613	1614	1615	1615C

Scott No.			Line Pair	Unused	Used

Americana Series Coil Stamps.

Scott No.			Line Pair	Unused	Used
❏ 1613	3.1¢	Guitar	.80	.26	.17
❏ 1614	7.7¢	Saxhorns	1.18	.32	.21
❏ 1615	7.9¢	Drum	.90	.32	.21
❏ 1615C	8.4¢	Piano	2.75	.32	.21

Scott No.			Line Pair	Unused	Used
❑ 1616	9¢	Capitol Dome (~1590)	.90	.31	.17
❑ 1617	10¢	Justice (~1592)	.90	.31	.17
❑ 1618	13¢	Liberty Bell (~1595)	.90	.31	.17

1622
(1622C, 1625)

1623
(1623B)

Scott No.			Plate Block	Unused	Used

1975–1977. Definitives.

❑ 1622	13¢	Flag & Ind. Hall, perf 11 x 10½	7.50 (20)	.35	.15
❑ 1622C	13¢	Flag & Ind. Hall (~1622), perf 11½	70.00 (20)	1.00	.72
❑ 1623	13¢	Flag & Capitol, perf 11 x 10½	—	.45	.15
		Booklet pane of 8 (7 x 1623, 1 x 1590)	—	33.00	—
❑ 1623B	13¢	Flag & Capitol (~1623), perf 10	—	1.10	.15
		Booklet pane of 8 (7 x 1623B, 1 x 1590A)	—	30.00	25.00

Scott No.			Line Pair	Unused	Used

Coil Stamps.

❑ 1625	13¢	Flag & Independence Hall (~1622)	6.00	.42	.17

1629–1531

1632

Scott No.			Plate Block	Unused	Used
1976.					
❑ 1629	13¢	Youthful Drummer	—	.45	.21
❑ 1630	13¢	Mature Drummer	—	.45	.21
❑ 1631	13¢	Fief Player	—	.45	.21
		Strip of 3, 1629–1631	4.00 (12)	.85	.47
❑ 1632	13¢	INTERPHIL '76	1.60	.35	.17

1633–1682

Scott No.	Plate Block	Unused	Used
❏ 1633–1682 13¢ Fifty State Flags	24.00 (20)	.65	.40

❏ 1633 Delaware

❏ 1634 Pennsylvania

❏ 1635 New Jersey

❏ 1636 Georgia

❏ 1637 Connecticut

❏ 1638 Massachusetts

❏ 1639 Maryland

❏ 1640 South Carolina

- ❏ 1641 New Hampshire
- ❏ 1642 Virginia
- ❏ 1643 New York
- ❏ 1644 North Carolina
- ❏ 1645 Rhode Island
- ❏ 1646 Vermont
- ❏ 1647 Kentucky
- ❏ 1648 Tennessee
- ❏ 1649 Ohio
- ❏ 1650 Louisiana
- ❏ 1651 Indiana
- ❏ 1652 Mississippi
- ❏ 1653 Illinois
- ❏ 1654 Alabama
- ❏ 1655 Maine
- ❏ 1656 Missouri
- ❏ 1657 Arkansas
- ❏ 1658 Michigan
- ❏ 1659 Florida
- ❏ 1660 Texas
- ❏ 1661 Iowa
- ❏ 1662 Wisconsin
- ❏ 1663 California
- ❏ 1664 Minnesota
- ❏ 1665 Oregon
- ❏ 1666 Kansas
- ❏ 1667 West Virginia
- ❏ 1668 Nevada
- ❏ 1669 Nebraska
- ❏ 1670 Colorado
- ❏ 1671 North Dakota
- ❏ 1672 South Dakota
- ❏ 1673 Montana
- ❏ 1674 Washington
- ❏ 1675 Idaho
- ❏ 1676 Wyoming
- ❏ 1677 Utah
- ❏ 1678 Oklahoma
- ❏ 1679 New Mexico
- ❏ 1680 Arizona
- ❏ 1681 Alaska
- ❏ 1682 Hawaii

1683

1684

1685

Scott No.			Plate Block	Unused	Used
❏ 1683	13¢	Telephone Centennial	1.50	.42	.15
❏ 1684	13¢	Commercial Aviation	4.00 (10)	.42	.15
❏ 1685	13¢	Chemistry	4.50 (12)	.45	.15

The Surrender of Lord Cornwallis at Yorktown
From a Painting by John Trumbull

1686

The Declaration of Independence, 4 July 1776 at Philadelphia
From a Painting by John Trumbull

1687

Washington Crossing the Delaware
From a Painting by Emanuel Leutze / Eastman Johnson

1688

Scott No.			Plate Block	Unused	Used
❏ 1686	13¢	Surrender at Yorktown, souvenir sheet	—	4.50	.45
❏ 1686a–e		Any single stamp	—	1.50	.75
❏ 1687	18¢	Declaration of Independence, souvenir sheet	—	6.10	4.50
❏ 1687a–e		Any single stamp	—	1.50	1.00
❏ 1688	24¢	Crossing the Delaware, souvenir sheet	—	9.00	7.00
❏ 1688a–e		Any single stamp	—	2.00	1.75

Washington Reviewing His Ragged Army at Valley Forge
From a Painting by William T. Trego

1689

1690

Scott No.			Plate Block	Unused	Used
❑ 1689	31¢	Valley Forge, souvenir sheet	—	11.00	7.50
❑ 1689a–e		Any single stamp	—	2.50	1.90
❑ 1690	13¢	Benjamin Franklin	1.50	.40	.16

1691–1694

1695–1698

Scott No.			Plate Block	Unused	Used
❑ 1691	13¢	Delegates Seated & Standing	—	2.10	.45
❑ 1692	13¢	Delegates Seated	—	2.10	.45
❑ 1693	13¢	Delegates at Desk	—	2.10	.45
❑ 1694	13¢	Seated at Large Chair	—	2.10	.45
		Strip of 4 (1691–1694)	12.50 (20)	3.00	1.50
❑ 1695	13¢	Olympics – Diving	—	1.20	.60
❑ 1696	13¢	Olympics – Skiing	—	1.20	.60
❑ 1697	13¢	Olympics – Running	—	1.20	.60
❑ 1698	13¢	Olympics – Skating	—	1.20	.60
		Block of 4 (1695–1698)	5.50 (20)	1.80	1.40

1701

1699   **1700**

1702

Scott No.			Plate Block	Unused	Used
❑ 1699	13¢	Clara Maass	6.00 (12)	.44	.15
❑ 1700	13¢	Adolph S. Ochs	2.00	.45	.15
❑ 1701	13¢	Christmas – Manger Scene	4.50 (12)	.42	.15
❑ 1702	13¢	Winter Pastimes (overall tagging)	4.50 (10)	.42	.15
❑ 1703	13¢	Winter Pastimes (~1702) (block tagging)	6.00 (10)	.42	.15

1705

1704

Scott No.			Plate Block	Unused	Used
1977.					
❑ 1704	13¢	Washington at Princeton	5.00 (10)	.47	.15
❑ 1705	13¢	Sound Recording	4.00	1.25	1.00

1706–1709

1710

1711

Scott No.			Plate Block	Unused	Used
❏ 1706	13¢	Zia Pot	—	.42	.15
❏ 1707	13¢	San Ildefonso Pot	—	.42	.15
❏ 1708	13¢	Hopi Pot	—	.42	.15
❏ 1709	13¢	Acoma Pot	—	.42	.15
		Block of 4 (1706–1709)	4.25	1.40	1.15
❏ 1710	13¢	Spirit of St. Louis	4.50 (12)	.42	.15
❏ 1711	13¢	Colorado Statehood	4.50	.42	.15

1712–1715

1716

1717–1720

1721

1722

Scott No.			Plate Block	Unused	Used
❏ 1712	13¢	Swallowtail	—	1.20	.46
❏ 1713	13¢	Checkerspot	—	1.20	.46
❏ 1714	13¢	Dogface	—	1.20	.46
❏ 1715	13¢	Orange-Tip	—	1.20	.46
		Block of 4 (1712–1715)	5.00 (12)	1.40	1.10
❏ 1716	13¢	Lafayette	2.00	.47	.15
❏ 1717	13¢	Seamstress	—	.47	.15
❏ 1718	13¢	Blacksmith	—	.47	.15
❏ 1719	13¢	Wheelwright	—	.47	.15
❏ 1720	13¢	Leatherworker	—	.47	.15
		Block of 4 (1717–1720)	5.00 (12)	1.40	1.00
❏ 1721	13¢	Peace Bridge	1.40	.40	.15
❏ 1722	13¢	Battle of Oriskany	4.00 (10)	.40	.15

1725

1723–24

1726

1727

US Bicentennial 13 cents

1728

1729

1730

Scott No.			Plate Block	Unused	Used
❏ 1723	13¢	Energy Conservation	—	.42	.17
❏ 1724	13¢	Energy Development	—	.42	.17
		Se-tenant pair (1723–1724)	4.50 (12)	.60	.36
❏ 1725	13¢	Alta, California	1.10	.35	.15
❏ 1726	13¢	Articles of Confederation	1.40	.42	.15
❏ 1727	13¢	Talking Pictures	1.50	.42	.15
❏ 1728	13¢	Surrender at Saratoga	3.50 (10)	.42	.15
❏ 1729	13¢	Christmas – Valley Forge	7.00 (20)	.42	.15
❏ 1730	13¢	Christmas – Mailbox	3.50 (10)	.42	.15

1731   **1732–1733**

Scott No.			Plate Block	Unused	Used
1978.					
❑ 1731	13¢	Carl Sandburg	2.00	.42	.15
❑ 1732	13¢	Captain James Cook	—	.42	.15
❑ 1733	13¢	Ships at Anchor	—	.42	.15
		Se-tenant pair (1732–1733)	9.00	.90	.62

1734

1735
(1736, 1743)

			Plate Block	Unused	Used
1978–1980.					
❑ 1734	13¢	Indian Head Cent	1.40	.40	.15
❑ 1735	(15¢)	"A" (photogravure)	1.80	.40	.15
Booklet Stamps.					
❑ 1736	(15¢)	"A" (~1735) (engraved)	—	.50	.15
		Booklet pane of 8	—	3.25	2.60

1737   **1738–1742**

Scott No.			Plate Block	Unused	Used
❑ 1737	15¢	Roses	—	.40	.15
		Booklet pane of 8	3.00	2.50	1.50
❑ 1738	15¢	Windmill – Virginia	—	.42	.15
❑ 1739	15¢	Windmill – Rhode Island	—	.42	.15
❑ 1740	15¢	Windmill – Massachusetts	—	.42	.15
❑ 1741	15¢	Windmill – Illinois	—	.42	.15
❑ 1742	15¢	Windmill – Texas	—	.42	.15
		Booklet pane of 10 (2 each 1738–1742)	—	4.50	4.00

Scott No.			Line Pair	Unused	Used

Coil Stamp.

❑ 1743	(15¢)	"A" (~1735) (engraved)	1.00	.42	.15

1744

Scott No.			Plate Block	Unused	Used

1978.

❑ 1744	13¢	Harriet Tubman	5.50 (12)	.48	.16

1745–1748

1749–1752

Scott No.			Plate Block	Unused	Used
❑ 1745	13¢	Quilt with Flowers	—	.36	.15
❑ 1746	13¢	Red & White Quilt	—	.36	.15
❑ 1747	13¢	Orange Striped Quilt	—	.36	.15
❑ 1748	13¢	Black Plaid Quilt	—	.36	.15
		Block of 4 (1745–1748)	5.75 (12)	1.10	.90
❑ 1749	13¢	Ballet	—	.36	.15
❑ 1750	13¢	Theater	—	.36	.15
❑ 1751	13¢	Folk Dance	—	.36	.15
❑ 1752	13¢	Modern Dance	—	.36	.15
		Block of 4 (1749–1752)	4.75 (12)	1.20	1.00

1753   1754   1755   1756

1757

Scott No.			Plate Block	Unused	Used
❑ 1753	13¢	French Alliance	1.40	.36	.15
❑ 1754	13¢	Cancer Detection	2.50	.40	.15
❑ 1755	13¢	Jimmie Rodgers	6.50 (12)	.52	.15
❑ 1756	15¢	George M. Cohan	7.50 (12)	.60	.15
❑ 1757	13¢	CAPEX, block of 8	3.25	1.50	1.25
❑ 1757a–h		Any single	—	.42	.21

Photography USA 15c

1758

Viking missions to Mars

Expanding human knowledge USA 15c

1759

1760–1763

Scott No.			Plate Block	Unused	Used
❑ 1758	15¢	Photography	5.00 (12)	.42	.15
❑ 1759	15¢	Viking Mission to Mars	1.50	.42	.15
❑ 1760	15¢	Great Gray Owl	—	.47	.15
❑ 1761	15¢	Saw-whet Owl	—	.47	.15
❑ 1762	15¢	Barred Owl	—	.47	.15
❑ 1763	15¢	Great Horned Owl	—	.47	.15
		Block of 4 (1760–1763)	1.75	1.50	.90

1764–1767

1768

1769

Scott No.			Plate Block	Unused	Used
❑ 1764	15¢	Giant Sequoia	—	.42	.16
❑ 1765	15¢	White Pine	—	.42	.16
❑ 1766	15¢	White Oak	—	.42	.16
❑ 1767	15¢	Gray Birch	—	.42	.16
		Block of 4 (1764–1767).00	5.75 (12)	1.50	1.34
❑ 1768	15¢	Christmas – Madonna	5.00 (12)	.46	.17
❑ 1769	15¢	Christmas – Rocking Horse	5.00 (12)	.46	.17

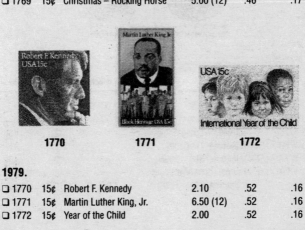

1770

1771

1772

1979.

❑ 1770	15¢	Robert F. Kennedy	2.10	.52	.16
❑ 1771	15¢	Martin Luther King, Jr.	6.50 (12)	.52	.16
❑ 1772	15¢	Year of the Child	2.00	.52	.16

1773

1774

1775–1778

Scott No.			Plate Block	Unused	Used
❑ 1773	15¢	John Steinbeck	2.00	.46	.15
❑ 1774	15¢	Albert Einstein	2.00	.46	.15
❑ 1775	15¢	Toleware – Straight Spout	—	.42	.15
❑ 1776	15¢	Toleware – Tea Caddy	—	.42	.15
❑ 1777	15¢	Toleware – Sugar Bowl	—	.42	.15
❑ 1778	15¢	Toleware – Curved Spout	—	.42	.15
		Block of 4 (1775–1778)	4.50 (10)	1.75	1.00

1779–82

1783–1786

1787

1788

Scott No.			Plate Block	Unused	Used
❑ 1779	15¢	Virginia Rotunda	—	.42	.16
❑ 1780	15¢	Baltimore Cathedral	—	.42	.16
❑ 1781	15¢	Boston State House	—	.42	.16
❑ 1782	15¢	Philadelphia Exchange	—	.42	.16
		Block of 4 (1779–1782)	2.50	2.00	1.50
❑ 1783	15¢	Persistent Trillium	—	.42	.15
❑ 1784	15¢	Hawaiian Wild Broadbean	—	.42	.15
❑ 1785	15¢	Contra Costa Wallflower	—	.42	.15
❑ 1786	15¢	Evening Primrose	—	.42	.15
		Block of 4 (1783–1786)	6.00 (12)	1.75	1.00
❑ 1787	15¢	Seeing for Me	10.00 (20)	.50	.15
❑ 1788	15¢	Special Olympics	4.00 (10)	.50	.15

I have not yet begun to fight

John Paul Jones
US Bicentennial 15c

1789
(1789A, 1789B)

1791–1794

1790

1795–1798

Scott No.			Plate Block	Unused	Used
❏ 1789	15¢	John Paul Jones, perf 11 x 12	4.75 (10)	.46	.16
❏ 1789A	15¢	Jones (~1789), perf 11	4.00 (10)	.55	.27
❏ 1789B	15¢	Jones (~1789), perf 12	11000.00	2000.00	750.00
❏ 1790	10¢	Olympics – Decathlon	4.00 (12)	.36	.16
❏ 1791	15¢	Olympics – Runners	—	.36	.16
❏ 1792	15¢	Olympics – Swimmers	—	.36	.16
❏ 1793	15¢	Olympics – Rowers	—	.36	.16
❏ 1794	15¢	Olympics – Equestrian	—	.36	.16
		Block of 4 (1791–1794)	6.00 (12)	2.00	1.40
❏ 1795	15¢	Olympics – Skater	—	.46	.16
❏ 1796	15¢	Olympics – Skier	—	.46	.16
❏ 1797	15¢	Olympics – Ski Jumper	—	.46	.16
❏ 1798	15¢	Olympics – Hockey	—	.46	.16
		Block of 4 (1795–1795)	6.00 (12)	2.00	1.75

1799

1800

1801

1802

Scott No.			Plate Block	Unused	Used
❏ 1799	15¢	Christmas – Madonna	5.00 (12)	.42	.15
❏ 1800	15¢	Gingerbread Santa	3.50 (12)	.42	.15
❏ 1801	15¢	Will Rogers	3.50 (12)	.42	.15
❏ 1802	15¢	Vietnam Veterans	3.50 (10)	.42	.15

1803

1804

1980.

❏ 1803	15¢	W. C. Fields	5.50 (12)	.42	.15
❏ 1804	15¢	Benjamin Banneker	7.00 (12)	.65	.15

1805–1810

Scott No.			Plate Block	Unused	Used
❑ 1805	15¢	Letters Preserve Memories	—	.42	.15
❑ 1806	15¢	P. S. Write Soon (violet & pink)	—	.42	.15
❑ 1807	15¢	Letters Lift Spirits	—	.42	.15
❑ 1808	15¢	P.S. (green & yellow green)	—	.42	.15
❑ 1809	15¢	Letters Shape Opinions	—	.42	.15
❑ 1810	15¢	P.S. (scarlet & blue)	—	.42	.15
		Strip of 6 (1805–1810)	19.50 (36)	3.00	2.80

1813

Scott No.			Line Pair	Unused	Used
1980. Americana Series Coil Stamps.					
❑ 1811	1¢	Inkwell (~1581)	.45	.26	.15
❑ 1813	3.5¢	Violins	1.00	.26	.15
❑ 1816	12¢	Torch of Liberty (~1594)	1.60	.37	.26

1818
(1819, 1820)

Scott No.	Plate Block	Unused	Used
1981.			
☐ 1818 (18¢) "B" (photogravure)	2.00	.50	.16
☐ 1819 (18¢) "B" (~1818) (engraved)	4.00	.42	.16
Booklet pane of 8	—	4.50	3.00

Scott No.	Line Pair	Unused	Used
Coil Stamp.			
☐ 1820 (18¢) "B" (~1818) (engraved)	1.50	.52	.17

| 1821 | 1822 | 1823 | 1824 |

Scott No.	Plate Block	Unused	Used
1980.			
☐ 1821 15¢ Francis Perkins	1.60	.42	.15
☐ 1822 15¢ Dolley Madison	2.00	.42	.15
☐ 1823 15¢ Emily Bissell	2.10	.50	.15
☐ 1824 15¢ Helen Keller – Anne Sullivan	2.50	.50	.15

1825

1826

1827–1830

1831

1832

1833

Scott No.			Plate Block	Unused	Used
❑ 1825	15¢	Veterans Administration	2.00	.42	.15
❑ 1826	15¢	General Bernardo de Galvez	2.00	.42	.15
❑ 1827	15¢	Brain Coral	—	.42	.15
❑ 1828	15¢	Elkhorn Coral	—	.42	.15
❑ 1829	15¢	Chalice Coral	—	.42	.15
❑ 1830	15¢	Finger Coral	—	.42	.15
		Block of 4 (1827–1830)	5.00 (12)	1.50	1.00
❑ 1831	15¢	Organized Labor	6.00 (12)	.47	.16
❑ 1832	15¢	Edith Wharton	2.00	.47	.15
❑ 1833	15¢	Learning Never Ends	3.10 (6)	.47	.15

1834–1837

1838–1841

Scott No.			Plate Block	Unused	Used
❏ 1834	15¢	Mask – Heiltsuk, Bella Bella	—	.42	.18
❏ 1835	15¢	Mask – Chilkat Tlingit	—	.42	.18
❏ 1836	15¢	Mask – Tlingit	—	.42	.18
❏ 1837	15¢	Mask – Bella Coola	—	.42	.18
		Block of 4 (1834–1837)	7.00 (10)	2.50	1.50
❏ 1838	15¢	Architecture – Smithsonian	—	.42	.18
❏ 1839	15¢	Architecture – Trinity Church	—	.42	.18
❏ 1840	15¢	Architecture – Penn Academy	—	.42	.18
❏ 1841	15¢	Architecture – Lyndhurst	—	.42	.18
		Block of 4 (1838–1841)	2.50	2.00	1.55

Christmas USA 15c

1842

USA 15c
Season's Greetings

1843

Scott No.			Plate Block	Unused	Used
❑ 1842	15¢	Christmas – Madonna & Child	4.50 (12)	.47	.15
❑ 1843	15¢	Christmas – Wreath & Drum	9.50 (20)	.42	.15

1844	**1845**	**1846**	**1847**	**1848**

1849	**1850**	**1851**	**1852**	**1853**

1980–1985. Great Americans Series.

❑ 1844	1¢	Dorothea Dix	2.40 (20)	.20	.15
❑ 1845	2¢	Igor Stravinsky	.50	.20	.15
❑ 1846	3¢	Henry Clay	.66	.20	.15
❑ 1847	4¢	Carl Schurz	.60	.20	.15
❑ 1848	5¢	Pearl Buck	.65	.20	.15
❑ 1849	6¢	Walter Lippmann	5.00 (20)	.20	.15
❑ 1850	7¢	Abraham Baldwin	5.00 (20)	.25	.15
❑ 1851	8¢	Henry Knox	1.10	.25	.15
❑ 1852	9¢	Sylvanus Thayer	6.00 (20)	.42	.20
❑ 1853	10¢	Richard Russell	7.00 (20)	.42	.20

1854	1855	1856	1857

1858	1859	1860	1861

1862	1863	1864	1865

Scott No.			Plate Block	Unused	Used
❏ 1854	11¢	Alden Partridge	2.50	.52	.14
❏ 1855	13¢	Crazy Horse	2.00	.40	.14
❏ 1856	14¢	Sinclair Lewis	10.00 (20)	.40	.14
❏ 1857	17¢	Rachel Carson	2.50	.48	.14
❏ 1858	18¢	George Mason	2.40	.45	.14
❏ 1859	19¢	Sequoyah	2.60	.46	.14
❏ 1860	20¢	Ralph Bunche	3.60	.50	.14
❏ 1861	20¢	Thomas H. Gallaudet	3.50	.50	.14
❏ 1862	20¢	Harry S. Truman	15.00 (20)	.50	.14
❏ 1863	22¢	John J. Audubon	15.00 (20)	.70	.14
❏ 1864	30¢	Frank C. Laubach	16.00 (20)	.70	.14
❏ 1865	35¢	Charles R. Drew M.D.	4.50	.90	.14

| 1866 | 1867 | 1868 | 1869 |

Scott No.			Plate Block	Unused	Used
❑ 1866	37¢	Robert Millikan	4.50	1.05	.16
❑ 1867	39¢	Grenville Clark	16.00 (20)	1.05	.16
❑ 1868	40¢	Lillian M. Gilbreth	22.00 (20)	1.05	.16
❑ 1869	50¢	Chester W. Nimitz	10.00	1.25	.16

NOTE: See Nos. 2168–2197 and 2933–2943 for other Great Americans Series stamps.

| 1874 | 1875 |

1876–1879

1981.

❑ 1874	15¢	Everett M. Dirksen	2.00	.46	.15
❑ 1875	15¢	Whitney Moore Young	1.90	.46	.15
❑ 1876	18¢	Rose	—	.46	.15
❑ 1877	18¢	Camellia	—	.46	.15
❑ 1878	18¢	Dahlia	—	.46	.15
❑ 1879	18¢	Lily	—	.46	.15
		Block of 4 (1876–1879)	2.50	2.00	1.45

1880–1889

Scott No.			Plate Block	Unused	Used
Booklet Pane.					
❑ 1880	18¢	Bighorn Sheep	—	.60	.15
❑ 1881	18¢	Mountain Lion	—	.60	.15
❑ 1882	18¢	Harbor Seal	—	.60	.15
❑ 1883	18¢	Bison	—	.60	.15
❑ 1884	18¢	Brown Bear	—	.60	.15
❑ 1885	18¢	Polar Bear	—	.60	.15
❑ 1886	18¢	Elk	—	.60	.15
❑ 1887	18¢	Moose	—	.60	.15
❑ 1888	18¢	White-tailed Deer	—	.60	.15
❑ 1889	18¢	Pronghorn Antelope	—	.60	.15
		Booklet pane of 10 (1880–1889)	—	11.00	7.75

1890

1891

981. Definitive.

Scott No.			Plate Block	Unused	Used
❑ 1890	18¢	Flag – Amber Waves of Grain	5.50 (20)	.60	.26

Scott No.			PNC Strip (5)	Unused	Used
Coil Stamp.					
❑ 1891	18¢	Flag – Sea to Shining Sea	1.00	.42	.15

1892	1893	1894
		(1895, 1896)

Scott No.			Plate Block	Unused	Used

1981. Definitives.

Scott No.			Plate Block	Unused	Used
❏ 1892	6¢	Numeral in Circle of Stars	—	1.00	.36
❏ 1893	18¢	Flag – Purple Mountain Majesties	—	.50	.18
		Booklet pane of 8 (two 1892; six 1893)	—	4.50	1.15
❏ 1894	20¢	Flag over Supreme Court	11.50 (20)	.95	.21

Scott No.			PNC Strip (5)	Unused	Used

1981. Coil Stamp.

Scott No.			PNC Strip (5)	Unused	Used
❏ 1895	20¢	Flag over Supreme Court (~1894)	12.00	.60	.20

Scott No.			Plate Block	Unused	Used

1981. Booklet Stamp.

Scott No.			Plate Block	Unused	Used
❏ 1896	20¢	Flag over Supreme Court (~1894)	—	.70	.20
		Booklet pane of 6	—	4.10	2.40
		Booklet pane of 10	—	6.00	4.00

	1897	1897A	1898	1898A	1899
	1900	1901	1902	1903	1904
	1905	1906	1907	1908	

Scott No.			PNC Strip (5)	Unused	Used

1981–1984. Transportation Series Coil Stamps.

			PNC Strip (5)	Unused	Used
❏ 1897	1¢	Omnibus	.47	.22	.15
❏ 1897A	2¢	Locomotive	.50	.22	.15
❏ 1898	3¢	Handcar	.75	.22	.15
❏ 1898A	4¢	Stagecoach	1.10	.22	.15
❏ 1899	5¢	Motorcycle	1.00	.22	.15
❏ 1900	5.2¢	Sleigh	5.00	.22	.15
❏ 1901	5.9¢	Bicycle	6.00	.26	.15
❏ 1902	7.4¢	Baby Buggy	6.75	.26	.15
❏ 1903	9.3¢	Mail Wagon	7.10	.26	.15
❏ 1904	10.9¢	Hansom Cab	12.00	.26	.15
❏ 1905	11¢	Caboose	3.50	.21	.15
❏ 1906	17¢	Electric Auto	2.50	.42	.15
❏ 1907	18¢	Surrey	2.75	.47	.15
❏ 1908	20¢	Fire Pumper	2.75	.52	.15

NOTE: Some values of the above exist Bureau precanceled. Prices are the same as unprecanceled examples. See Nos. 2123–2136, 2225–2231, 2252–2266, and 2451–2468 for other Transportation Series coil stamps.

1909   1910   1911

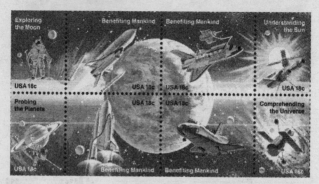

1912–1919

Scott No.			Plate Block	Unused	Used
1981.					
❏ 1909	$9.35	Express Mail	—	26.00	.14
		Booklet pane of 3	—	80.00	2.10
❏ 1910	18¢	American Red Cross	2.20	.52	.17
❏ 1911	18¢	Savings & Loan	1.80	.52	.17
❏ 1912	18¢	Exploring the Moon	—	.46	.17
❏ 1913	18¢	Shuttle Jettisoning Boosters	—	.46	.17
❏ 1914	18¢	Shuttle Deploying Satellite	—	.46	.17
❏ 1915	18¢	Understanding the Sun	—	.46	.17
❏ 1916	18¢	Probing the Planets	—	.46	.17
❏ 1917	18¢	Shuttle – Vertical Ascent	—	.46	.17
❏ 1918	18¢	Shuttle – Landing Gear Down	—	.46	.17
❏ 1919	18¢	Comprehending the Universe	—	.46	.17
		Block of 8 (1912–1919)	6.00 (8)	4.00	3.15

1920

1921–1924

1925　　　　　**1926**　　　　　**1927**

Scott No.			Plate Block	Unused	Used
❑ 1920	18¢	Professional Management	2.10	.55	.15
❑ 1921	18¢	Save Wetland Habitats	—	.55	.15
❑ 1922	18¢	Save Grassland Habitats	—	.55	.15
❑ 1923	18¢	Save Mountain Habitats	—	.55	.15
❑ 1924	18¢	Save Woodland Habitats	—	.55	.15
		Block of 4 (1921–1924)	2.50	1.75	1.50
❑ 1925	18¢	Disabled Persons	2.10	.50	.15
❑ 1926	18¢	Edna St. Vincent Millay	2.10	.60	.15
❑ 1927	18¢	Alcoholism	32.00 (20)	.60	.15

1928–1931

1934

1932   **1933**

Scott No.			Plate Block	Unused	Used
❏ 1928	18¢	NYU Library – New York	—	.52	.17
❏ 1929	18¢	Biltmore – Asheville, NC	—	.52	.17
❏ 1930	18¢	Palace of Arts – San Francisco	—	.52	.17
❏ 1931	18¢	Bank – Owatonna, MN	—	.52	.17
		Block of 4 (1928–1931)	2.90	2.00	1.80
❏ 1932	18¢	Babe Zaharias	3.60	.46	.17
❏ 1933	18¢	Bobby Jones	6.00	.95	.17
❏ 1934	18¢	Frederick Remington	1.70	1.10	.21

1935

1936

1937–1938

1939

1940

1941

Scott No.			Plate Block	Unused	Used
❑ 1935	18¢	James Hoban	2.50	.52	.16
❑ 1936	20¢	James Hoban	2.30	.52	.16
❑ 1937	18¢	Yorktown Map	—	.45	.16
❑ 1938	18¢	Virginia Capes Map	—	.45	.16
		Se-tenant pair (1937–1938)	3.00	1.50	.70
❑ 1939	(20¢)	Christmas – Madonna & Child	2.50	.52	.16
❑ 1940	(20¢)	Christmas – Teddy Bear	2.50	.52	.16
❑ 1941	20¢	John Hanson	2.50	.52	.16

1942–1945

1946
(1947, 1948)

Scott No.			Plate Block	Unused	Used
❑ 1942	20¢	Cactus – Barrel Cactus	—	.46	.17
❑ 1943	20¢	Cactus – Agave	—	.46	.17
❑ 1944	20¢	Cactus – Beavertail Cactus	—	.46	.17
❑ 1945	20¢	Cactus – Saguaro	—	.46	.17
		Block of 4 (1942–1945)	3.00	2.00	1.50
❑ 1946	(20¢)	"C" & Eagle	2.10	.52	.17

Scott No.			Line Pair	Unused	Used
Coil Stamp.					
❑ 1947	(20¢)	"C" & Eagle (~1946)	1.75	.74	.17

Scott No.			Plate Block	Unused	Used
Booklet Stamps.					
❑ 1948	(20¢)	"C" & Eagle (~1946)	—	.62	.17
		Booklet pane of 10	—	5.00	3.60

1949

Scott No.			Plate Block	Unused	Used
❑ 1949	20¢	Bighorn Sheep	—	.73	.18
		Booklet pane of 10	—	6.50	2.15

1950

1951
(1951A)

1952

1982.

❑ 1950	20¢	Franklin D. Roosevelt	2.10	.52	.17
❑ 1951	20¢	Love – Flowers	2.00	.52	.17
❑ 1952	20¢	George Washington	2.10	.52	.17

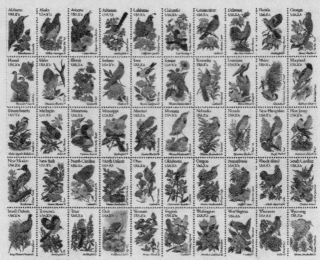

1953–2002

Scott No.		Plate Block	Unused	Used
❑ 1953– 20¢ 2002	State Birds & Flowers, perf 10½ x 11¼	—	35.00	—
❑ 1953– 2002 20¢	Any single stamp	—	1.40	.30
❑ 1953A– 2002A 20¢	State Birds & Flowers, perf 11¼ x 11	—	25.00	—
❑ 1953A– 2002A 20¢	Any single stamp	—	.60	.21

❑ 1953 Alabama   ❑ 1962 Georgia
❑ 1954 Alaska   ❑ 1963 Hawaii
❑ 1955 Arizona   ❑ 1964 Idaho
❑ 1956 Arkansas   ❑ 1965 Illinois
❑ 1957 California   ❑ 1966 Indiana
❑ 1958 Colorado   ❑ 1967 Iowa
❑ 1959 Connecticut   ❑ 1968 Kansas
❑ 1960 Delaware   ❑ 1969 Kentucky
❑ 1961 Florida   ❑ 1970 Louisiana

- ❏ 1971 Maine
- ❏ 1972 Maryland
- ❏ 1973 Massachusetts
- ❏ 1974 Michigan
- ❏ 1975 Minnesota
- ❏ 1976 Mississippi
- ❏ 1977 Missouri
- ❏ 1978 Montana
- ❏ 1979 Nebraska
- ❏ 1980 Nevada
- ❏ 1981 New Hampshire
- ❏ 1982 New Jersey
- ❏ 1983 New Mexico
- ❏ 1984 New York
- ❏ 1985 North Carolina
- ❏ 1986 North Dakota
- ❏ 1987 Ohio
- ❏ 1988 Oklahoma
- ❏ 1989 Oregon
- ❏ 1890 Pennsylvania
- ❏ 1991 Rhode Island
- ❏ 1992 South Carolina
- ❏ 1993 South Dakota
- ❏ 1994 Tennessee
- ❏ 1995 Texas
- ❏ 1996 Utah
- ❏ 1997 Vermont
- ❏ 1998 Virginia
- ❏ 1999 Washington
- ❏ 2000 West Virginia
- ❏ 2001 Wisconsin
- ❏ 2002 Wyoming

2003

2004

Scott No.			Plate Block	Unused	Used
❏ 2003	20¢	Netherlands	12.00 (20)	.55	.17
❏ 2004	20¢	Library of Congress	2.10	.55	.17

2005

Scott No.			PNC Strip (5)	Unused	Used
Coil Stamp.					
❏ 2005	20¢	Consumer Education	24.00	1.20	.17

2006–2009

2010

2011

2012

2013

2014

Scott No.			Plate Block	Unused	Used
1982.					
❑ 2006	20¢	Solar Energy	—	.52	.15
❑ 2007	20¢	Synthetic Fuels	—	.52	.15
❑ 2008	20¢	Breeder Reactor	—	.52	.15
❑ 2009	20¢	Fossil Fuels	—	.52	.15
		Block of 4 (2006–2009)	3.50	2.10	1.30
❑ 2010	20¢	Horatio Alger	2.00	.52	.15
❑ 2011	20¢	Aging Together	2.10	.52	.15
❑ 2012	20¢	The Barrymores	2.20	.52	.15
❑ 2013	20¢	Dr. Mary Walker	2.50	.55	.15
❑ 2014	20¢	International Peace Garden	2.50	.55	.15

2015

2016

2017

2018

2019–2022

Scott No.			Plate Block	Unused	Used
❏ 2015	20¢	America's Libraries	2.40	.50	.15
❏ 2016	20¢	Jackie Robinson	7.50	1.60	.18
❏ 2017	20¢	Touro Synagogue	17.50 (20)	.50	.15
❏ 2018	20¢	Wolf Trap Farm Park	2.10	.50	.15
❏ 2019	20¢	Architecture – Frank Lloyd Wright	—	.55	.15
❏ 2020	20¢	Architecture – Mies van der Rohe	—	.52	.15
❏ 2021	20¢	Architecture – Walter Gropius	—	.52	.15
❏ 2022	20¢	Architecture – Eero Saarinen	—	.52	.15
		Block of 4 (2019–2022)	4.50	3.10	1.45

2023

2024

2025

2026

2027–2030

2031

Scott No.			Plate Block	Unused	Used
❏ 2023	20¢	Francis of Assisi	2.50	.55	.15
❏ 2024	20¢	Ponce de Leon	12.50 (20)	.65	.15
❏ 2025	13¢	Christmas – Kitten & Puppy	1.90	.50	.15
❏ 2026	20¢	Christmas – Madonna & Child	13.00 (20)	.50	.15
❏ 2027	20¢	Christmas – Sledding	—	.65	.15
❏ 2028	20¢	Christmas – Snowman	—	.65	.15
❏ 2029	20¢	Christmas – Ice Skating	—	.65	.15
❏ 2030	20¢	Christmas – Trimming Tree	—	.65	.15
		Block of 4 (2027–2030)	4.10	3.15	1.60
❏ 2031	20¢	Science & Industry	2.10	.55	.15

2032–2035

Scott No.			Plate Block	Unused	Used
❑ 2032	20¢	Ballooning – Intrepid	—	.55	.15
❑ 2033	20¢	Ballooning – Hot Air Balloon	—	.55	.15
❑ 2034	20¢	Ballooning – Hot Air Balloon	—	.55	.15
❑ 2035	20¢	Ballooning – Explorer II	—	.55	.15
		Block of 4 (2032–2035)	3.00	2.00	1.50

2036

2037

2038

2039

2040

1983.

❑ 2036	20¢	USA – Sweden	2.40	.52	.15
❑ 2037	20¢	Civilian Conservation Corps	2.40	.52	.15
❑ 2038	20¢	Joseph Priestley	2.50	.52	.15
❑ 2039	20¢	Volunteer – Lend a Hand	12.00 (20)	.52	.15
❑ 2040	20¢	German Immigration	2.30	.52	.15

2041

2042

2043

2044

2045

2046

2047

Scott No.			Plate Block	Unused	Used
❑ 2041	20¢	Brooklyn Bridge	2.10	.50	.15
❑ 2042	20¢	Tennessee Valley Authority	14.00 (20)	.62	.15
❑ 2043	20¢	Physical Fitness	12.00 (20)	.60	.15
❑ 2044	20¢	Scott Joplin	2.50	.60	.15
❑ 2045	20¢	Medal of Honor	3.00	.65	.15
❑ 2046	20¢	Babe Ruth	10.50	3.00	.15
❑ 2047	20¢	Nathaniel Hawthorne	2.60	.60	.15

2048–2051

2052

CIVIL
SERVICE
1883
1983
USA 20c

2053

2054

Scott No.			Plate Block	Unused	Used
❏ 2048	13¢	Olympics – Discus	—	.55	.15
❏ 2049	13¢	Olympics – High Jump	—	.55	.15
❏ 2050	13¢	Olympics – Archery	—	.55	.15
❏ 2051	13¢	Olympics – Boxing	—	.55	.15
		Block of 4 (2048–2051)	3.00	2.50	1.15
❏ 2052	20¢	Treaty of Paris	2.75	.55	.15
❏ 2053	20¢	Civil Service	12.00 (20)	.60	.15
❏ 2054	20¢	Metropolitan Opera	2.10	.55	.15

2055–2058

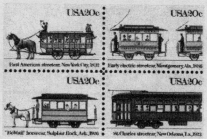

2059–2062

Scott No.			Plate Block	Unused	Used
❏ 2055	20¢	Charles Steinmetz	—	.60	.15
❏ 2056	20¢	Edwin Armstrong	—	.60	.15
❏ 2057	20¢	Nikola Tesla	—	.60	.15
❏ 2058	20¢	Philo T. Farnsworth	—	.60	.15
		Block of 4 (2055–2058)	4.10	2.50	2.00
❏ 2059	20¢	Streetcars – First American	—	.60	.15
❏ 2060	20¢	Streetcars – Electric Trolley	—	.60	.15
❏ 2061	20¢	Streetcars – Bobtail Horsecar	—	.60	.15
❏ 2062	20¢	Streetcars – St. Charles Coach	—	.60	.15
		Block of 4 (2059–2062)	3.50	3.00	2.20

NOTE. Prices for stamps from 1935 to date are for never-hinged (NH) examples.

| **2063** | **2064** | **2065** |

Scott No.			Plate Block	Unused	Used
❏ 2063	20¢	Christmas – Madonna	2.40	.60	.15
❏ 2064	20¢	Christmas – Santa Claus	12.00 (20)	.60	.15
❏ 2065	20¢	Martin Luther	2.40	.60	.15

2066

2067–70

1984.

❏ 2066	20¢	Alaska Statehood	2.25	.57	.15
❏ 2067	20¢	Olympics – Ice Dancing	—	.62	.15
❏ 2068	20¢	Olympics – Downhill Skiing	—	.62	.15
❏ 2069	20¢	Olympics – Cross Country Skiing	—	.62	.15
❏ 2070	20¢	Olympics – Hockey	—	.62	.15
		Block of 4 (2067–2070)	4.25	3.00	2.20

2071

2072

2073

2074

2075

2076–2079

2080

Scott No.			Plate Block	Unused	Used
❑ 2071	20¢	FDIC	2.40	.52	.15
❑ 2072	20¢	Love	13.50 (20)	.52	.15
❑ 2073	20¢	Carter G. Woodson	2.50	.52	.15
❑ 2074	20¢	Soil & Water Conservation	2.10	.52	.15
❑ 2075	20¢	Credit Union	2.10	.52	.15
❑ 2076	20¢	Orchids – Wild Pink	—	.62	.15
❑ 2077	20¢	Orchids – Yellow Lady Slipper	—	.62	.15
❑ 2078	20¢	Orchids – Spreading Pogonia	—	.62	.15
❑ 2079	20¢	Orchids – Pacific Calypso	—	.62	.15
		Block of 4 (2076–2079)	3.40	2.10	2.15
❑ 2080	20¢	Hawaii Statehood	2.50	.62	.15

2081

2082–2085

2086

2087

2088

Scott No.			Plate Block	Unused	Used
❑ 2081	20¢	National Archives	2.50	.60	.15
❑ 2082	20¢	Olympics – Men's Diving	—	.70	.15
❑ 2083	20¢	Olympics – Long Jump	—	.70	.15
❑ 2084	20¢	Olympics – Wrestling	—	.70	.15
❑ 2085	20¢	Olympics – Kayaking	—	.70	.15
		Block of 4 (2081–2084)	4.50	4.00	3.00
❑ 2086	20¢	Louisiana World's Exposition	4.00	.80	.15
❑ 2087	20¢	Health Research	3.00	.65	.15
❑ 2088	20¢	Douglas Fairbanks	16.00 (20)	.65	.15

2089

2090

2091

2092

2093

2094

2095

2096

2097

Scott No.			Plate Block	Unused	Used
❑ 2089	20¢	Jim Thorpe	3.10	.75	.15
❑ 2090	20¢	John McCormack	2.50	.60	.15
❑ 2091	20¢	St. Lawrence Seaway	2.50	.60	.15
❑ 2092	20¢	Preserving Wetlands	4.00	.75	.15
❑ 2093	20¢	Roanoke Voyages	3.00	.65	.15
❑ 2094	20¢	Herman Melville	2.40	.60	.15
❑ 2095	20¢	Horace Moses	16.00 (20)	.85	.15
❑ 2096	20¢	Smokey the Bear	3.00	.70	.15
❑ 2097	20¢	Roberto Clemente	12.00	2.40	.15

2098–2101

2102

2103

2104

2105

Scott No.			Plate Block	Unused	Used
❑ 2098	20¢	Beagle & Boston Terrier	—	.65	.15
❑ 2099	20¢	Retriever & Cocker Spaniel	—	.65	.15
❑ 2100	20¢	Malamute & Collie	—	.60	.15
❑ 2101	20¢	Coonhound & Foxhound	—	.60	.15
		Block of 4 (2098–2101)	4.00	3.00	2.50
❑ 2102	20¢	Crime Prevention	2.40	.60	.15
❑ 2103	20¢	Hispanic Americans	2.40	.60	.15
❑ 2104	20¢	Family Unity	17.00 (20)	.75	.15
❑ 2105	20¢	Eleanor Roosevelt	2.50	.55	.15

2106

2107

2108

Vietnam Veterans Memorial USA 20c

2109

Scott No.			Plate Block	Unused	Used
❑ 2106	20¢	Nation of Readers	2.50	.65	.15
❑ 2107	20¢	Christmas – Madonna & Child	2.10	.60	.15
❑ 2108	20¢	Christmas – Santa Claus	2.40	.60	.15
❑ 2109	20¢	Vietnam Veterans Memorial	4.00	.85	.15

2110

2111
(2112, 2113)

1985.

❑ 2110	22¢	Jerome Kern	2.75	.65	.15
❑ 2111	(22¢)	"D" & Eagle	30.00 (20)	.80	.15

Scott No.		PNC Strip (5)	Unused	Used
1985. Coil Stamp.				
❏ 2112 (22¢) "D" & Eagle (~2111)		9.00	.80	.15

2114
(2115)

Scott No.		Plate Block	Unused	Used
1985.				
❏ 2113 (22¢) "D" & Eagle (~2111)		—	.70	.15
Booklet pane of 10		—	10.00	4.00
❏ 2114 22¢ Flag over Capitol		3.00	.60	.15

Scott No.		PNC Strip (5)	Unused	Used
1985. Coil Stamps.				
❏ 2115 22¢ Flag over Capitol (~2114)		3.50	.60	.15
❏ 2115b With small letter "T" at bottom		3.75	.72	.30

2116

Scott No.		Plate Block	Unused	Used
1985.				
❏ 2116 22¢ Flag over Capitol		—	.82	.15
Booklet pane of 5		—	4.00	2.00

2117–2121

2122

Scott No.			Plate Block	Unused	Used
❑ 2117	22¢	Seashells – Frilled Dogwinkle	—	.70	.15
❑ 2118	22¢	Seashells – Reticulated Dogwinkle	—	.70	.15
❑ 2119	22¢	Seashells – New England Neptune	—	.70	.15
❑ 2120	22¢	Seashells – Calico Scallop	—	.70	.15
❑ 2121	22¢	Seashells – Lightning Whelk	—	.70	.15
		Booklet pane of 10 (2 each 2117–2121)	—	3.50	1.65
❑ 2122	$10.75	Express Mail (type I)	—	28.00	7.50
		Booklet pane of 3	—	80.00	10.00
❑ 2122b	$10.75	Express Mail (~2122) (type II)	—	38.00	12.00
		Booklet pane of 3	—	115.00	—

NOTE: Type I (Plate No. 11111) appears washed-out. Type II (Plate No. 22222) appears brighter and more intensely colored.

2123	2124	2125	2126	2127

2128	2129	2130	2131	2132
(2231)				

2133	2134	2135	2136

Scott No.			PNC Strip (5)	Unused	Used
Transportation Series Coil Stamps.					
❑ 2123	3.4¢	School Bus	1.10	.22	.15
❑ 2124	4.9¢	Buckboard	1.00	.22	.15
❑ 2125	5.5¢	Star Route Truck	2.10	.22	.15
❑ 2126	6¢	Tricycle	2.00	.22	.15
❑ 2127	7.1¢	Tractor	2.40	.30	.15
❑ 2128	8.3¢	Ambulance	1.80	.30	.15
❑ 2129	8.5¢	Tow Truck	3.10	.30	.15
❑ 2130	10.1¢	Oil Wagon	2.50	.30	.15
❑ 2131	11¢	Stutz Bearcat	2.00	.30	.15
❑ 2132	12¢	Stanley Steamer	2.50	.40	.15
❑ 2133	12.5¢	Pushcart	3.10	.32	.15
❑ 2134	14¢	Iceboat	2.50	.32	.15
❑ 2135	17¢	Dogsled	4.00	.60	.15
❑ 2136	25¢	Breadwagon	4.00	.65	.15

NOTE: Some values of the above exist Bureau precanceled. Prices are the same as unprecanceled examples.

See Nos. 1897–1908, 2225–2231, 2252–2266, and 2451–2468 for other Transportation Series coil stamps.

2137

2138–2141

2142

2143

2144

Scott No.			Plate Block	Unused	Used
1985.					
❑ 2137	22¢	Mary McLeod Bethune	4.00	.85	.15
❑ 2138	22¢	Broadbill Decoy	—	.85	.15
❑ 2139	22¢	Mallard Decoy	—	.85	.15
❑ 2140	22¢	Canvasback Decoy	—	.85	.15
❑ 2141	22¢	Redhead Decoy	—	.85	.15
		Block of 4 (2138–2141)	9.50	8.00	5.00
❑ 2142	22¢	Winter Special Olympics	2.50	.60	.15
❑ 2143	22¢	Love	3.00	.60	.15
❑ 2144	22¢	Rural Electrification	28.00 (20)	.75	.15

| | 2145 | | 2146 | | 2147 |

Scott No.			Plate Block	Unused	Used
❑ 2145	22¢	AMERIPEX	2.50	.60	.15
❑ 2146	22¢	Abigail Adams	3.00	.65	.15
❑ 2147	22¢	F. A. Bartholdi	3.00	.60	.15

| 2149 | 2149a | 2150 | 2150a |

Scott No.			PNC Strip (5)	Unused	Used
Coil Stamps.					
❑ 2149	18¢	George Washington	4.40	.70	.15
❑ 2149a	18¢	Washington & "Presorted First-Class"	4.00	.55	.15
❑ 2150	21.1¢	Envelopes	4.50	.70	.15
❑ 2150a	21.1¢	Envelopes & "ZIP + 4"	4.75	.70	.15

2152

2153

2154

2159

2155–2158

Scott No.			Plate Block	Unused	Used
1985.					
❏ 2152	22¢	Korean War Veterans	3.75	.80	.15
❏ 2153	22¢	Social Security	2.50	.60	.15
❏ 2154	22¢	World War I Veterans	3.60	.80	.15
❏ 2155	22¢	Quarter Horse	—	1.50	.15
❏ 2156	22¢	Morgan Horse	—	1.50	.15
❏ 2157	22¢	Saddlebred Horse	—	1.50	.15
❏ 2158	22¢	Appaloosa	—	1.50	.15
		Block of 4 (2155–2158)	14.00	11.00	7.00
❏ 2159	22¢	Public Education	5.75	1.30	1.00

2160–2163

2164

2165

2166

2167

Scott No.			Plate Block	Unused	Used
☐ 2160	22¢	Youth Year – YMCA	—	.70	.15
☐ 2161	22¢	Youth Year – Boy Scouts	—	.70	.15
☐ 2162	22¢	Youth Year – Big Brothers	—	.70	.15
☐ 2163	22¢	Youth Year – Campfire Girls	—	.70	.15
		Block of 4 (2160–2163)	7.50	5.00	3.15
☐ 2164	22¢	Help End Hunger	2.60	.60	.15
☐ 2165	22¢	Christmas – Madonna & Child	2.60	.60	.15
☐ 2166	22¢	Christmas – Poinsettia	2.60	.60	.15

1986.

☐ 2167	22¢	Arkansas Statehood	4.00	1.00	.15

2168 **2169** **2170** **2171** **2172**

2173 **2175** **2176** **2177** **2178**

2179 **2180** **2181** **2182**
(2197)
2183

Scott No.			Plate Block	Unused	Used

1986–1993. Great Americans Series.

❑ 2168	1¢	Margaret Mitchell	.70	.22	.15
❑ 2169	2¢	Mary Lyon	.60	.22	.15
❑ 2170	3¢	Paul Dudley White M.D.	1.00	.22	.15
❑ 2171	4¢	Father Flanagan	.80	.22	.15
❑ 2172	5¢	Hugo L. Black	1.50	.30	.15
❑ 2173	5¢	Luis Munoz Marin	.95	.21	.15
❑ 2175	10¢	Red Cloud	1.60	.35	.21
❑ 2176	14¢	Julia Ward Howe	2.30	.42	.21
❑ 2177	15¢	Buffalo Bill Cody	7.50	.70	.25
❑ 2178	17¢	Belva Ann Lockwood	2.50	.60	.25
❑ 2179	20¢	Virginia Apgar	3.00	.60	.15
❑ 2180	21¢	Chester Carlson	3.00	.60	.15
❑ 2181	23¢	Mary Cassatt	3.00	.60	.15
❑ 2182	25¢	Jack London	3.00	.60	.15
❑ 2183	28¢	Sitting Bull	4.50	.80	.15

Scott No.			Plate Block	Unused	Used
❏ 2184	29¢	Earl Warren	4.00	.90	.16
❏ 2185	29¢	Thomas Jefferson	4.00	.90	.16
❏ 2186	35¢	Dennis Chavez	4.75	1.30	.15
❏ 2187	40¢	Claire Chenault	6.00	.95	.35
❏ 2188	45¢	Dr. Harvey Cushing	5.25	1.20	.15
❏ 2189	52¢	Hubert Humphrey	8.75	1.50	.21
❏ 2190	56¢	John Harvard	8.50	1.40	.21
❏ 2191	65¢	H. H. "Hap" Arnold	8.50	1.60	.21
❏ 2192	75¢	Wendell Wilkie	9.00	1.80	.21
❏ 2193	$1	Bernard Revel	18.00	3.50	.40
❏ 2194	$1	Johns Hopkins	14.00	3.00	.40
❏ 2195	$2	William Jennings Bryan	22.00	5.00	.65
❏ 2196	$5	Bret Harte	46.00	11.50	2.50
❏ 2197	25¢	Jack London (~2182)	—	.80	.15
		Booklet pane of 6	—	4.10	2.75

NOTE: See Nos. 1844–1869 and 2933–2943 for other Great Americans Series stamps.

2198–2201

| 2202 | 2203 | 2204 |

Scott No.			Plate Block	Unused	Used
1986.					
❑ 2198	22¢	AMERIPEX – Vintage Hand Cancel	—	.70	.16
❑ 2199	22¢	AMERIPEX – Boy Stamp Collector	—	.70	.16
❑ 2200	22¢	AMERIPEX – Magnifying Glass	—	.70	.16
❑ 2201	22¢	AMERIPEX – Modern Hand Cancel	—	.70	.16
		Booklet pane of 4 (2198–2201)	—	2.70	2.00
❑ 2202	22¢	Love – Puppy	3.00	.70	.15
❑ 2203	22¢	Sojourner Truth	3.10	.75	.15
❑ 2204	22¢	Republic of Texas	2.60	.70	.15

2210

2205–2209

2211

Scott No.			Plate Block	Unused	Used
❏ 2205	22¢	Fish – Muskellunge	—	.72	.15
❏ 2206	22¢	Fish – Atlantic Cod	—	.72	.15
❏ 2207	22¢	Fish – Largemouth Bass	—	.72	.15
❏ 2208	22¢	Fish – Bluefin Tuna	—	.72	.15
❏ 2209	22¢	Fish – Catfish	—	.72	.15
		Booklet pane of 5 (2205–2209)	—	9.00	2.75
❏ 2210	22¢	Public Hospitals	3.00	.70	.15
❏ 2211	22¢	Duke Ellington	2.75	.70	.15

2216

2217

2218

2219

Scott No.			Plate Block	Unused	Used
☐ 2216	22¢	AMERIPEX – Presidents I	—	6.50	.15
☐ 2216a-i		Any single stamp	—	2.10	.50
☐ 2217	22¢	AMERIPEX – Presidents II	—	5.00	.15
☐ 2217a-i		Any single stamp	—	2.10	.50
☐ 2218	22¢	AMERIPEX – Presidents III	—	5.00	.15
☐ 2218a-i		Any single stamp	—	2.10	.60
☐ 2219	22¢	AMERIPEX – Presidents IV	—	5.00	.15
☐ 2219a-i		Any single stamp	—	2.10	.60

2220–2223

2224

Scott No.			Plate Block	Unused	Used
❑ 2220	22¢	Elisha Kane Kent	—	.60	.13
❑ 2221	22¢	Adolphus W. Greely	—	.60	.13
❑ 2222	22¢	Vilhjalmur Stefansson	—	.60	.13
❑ 2223	22¢	Peary & Henson	—	.60	.13
		Block of 4 (2220–2223)	6.00	4.00	3.50
❑ 2224	22¢	Statue of Liberty	3.25	.60	.13

2225

2226

2228

Scott No.			PNC Strip (5)	Unused	Used
1986–1987. Transportation Series Coil Stamps.					
❑ 2225	1¢	Omnibus, no ¢ symbol	.65	.22	.15
❑ 2226	2¢	Locomotive, no ¢ symbol	.75	.22	.15
❑ 2228	4¢	Stagecoach (~1898A)	1.55	.22	.15
❑ 2231	8.3¢	Ambulance (~2128)	9.00	.22	.15

NOTE: See Nos. 1897–1897A for designs similar to Nos. 2225–2226 except with ¢ symbol,

2235–2238

2239

2240–2243

Scott No.			Plate Block	Unused	Used
1986.					
❏ 2235	22¢	Navajo Carpet – Four Crosses	—	.70	.15
❏ 2236	22¢	Navajo Carpet – Vertical Diamonds	—	.70	.15
❏ 2237	22¢	Navajo Carpet – Lowe Art Museum	—	.70	.15
❏ 2238	22¢	Navajo Carpet – Eight Diamonds	—	.70	.15
		Block of 4 (2235–2238)	5.00	4.00	3.00
❏ 2239	22¢	T. S. Eliot	3.50	1.10	.16
❏ 2240	22¢	Highlander Figure	—	.65	.15
❏ 2241	22¢	Ship Figurehead	—	.65	.15
❏ 2242	22¢	Nautical Figure	—	.65	.15
❏ 2243	22¢	Cigar Store Figure	—	.65	.15
		Block of 4 (2240–2243)	4.50	2.10	2.00

2244   **2245**

Scott No.			Plate Block	Unused	Used
❑ 2244	22¢	Christmas – Madonna & Child	2.50	.65	.15
❑ 2245	22¢	Christmas – Village Scene	2.50	.65	.15

2246   **2247**   **2248**

2249   **2250**   **2251**

1987.

❑ 2246	22¢	Michigan Statehood	2.50	.65	.15
❑ 2247	22¢	Pan American Games	2.50	.65	.15
❑ 2248	22¢	Love	3.00	.65	.15
❑ 2249	22¢	Jean Baptiste Pointe du Sable	3.00	.65	.15
❑ 2250	22¢	Enrico Caruso	2.50	.65	.15
❑ 2251	22¢	Girl Scouts	3.00	.65	.15

Scott No.			PNC Strip (5)	Unused	Used

1987–1993. Transportation Series Coil Stamps.

❏ 2252	3¢	Conestoga Wagon	1.00	.22	.15
❏ 2253	5¢	Milk Wagon	1.50	.22	.15
❏ 2254	5.3¢	Elevator	2.40	.25	.15
❏ 2255	7.6¢	Carreta	3.00	.30	.15
❏ 2256	8.4¢	Wheelchair	2.40	.30	.15
❏ 2257	10¢	Canal Boat	4.00	.32	.15
❏ 2258	13¢	Police Wagon	6.00	.65	.15
❏ 2259	13.2¢	Coal Car	4.50	.40	.15
❏ 2260	15¢	Tug Boat	3.00	.40	.15
❏ 2261	16.7¢	Popcorn Wagon	4.00	.50	.15
❏ 2262	17.5¢	Racing Car	5.50	.50	.15
❏ 2263	20¢	Cable Car	4.75	.60	.15
❏ 2264	20.5¢	Fire Engine	9.00	1.15	.35
❏ 2265	21¢	Railroad Mail Car	6.50	.65	.40
❏ 2266	24.1¢	Tandem Bicycle	6.50	.60	.45

See Nos. 1897–1908, 2123–2136, 2225–2231, and 2451–2468 for other Transportation Series coil stamps.

2267–2274

Scott No.			Plate Block	Unused	Used
1987.					
❏ 2267	22¢	Congratulations!	—	.85	.15
❏ 2268	22¢	Get Well!	—	.85	.15
❏ 2269	22¢	Thank You!	—	.85	.15
❏ 2270	22¢	Love You, Dad!	—	.85	.15
❏ 2271	22¢	Best Wishes!	—	.85	.15
❏ 2272	22¢	Happy Birthday!	—	.80	.15
❏ 2273	22¢	Love You, Mother!	—	1.50	.15
❏ 2274	22¢	Keep in Touch!	—	1.40	.15
		Booklet pane of 10 (2267–2271)	—	15.00	3.00

| | 2275 | 2276 | 2277 (2279, 2282) | 2278 (2285A) |

Scott No.			Plate Block	Unused	Used
❏ 2275	22¢	United Way	2.50	.60	.15
❏ 2276	22¢	Flag & Fireworks	2.75	.60	.15
		Booklet pane of 20	—	11.00	.42
❏ 2277	(25¢)	"E" & Earth	4.10	.70	.22
❏ 2278	25¢	Flag & Clouds, perf 10	3.50	.70	.22

| 2280 | 2281 | 2283 | 2284 | 2285 |

Scott No.			PNC Strip (5)	Unused	Used
Coil Stamps.					
❏ 2279	(25¢)	"E" & Earth (~2277)	3.60	.70	.15
❏ 2280	25¢	Flag over Yosemite	4.50	.70	.15
❏ 2281	25¢	Honey Bee	3.50	.75	.15
Booklet Stamps.					
❏ 2282	(25¢)	"E" & Earth (~2277)	—	.75	.22
		Booklet pane of 10	—	7.50	4.00
❏ 2283	25¢	Pheasant	—	.85	.15
		Booklet pane of 10	—	7.25	4.00
❏ 2284	25¢	Grosbeak	—	.70	.16
❏ 2285	25¢	Owl	—	.80	.16
		Booklet pane of 10, (5 each 2284 & 2285)	—	6.00	5.00
❏ 2285A	25¢	Flag & Clouds (2278), perf 10x11	—	.80	.15
		Booklet pane of 6	—	4.65	3.50

2286–2335

Scott No.	Plate Block	Unused	Used

1987.

❏ 2286–2335	22¢	Wildlife, pane of 50	—	65.00	—
❏ 2286–2335		Any single stamp	—	.75	.20

❏ 2286 Barn Swallow
❏ 2287 Monarch Butterfly
❏ 2288 Bighorn Sheep
❏ 2289 Broad-tailed Hummingbird
❏ 2290 Cottontail
❏ 2291 Osprey
❏ 2292 Mountain Lion
❏ 2293 Luna Moth
❏ 2294 Mule Deer
❏ 2295 Gray Squirrel
❏ 2296 Armadillo
❏ 2297 Eastern Chipmunk
❏ 2298 Moose

❏ 2299 Black Bear
❏ 2300 Tiger Swallowtail
❏ 2301 Bobwhite
❏ 2302 Ringtail
❏ 2303 Red-wing Blackbird
❏ 2304 Lobster
❏ 2305 Black-tailed Jack Rabbit
❏ 2306 Scarlet Tanager
❏ 2307 Woodchuck
❏ 2308 Roseate Spoonbill
❏ 2309 Bald Eagle
❏ 2310 Alaskan Brown Bear
❏ 2311 Iiwi

❑ 2312 Badger
❑ 2313 Pronghorn
❑ 2314 River Otter
❑ 2315 Ladybug
❑ 2316 Beaver
❑ 2317 White-tail Deer
❑ 2318 Blue Jay
❑ 2319 Pika
❑ 2320 Buffalo
❑ 2321 Snowy Egret
❑ 2322 Gray Wolf
❑ 2323 Mountain Goat

❑ 2324 Deer Mouse
❑ 2325 Black-tailed Prairie Dog
❑ 2326 Box Turtle
❑ 2327 Wolverine
❑ 2328 Elk
❑ 2329 California Sea Lion
❑ 2330 Mockingbird
❑ 2331 Raccoon
❑ 2332 Bobcat
❑ 2333 Black-footed Ferret
❑ 2334 Canada Goose
❑ 2335 Red Fox

2336 **2337** **2338** **2339**

2340 **2341** **2342**

Scott No.			Plate Block	Unused	Used
❑ 2336	22¢	Delaware	4.00	.90	.16
❑ 2337	22¢	Pennsylvania	4.00	.90	.16
❑ 2338	22¢	New Jersey	4.00	.90	.16
❑ 2339	22¢	Georgia	4.00	.90	.16
❑ 2340	22¢	Connecticut	4.00	.90	.16
❑ 2341	22¢	Massachusetts	4.00	.90	.16
❑ 2342	22¢	Maryland	4.00	.90	.16

May 23, 1788
South Carolina

2343

June 21, 1788
New Hampshire

2344

June 25, 1788   USA
Virginia   25

2345

July 26, 1788   USA
New York   25

2346

November 21, 1789
North Carolina

2347

May 29, 1790
Rhode Island

2348

Friendship
with Morocco
1787–1987

USA 22

2349

William Faulkner

USA 22

2350

Scott No.			Plate Block	Unused	Used
❏ 2343	22¢	South Carolina	4.00	.90	.15
❏ 2344	22¢	New Hampshire	4.00	.90	.15
❏ 2345	22¢	Virginia	4.00	.90	.15
❏ 2346	22¢	New York	4.00	.90	.15
❏ 2347	22¢	North Carolina	4.00	.90	.15
❏ 2348	22¢	Rhode Island	4.00	.90	.15
❏ 2349	22¢	Friendship with Morocco	2.50	.60	.15
❏ 2350	22¢	William Faulkner	4.00	.60	.15

2351–2354

2355–2359

Scott No.			Plate Block	Unused	Used
❑ 2351	22¢	Lace	—	.60	.15
❑ 2352	22¢	Lace	—	.60	.15
❑ 2353	22¢	Lace	—	.60	.15
❑ 2354	22¢	Lace	—	.60	.15
		Block of 4 (2351–2354)	4.80	3.00	1.75
❑ 2355	22¢	Constitution – "Bicentennial"	—	.65	.15
❑ 2356	22¢	Constitution – "We the People"	—	.65	.15
❑ 2357	22¢	Constitution – "Establish Justice"	—	.65	.15
❑ 2358	22¢	Constitution – "And Secure"	—	.65	.15
❑ 2359	22¢	Constitution – "Do Ordain"	—	.65	.15
		Booklet pane of 5 (1255–2359)	—	6.00	1.10

2360

2361

2362–2366

2367

2368

Scott No.			Plate Block	Unused	Used
❑ 2360	22¢	U. S. Constitution	4.25	.90	.15
❑ 2361	22¢	CPAs	12.00	2.60	.15
❑ 2362	22¢	Stourbridge Lion	—	.80	.15
❑ 2363	22¢	Best Friend of Charleston	—	.80	.15
❑ 2364	22¢	John Bull	—	.80	.15
❑ 2365	22¢	Brother Jonathan	—	.80	.15
❑ 2366	22¢	Gowan & Marx	—	.80	.15
		Booklet pane of 5 (2362–2367)	—	4.00	3.00
❑ 2367	22¢	Christmas – Madonna & Child	2.60	.65	.40
❑ 2368	22¢	Christmas – Ornament	2.50	.65	.40

2369   2370   2371

2372–2375

Scott No.			Plate Block	Unused	Used
1988.					
❏ 2369	22¢	Olympics – Downhill Skier	3.25	.65	.16
❏ 2370	22¢	Australia Bicentennial	2.50	.60	.16
❏ 2371	22¢	James Weldon Johnson	3.00	.65	.16
❏ 2372	22¢	Cats – Siamese & Exotic Short Hair	—	.65	1.50
❏ 2373	22¢	Cats – Abyssinian & Himalayan	—	.65	1.50
❏ 2374	22¢	Cats – Maine Coon & Burmese	—	.65	1.50
❏ 2375	22¢	Cats – American Shorthair & Persian	—	.65	1.70
		Block of 4 (2372–2375)	5.00	3.00	2.00

2376

2377

2381–2385

2378

2379

2380

2381–2385

Scott No.			Plate Block	Unused	Used
❏ 2376	22¢	Knute Rockne	4.00	.85	.15
❏ 2377	25¢	Francis Ouimet	4.75	.90	.21
❏ 2378	25¢	Love – Rose	3.50	.70	.15
❏ 2379	45¢	Love – Rose	6.00	1.10	.15
❏ 2380	25¢	Olympics – Gymnast on Rings	3.50	.75	.15
❏ 2381	25¢	Autos – Locomobile	—	.60	.15
❏ 2382	25¢	Autos – Pierce Arrow	—	.60	.15
❏ 2383	25¢	Autos – Cord	—	.60	.15
❏ 2384	25¢	Autos – Packard	—	.60	.15
❏ 2385	25¢	Autos – Dusenberg	—	.60	.15
		Booklet pane of 5 (2381–2385)	—	9.00	1.50

2386–2389

2394

2390–2393

Scott No.			Plate Block	Unused	Used
❑ 2386	25¢	Nathaniel Palmer	—	.70	.15
❑ 2387	25¢	Lt. Charles Wilkes	—	.70	.15
❑ 2388	25¢	Richard E. Byrd	—	.70	.15
❑ 2389	25¢	Lincoln Ellsworth	—	.70	.15
		Block of 4 (2386–2389)	6.25	4.00	2.00
❑ 2390	25¢	Carousel – Deer	—	.80	.15
❑ 2391	25¢	Carousel – Horse	—	.80	.15
❑ 2392	25¢	Carousel – Camel	—	.80	.15
❑ 2393	25¢	Carousel – Goat	—	.80	.15
		Block of 4 (2390–2393)	6.00	4.50	2.75
❑ 2394	$8.75	Express Mail	100.00	25.00	8.00

2395

2396

2397

2398

2399

2400

Scott No.			Plate Block	Unused	Used
❑ 2395	25¢	Happy Birthday	—	.80	.15
❑ 2396	25¢	Best Wishes	—	.80	.15
		Booklet pane of 6 (3 each 2395 & 2396)	—	4.50	2.80
❑ 2397	25¢	Thinking of You	—	.70	.15
❑ 2398	25¢	Love You	—	.70	.15
		Booklet pane of 6 (3 each 2397 & 2398)	—	4.50	3.50
❑ 2399	25¢	Christmas – Madonna & Child	3.00	.70	.15
❑ 2400	25¢	Christmas – Winter Scene	3.00	.70	.15

2401

2402

2403

2404

2405–2409

Scott No.			Plate Block	Unused	Used
1989.					
❏ 2401	25¢	Montana	4.00	.90	.15
❏ 2402	25¢	A. Philip Randolph	4.00	.90	.15
❏ 2403	25¢	North Dakota Statehood	4.00	.90	.15
❏ 2404	25¢	Washington Statehood	3.75	.90	.15
❏ 2405	25¢	Steamboats – Experiment	—	.70	.15
❏ 2406	25¢	Steamboats – Phoenix	—	.70	.15
❏ 2407	25¢	Steamboats – New Orleans	—	.70	.15
❏ 2408	25¢	Steamboats – Washington	—	.70	.15
❏ 2409	25¢	Steamboats – Walk in the Water	—	.70	.15
		Booklet pane of 5 (2404–2409)	—	4.50	3.15

2410   2411

2412   2413   2414   2415

2416

Scott No.			Plate Block	Unused	Used
❑ 2410	25¢	World Stamp Expo '89	3.00	.70	.15
❑ 2411	25¢	Arturo Toscanini	3.00	.70	.15
❑ 2412	25¢	Bicentennial – House of Representatives	4.00	.70	.15
❑ 2413	25¢	Bicentennial – U. S. Senate	4.00	.70	.15
❑ 2414	25¢	Bicentennial – Executive Branch	4.00	.70	.15
❑ 2415	25¢	Bicentennial – Supreme Court	3.75	.70	.15
❑ 2416	25¢	South Dakota Statehood	3.75	.70	.15

2417

2418

2419

2420

2421

2422–2425

Scott No.			Plate Block	Unused	Used
❏ 2417	25¢	Lou Gehrig	5.00	1.00	.16
❏ 2418	25¢	Ernest Hemingway	3.50	.80	.16
❏ 2419	$2.40	Moon Landing	30.00	7.00	3.00
❏ 2420	25¢	Letter Carriers	2.50	.65	.15
❏ 2421	25¢	Bill of Rights	4.50	.90	.15
❏ 2422	25¢	Dinosaurs – Tyrannosaurus	—	.85	.15
❏ 2423	25¢	Dinosaurs – Pteranodon	—	.85	.15
❏ 2424	25¢	Dinosaurs – Stegosaurus	—	.85	.15
❏ 2425	25¢	Dinosaurs – Brontosaurus	—	.85	.15
		Block of 4 (2421–2425)	7.50	5.00	3.00

2426

2427

2428
(2429)

2431

2433

Scott No.			Plate Block	Unused	Used
❏ 2426	25¢	Southwest Carving	2.50	.60	.15
❏ 2427	25¢	Christmas – Madonna	3.00	.60	.15
❏ 2428	25¢	Christmas – Sleigh	3.00	.60	.15
❏ 2429	25¢	Christmas – Sleigh (~2428)	—	.60	.15
		Booklet pane of 10	—	12.00	4.00
❏ 2431	25¢	Eagle & Shield	—	.70	.15
		Booklet pane of 18	—	17.50	—
❏ 2433	$3.60	Lincoln Essays, souvenir sheet	—	18.00	9.50
❏ 2433a-d		Any single stamp	—	3.50	2.00

2434–2437

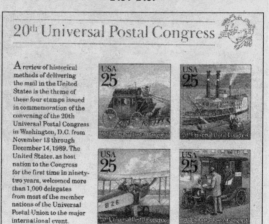

2438

Scott No.			Plate Block	Unused	Used
❏ 2434	25¢	Stagecoach	—	.60	.15
❏ 2435	25¢	Paddlewheel Steamer	—	.60	.15
❏ 2436	25¢	Biplane	—	.60	.15
❏ 2437	25¢	Automobile	—	.60	.15
		Block of 4 (2434–2437)	6.00	4.00	3.00
❏ 2438	$1	Souvenir sheet (~2434–2437)	—	5.00	1.20
❏ 2438a-d		Any single stamp	—	6.00	3.50

2440
(2441)

2439

2442

2443

2444

2445–2448

Scott No.			Plate Block	Unused	Used
1990.					
❏ 2439	25¢	Idaho Statehood	2.50	.70	.15
❏ 2440	25¢	Love	2.75	.70	.15
❏ 2441	25¢	Love (~2440)	—	.70	.15
		Booklet pane of 10	—	10.00	6.00
❏ 2442	25¢	Ida B. Wells	4.25	.90	.15
❏ 2443	25¢	Beach Umbrella	—	.65	.15
		Booklet pane of 10	—	4.00	3.00
❏ 2444	25¢	Wyoming Statehood	3.00	.75	.15
❏ 2445	25¢	Films – Wizard of Oz	—	1.65	.15
❏ 2446	25¢	Films – Gone With the Wind	—	1.65	.15
❏ 2447	25¢	Films – Beau Geste	—	1.65	.15
❏ 2448	25¢	Films – Stagecoach	—	1.65	.15
		Block of 4 (2445–2448)	8.00	7.00	4.00

2449

Scott No.			Plate Block	Unused	Used
❑ 2449	25¢	Marianne Moore	2.75	.65	.14

2451	2452 (2452B)	2452D	2453 (2454)	2457 (2458)

Scott No.			PNC Strip (5)	Unused	Used
1990. Transportation Series Coil Stamps.					
❑ 2451	4¢	Steam Carriage	1.00	.24	.15
❑ 2452	5¢	Circus Wagon (05) (engraved)	1.50	.25	.15
❑ 2452B	5¢	Circus Wagon (~2452) (05) (photogravure)	2.00	.25	.15
❑ 2452D	5¢	Circus Wagon (~2452) (5¢)	2.00	.25	.15
❑ 2453	5¢	Canoe, brown (engraved)	1.75	.25	.15
❑ 2454	5¢	Canoe, red (~2453) (photogravure)	2.25	.26	.15
❑ 2457	10¢	Tractor Trailer (engraved)	3.00	.26	.15
❑ 2458	10¢	Tractor Trailer (~2457) (photogravure)	3.75	.35	.15

| **2463** | **2464** | **2466** | **2468** |

Scott No.			PNC Strip (5)	Unused	Used
❏ 2463	20¢	Cog Railway	5.50	.55	.16
❏ 2464	23¢	Lunch Wagon	4.50	.65	.15
❏ 2466	32¢	Ferryboat	8.00	.85	.15
❏ 2468	$1	Seaplane	16.00	2.75	.50

NOTE: Some values of the above exist Bureau precanceled. Prices are the same as unprecanceled examples.

See Nos. 1897–1908, 2123–2136, and 2225–2231 for other Transportation Series coil stamps.

2470–2474

Scott No.			Plate Block	Unused	Used
1990.					
❏ 2470	25¢	Lighthouses – Admiralty Head	—	.74	.20
❏ 2471	25¢	Lighthouses – Cape Hatteras	—	.74	.15
❏ 2472	25¢	Lighthouses – West Quoddy Head	—	.74	.15
❏ 2473	25¢	Lighthouses – American Shoals	—	.74	.15
❏ 2474	25¢	Lighthouses – Sandy Hook	—	.74	.15
		Booklet pane of 5 (2470–2474)	—	7.50	3.00

2475

2476

2477
(3031, 3031A,
3044)

2478

2479

2480

2481

2482

Scott No.			Plate Block	Unused	Used
❏ 2475	25¢	Stylized Flag	—	.75	.17
		Booklet pane of 12	—	8.50	—
❏ 2476	1¢	Kestrel ("01" numeral)	.60	.25	.15
❏ 2477	1¢	Kestrel ("1¢" numeral)	.60	.25	.15
❏ 2478	3¢	Bluebird ("03" numeral)	.75	.25	.15
❏ 2479	19¢	Fawn	2.00	.60	.15
❏ 2480	30¢	Cardinal	3.00	.70	.15
❏ 2481	45¢	Sunfish	5.50	1.00	.30
❏ 2482	$2	Bobcat	20.00	4.00	.90

2483
(3048, 3053)

1991–1995. Booklet Stamps.

❏ 2483	20¢	Blue Jay	—	.75	.15
		Booklet pane of 10	—	6.50	2.00

Scott No.			Plate Block	Unused	Used
❏ 2484	29¢	Wood Duck, black numerals	—	.80	.15
		Booklet pane of 10	—	7.50	5.70
❏ 2485	29¢	Wood Duck, red numerals	—	.90	.15
		Booklet pane of 10	—	7.00	5.25
❏ 2486	29¢	African Violets	—	.92	.21
		Booklet pane of 10	—	9.10	5.50
❏ 2487	32¢	Peach	—	.87	.15
❏ 2488	32¢	Pear	—	.90	.15
		Booklet pane of 10 (5 each of 2487–2488)	—	8.00	6.30
❏ 2489	29¢	Red Squirrel	—	.80	.15
		Booklet pane of 18	—	16.00	—
❏ 2490	29¢	Red Rose	—	.82	.15
		Booklet pane of 18	—	14.00	—
❏ 2491	29¢	Pine Cone	—	.90	.27
		Booklet pane of 18	—	13.00	—
❏ 2492	32¢	Pink Rose	—	.90	.15
		Booklet pane of 20	—	16.00	—
		Booklet pane of 18	—	14.00	—
		Booklet pane of 16	—	12.00	—
		Booklet pane of 14	—	20.00	—
❏ 2493	32¢	Peach (~2487)	—	.94	.25
❏ 2494	32¢	Pear (~2488)	—	.80	.15
		Booklet pane of 20 (10 each 2493–2494)	—	18.00	—

Scott No.			PNC Strip (5)	Unused	Used

1995. Coil Stamps.

❏ 2495	32¢	Peach (~2487)	—	1.10	.15
❏ 2495A	32¢	Pear (~2488)	—	1.15	.15
		Se-tenant pair (2495–2495A)	12.00	5.00	—

2496–2500

Scott No.			Plate Block	Unused	Used

1990.

❏ 2496	25¢	Olympians – Jesse Owens	—	.74	.15
❏ 2497	25¢	Olympians – Ray Ewry	—	.74	.15
❏ 2498	25¢	Olympians – Hazel Wightman	—	.74	.15
❏ 2499	25¢	Olympians – Eddie Eagan	—	.74	.15
❏ 2500	25¢	Olympians – Helene Madison	—	.74	.15
		Strip of 5 (2496–2500)	12.00 (10)	4.20	3.00

2501–2505

2506–2507

Scott No.			Plate Block	Unused	Used
❏ 2501	25¢	Headdress – Assiniboine	—	.84	.20
❏ 2502	25¢	Headdress – Cheyenne	—	.84	.20
❏ 2503	25¢	Headdress – Comanche	—	.84	.20
❏ 2504	25¢	Headdress – Flathead	—	.84	.20
❏ 2505	25¢	Headdress – Shoshone	—	.84	.20
		Booklet pane of 10 (5 each 2501–2505)	—	11.00	6.00
❏ 2506	25¢	Micronesia	—	1.10	.40
❏ 2507	25¢	Marshall Islands	—	1.10	.40
		Se-tenant pair (2506–2507)	3.50	3.00	.80

2508–2511

2512

2513

Scott No.			Plate Block	Unused	Used
❑ 2508	25¢	Killer Whale	—	.70	.15
❑ 2509	25¢	Northern Sea Lion	—	.70	.15
❑ 2510	25¢	Sea Otter	—	.70	.15
❑ 2511	25¢	Dolphin	—	.70	.15
		Block of 4 (2508–2511)	4.00	3.00	1.65
❑ 2512	25¢	Grand Canyon	3.00	.80	.15
❑ 2513	25¢	Dwight D. Eisenhower	4.50	.90	.15

2514

2515
(2516)

2517
(2518–2520)

2522

2521

Scott No.			Plate Block	Unused	Used
❏ 2514	25¢	Christmas – Madonna	3.00	.70	.15
❏ 2515	25¢	Christmas Tree	3.00	.70	.15
❏ 2516	25¢	Christmas Tree	—	.70	.15
		Booklet pane of 10	—	8.00	4.10
❏ 2517	(29¢)	"F" & Flower	4.10	.80	.15

Scott No.			PNC Strip (5)	Unused	Used
Coil Stamp.					
❏ 2518	(29¢)	"F" & Flower (~2517)	4.75	.80	.15

Scott No.			Plate Block	Unused	Used
1991.					
❏ 2519	(29¢)	"F" & Flower (~2517)	—	.70	.15
		Booklet pane of 10	—	25.00	14.00
❏ 2520	(29¢)	"F" & Flower (~2517)	—	.80	.15
		Booklet pane of 10	—	24.00	14.00

NOTE: No. 2519 has a pale green leaf; No. 2520, a bright green leaf.

❏ 2521	(4¢)	Make Up Rate	.75	.23	.15
❏ 2522	(29¢)	"F" & Stylized Flag	—	.74	.15
		Booklet pane of 10	—	9.00	—

2523	**2524**	**2528**	**2529**
(2523A)	(2524A, 2525–2527)		(2529C)

Scott No.			PNC Strip (5)	Unused	Used

1991. Coil Stamps.

| ❏ 2523 | 29¢ | Flag over Mt. Rushmore (engraved) | 6.50 | .84 | .15 |
| ❏ 2523A | 29¢ | Flag over Mt. Rushmore (photogravure) | 6.00 | .80 | .14 |

Scott No.			Plate Block	Unused	Used

1991. Sheet Stamps.

| ❏ 2524 | 29¢ | Tulip, perforated 11 | 3.10 | .75 | .15 |
| ❏ 2524A | 29¢ | Tulip, perforated 13 x 12½ | 4.15 | .85 | .15 |

Scott No.			PNC Strip (5)	Unused	Used

1991. Coil Stamps.

| ❏ 2525 | 29¢ | Tulip (~2524), rouletted | 7.00 | .90 | .15 |
| ❏ 2526 | 29¢ | Tulip (~2524), perforated 10 | 7.00 | .90 | .15 |

Scott No.			Plate Block	Unused	Used

1991. Booklet Stamps.

❏ 2527	29¢	Tulip (~2524)	—	.85	.15
		Booklet pane of 10	—	8.00	4.00
❏ 2528	29¢	Flag & Olympic Rings	—	.92	.15
		Booklet pane of 10	—	9.00	4.00

Scott No.			PNC Strip (5)	Unused	Used

1991. Coil Stamps.

| ❏ 2529 | 19¢ | Fishing Boat | 4.75 | .62 | .15 |
| ❏ 2529C | 19¢ | Fishing Boat (~2529) | 9.00 | .94 | .15 |

NOTE: No. 2529C contains only one loop of rope on the dock pole.

2530

2531

2531A

2532

2533

2534

2535
(2535A, 2536)

2537

Scott No.			Plate Block	Unused	Used
1991. Booklet Stamp.					
❏ 2530	19¢	Ballooning	—	.60	.20
		Booklet pane of 10	—	5.00	3.00
1991.					
❏ 2531	29¢	Flags on Parade	3.50	.84	.15
❏ 2531A	29¢	Torch of Liberty	—	.90	.15
❏ 2532	50¢	Switzerland	6.50	1.40	.15
❏ 2533	29¢	Vermont Statehood	6.50	1.20	.15
❏ 2534	29¢	Savings Bonds	3.25	.80	.15
❏ 2535	29¢	Love, perforated 12½ x 13	3.25	.80	.15
❏ 2535A	29¢	Love, perforated 11 (all sides)	4.50	.90	.15
❏ 2536	29¢	Love, perforated 11 (2 or 3 sides)	—	.90	.16
		Booklet pane of 10	—	7.50	3.00
❏ 2537	52¢	Love Birds	6.50	1.30	.15

2538

2539

2540

2541

2542

2543   2544   2544A

Scott No.			Plate Block	Unused	Used
❏ 2538	29¢	William Saroyan	3.00	.70	.15
❏ 2539	$1	Olympic Rings	9.50	2.10	.62
❏ 2540	$2.90	Eagle & Olympic Rings	31.00	7.80	2.50
❏ 2541	$9.95	Express Mail	100.00	25.00	10.00
❏ 2542	$14	Express Mail	140.00	30.00	18.00
❏ 2543	$2.90	Futuristic Spacecraft	33.00	7.00	2.50
❏ 2544	$3	Space Shuttle "Enterprise"	30.00	6.50	2.50
❏ 2544A	$10.75	Shuttle Blasting Off	110.00	24.00	8.50

2545–2549

2550

2551
(2552)

Scott No.			Plate Block	Unused	Used
❏ 2545	29¢	Fishing Flies – Royal Wulff	—	.90	.15
❏ 2546	29¢	Fishing Flies – Jock Scott	—	.90	.15
❏ 2547	29¢	Fishing Flies – Apte Tarpon Fly	—	.90	.15
❏ 2548	29¢	Fishing Flies – Lefty's Deceiver	—	.90	.15
❏ 2549	29¢	Fishing Flies – Muddler Minnow	—	.90	.15
		Booklet pane of 5 (2545–2549)	—	7.50	4.10
❏ 2550	29¢	Cole Porter	4.00	.85	.15
❏ 2551	29¢	Desert Storm	3.50	.72	.15
❏ 2552	29¢	Desert Storm, booklet stamp	—	.72	.15
		Booklet pane of 5	—	4.50	3.10

2553–2557

NUMISMATICS

2558

Scott No.			Plate Block	Unused	Used
❑ 2553	29¢	Olympics – High Jump	—	.80	.15
❑ 2554	29¢	Olympics – Discus	—	.80	.15
❑ 2555	29¢	Olympics – Sprint	—	.80	.15
❑ 2556	29¢	Olympics – Javelin	—	.80	.15
❑ 2557	29¢	Olympics – Hurdles	—	.80	.15
		Strip of 5 (2553–2557)	9.00 (10)	4.10	3.30
❑ 2558	29¢	Numismatics	4.10	.70	.15

2559

2560

2561

Scott No.			Plate Block	Unused	Used
❑ 2559	29¢	World War II, 1941, pane of 10	—	8.00	6.00
❑ 2559a–j	29¢	Any single stamp	—	.70	.15
❑ 2560	29¢	Basketball	4.25	.75	.15
❑ 2561	29¢	District of Columbia	3.00	.75	.15

2562–2566

2567

Scott No.			Plate Block	Unused	Used
1991.					
❏ 2562	29¢	Comedians – Laurel & Hardy	—	.74	.15
❏ 2563	29¢	Comedians – Bergen & McCarthy	—	.74	.15
❏ 2564	29¢	Comedians – Jack Benny	—	.74	.15
❏ 2565	29¢	Comedians – Fanny Brice	—	.74	.15
❏ 2566	29¢	Comedians – Abbott & Costello	—	.74	.15
		Booklet pane of 10 (2 each 1561–2566)	—	4.60	3.20
❏ 2567	29¢	Jan E. Matzeliger	4.10	.70	.15

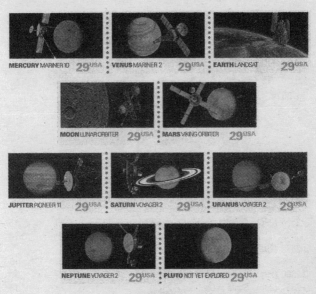

2568–2577

Scott No.			Plate Block	Unused	Used
❏ 2568	29¢	Mercury	—	.90	.15
❏ 2569	29¢	Venus	—	.90	.15
❏ 2570	29¢	Earth	—	.90	.15
❏ 2571	29¢	Moon	—	.90	.15
❏ 2572	29¢	Mars	—	.90	.15
❏ 2573	29¢	Jupiter	—	.90	.15
❏ 2574	29¢	Saturn	—	.90	.15
❏ 2575	29¢	Uranus	—	.90	.15
❏ 2576	29¢	Neptune	—	.90	.15
❏ 2577	29¢	Pluto	—	.90	.15
		Booklet pane of 10 (2568–2577)	—	13.50	3.50

2578

2579
(2580–2581)

2582

2583

2584

2585

Scott No.		Plate Block	Unused	Used
❏ 2578 (29¢)	Christmas – Madonna & Child	3.00	.80	.15
	Booklet pane of 10	—	7.50	3.10
❏ 2579 (29¢)	Santa in Chimney, perforated all sides	3.00	.70	.15
❏ 2580 (29¢)	Santa in Chimney (~2579)	—	1.20	.15
❏ 2581 (29¢)	Santa in Chimney (~2579)	—	1.20	.15
	Booklet pane of 4 (2 each of 2580–2581)	—	10.00	1.10

NOTE: Examples of 2580 contain part of an extra brick on the left side of the top row of bricks; examples of 2581 do not. Nos. 2580–2581 are booklet stamps and contain perforations on only 2 or 3 sides.

❏ 2582 (29¢)	Santa with List	—	.70	.15
	Booklet pane of 4	—	3.00	1.00
❏ 2583 (29¢)	Santa and Package	—	.70	.15
	Booklet pane of 4	—	3.00	1.00
❏ 2584 (29¢)	Santa and Fireplace	—	.70	.15
	Booklet pane of 4	—	3.00	1.00
❏ 2585 (29¢)	Santa and Sleigh	—	.70	.15
	Booklet pane of 4	—	3.00	1.00

| 2587 | 2590 | 2592 |

Scott No.			Plate Block	Unused	Used

1994–1995.

❏ 2587	32¢	James Polk	4.00	.80	.16
❏ 2590	$1	Surrender of General Burgoyne	11.00	2.50	.95
❏ 2592	$5	Washington & Jackson	42.00	10.00	3.00

| **2593** | **2595** |
| (2593B, 2594) | (2596–2597) |

1992–1993. Booklet Stamps.

❏ 2593	29¢	Flag, black numeral, perforated 10	—	.80	.15
		Booklet pane of 10	—	7.00	4.50
❏ 2593B	29¢	Flag (~2593), black numeral, perforated 11 x 10	—	1.00	.62
		Booklet pane of 10	—	21.00	6.00
❏ 2594	29¢	Flag (~2593, red numeral	—	.90	.22
		Booklet pane of 10	—	7.00	3.50
❏ 2595	29¢	Eagle & Shield, brown numeral	—	.90	.27
		Booklet pane of 17	—	14.00	—
❏ 2596	29¢	Eagle & Shield (~2595), green numeral	—	.92	.26
		Booklet pane of 17	—	14.00	—
❏ 2597	29¢	Eagle & Shield (~2595), red numeral	—	.92	.27
		Booklet pane of 17	—	14.00	—

2598	2599

Scott No.			Plate Block	Unused	Used
❏ 2598	29¢	Eagle with Wings Upraised	—	.90	.26
		Booklet pane of 18	—	13.00	—
❏ 2599	29¢	Statue of Liberty	—	.92	.21
		Booklet pane of 18	—	15.00	—

2602	2603 (2604)	2605	2606 (2607–2608)	2609

Scott No.			PNC Strip (5)	Unused	Used

1991–1993. Coil Stamps.

			PNC Strip (5)	Unused	Used
❏ 2602	(10¢)	Bulk Rate USA, "USA" in red	3.10	.25	.16
❏ 2503	(10¢)	USA Bulk Rate, "USA" in blue, bright gold	2.50	.25	.16
❏ 2504	(10¢)	USA Bulk Rate (~2504), "USA" in blue & dull gold	3.00	.25	.16

NOTE: See Nos. 3270–3271 for Eagle & Shield stamps inscribed "USA Presort Std."

❏ 2605	23¢	Flag Presorted First–Class	5.50	.65	.16
❏ 2606	23¢	Flag & Chrome, bright blue	5.50	.65	.16
❏ 2607	23¢	Flag & Chrome (~2606), dark blue	6.00	.65	.16
❏ 2608	23¢	Flag & Chrome (~2606), violet blue	6.00	.65	.16
❏ 2609	29¢	Flag & White House	6.00	.75	.16

2611–2615

2616 **2617** **2618**

Scott No.			Plate Block	Unused	Used
1992.					
❑ 2611	29¢	Olympics – Hockey	—	.74	.15
❑ 2612	29¢	Olympics – Figure Skating	—	.74	.15
❑ 2613	29¢	Olympics – Speed Skating	—	.74	.15
❑ 2614	29¢	Olympics – Downhill Skiing	—	.74	.15
❑ 2615	29¢	Olympics – Bobsledding	—	.74	.15
		Strip of 5 (2611–2615)	9.00 (10)	4.00	2.50
❑ 2616	29¢	World Columbian Stamp Expo	3.50	.70	.16
❑ 2617	29¢	W. E. B. DuBois	4.00	.80	.16
❑ 2618	29¢	Love	3.00	.72	.16

2619

2620–2623

Scott No.			Plate Block	Unused	Used
❑ 2619	29¢	Olympic Baseball	4.50	.95	.15
❑ 2620	29¢	Seeking Isabella's Support	—	.75	.15
❑ 2621	29¢	Crossing the Atlantic	—	.75	.15
❑ 2622	29¢	Approaching Land	—	.75	.15
❑ 2623	29¢	Coming Ashore	—	.75	.15
		Block of 4 (2620–2623)	4.00	3.60	2.10

2624   2625

2626   2627

Scott No.		Plate Block	Unused	Used
1992. Columbian Souvenir Sheets.				
☐ 2624 $1.05	Sheet of 3 (1¢, 4¢ & $1 denominations)	—	2.50	2.10
☐ 2625 $4.05	Sheet of 3 (2¢, 3¢ & $4 denominations)	—	2.50	2.10
☐ 2626 85¢	Sheet of 3 (5¢, 30¢ & 50¢ denominations)	—	2.50	2.10
☐ 2627 $3.14	Sheet of 3 (6¢, 8¢ & $3 denominations)	—	7.00	6.00

| | 2628 | | 2629 | |

Scott No.		Plate Block	Unused	Used
❑ 2628 $2.25	Sheet of 3			
	(10¢, 15¢ & $2 denominations)	—	5.50	.70
❑ 2629 $5	Sheet of 1 ($5 denomination)	—	12.00	9.00
	Set of 6 sheets	—	42.00	—

2630

2631–2634

2635

2636

Scott No.			Plate Block	Unused	Used
❏ 2630	29¢	N. Y. Stock Exchange	3.25	.74	.15
❏ 2631	29¢	Cosmonaut	—	.74	.15
❏ 2632	29¢	Astronaut	—	.74	.15
❏ 2633	29¢	Apollo Spacecraft	—	.74	.15
❏ 2634	29¢	Soyuz Spacecraft	—	.74	.15
		Block of 4 (2631–2634)	4.00	2.00	1.10
❏ 2635	29¢	Alaska Highway	3.50	.75	.15
❏ 2636	29¢	Kentucky Statehood	3.10	.75	.15

2637–2641

2642–2646

Scott No.			Plate Block	Unused	Used
❑ 2637	29¢	Olympics – Soccer	—	.72	.16
❑ 2638	29¢	Olympics – Gymnastics	—	.72	.16
❑ 2639	29¢	Olympics – Volleyball	—	.72	.16
❑ 2640	29¢	Olympics – Boxing	—	.72	.16
❑ 2641	29¢	Olympics – Diving	—	.72	.16
		Strip of 5 (2637–2641)	10.00 (10)	4.00	3.00
❑ 2642	29¢	Ruby-throated Hummingbird	—	.63	.15
❑ 2643	29¢	Broad-billed Hummingbird	—	.63	.15
❑ 2644	29¢	Costa's Hummingbird	—	.63	.15
❑ 2645	29¢	Rufous Hummingbird	—	.63	.15
❑ 2646	29¢	Calliope Hummingbird	—	.63	.15
		Booklet pane of 5 (2642–2646)	—	4.50	3.00

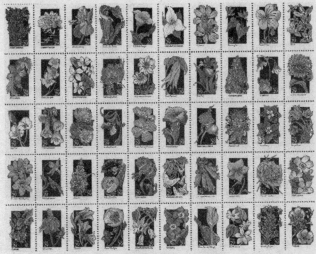

2647–2696

Scott No.		Plate Block	Unused	Used
❏ 2647–2696	29¢ Wildflowers, pane of 50	—	41.00	—
❏ 2647–2696	Any single stamp	—	1.20	.64

❏ 2647 Indian Paintbrush
❏ 2648 Fragrant Water Lily
❏ 2649 Meadow Beauty
❏ 2650 Jack-in-the-Pulpit
❏ 2651 California Poppy
❏ 2652 Large Flower Trillium
❏ 2653 Tickseed
❏ 2654 Shooting Star
❏ 2655 Stream Violet
❏ 2656 Bluets
❏ 2657 Herb Robert
❏ 2658 Marsh Marigold
❏ 2659 Sweet White Violet
❏ 2660 Claret Cup Cactus
❏ 2661 White Mountain Avens

❏ 2662 Sessile Bellwort
❏ 2663 Blue Flag
❏ 2664 Harlequin Lupine
❏ 2665 Twin Flower
❏ 2666 Common Sunflower
❏ 2667 Sego Lily
❏ 2668 Virginia Bluebells
❏ 2669 Ohi'a Lehua
❏ 2670 Rosebud Orchid
❏ 2671 Showy Evening Primrose
❏ 2672 Fringed Gentian
❏ 2673 Yellow Lady's Slipper
❏ 2674 Passion Flower
❏ 2675 Bunch Berry
❏ 2676 Pasque Flower

- ❏ 2677 Round-Lobed Hepatica
- ❏ 2678 Wild Columbine
- ❏ 2679 Firewood
- ❏ 2680 Indian Pond Lily
- ❏ 2681 Turk's Cap Lily
- ❏ 2682 Dutchman's Breeches
- ❏ 2683 Trumpet Honeysuckle
- ❏ 2684 Jacob's Ladder
- ❏ 2685 Plains Prickly Pear
- ❏ 2686 Mots Campion

- ❏ 2687 Bearberry
- ❏ 2688 Mexican Hat
- ❏ 2689 Harebell
- ❏ 2690 Desert Five Spot
- ❏ 2691 Smooth Solomon's Seal
- ❏ 2692 Red Maids
- ❏ 2693 Yellow Skunk Cabbage
- ❏ 2694 Rue Anemone
- ❏ 2695 Standing Cypress
- ❏ 2696 Wild Flax

2697

Scott No.			Plate Block	Unused	Used
❏ 2697	29¢	World War II, 1942, pane of 10	—	11.00	6.00
❏ 2697a–j	29¢	Any single stamp	—	.80	.25

2698

2699

2700–2703

2704

Scott No.			Plate Block	Unused	Used
❑ 2698	29¢	Dorothy Parker	3.10	.74	.16
❑ 2699	29¢	Theodore von Kármán	2.20	.74	.16
❑ 2700	29¢	Minerals – Azurite	—	.74	.16
❑ 2701	29¢	Minerals – Copper	—	.74	.16
❑ 2702	29¢	Minerals – Variscite	—	.74	.16
❑ 2703	29¢	Minerals – Wulfenite	—	.74	.16
		Block of 4 (2700–2703)	4.50	3.00	2.10
❑ 2704	29¢	Juan Rodríguez Cabrillo	3.40	.70	.16

CHRISTMAS
29
USA

Bellini, 1490, National Gallery

2710

2705–2709

Scott No.			Plate Block	Unused	Used
❑ 2705	29¢	Giraffe	—	.72	.16
❑ 2706	29¢	Giant Panda	—	.72	.16
❑ 2707	29¢	Flamingo	—	.72	.16
❑ 2708	29¢	King Penguins	—	.72	.16
❑ 2709	29¢	White Bengal Tiger	—	.72	.16
		Booklet pane of 5 (2705–2709)	—	4.50	3.00
❑ 2710	29¢	Christmas – Madonna & Child	—	.60	.16
		Booklet pane of 10	—	7.00	5.50

2719

2711–2714
(2715–2718)

2720

Scott No.			Plate Block	Unused	Used
❏ 2711	29¢	Christmas – Horse, perf 11½ x 11	—	.72	.15
❏ 2712	29¢	Christmas – Locomotive, perf 11½ x 11	—	.72	.15
❏ 2713	29¢	Christmas – Fire Pumper, perf 11½ x 11	—	.72	.15
❏ 2714	29¢	Christmas – Boat, perf 11½ x 11	—	.72	.15
		Block of 4 (2711–2714)	—	4.00	2.75

1992. Booklet Stamps.

❏ 2715	29¢	Christmas – Horse (~2711), perf 11	—	.82	.15
❏ 2716	29¢	Christmas – Locomotive (~2712), perf 11	—	.82	.15
❏ 2717	29¢	Christmas – Fire Pumper (~2713), perf 11	—	.82	.15
❏ 2718	29¢	Christmas – Boat (~2714), perf 11	—	.82	.15
		Booklet pane of 4 (2715–2718)	—	5.00	1.10
❏ 2719	29¢	Christmas – Locomotive (~2712), self-adhesive	—	.52	.15
		Booklet pane of 18	—	17.00	—
❏ 2720	29¢	Year of the Rooster	3.50	.90	.15

2721

2722

2723
(2723A)

Scott No.			Plate Block	Unused	Used
1993.					
❏ 2721	29¢	Elvis (no "Presley")	3.50	.90	.22
❏ 2722	29¢	Oklahoma! (no black frameline)	3.00	.72	.22

NOTE: See also No. 2769.

❏ 2723	29¢	Hank Williams, perf 10	4.00	1.00	.22
❏ 2723A	29¢	Hank Williams, perf 11.2 x 11.4	130.00	23.00	12.50

NOTE: The inscription on Nos. 2723 and 2723A measures 27½ mm. See also Nos. 2771 and 2775.

2724–2730
(2731–2737)

Scott No.			Plate Block	Unused	Used
❏ 2724	29¢	Elvis (with "Presley")	—	.80	.17
❏ 2725	29¢	Bill Haley	—	.80	.17
❏ 2726	29¢	Clyde McPhatter	—	.80	.17
❏ 2727	29¢	Ritchie Valens	—	.80	.17
❏ 2728	29¢	Otis Redding	—	.80	.17
❏ 2729	29¢	Buddy Holly	—	.80	.17
❏ 2730	29¢	Dinah Washington	—	.80	.17
		Strip of 7 (2724–2730)	12.50 (10)	11.00	4.00

NOTE: Nos. 2724–2730 lack a black frameline around stamps. See also No. 2731–2737.

Scott No.			Plate Block	Unused	Used
❏ 2731	29¢	Elvis (~2724) (with "Presley")	—	.78	.21
❏ 2732	29¢	Bill Haley (~2725)	—	.78	.21
❏ 2733	29¢	Clyde McPhatter (~2726)	—	.78	.21
❏ 2734	29¢	Ritchie Valens (~2727)	—	.78	.21
❏ 2735	29¢	Otis Redding (~2728)	—	.78	.21
❏ 2736	29¢	Buddy Holly (~2729)	—	.78	.21
❏ 2737	29¢	Dinah Washington (~2730)	—	.78	.21
		Booklet pane of 8 (1 x 2731; 2 each 2737)		6.50	4.20
		Booklet pane of 4 (2731 & 2735–2737)	—	3.75	3.00

NOTE: Nos. 2731–2737 have a black frameline around stamps.

2741–2745

❏ 2741	29¢	Planet & Rings	—	.72	.17
❏ 2742	29¢	Flying Saucers	—	.72	.17
❏ 2743	29¢	Jet Backpacks	—	.72	.17
❏ 2744	29¢	Winged Spacecraft	—	.72	.17
❏ 2745	29¢	Stubby-winged Spacecraft	—	.72	.17
		Booklet pane of 5 (2741–2745)	—	4.00	3.15

2747

2748

2746

2749

2750–2753

2754

Scott No.			Plate Block	Unused	Used
❑ 2746	29¢	Percy Lavon Julian	3.50	.72	.15
❑ 2747	29¢	Oregon Trail	3.50	.72	.15
❑ 2748	29¢	World University Games	3.50	.72	.15
❑ 2749	29¢	Grace Kelly	3.50	.72	.15
❑ 2750	29¢	Clown	—	.72	.15
❑ 2751	29¢	Ringmaster	—	.72	.15
❑ 2752	29¢	Trapeze Artist	—	.72	.15
❑ 2753	29¢	Elephant	—	.72	.15
		Block of 4 (2750–2753)	8.00 (6)	3.50	3.00
❑ 2754	29¢	Cherokee Strip	2.00	.65	.15

2755

2756–2759

2760–2764

Scott No.			Plate Block	Unused	Used
❏ 2755	29¢	Dean Acheson	3.25	.80	.16
❏ 2756	29¢	Steeplechase	—	.80	.16
❏ 2757	29¢	Thoroughbred Racing	—	.80	.16
❏ 2758	29¢	Harness Racing	—	.80	.16
❏ 2759	29¢	Polo	—	.80	.16
		Block of 4 (2554–2557)	4.00	3.50	2.70
❏ 2760	29¢	Hyacinth	—	.75	.15
❏ 2761	29¢	Daffodil	—	.75	.15
❏ 2762	29¢	Tulip	—	.75	.15
❏ 2763	29¢	Iris	—	.75	.15
❏ 2764	29¢	Lilac	—	.75	.15
		Booklet pane of 5 (2760–2764)	—	4.10	1.60

2765

2766

Scott No.			Plate Block	Unused	Used
❏ 2765	29¢	World War II, 1943, pane of 10	—	11.00	6.00
❏ 2765a–j	29¢	Any single stamp	—	.90	.22
❏ 2766	29¢	Joe Louis	4.00	1.00	.20

2767–2770

Scott No.			Plate Block	Unused	Used
❑ 2767	29¢	Show Boat	—	.72	.16
❑ 2768	29¢	Porgy & Bess	—	.72	.16
❑ 2769	29¢	Oklahoma! (~2722)			
		(black frameline)	—	.72	.16
❑ 2770	29¢	My Fair Lady	—	.72	.16
		Booklet pane of 4			
		(2767–2770)	—	3.60	2.20

2771–2774
(2775–2778)

2779–2782

Scott No.			Plate Block	Unused	Used
❑ 2771	29¢	Hank Williams (~2723) (no frameline)	—	.73	.15
❑ 2772	29¢	Patsy Cline (no frameline)	—	.73	.15
❑ 2773	29¢	Carter Family (no frameline)	—	.73	.15
❑ 2774	29¢	Bob Wills (no frameline)	—	.73	.15
		Block or strip of 4 (2771–2774)	5.00	4.00	2.40

NOTE: The inscription on No. 2771 measures 27mm. See also Nos. 2723, 2723A and 2778.

Scott No.			Plate Block	Unused	Used
❑ 2775	29¢	Hank Williams (~2723) (black frameline)	—	.70	.15
❑ 2776	29¢	Patsy Cline (~2772) (black frameline)	—	.70	.15
❑ 2777	29¢	Carter Family (~2773) (black frameline)	—	.70	.15
❑ 2778	29¢	Bob Wills (~2774) (black frameline)	—	.70	.15
		Booklet pane of 4 (2775–2778)	—	4.00	1.00

NOTE: The inscription on No. 2775 measures 22mm. See also Nos. 2723, 2723A and 2771.

Scott No.			Plate Block	Unused	Used
❑ 2779	29¢	Benjamin Franklin	—	.52	.15
❑ 2780	29¢	Drummer	—	.52	.15
❑ 2781	29¢	Charles Lindbergh	—	.52	.15
❑ 2782	29¢	Rare Stamps	—	.52	.15
		Block of 4 (2779–2782)	5.00	3.40	2.60

2783–84

2785–2788

Scott No.			Plate Block	Unused	Used
❏ 2783	29¢	Deafness – Mother & Child	—	.70	.15
❏ 2784	29¢	American Sign Language	—	.70	.15
		Se-tenant pair (2783–2784)	3.00	.70	.45
❏ 2785	29¢	Rebecca of Sunnybrook Farm	—	.55	.15
❏ 2786	29¢	Little House on the Prairie	—	.55	.15
❏ 2787	29¢	Huckleberry Finn	—	.55	.15
❏ 2788	29¢	Little Women	—	.55	.15
		Block of 4 (2785–2788)	5.00	4.00	2.75

2789

2791–2794
(2795–2803)

Scott No.			Plate Block	Unused	Used
❑ 2789	29¢	Christmas – Madonna & Child	3.10	.60	.15
❑ 2790	29¢	Madonna & Child (~2789)	—	.60	.15
		Booklet pane of 4	—	3.60	2.10

NOTE: The design of No.2789 is slightly cropped in No. 2790, the booklet version.

❑ 2791	29¢	Christmas – Jack in the Box	—	.60	.15
❑ 2792	29¢	Christmas – Reindeer	—	.60	.15
❑ 2793	29¢	Christmas – Snowman	—	.60	.15
❑ 2794	29¢	Christmas – Toy Soldier	—	.60	.15
		Block or strip of 4 (2791–2794)	4.10	3.75	3.00
❑ 2795	29¢	Toy Soldier (~2794)	—	.90	.15
❑ 2796	29¢	Snowman (~2793)	—	.90	.15
❑ 2797	29¢	Reindeer (~2792)	—	.90	.15
❑ 2798	29¢	Jack in the Box (~2791)	—	.90	.15
		Booklet pane of 10 (2 or 3 of each design)	—	5.00	3.00
❑ 2799	29¢	Snowman (~2793) self-adhesive	—	.60	.15
❑ 2800	29¢	Toy Soldier (~2794) self-adhesive	—	.60	.15
❑ 2801	29¢	Jack in the Box (~2791) self-adhesive	—	.60	.15
❑ 2802	29¢	Reindeer (~2792) self-adhesive	—	.60	.15
		Booklet pane of 12 (3 each 2799–2802)	—	4.50	—

NOTE: Nos. 2799–2802 measure 19½ x 26½ mm.

Scott No.			Plate Block	Unused	Used
❑ 2803	29¢	Snowman (~2793)			
		self-adhesive	—	.50	.15
		Booklet pane of 18	—	15.00	—

NOTE: No. 2803 measures 17 x 20 mm.

2804

2805

2806

❑ 2804	29¢	Mariana Islands	3.50	.62	.15
❑ 2805	29¢	Columbus Landing	3.25	.62	.15
❑ 2806	29¢	AIDS Awareness	3.50	.62	.15
❑ 2806b	29¢	Booklet pane of 5 (~2806)	—	4.00	2.50

2807–2811

1994.

❑ 2807	29¢	Slalom	—	.55	.15
❑ 2808	29¢	Luge	—	.55	.15
❑ 2809	29¢	Ice Dancing	—	.55	.15
❑ 2810	29¢	Skiing	—	.55	.15
❑ 2811	29¢	Hockey	—	.55	.15
		Strip of 5 (2807–2811)	4.50 (10)	3.75	2.60

2812

2813

2814
(2814C)

2815

2816

2817

2818

Scott No.			Plate Block	Unused	Used
❑ 2812	29¢	Edward R. Murrow	3.40	.70	.16
❑ 2813	29¢	Love – Sunshine Heart	6.00	.70	.16
		Booklet pane of 18	—	14.00	—
❑ 2814	29¢	Love – Dove (photogravure)	—	.60	.15
		Booklet pane of 10	—	7.50	4.00
❑ 2814C	29¢	Love (~2814) (lithographed & engraved)	4.00	.50	.16
❑ 2815	52¢	Love – Doves	5.00	.90	.16
❑ 2816	29¢	Dr. Allison Davis	3.50	.62	.16
❑ 2817	29¢	Year of the Dog	5.00	.67	.16
❑ 2818	29¢	Buffalo Soldiers	3.50	.67	.16

2819–2828

Scott No.			Plate Block	Unused	Used
❏ 2819	29¢	Rudolph Valentino	—	.62	.16
❏ 2820	29¢	Clara Bow	—	.62	.16
❏ 2821	29¢	Charlie Chaplin	—	.62	.16
❏ 2822	29¢	Lon Chaney	—	.62	.16
❏ 2823	29¢	John Gilbert	—	.62	.16
❏ 2824	29¢	Zasu Pitts	—	.62	.16
❏ 2825	29¢	Harold Lloyd	—	.62	.16
❏ 2826	29¢	Keystone Cops	—	.62	.16
❏ 2827	29¢	Theda Bara	—	.62	.16
❏ 2828	29¢	Buster Keaton	—	.62	.16
		Block of 10 (2819–2828)	10.00 (10)	8.00	6.50

2829–2833

2837

Scott No.			Plate Block	Unused	Used
☐ 2829	29¢	Lily	—	.72	.17
☐ 2830	29¢	Zinnia	—	.72	.17
☐ 2831	29¢	Gladiola	—	.72	.17
☐ 2832	29¢	Marigold	—	.72	.17
☐ 2833	29¢	Rose	—	.72	.17
		Booklet pane of 5 (2830–2833)	—	4.20	.17
☐ 2834	29¢	World Cup Soccer	3.50	.84	.17
☐ 2835	40¢	World Cup Soccer	4.50	1.00	.17
☐ 2836	50¢	World Cup Soccer	6.00	1.40	.17
☐ 2837	$1.19	Souvenir Sheet of 3 (2834–2836)	—	4.20	3.15

2838

Scott No.			Plate Block	Unused	Used
❏ 2838	29¢	World War II, 1944, pane of 10	—	8.00	6.10
❏ 2838a–j		Any single stamp	—	1.00	.21

2839

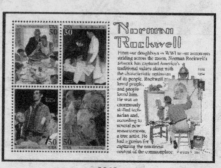

2840

Scott No.			Plate Block	Unused	Used
❏ 2839	29¢	Norman Rockwell	3.50	.86	.17
❏ 2840	50¢	Rockwell souvenir sheet	—	5.50	3.00
❏ 2840a–d	50¢	Any single stamp	—	.80	.15

2841

2842

2848

2843–2847

Scott No.			Plate Block	Unused	Used
❏ 2841	29¢	Moon Landing	—	1.00	.17
❏ 2842	$9.95	Moon Landing	100.00	26.00	8.00
❏ 2843	29¢	Hudson's General	—	.87	.17
❏ 2844	29¢	McQueen's Jupiter	—	.87	.17
❏ 2845	29¢	Eddy's No. 242	—	.87	.17
❏ 2846	29¢	Ely's No. 10	—	.87	.17
❏ 2847	29¢	Buchanan's No. 999	—	.87	.17
		Booklet pane of 5 (2843–2847)	—	5.00	2.10
❏ 2848	29¢	George Meany	35.00	.82	.22

2849–2853

Scott No.			Plate Block	Unused	Used
1995.					
❏ 2849	29¢	Al Jolson	—	.80	.20
❏ 2850	29¢	Bing Crosby	—	.80	.20
❏ 2851	29¢	Ethel Waters	—	.80	.20
❏ 2852	29¢	Nat "King" Cole	—	.80	.20
❏ 2853	29¢	Ethel Merman	—	.80	.20
		Strip of 5 (2849–2853)	6.50 (10)	3.10	1.65

2854–2861

Scott No.			Plate Block	Unused	Used
❏ 2854	29¢	Bessie Smith	—	.72	.16
❏ 2855	29¢	Muddy Waters	—	.72	.16
❏ 2856	29¢	Billie Holiday	—	.72	.16
❏ 2857	29¢	Robert Johnson	—	.72	.16
❏ 2858	29¢	Jimmy Rushing	—	.72	.16
❏ 2859	29¢	"Ma" Rainey	—	.72	.16
❏ 2860	29¢	Mildred Bailey	—	.72	.16
❏ 2861	29¢	Howlin' Wolf	—	.72	.16
		Block of 9 (2854–3861 + any 1 extra stamp)	14.00 (10)	8.75	6.50

2862

2863–2866

2867–2868

Scott No.			Plate Block	Unused	Used
❑ 2862	29¢	James Thurber	3.25	.72	.17
❑ 2863	29¢	Motorboat & Diver	—	.72	.17
❑ 2864	29¢	Three–masted Ship	—	.72	.17
❑ 2865	29¢	Diver & Sunken Wheel	—	.72	.17
❑ 2866	29¢	Fish & Coral	—	.72	.17
		Block of 4 (2863–2866)	4.00	3.50	2.50
❑ 2867	29¢	Black-necked Crane	—	.80	.17
❑ 2868	29¢	Whooping Crane	—	.80	.17
		Se-tenant pair (2867–2868)	3.50	2.00	1.20

2869

2869g

2870g

Scott No.			Plate Block	Unused	Used
❑ 2869	29¢	Legends of the West	—	16.00	14.00
❑ 2869a–j	29¢	Any single stamp	—	.82	.15
❑ 2870	29¢	Recalled Legends	—	210.00	—
❑ 2870a–j	29¢	Any single stamp	—	11.00	8.75

NOTE: The Bill Pickett stamps in Nos. 2869 and 2870 differ. The Pickett stamp in No. 2870 shows a handkerchief in the vest pocket. Other stamps in the two panes are similar except that the framelines on No. 2869 are thicker than on No. 2870.

2871
(2871A) **2872** **2873** **2874**

2875

Scott No.			Plate Block	Unused	Used
❏ 2871	29¢	Madonna & Child, perf 11½	3.00	.72	.15
❏ 2871A	29¢	Madonna & Child (~2871), perf 9½ x 11	—	.93	.21
		Booklet pane of 10	—	7.50	4.00
❏ 2872	29¢	Teddy Bear in Stocking	3.25	.72	.17
❏ 2872a	29¢	Booklet pane of 20	—	14.00	8.00
❏ 2873	29¢	Santa Claus	—	1.60	.17
		Booklet pane of 12	—	11.50	6.50
❏ 2874	29¢	Cardinal	—	1.10	.36
		Booklet pane of 18	—	16.00	—
❏ 2875	$2	B.E.P. souvenir sheet	—	20.00	—
		Single stamp	—	2.75	1.60

| | | **2876** | | | **2877**
(2878) | **2879**
(2880) | **2881**
(2882–2887,
2889–2892) |

Scott No.			Plate Block	Unused	Used
☐ 2876	29¢	Year of the Boar	4.25	.93	.21
☐ 2877	(4¢)	G Rate Make-up Stamp	.70	.20	.15
☐ 2878	(4¢)	G Rate Make-up Stamp (~2877)	.85	.21	.15

NOTE: No. 2877 is printed with bright blue; No. 2878 is printed with dark blue.

Scott No.			Plate Block	Unused	Used
☐ 2879	(20¢)	Yellow with Black G	5.00	.62	.15
☐ 2880	(20¢)	Yellow with Red G (~2879)	8.00	.62	.15
☐ 2881	(32¢)	White with Black G, perf 11.2 x 11.1	10.00	.90	.15
		Booklet pane of 10	—	8.00	4.10
☐ 2882	(32¢)	White with Red G (~2881)	5.00	.90	.17

Booklet Stamps.

Scott No.			Plate Block	Unused	Used
☐ 2883	(32¢)	White with Black G (~2881), perf 10 x 9.9	—	1.25	.21
		Booklet pane of 10	—	10.00	3.60
☐ 2884	(32¢)	White with Blue G (~2881)	—	1.10	.22
		Booklet pane of 10	—	8.50	4.60
☐ 2885	(32¢)	White with Red G (~2881)	—	1.15	.17
		Booklet pane of 10	—	11.00	4.10
☐ 2886	(32¢)	White with Black G (~2881), self-adhesive		.80	.17
		Booklet pane of 18	—	18.00	—
		PNC strip of 5 (see note)	3.50	—	—

NOTE: No.2886 also exists as a coil stamp. Booklet examples and coil examples alike possess straight die cutting and, therefore, are indistinguishable once removed from their backing paper.

Scott No.		Plate Block	Unused	Used
❏ 2887 (32¢)	White with Black G (~2881), self-adhesive	—	1.10	.17
	Booklet pane of 18	—	17.00	—

NOTE: No. 2887 contains noticeable blue shading in the white stripes below the field of stars; No. 2886 does not.

2888

2893

Scott No.		PNC Strip (5)	Unused	Used
Coil Stamps.				
❏ 2888 (25¢)	Blue with Black G	7.00	.75	.30
❏ 2889 (32¢)	White with Black G (~2881)	12.00	2.10	.21
❏ 2890 (32¢)	White with Blue G (~2881)	8.00	.85	.26
❏ 2891 (32¢)	White with Red G (~2881)	8.00	1.00	.26
❏ 2892 (32¢)	White with Red G (~2881), rouletted	10.00	1.00	.26
❏ 2893 (5¢)	Green with Black G	2.50	.50	.25

2897
(2913–2915, 2920, 3113)

Scott No.		Plate Block	Unused	Used
1995.				
❏ 2897 32¢	Flag over Porch, perforated	4.10	.85	.17

2902	**2903**	**2905**	**2908**	**2911**
(2902B)	(2904, 2904A)	(2906)	(2909–2910)	(2912, 2912A, 3132)

Scott No.		PNC Strip (5)	Unused	Used

Coil Stamps.

		PNC Strip (5)	Unused	Used
❑ 2902 (5¢)	Butte, Non-Profit, perforated	1.60	.20	.17
❑ 2902B (5¢)	Butte, Non-Profit, die cut	2.10	.26	.17
❑ 2903 (10¢)	Mountain, purple cast, perforated	2.10	.20	.17
❑ 2904 (10¢)	Mountain, bluish cast (~2903), perforated	2.75	.21	.17
❑ 2904A (10¢)	Mountain, purple cast (~2903), die cut	3.25	.24	.17
❑ 2905 (10¢)	Automobile, Bulk rate, perforated	3.00	.31	.17
❑ 2906 (10¢)	Automobile (~2905), die cut	2.40	.31	.17
❑ 2908 (15¢)	Tail Fin, orange-yellow cast, perforated	3.75	.41	.17
❑ 2909 (15¢)	Tail Fin (~2908), buff cast, perforated	3.25	.41	.17
❑ 2910 (15¢)	Tail Fin (~2908), self-adhesive	3.50	.60	.17
❑ 2911 (25¢)	Juke Box, perforated	6.00	.77	.26
❑ 2912 (25¢)	Juke Box (~2911), perforated	6.00	.72	.26
❑ 2912A (25¢)	Juke Box (~2911), die cut	6.00	.72	.26
❑ 2913 32¢	Flag over Porch (~2897), perforated	6.50	.93	.26
❑ 2914 32¢	Flag over Porch (~2897), perforated	7.75	.90	.26

NOTE: The tan color on No. 2913 appears tan; it appears yellow brown on No. 2914.

❑ 2915 32¢	Flag over porch, die cut (~2897)	13.00	1.10	.26

2919

Scott No.			Plate Block	Unused	Used
Booklet Stamps.					
❑ 2916	32¢	Flag over Porch (~2897), water-activated gum	—	.98	.16
		Booklet pane of 10	—	8.00	4.00
❑ 2919	32¢	Flag over Field, self adhesive	—	1.00	.26
		Booklet pane of 18	—	14.50	.16
❑ 2920	32¢	Flag over Porch (~2897), self-adhesive	—	1.00	.26
		Booklet pane of 20	—	16.50	—

2933	**2934**	**2935**	**2936**	**2938**

1995–1996. Great Americans Series.

Scott No.			Plate Block	Unused	Used
❑ 2933	32¢	Milton Hershey	3.75	.80	.21
❑ 2934	32¢	Cal Farley	3.75	.80	.17
❑ 2935	32¢	Henry R. Luce	3.40	.80	.21
❑ 2936	32¢	Lila & DeWitt Wallace	3.50	.80	.21
❑ 2938	46¢	Ruth Benedict	4.50	1.00	.21

| 2940 | 2941 | 2942 | 2943 |

Scott No.			Plate Block	Unused	Used
❏ 2940	55¢	Alice Hamilton M.D.	6.00	1.50	.30
❏ 2941	55¢	Justin S. Morrill	5.50	1.50	.30
❏ 2942	77¢	Mary Breckinridge	7.00	1.50	.30
❏ 2943	78¢	Alice Paul	8.00	1.50	.30

| 2948 | 2949 | 2950 |

1995.

❏ 2948	(32¢)	Love – Cherub, perforated	3.50	.70	.22
❏ 2949	(32¢)	Love – Cherub, self-adhesive	—	.94	.22
		Booklet pane of 20	—	15.00	—
❏ 2950	32¢	Florida Statehood	4.60	1.00	.18

2951–2954

| | | | 2955 | 2956 | 2957 (2959) | 2958 (2960) |

2955

2956

2957
(2959)

2958
(2960)

Scott No.			Plate Block	Unused	Used
❏ 2951	32¢	Globe in a Tub	—	.72	.16
❏ 2952	32¢	Sun & Electrical Cord	—	.72	.16
❏ 2953	32¢	Planting a Tree	—	.72	.16
❏ 2954	32¢	Clean-up at the Beach	—	.72	.16
		Block of 4 (2952–2954)	4.00	2.50	1.60
❏ 2955	32¢	Richard M. Nixon	3.50	.82	.17
❏ 2956	32¢	Bessie Coleman	3.50	.82	.17
❏ 2957	32¢	Love – Cherub, perforated	3.00	.82	.17
❏ 2958	55¢	Love – Cherubs, perforated	4.00	1.30	.17
❏ 2959	32¢	Love – Cherub, self-adhesive	—	.95	.17
		Booklet pane of 10	—	7.50	—
❏ 2960	55¢	Love – Cherubs, self-adhesive	—	1.60	.15
		Booklet pane of 20	—	21.00	—

2966

2967

2968

2961–2965

Scott No.			Plate Block	Unused	Used
❏ 2961	32¢	Volleyball	—	.80	.15
❏ 2962	32¢	Softball	—	.80	.15
❏ 2963	32¢	Bowling	—	.80	.15
❏ 2964	32¢	Tennis	—	.80	.15
❏ 2965	32¢	Golf	—	.80	.15
		Strip of 5 (2961–2965)	6.00 (10)	3.10	1.60
❏ 2966	32¢	POW – MIA	4.00	.84	.21
❏ 2967	32¢	Marilyn Monroe	5.50	1.00	.21
❏ 2968	32¢	Texas Statehood	3.75	1.00	.21

2969–2973

2974

Scott No.			Plate Block	Unused	Used
❑ 2969	32¢	Split Rock Lighthouse	—	.92	.21
❑ 2970	32¢	St. Joseph Lighthouse	—	.92	.21
❑ 2971	32¢	Spectacle Reef Lighthouse	—	.92	.21
❑ 2972	32¢	Marblehead Lighthouse	—	.92	.21
❑ 2973	32¢	Thirty Mile Point Lighthouse	—	.92	.21
		Booklet pane of 5 (2969–1973)	—	4.50	1.60
❑ 2974	32¢	United Nations	3.60	.80	.17

2975

Scott No.			Plate Block	Unused	Used
❑ 2975	32¢	Civil War, pane of 20	—	24.00	16.00
❑ 2975a–t		Any single stamp	—	.80	.17

2976–2979

2980

Scott No.			Plate Block	Unused	Used
❑ 2976	32¢	Carousel Horse – Gold	—	.80	.17
❑ 2977	32¢	Carousel Horse – Black & Gold	—	.80	.17
❑ 2978	32¢	Carousel Horse – Silver	—	.80	.17
❑ 2979	32¢	Carousel Horse – Brown	—	.80	.17
		Block of 4 (2976–2979)	4.75	3.50	2.50
❑ 2980	32¢	Women's Suffrage	3.50	.80	.17

2981

2982

Scott No.			Plate Block	Unused	Used
❑ 2981	32¢	World War II ,1945, pane of 10	—	10.00	6.00
❑ 2981a–j	32¢	Any single stamp	—	.90	.17
❑ 2982	32¢	Louis Armstrong (white "32¢")	4.75	1.00	.22

2983–2992

Scott No.			Plate Block	Unused	Used
❏ 2983	32¢	Coleman Hawkins	—	.82	.17
❏ 2984	32¢	Louis Armstrong (black "32¢")	—	.82	.17
❏ 2985	32¢	James P. Johnson	—	.82	.17
❏ 2986	32¢	Jelly Roll Morton	—	.82	.17
❏ 2987	32¢	Charlie Parker	—	.82	.17
❏ 2988	32¢	Eubie Blake	—	.82	.17
❏ 2989	32¢	Charles Mingus	—	.82	.17
❏ 2990	32¢	Thelonious Monk	—	.82	.17
❏ 2991	32¢	John Coltrane	—	.82	.17
❏ 2992	32¢	Errol Garner	—	.82	.17
		Block of 10 (2983–2992)	12.50 (10)	11.00	7.75

2993–2997

2998

2999

Scott No.			Plate Block	Unused	Used
❏ 2993	32¢	Aster	—	.80	.16
❏ 2994	32¢	Chrysanthemum	—	.80	.16
❏ 2995	32¢	Dahlia	—	.80	.16
❏ 2996	32¢	Hydrangea	—	.80	.16
❏ 2997	32¢	Rudbeckia	—	.80	.16
		Booklet pane of 5 (2993–2997)	—	4.50	1.60
❏ 2998	60¢	Eddie Rickenbacker	7.50	1.50	.60
❏ 2999	32¢	Republic of Palau	3.50	.80	.17

3000

3001

3002

Scott No.			Plate Block	Unused	Used
❑ 3000	32¢	Comic Strip Classics	—	18.00	12.00
❑ 3000a–t	32¢	Any single stamp	—	.85	.17
❑ 3001	32¢	U.S. Naval Academy	3.25	.80	.17
❑ 3002	32¢	Tennessee Williams	4.60	1.10	.17

3003
(3003A)

3004–3007
(3008–3011, 3014–3017)

3012
(3018)

3013

Scott No.			Plate Block	Unused	Used
❑ 3003	32¢	Madonna & Child, perf 11.2	3.50	.75	.17
❑ 3003A	32¢	Madonna & Child, perf 9.8 x 11.9	—	.76	.17
		Booklet pane of 10	—	8.50	4.10
❑ 3004	32¢	Santa & Chimney, perforated	—	.72	.17
❑ 3005	32¢	Jack-in-the-Box, perforated	—	.72	.17
❑ 3006	32¢	Boy & Christmas Tree, perforated	—	.72	.17
❑ 3007	32¢	Santa in Workshop, perforated	—	.75	.17
		Block or strip of 4	3.50	.75	.16
		Booklet pane of 10 (2 or 3 each 3004–3007)	—	8.50	5.50
❑ 3008	32¢	Santa in Workshop (~3007), self-adhesive	—	.80	.17
❑ 3009	32¢	Jack-in-the-Box (~3005), self-adhesive	—	.80	.17
❑ 3010	32¢	Santa & Chimney (~3004), self-adhesive	—	.80	.17
❑ 3011	32¢	Boy & Christmas Tree (~3006), self-adhesive	—	.80	.17
		Booklet pane of 20 (5 each 3008–3011)	—	19.00	—
❑ 3012	32¢	Christmas – Midnight Angel	—	.80	.17
		Booklet pane of 20	—	14.00	—
❑ 3013	32¢	Christmas – Children Sledding	—	1.25	.17
		Booklet pane of 18	—	16.00	—

Scott No.			PNC Strip (5)	Unused	Used

Coil Stamps.

❏ 3014	32¢	Santa in Workshop (~3007), self-adhesive	—	.80	.17
❏ 3015	32¢	Jack-in-the-Box (~3005), self-adhesive	—	.80	.17
❏ 3016	32¢	Santa & Chimney (~3004), self-adhesive	—	.80	.17
❏ 3017	32¢	Boy & Christmas Tree (~3006), self-adhesive	—	.80	.17
		Strip of 4 (3014–3017)	7.00	3.10	—
❏ 3018	32¢	Christmas – Midnight Angel, self-adhesive	10.00	3.00	.17

3019–3023

Scott No.			Plate Block	Unused	Used

1995.

❏ 3019	32¢	1893 Duryea	—	.82	.17
❏ 3020	32¢	1894 Haynes	—	.82	.17
❏ 3021	32¢	1898 Columbia	—	.82	.17
❏ 3022	32¢	1899 Winton	—	.82	.17
❏ 3023	32¢	1901 White	—	.82	.17
		Strip of 5 (3019–3023)	9.50 (10)	4.60	.17

3831

3834

3833

3832

3835

3835

3836

3837

3838

3839

3840-43

3840-43

A-2

3844

3851

3854

3845

3852

3855

3856

3846

3853

3855-56

3847

3857-61

3848

3849

 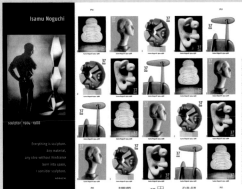

3850

3857-61

3862

3863

3865

3865-68

3869

3870

3871

3872

ART OF THE AMERICAN INDIAN

Mimbres bowl USA37

Kutenai parfleche USA37

Tlingit sculptures USA37

Ho-Chunk bag USA37

Seminole doll USA37

Mississippian effigy USA37

Acoma pot USA37

Navajo weaving USA37

Seneca carving USA37

Luiseño basket USA37

3873a-j

3874

3875

3876

3876

CLOUDSCAPES

© 2003
USPS

37
x 15
$5.55

| Cirrus radiatus | Cirrostratus fibratus | Cirrocumulus undulatus | Cumulonimbus mammatus | Cumulonimbus incus |

| Altocumulus stratiformis | Altostratus translucidus | Altocumulus undulatus | Altocumulus castellanus | Altocumulus lenticularis |

| Stratocumulus undulatus | Stratus opacus | Cumulus humilis | Cumulus congestus | Cumulonimbus with tornado |

V 11111   V 11111

3878

3877

3879

3880

3881

3882

3887

3888

3889

3890

3891

3892

3883-3886

3893

3894

3024

3025–3029

3030

Scott No.			Plate Block	Unused	Used
1996.					
❑ 3024	32¢	Utah Statehood	3.50	.78	.21
❑ 3025	32¢	Crocus	—	.78	.21
❑ 3026	32¢	Winter Aconite	—	.78	.21
❑ 3027	32¢	Pansy	—	.78	.21
❑ 3028	32¢	Snowdrop	—	.78	.21
❑ 3029	32¢	Anemone	—	.78	.21
		Booklet pane of 5 (3024–3029)	—	4.10	1.60
❑ 3030	32¢	Love – Cherub, self adhesive	—	15.00	—
		Booklet pane of 15	—	15.00	—
		Booklet pane of 20	—	18.00	—

| **3032** | **3033** | **3036** |
| (3045) | | |

Scott No.			Plate Block	Unused	Used
❑ 3031	1¢	Kestrel, die cut 10½ ("1¢")	.65	.22	.17
❑ 3031A	1¢	Kestrel, die cut 11½ ("1¢")	.65	.22	.17
❑ 3032	2¢	Woodpecker	.70	.18	.17
❑ 3033	3¢	Blue Bird ("3¢")	.80	.22	.17
❑ 3036	$1	Red Fox	10.00	2.20	.17

NOTE: See Nos. 2476 and 2478 for 1¢ and 3¢ stamps denominated "01" and "03."

Scott No.			PNC Strip (5)	Unused	Used
Coil Stamps.					
❑ 3044	1¢	Kestrel ("1¢")	.65	.22	.15
❑ 3045	2¢	Woodpecker	.85	.22	.15

| **3048** | **3049** |
| | (3054) |

Scott No.			Plate Block	Unused	Used
1996. Booklet Stamps.					
❑ 3048	20¢	Blue Jay (~2483), self-adhesive	—	.70	.15
		Booklet pane of 10	—	6.50	—
❑ 3049	32¢	Yellow Rose (~2490), self-adhesive	—	1.00	.15
		Booklet pane of 20	—	17.00	—

3050
(3051, 3055)

3052
(3052E)

Scott No.			Plate Block	Unused	Used
❑ 3050	20¢	Pheasant, die cut 11½	—	.64	.17
		Booklet pane of 10	—	5.50	—
❑ 3051	20¢	Pheasant (~3050), die cut 10½ x 11	—	1.10	.17
		Booklet pane of 5 (& one 3051a)	—	5.00	.17
❑ 3051a	20¢	Pheasant, die cut 10½	—	.78	.17
❑ 3052	32¢	Coral Pink Rose, die cut 11½ x 11½	—	.76	.17
		Booklet pane of 20	—	14.00	—
❑ 3052E	32¢	Coral Pink Rose (~3052), die cut 10½ x 10½	—	.78	.17
		Booklet pane of 20	—	16.00	—

Scott No.			PNC Strip (5)	Unused	Used
Coil Stamps.					
❑ 3053	20¢	Blue Jay (~2483), die cut 11½	4.75	.86	.17
❑ 3054	32¢	Yellow Rose (~2490), die cut 9½	7.25	.92	.17
❑ 3055	20¢	Pheasant (~3051), die cut 9½	4.25	.72	.17

3058

3061–3064

3059

3060

3065

3066

3067

Scott No.			Plate Block	Unused	Used
1996.					
☐ 3058	32¢	Ernest E. Just	4.00	.92	.21
☐ 3059	32¢	Smithsonian Institution	4.00	.90	.21
☐ 3060	32¢	Year of the Rat	4.25	1.10	.21
☐ 3061	32¢	Edweard Muybridge	—	.72	.17
☐ 3062	32¢	Ottmar Mergenthaler	—	.72	.17
☐ 3063	32¢	Frederick E. Ives	—	.72	.17
☐ 3064	32¢	William Dickson	—	.72	.17
		Block of 4 (3061–3064)	4.10	3.60	2.10
☐ 3065	32¢	Fulbright Scholarships	4.10	1.00	.21
☐ 3066	50¢	Jacqueline Cochran	5.50	1.20	.21
☐ 3067	32¢	Marathon	3.50	.80	.21

3069

3070
(3071)

3068

3072–3076

Scott No.			Plate Block	Unused	Used
❑ 3068	32¢	Olympics 1996, pane of 20	—	18.00	13.00
		Any single stamp	—	.75	.17
❑ 3069	32¢	Georgia O'Keeffe	4.50	1.00	.21
❑ 3070	32¢	Tennessee, perforated	3.50	.80	.21
❑ 3071	32¢	Tennessee (~3070), self-adhesive	—	.92	.26
		Booklet pane of 20	—	14.00	—
❑ 3072	32¢	Fancy Dance	—	.70	.15
❑ 3073	32¢	Butterfly Dance	—	.70	.15
❑ 3074	32¢	Traditional Dance	—	.70	.15
❑ 3075	32¢	Raven Dance	—	.70	.15
❑ 3076	32¢	Hoop Dance	—	.70	.15
		Strip of 5 (3072–3076)	11.50 (10)	4.00	2.10

3077–3080

3081

3082

Scott No.			Plate Block	Unused	Used
❑ 3077	32¢	Eohippus	—	.80	.17
❑ 3078	32¢	Woolly Mammoth	—	.80	.17
❑ 3079	32¢	Mastodon	—	.80	.17
❑ 3080	32¢	Saber-tooth Cat	—	.80	.17
		Block of 4 (3077–3080)	4.00	3.50	2.00
❑ 3081	32¢	Breast Cancer Awareness	4.50	1.10	.21
❑ 3082	32¢	James Dean	4.50	1.15	.21

3083–3086

3087

3088
(3089)

3089

Scott No.			Plate Block	Unused	Used
❏ 3083	32¢	Mighty Casey	—	.78	.17
❏ 3084	32¢	Paul Bunyan	—	.78	.17
❏ 3085	32¢	John Henry	—	.78	.17
❏ 3086	32¢	Pecos Bill	—	.78	.17
		Block of 4 (3083–3086)	4.00	3.50	1.80
❏ 3087	32¢	Discus Thrower	4.00	.90	.21
❏ 3088	32¢	Iowa Statehood, water activated	3.10	.80	.21
❏ 3089	32¢	Iowa (~3088), self-adhesive	—	.70	.15
		Booklet pane of 20	—	20.00	—
❏ 3090	32¢	RFD – Rural Free Delivery	3.80	.78	.22

3091–3095

Scott No.			Plate Block	Unused	Used
❑ 3091	32¢	Riverboat – Robert E. Lee	—	.72	.17
❑ 3092	32¢	Riverboat – Sylvan Dell	—	.72	.17
❑ 3093	32¢	Riverboat – Far West	—	.72	.17
❑ 3094	32¢	Riverboat – Rebecca Everingham	—	.72	.17
❑ 3095	32¢	Riverboat – Bailey Gatzert	—	.72	.17
		Strip of 5 (3091–3096)	10.50 (10)	6.00	—

3096–3099

3100–3103

Scott No.			Plate Block	Unused	Used
❑ 3096	32¢	Count Basie	—	.78	.17
❑ 3097	32¢	Tommy & Jimmy Dorsey	—	.78	.17
❑ 3098	32¢	Glenn Miller	—	.78	.17
❑ 3099	32¢	Benny Goodman	—	.78	.17
		Block or strip of 4 (3096–3099)	4.50	4.00	2.00
❑ 3100	32¢	Harold Arlen	—	.80	.15
❑ 3101	32¢	Johnny Mercer	—	.80	.15
❑ 3102	32¢	Dorothy Fields	—	.80	.15
❑ 3103	32¢	Hoagy Carmichael	—	.80	.15
		Block or strip of 4 (3100–3103)	4.75	4.10	2.10

3104

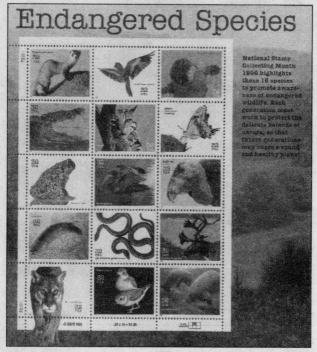

3105

Scott No.			Plate Block	Unused	Used
❏ 3104	23¢	F. Scott Fitzgerald	3.10	.70	.17
❏ 3105	32¢	Endangered Species, pane of 15	—	14.00	8.50
❏ 3105a–o		Any single stamp	—	.80	.21

3106

3107
(3112)

3108–3111
(3113–3116)

Scott No.			Plate Block	Unused	Used
❏ 3106	32¢	Computer Technology	3.50	.80	.21
❏ 3107	32¢	Christmas – Madonna & Child	3.00	.80	.21
❏ 3108	32¢	Family & Fireplace	—	.80	.21
❏ 3109	32¢	Decorating Christmas Tree	—	.80	.21
❏ 3110	32¢	Dreaming of Santa	—	.80	.21
❏ 3111	32¢	Christmas Shopping	—	.80	.21
		Block or strip of 4 (3108–3111)	4.00	3.00	1.90
❏ 3112	32¢	Madonna & Child (~3107), self-adhesive	—	.75	.17
		Booklet pane of 20	—	16.00	—
❏ 3113	32¢	Family & Fireplace (~3108), self-adhesive	—	.75	.21
❏ 3114	32¢	Decorating Tree (~3109), self-adhesive	—	.75	.21
❏ 3115	32¢	Dreaming of Santa (~3110), self-adhesive	—	.75	.21
❏ 3116	32¢	Christmas Shopping (~3111), self-adhesive	—	.75	.21
		Booklet pane of 20 (5 each of 3113–3116)	—	17.00	—

3117

3118

3119

Scott No.			Plate Block	Unused	Used
❏ 3117	32¢	Christmas – Skaters	—	.98	.17
		Booklet pane of 18	—	16.00	—
❏ 3118	32¢	Hanukkah	3.50	.85	.17
❏ 3119	$1	Cycling, souvenir sheet of 2	—	3.00	1.24
		Either single stamp	—	2.10	.92

3120

3121

3122

3123

3124

3125

Scott No.			Plate Block	Unused	Used
1997.					
❏ 3120	32¢	Year of the Ox	3.20	.93	.21
❏ 3121	32¢	Benjamin O. Davis, Sr.	3.20	.93	.21
❏ 3122	32¢	Statue of Liberty	—	.93	.21
		Booklet pane of 20	—	17.00	—
❏ 3123	32¢	Swans	—	1.10	.26
		Booklet pane of 20	—	17.00	—
❏ 3124	55¢	Swans	—	1.60	.26
		Booklet pane of 20	—	28.00	—
❏ 3125	32¢	Helping Children Learn	3.00	.80	.21

3126
(3128)

3127
(3129)

3130

3131

Scott No.			Plate Block	Unused	Used
❏ 3126	32¢	Citron	—	.92	.26
❏ 3127	32¢	Flowering Pineapple	—	.92	.26
		Booklet pane of 20 (10 each 3126–3127)	—	16.00	—
❏ 3128	32¢	Citron (~3126)	—	.92	.32
❏ 3129	32¢	Flowering Pineapple (~3127)	—	.86	.32
		Booklet pane of 5 (2 of 3128; 3 of 3129)	—	6.80	—

NOTE: Nos. 3126–3127 measure 19½ x 26½ mm; Nos. 3128–3129 measure 18½ x 24 mm.

❏ 3130	32¢	Pacific 97 – Ship	—	1.00	.17
❏ 3131	32¢	Pacific 97 – Stagecoach	—	1.00	.17
		Se-tenant pair (3130–3131)	4.00	1.30	.17

Scott No.		PNC Strip (5)	Unused	Used

Coil Stamps. Linerless Self-Adhesive.

❏ 3132	(25¢)	Jukebox (~2911)	15.00	1.00	.47
❏ 3133	32¢	Flag over Porch (~2897)	7.50	1.00	.32

NOTE: Nos. 3121 and 3122 are not mounted on backing paper (liner) as are other self-adhesive coil stamps.

3134

3135

3136

Scott No.			Plate Block	Unused	Used
1997.					
❏ 3134	32¢	Thornton Wilder	3.25	.74	.21
❏ 3135	32¢	Raoul Wallenberg	3.10	.75	.25
❏ 3136	32¢	Dinosaurs, pane of 15	—	12.00	—
❏ 3136a–o		Any single stamp	—	—	.21

3137
(3138)

Scott No.			Plate Block	Unused	Used
❏ 3137	32¢	Bugs Bunny		.50	.16
		Pane of 10	—	8.00	—

NOTE: Die cutting on No. 3137 does not cut into backing.

❏ 3138	32¢	Bugs Bunny (~3137)	—	3.80	.21
		Pane of 10	—	225.00	—

NOTE: Die cutting on No. 3138 cuts through the backing. Used examples of Nos. 3137 and 3138 are identical in appearance. Once removed from backing paper they cannot be distinguished from one another.

❏ 3138c		Booklet pane of 10, right stamp w/o die cut	—	190.00	—

3139

3140

Scott No.			Plate Block	Unused	Used
❑ 3139	50¢	Franklin, pane of 12	—	15.00	—
❑		Single stamp	—	1.80	.80
❑ 3140	60¢	Washington, pane of 12	—	20.00	—
		Single stamp	—	2.00	.90

3141

3142

Scott No.			Plate Block	Unused	Used
❏ 3141	32¢	Marshall Plan	3.40	.80	.21
❏ 3142	32¢	Classic Aircraft, pane of 20	—	17.00	14.00
❏ 3142a–t		Any single stamp	—	.80	.15

3143–3146

Scott No.			Plate Block	Unused	Used
❏ 3143	32¢	Bear Bryant	—	.75	.16
❏ 3144	32¢	Pop Warner	—	.75	.16
❏ 3145	32¢	Vince Lombardi	—	.75	.16
❏ 3146	32¢	George Halas	—	.75	.16
		Block of 4 (3143–3146)	4.00	3.50	2.25
❏ 3147	32¢	Vince Lombardi	2.00	.65	.32
❏ 3148	32¢	Bear Bryant	2.00	.65	.32
❏ 3149	32¢	Pop Warner	2.00	—	.32
❏ 3150	32¢	George Halas	2.00	—	.32

NOTE: Nos. 3147–3150 were issued in individual (not se-tenant) panes and stamps contain a red stripe above the coach's name. Nos. 3143–3146 were issued in se-tenant panes and do not contain a red stripe above the coach's name.

3151

Scott No.			Plate Block	Unused	Used
❑ 3151	32¢	American Dolls, pane of 15	—	15.00	11.00
❑ 3151a–o		Any single stamp	—	.82	.26

3152   3153

3154–3157

Scott No.			Plate Block	Unused	Used
❑ 3152	32¢	Humphrey Bogart	4.00	.90	.21
❑ 3153	32¢	Stars & Strips Forever	3.80	.82	.21
❑ 3154	32¢	Lily Pons	—	.16	.15
❑ 3155	32¢	Richard Tucker	—	.16	.15
❑ 3156	32¢	Lawrence Tibbett	—	.16	.15
❑ 3157	32¢	Rosa Ponselle	—	.16	.15
		Block or strip of 4 (3154–3157)	4.50	3.50	2.10

3158–3165

3166

3167

Scott No.			Plate Block	Unused	Used
❏ 3158	32¢	Leopold Stokowski	—	.78	.17
❏ 3159	32¢	Arthur Fiedler	—	.78	.17
❏ 3160	32¢	George Szell	—	.78	.17
❏ 3161	32¢	Eugene Ormandy	—	.78	.17
❏ 3162	32¢	Samuel Barber	—	.78	.17
❏ 3163	32¢	Ferde Grofé	—	.78	.17
❏ 3164	32¢	Charles Ives	—	.78	.17
❏ 3165	32¢	Louis Moreau Gottschalk	—	.78	.17
		Block of 8 (3158–3163)	10.00 (8)	8.00	4.10
❏ 3166	32¢	Padre Félix Varela	3.25	.75	.21
❏ 3167	32¢	U.S. Air Force	3.25	.82	.26

3168–3172

3173   **3174**   **3175**

3176   **3177**

Scott No.			Plate Block	Unused	Used
❑ 3168	32¢	Phantom of the Opera	—	.77	.17
❑ 3169	32¢	Dracula	—	.77	.17
❑ 3170	32¢	Frankenstein	—	.77	.17
❑ 3171	32¢	The Mummy	—	.77	.17
❑ 3172	32¢	Wolf Man	—	.77	.17
		Strip of 5 (3168–3172)	10.00	4.50	3.00
❑ 3173	32¢	Supersonic Flight	3.10	.78	.21
❑ 3174	32¢	Women in the Military	3.75	.78	.21
❑ 3175	32¢	Kwanzaa	3.10	.78	.21
❑ 3176	32¢	Christmas – Madonna & Child	—	.78	.21
		Booklet pane of 20	—	15.00	—
❑ 3177	32¢	Christmas – Holly	—	.90	.21
		Booklet pane of 20	—	14.50	—

3178

3179

3180

3181

Scott No.			Plate Block	Unused	Used
❑ 3178	$3	Mars Rover, souvenir sheet	—	7.10	3.10
1998.					
❑ 3179	32¢	Year of the Tiger	3.75	.92	.25
❑ 3180	32¢	Alpine Skiing	4.15	.92	.25
❑ 3181	32¢	Madam C.J. Walker	4.10	.92	.25

3182

3183

3184

3185

Scott No.			Plate Block	Unused	Used
Celebrate the Century.					
❑ 3182	32¢	1900s, pane of 15	—	10.00	9.00
❑ 3182a–o		Any single stamp	—	.90	.17
❑ 3183	32¢	1910s, pane of 15	—	11.50	9.10
❑ 3183a–o		Any single stamp	—	.82	.17
❑ 3184	32¢	1920s, pane of 15	—	12.00	9.50
❑ 3184a–o		Any single stamp	—	.82	.17
❑ 3185	32¢	1930s, pane of 15	—	11.00	9.00
❑ 3185a–o		Any single stamp	—	.82	.17

3186

3187

3188

3189

Scott No.			Plate Block	Unused	Used
❏ 3186	33¢	1940s, pane of 15	—	12.50	10.00
❏ 3186a–o		Any single stamp	—	.80	.75
❏ 3187	33¢	1950s, pane of 15	—	12.50	10.00
❏ 3187a–o		Any single stamp	—	.80	.17
❏ 3188	33¢	1960s, pane of 15	—	12.50	9.50
❏ 3188a–o		Any single stamp	—	.80	.17
❏ 3189	33¢	1970s, pane of 15	—	12.50	10.00
❏ 3189a–o		Any single stamp	—	.80	.17

3190   **3191**

Scott No.			Plate Block	Unused	Used
☐ 3190	33¢	1980s, pane of 15	—	12.50	10.00
☐ 3190a–o		Any single stamp	—	.80	.17
☐ 3191	33¢	1990s, pane of 15	—	12.50	10.00
☐ 3191a–o		Any single stamp	—	.80	.17

3192

3193–3197

3198–3202

Scott No.			Plate Block	Unused	Used
1998.					
❏ 3192	32¢	Remember the Maine	4.00	1.00	.21
❏ 3193	32¢	Southern Magnolia	—	1.00	.21
❏ 3194	32¢	Blue Paloverde	—	1.00	.21
❏ 3195	32¢	Yellow Poplar	—	1.00	.21
❏ 3196	32¢	Prairie Crab Apple	—	1.00	.21
❏ 3197	32¢	Pacific Dogwood	—	1.00	.21
		Strip of 5 (3193-3197)	10.00 (10)	3.50	—
❏ 3198	32¢	Black Cascade, 13 Verticals, 1959	—	1.00	.21
❏ 3199	32¢	Untitled, 1965	—	1.00	.21
❏ 3200	32¢	Rearing Stallion, 1928	—	1.00	.21
❏ 3201	32¢	Portrait of a Young Man, c. 1945	—	1.00	.21
❏ 3202	32¢	Un Effet du Japonais, 1945	—	1.00	.21
		Strip of 5 (3198-3202)	9.00	2.50	1.45

3203

3204
(3205)

Scott No.			Plate Block	Unused	Used
❏ 3203	32¢	Cinco de Mayo	3.75	.80	.21
❏ 3204	32¢	Sylvester & Tweety	—	.80	.21
		Pane of 10	—	5.00	—
❏ 3205	32¢	Sylvester & Tweety	—	.80	.21
		Pane of 10	—	6.50	—

NOTE: The stamp in the right panel of No. 3204 contains a die cut; the stamp in the right panel of No. 3205 does not.

3206

Scott No.			Plate Block	Unused	Used
❏ 3206	32¢	Wisconsin Statehood	3.00	.70	.15

3207
(3207A)

3208
(3208A)

Scott No.			PNC Strip (5)	Unused	Used

Coil Stamps.

❏ 3207	(5¢)	Wetlands—Nonprofit Org.	2.20	.25	.19
❏ 3207A	(5¢)	Wetlands (~3207), self-adhesive	2.20	.25	.19
❏ 3208	(25¢)	Diner—Presorted First-Class	6.50	.75	.19
❏ 3208A	(25¢)	Diner (3208), self-adhesive	6.50	.75	.19

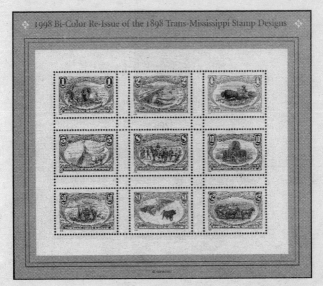

1998 Bi-Color Re-Issue of the 1898 Trans-Mississippi Stamp Designs

3209

Scott No.			Plate Block	Unused	Used
1998.					
☐ 3209		1989 Trans-Mississippi reissue Sheet of 9	—	9.00	6.75
☐ 3209a	1¢	Marquette on the Mississippi	—	.22	.17
☐ 3209b	2¢	Farming in the West	—	.22	.17
☐ 3209c	4¢	Indian Hunting Buffalo	—	.22	.17
☐ 3209d	5¢	Fremont on Rocky Mountains	—	.22	.17
☐ 3209e	8¢	Troops Guarding Train	—	.22	.17
☐ 3209f	10¢	Hardships of Emigration	—	.22	.17
☐ 3209g	50¢	Western Mining Prospector	—	1.00	.26
☐ 3209h	$1	Western Cattle in Storm	—	2.75	.84
☐ 3209l	$2	Mississippi Bridge	—	2.50	1.70

NOTE: The reissued stamps are bicolor and contain the date "1998" in the lower right corner. Stamps of the original issue of 1898 are monocolor and contain no date at lower right. Once separated from their respective sheets, Nos. 3209h and 3210 are indistinguishable.

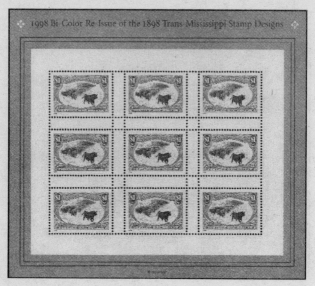

3210

Scott No.			Plate Block	Unused	Used
❑ 3210	$1	Cattle in Storm, sheet of 9	—	24.00	14.00

3211

3212–3215

Scott No.			Plate Block	Unused	Used
❑ 3211	32¢	Berlin Airlift	3.25	.80	.21
❑ 3212	32¢	Leadbelly	—	.80	.21
❑ 3213	32¢	Woody Guthrie	—	.80	.21
❑ 3214	32¢	Sonny Terry	—	.80	.21
❑ 3215	32¢	Josh White	—	.80	.21
		Block or strip of 4 (3212-3215)	4.50	4.10	2.10

3216–3219

3220   **3221**

Scott No.			Plate Block	Unused	Used
❑ 3216	32¢	Mahalia Jackson	—	.80	.21
❑ 3217	32¢	Roberta Martin	—	.80	.21
❑ 3218	32¢	Clara Ward	—	.80	.21
❑ 3219	32¢	Sister Rosetta	—	.80	.21
		Block or strip of 4 (3216–3219)	4.00	3.75	2.00
❑ 3220	32¢	Spanish Settlement	4.00	.92	.22
❑ 3221	32¢	Stephen Vincent Benét	—	.92	.22

3222–3225

3226

3227

3228
(3229)

Scott No.			Plate Block	Unused	Used
❏ 3222	32¢	Antillean Euphonia	—	.72	.17
❏ 3223	32¢	Green-throated Carib	—	.72	.17
❏ 3224	32¢	Crested Honeycreeper	—	.72	.17
❏ 3225	32¢	Cardinal Honeyeater	—	.72	.17
		Block of 4 (3222–3225)	4.25	3.75	2.10
❏ 3226	32¢	Alfred Hitchcock	3.50	.76	.21
❏ 3227	32¢	Organ & Tissue Donation	4.00	.76	.21

Scott No.			PNC Strip (5)	Unused	Used

Coil Stamps.

❏ 3228	(10¢)	Bicycle Handlebar, self-adhesive	4.00	.40	.15
❏ 3229	(10¢)	Bicycle (~3228), water-activated gum	4.00	.42	.15

3230–3234

3235

Scott No.			Plate Block	Unused	Used
1998.					
❏ 3230	32¢	Bright Eyes - Dog	—	.80	.17
❏ 3231	32¢	Bright Eyes - Fish	—	.80	.17
❏ 3232	32¢	Bright Eyes - Cat	—	.80	.17
❏ 3233	32¢	Bright Eyes - Parakeet	—	.80	.17
❏ 3234	32¢	Bright Eyes - Hamster	—	.80	.17
		Strip of 5 (3230–3234)	8.00 (10)	2.40	—
❏ 3235	32¢	Klondike Gold Rush	4.10	.94	.21

3236

Scott No.			Plate Block	Unused	Used
❏ 3236	32¢	American Art, pane of 20	—	24.00	12.50
❏ 3236a–t		Any single stamp	—	.80	.17

3237

3238–3242

3243

3244

Scott No.			Plate Block	Unused	Used
❑ 3237	32¢	Ballet	3.50	.82	.21
❑ 3238	32¢	Futuristic Truck	—	.82	.21
❑ 3239	32¢	Pod-craft in Flight	—	.82	.21
❑ 3240	32¢	Observer in Space Suit	—	.82	.21
❑ 3241	32¢	Planet Rover	—	.82	.21
❑ 3242	32¢	Spaceport Dome	—	.82	.21
		Strip of 5 (3238-3242)	—	3.00	2.10
❑ 3243	32¢	Giving & Sharing	4.50	.70	.17
❑ 3244	32¢	Christmas - Madonna & Child	—	.72	.17
		Booklet pane of 20	—	12.50	—

3245–3248
(3249–3252)

3257
(3258)

Scott No.			Plate Block	Unused	Used
❏ 3245	32¢	Evergreen Wreath	—	.82	.17
❏ 3246	32¢	Victorian Wreath	—	.82	.17
❏ 3247	32¢	Chili Pepper Wreath	—	.82	.17
❏ 3248	32¢	Tropical Wreath	—	.82	.17
		Booklet pane of 20 (3245-3248)	—	6.00	—
❏ 3249	32¢	Evergreen Wreath (~3245)	—	.74	.17
❏ 3250	32¢	Victorian Wreath (~3246)	—	.74	.17
❏ 3251	32¢	Chili Pepper Wreath (~3247)	—	.74	.17
❏ 3252	32¢	Tropical Wreath (~3248)	—	.74	.17
		Block or strip of 4 (3249–3252)	4.00	2.20	—

NOTE: Nos. 3249–3252 measure 23 x 30 mm.

❏ 3257	(1¢)	Weather Vane, white "U.S.A."	.60	.24	.16
❏ 3258	(1¢)	Weather Vane, blue "U.S.A."	.60	.24	.16

3259
(3263, 3353)

3260
(3264–3269)

3261

3262

Scott No.			Plate Block	Unused	Used
❏ 3259	22¢	Uncle Sam	2.40	.50	.21
❏ 3260	(33¢)	Uncle Sam's Hat	4.00	.50	.21
❏ 3261	$3.20	Space Shuttle	30.00	7.00	2.40
❏ 3262	$11.75	Space Shuttle Piggyback	110.00	24.00	9.00

Scott No.			PNC Strip (5)	Unused	Used
Coil Stamps.					
❏ 3263	22¢	Uncle Sam (~3259)	5.00	.70	.17
❏ 3264	(33¢)	Uncle Sam's Hat (~3260), water-activated gum	8.00	.82	.17
❏ 3265	(33¢)	Hat (~3260), self-adhesive, square corners	8.00	.92	.21
❏ 3266	(33¢)	Hat (~3260), self-adhesive, rounded corners	8.50	1.10	.26

Scott No.			Plate Block	Unused	Used
Booklet Stamps.					
❏ 3267	(33¢)	Hat (~3260), die cut 9.9	—	.84	.17
		Booklet pane of 10	—	8.00	—
❏ 3268	(33¢)	Hat (~3260), die cut 11 or 11½	—	1.00	.17
		Booklet pane of 10	—	9.50	—
		Booklet pane of 20	—	15.00	—

Scott No.		Plate Block	Unused	Used
❏ 3269 (33¢)	Hat (~3260), die cut 8	—	.80	.17
	Booklet pane of 10	—	8.10	—
	Booklet pane of 18	—	18.00	—

3270
(3271)

Scott No.		PNC Strip (5)	Unused	Used

Coil Stamps.

❏ 3270 (10¢)	Eagle & Shield, water-activated gum, perforated	4.00	.27	.20
❏ 3271 (10¢)	Eagle & Shield, self-adhesive, die cut	4.10	.27	.20

NOTE: See Nos. 2602–2604 for Eagle & Shield stamps inscribed "USA Bulk Rate" or "Bulk Rate USA."

3272

3273

Scott No.			Plate Block	Unused	Used

1999.

❏ 3272	33¢	Year of the Rabbit	3.50	.85	.22
❏ 3273	33¢	Malcolm X	4.10	.94	.21

3274   **3275**   **3276**   **3277**
(3278,
3279–3282)

Scott No.			Plate Block	Unused	Used
❑ 3274	33¢	Love - Lacy Valentine	—	.95	.21
		Booklet pane of 20	—	16.00	—
❑ 3275	55¢	Love - Lacy Valentine	—	1.10	.21
❑ 3276	33¢	Hospice Care	3.50	.83	.21
❑ 3277	33¢	Flag & City, water-activated gum, perforated	7.50	.83	.21
❑ 3278	33¢	Flag & City (~3277), self-adhesive, black date	—	.83	.20
		Booklet pane of 10	—	9.00	—
		Booklet pane of 20	—	15.00	—
❑ 3279	33¢	Flag & City (~3277), self-adhesive, red date	—	.94	.21
		Booklet pane of 10	—	8.00	—

Scott No.			PNC Strip (5)	Unused	Used

Coil Stamps.

❑ 3280	33¢	Flag & City (~3277), water-activated gum, perforated	7.00	.95	.21
❑ 3281	33¢	Flag & City (~3277), self-adhesive, square corners	7.25	.94	.21
❑ 3282	33¢	Flag & City (~3277), self-adhesive, rounded corners	8.75	.95	.25

| 3283 | 3286 | 3287 |

3288–3292

Scott No.			Plate Block	Unused	Used
1999.					
❑ 3283	33¢	Flag & Chalkboard, self-adhesive	—	.98	.25
		Booklet pane of 18	—	15.00	—
❑ 3286	33¢	Irish Immigration	4.00	.84	.23
❑ 3287	33¢	Alfred Lunt & Lynn Fontanne	3.75	.84	.23
❑ 3288	33¢	Arctic Hare	—	.84	.23
❑ 3289	33¢	Arctic Fox	—	.84	.23
❑ 3290	33¢	Snowy Owl	—	.84	.23
❑ 3291	33¢	Polar Bear	—	.84	.23
❑ 3292	33¢	Gray Wolf	—	.84	.23
		Strip of 5 (3288-3293)	7.50 (10)	4.50	1.65

3293

Scott No.			Plate Block	Unused	Used
❏ 3293	33¢	Sonoran Desert, pane of 10	—	8.00	—
❏ 3293a–j		Any single stamp	—	.84	.22

3294–3297
(3298–3301, 3302–3305)

Scott No.			Plate Block	Unused	Used
❏ 3294	33¢	Blueberries	—	.85	.17
❏ 3295	33¢	Raspberries	—	.85	.17
❏ 3296	33¢	Strawberries	—	.85	.17
❏ 3297	33¢	Blackberries	—	.85	.17
		Booklet pane of 20 (3294-3297)	—	15.00	—

NOTE: Nos. 3294–3297 exist dated either 1999 or 2000. Prices are the same for both. Nos. 3294–3297 are die cut 11½ x 11½. Nos. 3298–3301 are die cut 9½ x 10.

❏ 3298	33¢	Blueberries (~3294)	—	.76	.17
❏ 3299	33¢	Raspberries (~3295)	—	.76	.17
❏ 3300	33¢	Strawberries (~3296)	—	.76	.17
❏ 3301	33¢	Blackberries (~3297)	—	.76	.17
		Booklet pane (3298-3301)	—	4.00	—

Scott No.			PNC Strip (5)	Unused	Used

Coil Stamps.

❏ 3302	33¢	Blueberries (~3294)	—	.78	.18
❏ 3303	33¢	Raspberries (~3295)	—	.78	.18
❏ 3304	33¢	Strawberries (~3296)	—	.78	.18
❏ 3305	33¢	Blackberries (~3297)	—	.78	.18
		Strip of 4 (3302-3305)	4.75	3.00	—

NOTE: See also Nos. 3404–3407. Nos. 3302–3305 contain straight edges at top and bottom; Nos. 3404–3407 contain straight edges at sides.

3306
(3307)

Scott No.			Plate Block	Unused	Used
1999.					
❏ 3306	33¢	Daffy Duck	—	.87	.18
		Pane of 10	—	7.00	—
❏ 3307	33¢	Daffy Duck	—	.84	.18
		Pane of 10, right stamp w/o die cut	—	7.75	—

3308   3309

3310–3313

Scott No.			Plate Block	Unused	Used
❑ 3308	33¢	Ayn Rand	3.50	.84	.21
❑ 3309	33¢	Cinco de Mayo	3.50	.84	.21
❑ 3310	33¢	Bird of Paradise	—	.84	.21
❑ 3311	33¢	Royal Poinciana	—	.84	.21
❑ 3312	33¢	Gloriosa	—	.84	.21
❑ 3313	33¢	Chinese Hibiscus	—	.84	.21
		Booklet pane of 20 (3310-3315)	—	15.00	—

3314

3315

3316

3317–3320

Scott No.			Plate Block	Unused	Used
❏ 3314	33¢	John & William Bartram	3.60	.84	.21
❏ 3315	33¢	Prostate Cancer Awareness	3.60	.84	.21
❏ 3316	33¢	California Gold Rush	3.60	.84	.21
❏ 3317	33¢	Fish - Yellow & Red Fish	—	.84	.21
❏ 3318	33¢	Fish - Fish & Thermometer	—	.84	.21
❏ 3319	33¢	Fish - Blue Fish	—	.84	.21
❏ 3320	33¢	Fish - Hermit Crab	—	.84	.21
		Strip of 4 (3317-3320)	—	3.00	—

3321–3324

3325–3328

Scott No.			Plate Block	Unused	Used
❑ 3321	33¢	Extreme Sports – Skateboarding	—	.87	.17
❑ 3322	33¢	Extreme Sports – BMX Biking	—	.87	.17
❑ 3323	33¢	Extreme Sports – Snowboarding	—	.87	.17
❑ 3324	33¢	Extreme Sports – Inline Skating	—	.87	.17
		Block of 4 (3321–3324)	4.00	3.25	—
❑ 3325	33¢	Free-blown Glass	—	.87	.17
❑ 3326	33¢	Mold-blown Glass	—	.87	.17
❑ 3327	33¢	Pressed Glass	—	.87	.17
❑ 3328	33¢	Art Glass	—	.87	.17
		Block or strip of 4 (3225–3228)	3.50	2.60	1.40

3329

3330

3331

3332

3333–3337

Scott No.			Plate Block	Unused	Used
❑ 3329	33¢	James Cagney	3.50	.80	.24
❑ 3330	33¢	General Billy Mitchell	6.00	.80	.24
❑ 3331	33¢	Honoring Those Who Served	3.50	.80	.24
❑ 3332	45¢	Universal Postal Union	4.50	1.00	.50
❑ 3333	33¢	Trains – the "Daylight"	—	.76	.21
❑ 3334	33¢	Trains – the "Congressional"	—	.76	.18
❑ 3335	33¢	Trains – the "20th Century Limited"	—	.76	.18
❑ 3336	33¢	Trains – the "Hiawatha"	—	.76	.18
❑ 3337	33¢	Trains – the "Super Chief"	—	.76	.18
		Strip of 5 (3333–3337)	10.00 (10)	4.50	1.50

3338

3339–3344

Scott No.			Plate Block	Unused	Used
❏ 3338	33¢	Frederick Law Olmsted	3.50	.80	.21
❏ 3339	33¢	Max Steiner	—	.80	.21
❏ 3340	33¢	Dmitri Tiomkin	—	.80	.21
❏ 3341	33¢	Bernard Herrmann	—	.80	.21
❏ 3342	33¢	Franz Waxman	—	.80	.21
❏ 3343	33¢	Alfred Newman	—	.80	.21
❏ 3344	33¢	Erich Wolfgang Korngold	—	.80	.21
		Block of 6 (3339–3344)	6.50 (6)	5.50	4.00

3345–3350

Scott No.			Plate Block	Unused	Used
❏ 3345	33¢	Ira & George Gershwin	—	.76	.18
❏ 3346	33¢	Lerner & Loewe	—	.76	.18
❏ 3347	33¢	Lorenz Hart	—	.76	.18
❏ 3348	33¢	Rodgers & Hammerstein	—	.76	.18
❏ 3349	33¢	Meredith Willson	—	.76	.18
❏ 3350	33¢	Frank Loesser	—	.76	.18
		Block of 6 (3345–3350)	6.00 (6)	4.75	3.00

INSECTS & SPIDERS

3351

Scott No.			Plate Block	Unused	Used
❏ 3351	33¢	Insects & Spiders, pane of 20	—	16.50	10.00
❏ 3351a–t		Any single stamp	—	.85	.22

3352

Scott No.			Plate Block	Unused	Used
❏ 3352	33¢	Hanukkah	3.50	.80	.22

Scott No.			PNC Strip (5)	Unused	Used

Coil Stamp.

❏ 3353	22¢	Uncle Sam (~3259), water-activated gum, perforated	5.25	.70	.16

3354   **3355**

Scott No.			Plate Block	Unused	Used
1999.					
❏ 3354	33¢	NATO 50th Anniversary	3.50	.84	.21
❏ 3355	33¢	Christmas – Madonna & Child	—	.84	.21
		Booklet pane of 20	—	15.50	—

3356–3359
(3360–3363, 3364–3367)

Scott No.			Plate Block	Unused	Used
❑ 3356	33¢	Leaping Stag, maroon & gold	—	.85	.21
❑ 3357	33¢	Leaping Stag, blue & gold	—	.85	.21
❑ 3358	33¢	Leaping Stag, violet & gold	—	.85	.21
❑ 3359	33¢	Leaping Stag, green & gold	—	.85	.21
		Block or strip of 4			
		(3356–3359)	5.00	3.25	—
❑ 3360	33¢	Stag, maroon & gold (~3356)	—	.85	.21
❑ 3361	33¢	Stag, blue & gold (~3357)	—	.85	.21
❑ 3362	33¢	Stag, violet & gold (~3358)	—	.85	.21
❑ 3363	33¢	Stag, green & gold (3359)	—	.85	.21
		Booklet pane of 20			
		(3360–3363)	—	17.00	—

NOTE: The frameline on Nos. 3356–3369 is narrower than the frameline on Nos. 3360–3363.

❑ 3364	33¢	Stag, maroon & gold (~3356)	—	.86	.21
❑ 3365	33¢	Stag, blue & gold (~3357)	—	.86	.21
❑ 3366	33¢	Stag, violet & gold (~3358)	—	.86	.21
❑ 3367	33¢	green & gold (3359)	—	.86	.21
		Booklet pane of 20			
		(3364–3367)	—	12.75	—

NOTE: Nos. 3364–3367 measure 21 x 18 mm.

3368

3369

3370

3371

Scott No.			Plate Block	Unused	Used
❏ 3368	33¢	Kwanzaa	3.50	.82	.23
❏ 3369	33¢	Infant New Year	3.50	.82	.23
❏ 3370	33¢	Year of the Dragon	3.50	.82	.23
❏ 3371	33¢	Patricia Roberts Harris	3.50	.82	.23

3372

3373–3377

Scott No.			Plate Block	Unused	Used
❑ 3372	33¢	Los Angeles Class Submarine	3.50	.84	.23
❑ 3373	22¢	S Class Submarine	—	.84	.23
❑ 3374	33¢	Los Angeles Class Submarine	—	.84	.23
❑ 3375	55¢	Ohio Class Submarine	—	1.30	.45
❑ 3376	60¢	USS Holland	—	1.30	.45
❑ 3377	$3.20	Gato Class Submarine	—	3.00	2.10
		Booklet pane of 5 (3373–3377)		14.00	2.50
		Intact booklet with 2 panes (3373–3377)		17.00	—

NOTE: No. 3372 contains microprinted letters "USPS" at the base of its conning tower; No. 3374 does not. Each of the two booklet panes in the booklet contain a different marginal text.

3378

3379–3383

Scott No.			Plate Block	Unused	Used
❏ 3378	33¢	Rain Forest, pane of 10	—	8.00	—
❏ 3378a–j		Any single stamp	—	.90	.21
❏ 3379	33¢	Nevelson – Silent Music I	—	.90	.21
❏ 3380	33¢	Nevelson – Royal Tide I	—	.90	.21
❏ 3381	33¢	Nevelson – Black Chord	—	.90	.21
❏ 3382	33¢	Nevelson – Nightsphere Light	—	.90	.21
❏ 3383	33¢	Nevelson – Wedding Chapel I	—	.90	.21
		Strip of 5 (3379–3381)	16.00 (10)	4.00	2.10

3384–3388

3389

3390

Scott No.			Plate Block	Unused	Used
❑ 3384	33¢	Eagle Nebula	—	.81	.22
❑ 3385	33¢	Ring Nebula	—	.81	.22
❑ 3386	33¢	Lagoon Nebula	—	.81	.22
❑ 3387	33¢	Egg Nebula	—	.81	.22
❑ 3388	33¢	Galaxy NGC 1316	—	.81	.22
		Strip of 5 (3384–3388)	15.00 (10)	4.10	2.10
❑ 3389	33¢	American Samoa	3.25	.80	.24
❑ 3390	33¢	Library of Congress	3.50	.83	.24

3391
(3392)

Scott No.			Plate Block	Unused	Used
❑ 3391	33¢	Roadrunner & Wile E. Coyote	—	.86	.32
		Pane of 10	—	7.50	—
❑ 3392	33¢	Roadrunner & Wile E. Coyote	—	.82	.22
		Pane of 10, right stamp			
		w/o die cut	—	10.00	—

3393–3396

3397

3398

Scott No.			Plate Block	Unused	Used
❏ 3393	33¢	Major General John Hines	—	.84	.22
❏ 3394	33¢	General Omar Bradley	—	.84	.22
❏ 3395	33¢	Sergeant Alvin York	—	.84	.22
❏ 3396	33¢	Second Lt. Audie Murphy	—	.84	.22
		Block or strip of 4 (3393–3396)	3.60	3.00	2.00
❏ 3397	33¢	Summer Sports – Runners	—	.80	.21
❏ 3398	33¢	Adoption	—	.80	.21

3399–3402

Scott No.			Plate Block	Unused	Used
❏ 3399	33¢	Basketball	—	.82	.18
❏ 3400	33¢	Football	—	.82	.18
❏ 3401	33¢	Soccer	—	.82	.18
❏ 3402	33¢	Baseball	—	.82	.18
		Block or strip of 4			
		(3399–3402)	4.00	3.00	2.10

THE STARS AND STRIPES

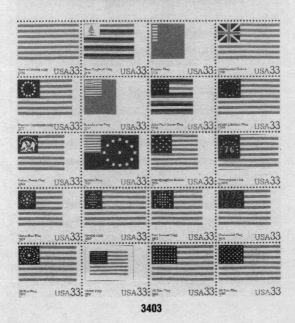

3403

Scott No.			Plate Block	Unused	Used
❏ 3403	33¢	American Flags, pane of 20	—	16.00	11.00
❏ 3403a–t	33¢	Any single stamp	—	.82	.22

Scott No.			PNC Strip (5)		
Coil Stamps.					
❏ 3404	33¢	Blueberries (~3294)	—	.82	.21
❏ 3405	33¢	Strawberries (~3296)	—	.82	.21
❏ 3406	33¢	Blackberries (~3297)	—	.82	.21
❏ 3407	33¢	Raspberries (~3295)	—	.82	.21
		Strip of 4 (3404–3407)	—	4.00	—

NOTE: Nos. 3404–3407 contain straight edges at sides; Nos. 3302–3305 contain straight edges at top and bottom.

3408

Scott No.			Plate Block	Unused	Used
2000.					
❑ 3408	33¢	Baseball, pane of 20	—	15.75	—
❑ 3408a–t	33¢	Any single stamp	—	.85	.22

3409

	3410		**3411**	
Scott No.		Plate Block	Unused	Used
❏ 3409 60¢	Probing the Vastness of Space, souvenir sheet of 6	—	8.50	—
	Any single stamp	—	.88	.22
❏ 3410 $1.00	Exploring the Solar System, souvenir sheet of 5	—	11.50	—
	Any single stamp	—	1.10	.80
❏ 3411 $3.20	Escaping the Gravity of Earth, souvenir sheet of 2	—	15.00	—
	Any single stamp	—	4.15	2.00

3412

3413

Scott No.		Plate Block	Unused	Used
❏ 3412 $11.75	Space Achievement & Exploration, souvenir sheet of 1	—	25.00	18.50
❏ 3413 $11.75	Landing on the Moon, souvenir sheet of 1	—	25.00	18.50

3414–3417

Scott No.			Plate Block	Unused	Used
❏ 3414	33¢	Space Figures	—	.82	.17
❏ 3415	33¢	Heart	—	.82	.17
❏ 3416	33¢	Mommy Are We There Yet	—	.82	.17
❏ 3417	33¢	Space Dog	—	.82	.17
		Strip of 4 (3414–3417)	7.00 (8)	3.20	—

3420 **3426** **3431** **3432**

Distinguished Americans Series.

			Plate Block	Unused	Used
❏ 3420	10¢	General Joseph W. Stillwell	1.15	.25	.20
❏ 3426	33¢	Claude Pepper	3.40	.80	.20
❏ 3431	76¢	Hattie W. Caraway	6.50	1.50	.32
❏ 3432	83¢	Edna Ferber	7.25	1.50	.64

3438

3439–3443

Scott No.			Plate Block	Unused	Used
2000.					
❏ 3438	33¢	California Statehood	3.00	.83	.22
❏ 3439	33¢	Fanfin Anglefish	—	.83	.22
❏ 3440	33¢	Sea Cucumber	—	.83	.22
❏ 3441	33¢	Fangtooth	—	.83	.22
❏ 3442	33¢	Amphipod	—	.83	.22
❏ 3443	33¢	Medusa	—	.83	.22
		Strip of 5 (3438–3443)	8.75 (10)	4.00	—

| | **3444** | **3445** | **3446** |

Scott No.			Plate Block	Unused	Used
❑ 3444	33¢	Thomas Wolfe	3.15	.82	.26
❑ 3445	33¢	White House	3.15	.82	.26
❑ 3446	33¢	Edward G. Robinson	3.15	.82	.26

3447

Scott No.		PNC Strip (5)	Unused	Used
Coil Stamp.				
❑ 3447 (10¢)	New York Public Library Lion	2.50	.40	.22

3448
(3449–3450)

3451

Scott No.		Plate Block	Unused	Used
2000.				
❑ 3448 (34¢)	Flag over Farm, water-activated gum	3.50	.80	.31
❑ 3449 (34¢)	Flag over Farm (~3448), self-adhesive, die cut 11½	4.50	.88	.27
❑ 3450 (34¢)	Flag over Farm (~3448), self-adhesive, die cut 8	—	.88	.17
	Booklet pane of 8	—	.88	—
❑ 3451 (34¢)	Statue of Liberty, self-adhesive	—	.88	.17
	Booklet pane of 20	—	3.10	—

3452
(3453)

Scott No.		PNC Strip (5)	Unused	Used
Coil Stamps.				
❑ 3452 (34¢)	Statue of Liberty, water-activated gum	9.00	.90	.17
❑ 3453 (34¢)	Statue of Liberty, self-adhesive	9.00	.90	.17

3454–3457
(3458–3461)

3466
(3476–3477)

Scott No.		Plate Block	Unused	Used
2000.				
❏ 3454 (34¢)	Flower – Purple	—	.85	.21
❏ 3455 (34¢)	Flower – Tan	—	.85	.21
❏ 3456 (34¢)	Flower – Green	—	.85	.21
❏ 3457 (34¢)	Flower – Red	—	.85	.21
	Booklet pane of 20 (3454–3457)	—	16.00	—
❏ 3458 (34¢)	Flower – Purple (~3454)	—	.82	.19
❏ 3459 (34¢)	Flower – Tan (~3455)	—	.82	.19
❏ 3460 (34¢)	Flower – Green (~3456)	—	.82	.19
❏ 3461 (34¢)	Flower – Red (~3457)	—	.82	.19
	Booklet pane of 6 (3458–3461)	—	3.10	—

Scott No.		PNC Strip (5)	Unused	Used
Coil Stamps.				
❏ 3462 (34¢)	Flower – Green (~3456)	—	.80	.17
❏ 3463 (34¢)	Flower – Red (~3457)	—	.80	.17
❏ 3464 (34¢)	Flower – Tan (~3455)	—	.80	.17
❏ 3465 (34¢)	Flower – Purple (~3454)	—	.80	.17
	Strip of 4 (3462–3465)	3.10	.80	—
❏ 3466 34¢	Statue of Liberty, self-adhesive, rounded corners	4.50	.80	.17

See also No. 3477.

3467
(3468, 3475,
3484, 3484A)

3468A
(3475A)

3469
(3470, 3495)

3471

3472

3473

Scott No.			Plate Block	Unused	Used
2001.					
☐ 3467	21¢	Buffalo, water activated gum	5.00	.95	.16
☐ 3468	21¢	Buffalo, self-adhesive	2.25	.52	.21
☐ 3468A	23¢	George Washington, self-adhesive	2.40	.55	.18
☐ 3469	34¢	Flag over Farm, water-activated gum	2.10	.42	.18
☐ 3470	34¢	Flag over Farm (~3470), self-adhesive, die cut 11½	3.25	.75	.18
☐ 3471	55¢	Art Deco Eagle	5.00	1.25	.18
☐ 3471A	57¢	Art Deco Eagle (~3471)	5.00	1.25	.18
☐ 3472	$3.50	Capitol Dome	32.00	7.50	3.00
☐ 3473	$12.25	Washington Monument	125.00	25.00	10.00

3487–3490

Scott No.			PNC Strip (5)	Unused	Used
Coil Stamps.					
❏ 3475	21¢	Buffalo (~3467), self-adhesive	5.50	.60	.17
❏ 3475A	23¢	George Washington (~3468A), self-adhesive	3.50	.62	.17
❏ 3476	34¢	Statue of Liberty (~3466), water-activated gum	7.50	.76	.17
❏ 3477	34¢	Liberty (~3466), self-adhesive, square corners	6.50	.76	.17
❏ 3478	34¢	Flower – Green	—	.76	.17
❏ 3479	34¢	Flower – Red	—	.76	.17
❏ 3480	34¢	Flower – Tan	—	.76	.17
❏ 3481	34¢	Flower – Purple	—	.76	.17
		Strip of 4 (3478–3481)	6.50	2.50	—

3482
(3483)

Scott No.			Plate Block	Unused	Used
2001.					
❏ 3482	20¢	George Washington, self-adhesive, die cut 11½	—	.55	.17
		Booklet pane of 10	—	4.50	—
❏ 3483	20¢	Washington (~3482), self-adhesive, die cut 10½ x 11½	—	.67	.17
		Booklet pane of 10	—	12.50	—

3485 **3491** **3492**
(3493) (3494)

Scott No.			Plate Block	Unused	Used
❏ 3484	21¢	Buffalo (~3467), self-adhesive, die cut 11½	—	.60	.17
		Booklet pane of 10	—	5.50	—
❏ 3484A	21¢	Buffalo (~3467), self-adhesive, die cut 10½ x 11½	—	.78	.17
		Booklet pane of 10	—	12.00	—
❏ 3485	34¢	Statue of Liberty, self-adhesive, die cut 11	—	.82	.17
		Booklet pane of 10	—	8.00	—
		Booklet pane of 20	—	16.00	—
❏ 3487	34¢	Flower – Purple (~3481)	—	.75	.25
❏ 3488	34¢	Flower – Tan (~3480)	—	.75	.25
❏ 3489	34¢	Flower – Green (~3478)	—	.70	.24
❏ 3490	34¢	Flower – Red (~3479)	—	.70	.24
		Booklet pane of 20 (3487–3480)	—	16.50	—
❏ 3491	34¢	Apple, self-adhesive, die cut 11½	—	.76	.17
❏ 3492	34¢	Orange, self-adhesive, die cut 11½	—	.76	.17
		Booklet pane of 20 (3491–3492)	—	16.50	—
❏ 3493	34¢	Apple (~3491), self-adhesive, die cut 10½ x 11½	—	.81	.17
❏ 3494	34¢	Orange (~3492)), self-adhesive, die cut 10½ x 11½	—	.81	.17
		Booklet pane of 20 (3493–3494)	—	3.50	—
❏ 3495	34¢	Flag over Farm (~3469), self-adhesive, die cut 8	—	.72	.17
		Booklet pane of 18	—	12.00	—

3496

3497
(3498)

3499

3500

3501

Scott No.			Plate Block	Unused	Used
❏ 3496	(34¢)	Love – Rose	—	.75	.17
		Booklet pane of 20	—	16.00	—
❏ 3497	34¢	Love – Rose	—	.77	.17
		Booklet pane of 20	—	15.00	—
❏ 3498	34¢	Love – Rose	—	.75	.17
		Booklet pane of 20	—	6.00	.17

NOTE: No. 3497 measures 19½ x 26½ mm; No. 3498 measures 18 x 21 mm.

❏ 3499	55¢	Love – Rose	5.50	1.00	.36

NOTE: No. 3551 for 57c stamp of similar design.

❏ 3500	34¢	Year of the Snake	3.10	.78	.22
❏ 3501	34¢	Roy Wilkins	3.00	.78	.22

3502

3503

3504

Scott No.			Plate Block	Unused	Used
❏ 3502	34¢	Illustrators, pane of 20	—	18.00	—
❏ 3502a–t		Any single stamp	—	.82	.17
❏ 3503	34¢	Diabetes Awareness	3.25	.82	.17
❏ 3504	34¢	Nobel Prize 1901–2001	3.25	.82	.17

3505

Scott No.			Plate Block	Unused	Used
❏ 3505	34¢	Pan American Inverts, souvenir sheet	—	8.00	7.00
❏ 3505a	1¢	Ship Inverted	—	.37	.27
❏ 3505b	2¢	Train Inverted	—	.37	.27
❏ 3505c	4¢	Automobile Inverted	—	.37	.27
❏ 3505d	80¢	Exposition Seal	—	1.65	1.20

NOTE: Nos. 3505a–3505c can be distinguished from the original errors by the date 2001 at lower left.

3506

3507

3508

3509

Scott No.			Plate Block	Unused	Used
☐ 3506	34¢	Great Plains Prairie, pane of 10	—	7.50	—
☐ 3506a–j		Any single stamp	—	.76	.17
☐ 3507	34¢	Snoopy	4.00	.76	.17
☐ 3508	34¢	Honoring Veterans	3.00	.76	.17
☐ 3509	34¢	Frida Kahlo	3.00	.76	.17

3510–3519

Scott No.			Plate Block	Unused	Used
❏ 3510	34¢	Ebbetts Field	—	.78	.21
❏ 3511	34¢	Tiger Stadium	—	.78	.21
❏ 3512	34¢	Crosley Field	—	.78	.21
❏ 3513	34¢	Yankee Stadium	—	.78	.21
❏ 3514	34¢	Polo Grounds	—	.78	.21
❏ 3515	34¢	Forbes Field	—	.78	.21
❏ 3516	34¢	Fenway Park	—	.78	.21
❏ 3517	34¢	Comisky Park	—	.78	.21
❏ 3518	34¢	Shibe Park	—	.78	.21
❏ 3519	34¢	Wrigley Field	—	.78	.21
		Block of 10 (3510–3519)	8.00 (10)	4.80	—

3520

3521

3522

Scott No.		PNC Strip (5)	Unused	Used
Coil Stamp.				
❏ 3520 (10¢)	Atlas Statue, self-adhesive	3.75	.28	.22

Scott No.		Plate Block	Unused	Used
2001.				
❏ 3521 34¢	Leonard Bernstein	3.00	.62	.18

Scott No.		PNC Strip (5)	Unused	Used
Coil Stamp.				
❏ 3522 (15¢)	Woody Wagon, self-adhesive	3.50	.52	.17

3523

Scott No.		Plate Block	Unused	Used
2001.				
❏ 3523 34¢	Lucille Ball	3.40	.77	.22

AMISH QUILT 34 USA   AMISH QUILT 34 USA   AMISH QUILT 34 USA   AMISH QUILT 34 USA

3524–3527

Venus Flytrap   Yellow Trumpet   Cobra Lily   English Sundew   Venus Flytrap

3528–3531

Scott No.			Plate Block	Unused	Used
❏ 3524	34¢	Amish quilt – Diamond in Square	—	.67	.18
❏ 3525	34¢	Amish quilt – Starburst	—	.67	.18
❏ 3526	34¢	Amish quilt – Diamond Pattern	—	.67	.18
❏ 3427	34¢	Amish quilt – Double Ninepatch Pattern	—	.67	.18
		Block or strip of 4 (3424–3427)	3.60	3.15	—
❏ 3528	34¢	Venus Flytrap	—	.75	.18
❏ 3529	34¢	Yellow Trumpet	—	.75	.18
❏ 3530	34¢	Cobra Lily	—	.75	.18
❏ 3531	34¢	English Sundew	—	.75	.18
		Block or strip of 4 (3528–3531)	3.40	3.10	—

3532

3533

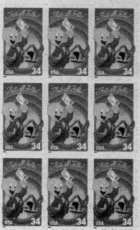

3534
(3535)

Scott No.			Plate Block	Unused	Used
❑ 3532	34¢	Eid Mubarak	3.40	.75	.22
❑ 3533	34¢	Enrico Fermi	3.40	.75	.22
❑ 3534	34¢	Porky Pig	—	.74	.22
		Pane of 10	—	7.40	.22
❑ 3535	34¢	Porky Pig	—	.85	.30
		Pane of 10, right stamp w/o die cut	—	9.75	—

3536

3537–3540
(3541–3544)

Scott No.			Plate Block	Unused	Used
❏ 3536	34¢	Christmas – Madonna & Child	—	.90	.17
		Booklet pane of 20	—	15.00	—
❏ 3537	34¢	Santa & Rocking Horse, black inscription	—	.74	.17
❏ 3538	34¢	Santa & Tree on Shoulder, black inscription	—	.74	.17
❏ 3539	34¢	Santa Holding Tree, black inscription	—	.74	.17
❏ 3540	34¢	Santa Garland on Cap, black inscription	—	.74	.17
		Block of 4 (3537–3540)	4.00	3.00	—
		Booklet pane of 5 (5 of 3540)	—	13.50	—

NOTE: Year date at lower right is smaller on booklet stamps than on those from pane of 20.

❏ 3541	34¢	Santa & Rocking Horse, red & green inscription	—	.67	.17
❏ 3542	34¢	Santa & Tree on Shoulder, red & green inscription	—	.67	.17
❏ 3543	34¢	Santa Holding Tree, red & green inscription	—	.67	.17
❏ 3544	34¢	Santa Garland on Cap, red & green inscription	—	.67	.17
		Booklet pane of 10 (3541–3544)	—	3.50	—

3545

3546

3547

3548

3549
(3550–3550A)

Scott No.			Plate Block	Unused	Used
❏ 3545	34¢	James Monroe	4.00	.90	.22
❏ 3546	34¢	We Give Thanks	4.00	.90	.22
❏ 3547	34¢	Hanukkah (~ 3118)	3.40	.78	.22
❏ 3548	34¢	Kwanzaa (~3175)	3.40	.78	.22
❏ 3549	34¢	United We Stand	—	.78	.22
		Booklet Pane of 20	—	15.00	—

Scott No.			PNC Strip (5)	Unused	Used

Coils Stamps.

❏ 3550	34¢	United We Stand (~3549), self-adhesive, square corners	8.00	.90	.17
❏ 3550A	34¢	United We Stand (~3549), self-adhesive, rounded corners	8.50	.90	.17

Scott No.			Plate Block	Unused	Used

2001.

❏ 3551	57¢	Love – Rose (~3499)	5.50	1.15	.41

3552–3555

3556

3557

3558

3559

3560

Scott No.			Plate Block	Unused	Used
☐ 3552	34¢	Olympics – Ski Jumping	—	.76	.17
☐ 3553	34¢	Olympics – Snowboarding	—	.76	.17
☐ 3554	34¢	Olympics – Ice Hockey	—	.76	.17
☐ 3555	34¢	Olympics – Figure Skating	—	.76	.17
		Block or strip of 4 (3551–3555)	3.50	.76	—
☐ 3556	34¢	Mentoring a Child	3.15	.75	.21
☐ 3557	34¢	Langston Hughes	3.15	.75	.21
☐ 3558	34¢	Happy Birthday	3.15	.75	.21
☐ 3559	34¢	Year of the Horse	3.15	.75	.21
☐ 3560	34¢	West Point	3.15	.75	.21

3561–3610

Scott No.			Plate Block	Unused	Used
❏ 3561–					
3610	34¢	Greetings from America	—	36.00	—
		Any single stamp	—	.80	.22

3611

3612

3613
(3614)

Scott No.			Plate Block	Unused	Used
❏ 3611	34¢	Pine Forest, pane of 10	—	7.20	—
❏ 3611a–j		Any single stamp	—	.78	.17

Scott No.			PNC Strip (5)	Unused	Used
Coil Stamp.					
❏ 3612	(5¢)	American Toleware	2.30	.21	.17
2002.					
❏ 3613	3¢	Red, white & blue Star	4.50	.20	.17
❏ 3614	3¢	Red, white & blue Star (~3613)	3.10	.20	.17

NOTE: On No. 3613 the date appears at lower left; on No. 3614 it appears at lower right.

3620
(3621–3625)

3626–3629

Scott No.		Plate Block	Unused	Used
❑ 3620 (37¢)	Flag, water activated	7.00	.75	.17
❑ 3621 (37¢)	Flag (~3620), self-adhesive	3.00	.75	.17

Scott No.		PNC Strip (5)	Unused	Used
❑ 3622 (37¢)	Flag (~3620), self-adhesive	7.00	.75	.17

Scott No.		Plate Block	Unused	Used
❑ 3623 (37¢)	Flag (~3620), die cut 11.25	—	.75	.18
	Booklet pane of 20	—	15.00	—
❑ 3624 (37¢)	Flag (~3620), die cut 10½ x 10¾	—	.77	.17
	Booklet pane of 4	—	2.00	—
	Booklet pane of 20	—	15.25	—
❑ 3625 (37¢)	Flag (~3620), die cut 8	—	.75	.17
	Booklet pane of 18	—	14.00	—
❑ 3626 (37¢)	Mail Wagon	—	.80	.17
❑ 3627 (37¢)	Locomotive	—	.80	.17
❑ 3628 (37¢)	Automobile	—	.80	.17
❑ 3629 (37¢)	Fire Engine	—	.80	.17
	Booklet pane of 20 (3626-3629)	—	15.00	—

3630
(3631–3636)

Scott No.			Plate Block	Unused	Used
❏ 3630	37¢	Flag	3.00	.77	.17

Scott No.			PNC Strip (5)	Unused	Used
❏ 3631	37¢	Flag (~3630), water activated	7.00	.77	.17
❏ 3632	37¢	Flag (~3630), self-adhesive, die cut 10	7.50	.77	.17
❏ 3633	37¢	Flag (~3630), self-adhesive, die cut 8	6.00	.77	.17

Scott No.			Plate Block	Unused	Used
❏ 3635	37¢	Flag (~3630), die cut 11.25	—	.78	.17
		Booklet pane of 20	—	14.00	—
❏ 3636	37¢	Flag (~3630), die cut 10½ x 10¾	—	1.10	.17
		Booklet pane of 20	—	13.50	—

3638–3641

Scott No.			PNC Strip (5)	Unused	Used
Coil Stamp.					
❏ 3638	37¢	Locomotive	—	.75	.17
❏ 3639	37¢	Mail Wagon	—	.75	.17
❏ 3640	37¢	Fire Engine	—	.75	.17
❏ 3641	37¢	Automobile	—	.75	.17
		Strip of 4 (3638–3642)	12.50	.75	—

Scott No.			Plate Block	Unused	Used
❏ 3642	37¢	Mail Wagon (~3639)	—	.75	.17
❏ 3643	37¢	Locomotive (~3638)	—	.75	.17
❏ 3644	37¢	Automobile (~3641)	—	.75	.17
❏ 3644	37¢	Fire Engine (~3640)	—	.75	.17
		Booklet pane of 4 (3642-3644)	—	4.50	—
		Booklet pane of 20 (3642-3644)	—	13.50	—

3646

3647

3648

❏ 3646	60¢	Eagle	5.50	1.20	.44
❏ 3647	$3.85	Jefferson Memorial	34.00	7.10	3.25
❏ 3648	$13.65	Capitol Dome	100.00	29.00	9.00

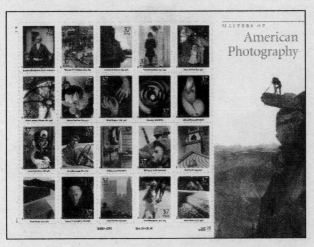

3649

3650

3651

Scott No.			Plate Block	Unused	Used
❏ 3649	37¢	Photography, pane of 20	—	14.00	—
❏ 3649a–t		Any single stamp	—	.77	.17
❏ 3650	37¢	John James Audubon	3.60	.77	.17
❏ 3651	37¢	Harry Houdini	3.60	.77	.17

3652

3653   **3654**   **3655**   **3656**

Scott No.			Plate Block	Unused	Used
❑ 3652	37¢	Andy Warhol	3.75	.72	.27
❑ 3653-56	37¢	Teddy Bears	3.60	.72	.27

3657   **3658**   **3659**

Scott No.			Plate Block	Unused	Used
❑ 3657	37¢	Love Pane of 20	14.00	.72	.28
❑ 3658	60¢	Love SA	6.00	1.10	.36
❑ 3659	37¢	Ogden Nash SA	4.50	.85	.37

3660

| **3661** | **3662** | **3663** | **3664** |

Scott No.			Plate Block	Unused	Used
❏ 3660	37¢	Duke Kahanamoku	12.00	3.30	.60
❏ 3661-64	37¢	American Bats	3.30	2.00	1.00

| **3665** | **3666** | **3667** | **3668** |

Scott No.			Plate Block	Unused	Used
❏ 3665	37¢	Nellie Bly	—	2.70	2.00
❏ 3666	37¢	Ida M. Tarbell	—	2.70	2.00
❏ 3667	37¢	Ethel L. Payne	—	2.70	2.00
❏ 3668	37¢	Marguerite Higgins	—	2.70	2.00
		(block of 4)	4.00	—	—

3669

3670-71

Scott No.			Plate Block	Unused	Used
❑ 3669	37¢	Irving Berlin	3.75	.94	.27
❑ 3670	37¢	Neuter and Spay	3.25	1.00	.72
❑ 3671	37¢	Neuter and Spay	3.25	1.00	.72

3672

3673

3674

3675

Scott No.			Plate Block	Unused	Used
❑ 3672	37¢	Hanukkah SA	3.50	.82	.26
❑ 3673	37¢	Kwanzaa SA	3.50	.82	.26
❑ 3674	37¢	Islamic Festival	3.50	.82	.26
❑ 3675	37¢	Madonna	3.50	.82	.26
		(pane of 20)	14.50	—	—

3676

3677

3678

3679

3680

3681

3682

3683

Scott No.			Plate Block	Unused	Used
❏ 3676-79	37¢	Snowman	2.75	2.60	1.80
❏ 3680-83	37¢	Snowman (strip of 5)	8.00	2.60	1.00

3684

3685

3686

3687

3688

3689

3690

3691

Scott No.			Plate Block	Unused	Used
❏ 3684-87	37¢	Snowman	2.75	2.60	—
❏ 3688-91	37¢	Snowman	3.50	—	—

3692

3693

3694

3695

Scott No.			Plate Block	Unused	Used
❑ 3692	37¢	Cary Grant	3.25	.82	.26
❑ 3693	5¢	Sea Coast (strip of 5)	2.40	.28	.22
❑ 3694	37¢	Hawaiian Missionary	—	3.00	1.60
❑ 3695	37¢	Happy Birthday	3.00	.80	.22

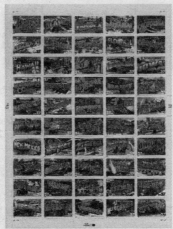

3696-3745

3746

3747

3748

Scott No.			Plate Block	Unused	Used
❑ 3696-3745	37¢	Greetings From America (sheet of 50 singles)	35.00	—	—
❑ 3746	37¢	Thurgood Marshall SA	3.15	.82	.27
❑ 3747	37¢	Year of the Ram SA	3.15	.82	.27
❑ 3748	37¢	Zora Neale Hurston SA	3.15	.82	.27

| 3751 | 3757 | 3766 | 3769 | 3770 |

Scott No.			Plate Block	Unused	Used
❑ 3751	10¢	U.S. Clock	.90	.22	.17
❑ 3757	1¢	Tiffany Lamp		.22	.17
❑ 3766	$1	Wisdom	8.00	2.00	.75
❑ 3769	10¢	New York Public Library	—	.25	.17
❑ 3770	10¢	Atlas	—	.25	.20

| 3771 | 3772 |

Scott No.			Plate Block	Unused	Used
❑ 3771	80¢	Special Olympics	—	1.60	.50
❑ 3772	37¢	American Filmmaking		4.50	3.10
		(sheets of 10)	7.20	—	—

3773   **3774**   **3775**

3776–80

Scott No.			Plate Block	Unused	Used
❑ 3773	37¢	Ohio Statehood	3.75	.70	.22
❑ 3774	37¢	Pelican Island	3.75	.70	.22
❑ 3775	50¢	Seacoast	—	.21	.17
		(strip of 5)	1.60	—	—
❑ 3776–80	37¢	Old Glory	—	.21	.17
		(strip of 5)	3.60	—	—

3781   **3782**

Scott No.			Plate Block	Unused	Used
❑ 3781	37¢	Cesar Chavez SA	3.35	.54	.32
❑ 3782	37¢	Louisiana Purchase SA	3.25	.54	.32

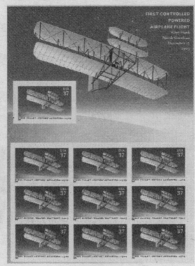

3783

3784

3784A

3785

Scott No.			Plate Block	Unused	Used
❏ 3783	37¢	First Flight	7.50	.52	.32
❏ 3784	37¢	Purple Heart	3.60	.80	.26
❏ 3785	37¢	Sea Coast	3.60	.80	.26

3786

3787–91

Scott No.			Plate Block	Unused	Used
❑ 3786	37¢	Audrey Hepburn	3.50	.80	.26
❑ 3787–91	37¢	Cape Henry Lighthouse	7.75	.80	.26

3792-96

3797–3801

Scott No.			Plate Block	Unused	Used
❏ 3792–96	25¢	Presorted First Class	8.00	5.50	—
❏ 3797–3801	25¢	Presorted (strip of 10)	—	8.00	4.60

3802

3803

3804

3805

3806

3807

Scott No.			Plate Block	Unused	Used
❏ 3802	37¢	Arctic Tundra (strip of 10)	—	8.00	—
❏ 3803	37¢	Korean War	4.75	.70	.25
❏ 3804–07	37¢	Mary Cassatt	4.00	.70	.25

3808–11

3812   3813   3814–18

Scott No.			Plate Block	Unused	Used
❏ 3808–11	37¢	Early Football Heroes	8.00	3.50	—
❏ 3812	37¢	Roy Acuff	4.00	3.25	1.20
❏ 3813	37¢	District of Columbia	8.00	.75	.26
❏ 3814–18	37¢	Reptile (strip of 5)	7.40	.75	.26

3819

3820

3821   **3822**   **3823**   **3824**

3821–24   **3825**   **3826**   **3827**   **3828**

Scott No.			Plate Block	Unused	Used
❑ 3819	37¢	Washington	7.00	.50	.28
❑ 3820	37¢	J. Gossaett Christmas	7.00	.75	.28
❑ 3821–24	37¢	Christmas (strip of 4)	—	8.00	.28
❑ 3821	37¢	Christmas	—	.62	.28
❑ 3822	37¢	Christmas	—	.62	.28
❑ 3823	37¢	Christmas	—	.62	.28
❑ 3824	37¢	Christmas	—	.62	.28
❑ 3825	37¢	ChristmasSA	—	.62	.28
❑ 3826	37¢	ChristmasSA	—	.62	.28
❑ 3827	37¢	ChristmasSA	—	.62	.28
❑ 3828	37¢	ChristmasSA	—	.62	.28

3829

3830

3831

3832

3833

3834

Scott No.			Plate Block	Unused	Used
❑ 3829	37¢	Egret	7.00	.70	.25
❑ 3830	37¢	American Flag	7.00	.70	.25
❑ 3831	37¢	Pacific Coral Reefs	—	.70	.25
❑ 3832	37¢	Year of the Monkey	3.75	.70	.25
❑ 3833	37¢	Candy Hearts Love	—	.70	.25
❑ 3834	37¢	Paul Robeson	3.75	.70	.25

3835

3835 (sheet)

3836

3838

3839

Scott No.			Plate Block	Unused	Used
❏ 3835	37¢	Dr. Seuss	3.60	.70	.25
❏ 3836	37¢	Garden Blossoms	3.60	.70	.25
❏ 3838	37¢	U. S. Air Force Academy	3.60	.70	.25
❏ 3839	37¢	Henry Mancini	3.60	.70	.25

3840–3843

3855

3856

Scott No.			Plate Block	Unused	Used
❏ 3840	37¢	Martha Graham	—	.70	.25
❏ 3841	37¢	Alvin Ailey	—	.70	.25
❏ 3842	37¢	Agnes de Mille	—	.70	.25
❏ 3843	37¢	George Balanchine	—	.70	.25
❏ 3855	37¢	Lewis	—	.70	.25
❏ 3856	37¢	Clark	—	.70	.25

3857–3861

3857–3861 (pane)

Scott No.			Plate Block	Unused	Used
❏ 3857	37¢	Isamu Noguchi-Akari	—	.70	.25
❏ 3858	37¢	Isamu Noguchi-Margaret La Farge Osborn	—	.70	.25
❏ 3859	37¢	Isamu Noguchi-Black Sun	—	.70	.25
❏ 3860	37¢	Isamu Noguchi-Mother & Child	—	.70	.25
❏ 3861	37¢	Isamu Noguchi-Figure	—	.70	.25

3862

3863

3864

3865

Scott No.			Plate Block	Unused	Used
❏ 3862	37¢	World War II Memorial	—	.70	.25
❏ 3863	37¢	Summer Olympic Games	—	.70	.25
❏ 3864	5¢	Sea Coast	—	.30	.15
❏ 3865	37¢	Art of Disney-Goofy, Mickey, Donald	—	.70	.25

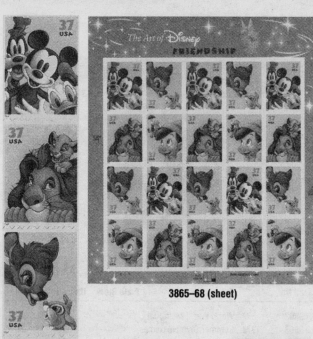

3865–68 (sheet)

3865-3868

3869

3870

Scott No.			Plate Block	Unused	Used
❏ 3866	37¢	Art of Disney-Bambi, Thumper	—	.70	.25
❏ 3867	37¢	Art of Disney-Mufasa, Simba	—	.70	.25
❏ 3868	37¢	Art of Disney-Jiminy, Pinocchio	—	.70	.25
❏ 3869	37¢	USS Constellation	—	.70	.25
❏ 3870	37¢	Buckminster Fuller	—	.70	.25

3871

3872

ART OF THE AMERICAN INDIAN

3873 a–j

3874

3875

Scott No.			Plate Block	Unused	Used
❑ 3871	37¢	James Baldwin	—	.70	.25
❑ 3872	37¢	Martin Johnson Heade	—	.70	.25
❑ 3873	37¢	American Indian Art	—	.70	.25
❑ 3874	37¢	Sea Coast	—	.30	.15
❑ 3875	37¢	Sea Coast	—	.30	.15

3876

3876 (sheet)

3877

3878

Scott No.			Plate Block	Unused	Used
❏ 3876	37¢	John Wayne	—	.70	.25
❏ 3877	37¢	Sickle Cell	—	.70	.25
❏ 3878	37¢	Cloudscapes	—	.70	.25

3879   **3880**   **3881**

3882

3883–3886

Scott No.			Plate Block	Unused	Used
❏ 3879	37¢	Madonna & Child	—	.70	.25
❏ 3880	37¢	Hanukkah	—	.70	.25
❏ 3881	37¢	Kwanzaa	—	.70	.25
❏ 3882	37¢	Moss Hart	—	.70	.25
❏ 3883–86	37¢	Holiday Ornaments	—	.70	.25

SEMIPOSTAL STAMPS

NOTE: The listings include the initial postage value and surtax. The postage value changes to match first class postage as rates increase. In most cases, the surtax decreases by a corresponding amount. When the surtax falls below a certain amount, the Postal Service raises the price of a stamp, such as was the case for the Breast Cancer stamp, which rose from 40¢ to 45¢.

B1

Scott No.			Plate Block	Unused	Used
1998.					
❏ B1	(32¢+8¢)	Breast Cancer	19.00	.76	.21

B2

2002.					
❏ B2	(34¢+11¢)	Heroes of 2001	4.50	.76	.21

AIRMAIL STAMPS

C1
(C2–C3)

Scott No.			Plate Block	Unused	Used
1918. (NH Add 60%)					
❏ C1	6¢	Orange	1400.00 (6)	64.00	31.00
❏ C2	16¢	Green (~C1)	2400.00 (6)	85.00	40.00
❏ C3	24¢	Carmine & Blue (~C1)	2600.00 (12)	85.00	42.00

C4   **C5**   **C6**

1923. (NH Add 60%)					
❏ C4	8¢	Dark Green	520.00 (6)	20.00	12.00
❏ C5	16¢	Dark Blue	3000.00 (6)	86.00	32.00
❏ C6	24¢	Carmine	4000.00 (6)	96.00	30.00

C7
(C8–C9)

1926–1927. (NH Add 60%)					
❏ C7	10¢	Biplanes & Map	80.00 (6)	2.60	.42
❏ C8	15¢	Biplanes & Map (~C7)	80.00 (6)	3.15	2.50
❏ C9	20¢	Biplanes & Map (~C7)	200.00 (6)	10.00	2.10

C10

Scott No.			Plate Block	Unused	Used
1927. (NH Add 60%)					
❑ C10	10¢	Lindbergh	260.00 (6)	7.40	2.10
		Booklet Pane of 3	150.00	81.00	2.50

C11

1928. (NH Add 50%)					
❑ C11	5¢	Beacon	285.00 (8)	4.60	.72

C12
(C16)

1930. Flat Plate Press. (NH Add 60%)					
❑ C12	5¢	Winged Globe, perf 11	280.00 (6)	10.75	.75

C13

C14

C15

Scott No.			Plate Block	Unused	Used
1930. (NH Add 50%)					
❑ C13	65¢	Graf Zeppelin	3500.00 (6)	270.00	210.00
❑ C14	$1.30	Graf Zeppelin	9200.00 (6)	600.00	420.00
❑ C15	$2.60	Graf Zeppelin	14000.00 (6)	850.00	640.00

C17

1931–1932. Rotary Press. (NH Add 60%)					
❑ C16	5¢	Winged Globe (~C12), perf 10½ x 11	130.00	6.40	.55
❑ C17	8¢	Winged Globe, perf 10½ x 11	54.00	2.15	.45

C18

1933. (NH Add 50%)					
❑ C18	50¢	Zeppelin	1250.00 (6)	86.00	80.00

C19

Scott No.			Plate Block	Unused	Used
1934. (NH Add 30%)					
❏ C19	6¢	Winged Globe	41.00	2.60	.22

NOTE: Prices for stamps from 1935 forward are for never-hinged (NH) examples.

C20   **C21**   **C22**

1935–1937.					
❏ C20	25¢	Pan-Am Clipper	36.00 (6)	1.50	1.10
❏ C21	20¢	Pan-Am Clipper	161.00 (6)	8.75	1.50
❏ C22	50¢	Clipper	165.00 (6)	9.00	5.75

C23   **C24**

1938.					
❏ C23	6¢	Eagle & Shield	15.00	.48	.20
1939.					
❏ C24	30¢	Transatlantic Airmail	250.00 (6)	9.50	1.35

C25
(C26–C31)

Scott No.			Plate Block	Unused	Used
1941–1944. Transport Plane Series.					
❑ C25	6¢	Carmine	3.50	.22	.16
❑ C26	8¢	Olive Green (~C25)	1.96	.26	.20
❑ C27	10¢	Violet (~C25)	10.00	1.40	.21
❑ C28	15¢	Brown Carmine (~C25)	14.00	3.20	.35
❑ C29	20¢	Bright Green (~C25)	10.50	2.10	.35
❑ C30	30¢	Blue (~C25)	13.00	3.00	.42
❑ C31	50¢	Orange (~C25)	78.00	12.50	3.60

C32   **C33**   **C34**
(C37)

C35   **C36**

1946–1947.					
❑ C32	5¢	DC-4 Skymaster, large	.90	.23	.17
❑ C33	5¢	DC-4 Skymaster, small	.75	.21	.17
❑ C34	10¢	Pan American Union Building	1.45	.32	.17
❑ C35	15¢	New York Skyline	2.00	.45	.17
❑ C36	25¢	Golden Gate	4.40	1.00	.17

Scott No.			Line Pair	Unused	Used
1948. Coil Stamp.					
❑ C37	5¢	DC-4 Skymaster (~C33)	9.00	1.15	.90

C38

Scott No.			Plate Block	Unused	Used
1948.					
❑ C38	5¢	New York City	4.50	.26	.18

C39
(C41)

C40

1949.					
❑ C39	6¢	DC-4 Skymaster	.96	.24	.18
❑ C40	6¢	Alexandria	.95	.26	.18

Scott No.			Line Pair	Unused	Used
1949. Coil Stamp.					
❑ C41	6¢	DC-4 Skymaster (~C39)	14.00	3.10	.18

C42

C43

C44

C45

Scott No.			Plate Block	Unused	Used
1949.					
❏ C42	10¢	UPU Centennial	1.50	.32	.25
❏ C43	15¢	UPU Centennial	2.00	.40	.30
❏ C44	25¢	UPU Centennial	5.50	.75	.48
❏ C45	6¢	Wright Brothers	1.60	.30	.18

C46

C47

C48
(C50)

			Plate Block	Unused	Used
1952.					
❏ C46	80¢	Diamond Head	30.00	7.00	1.50
1953.					
❏ C47	6¢	Wright Brothers	.85	.24	.18
1954.					
❏ C48	4¢	Eagle in Flight	1.80	.24	.17

C49

C51
(C52, C60–C61)

1957.

❑ C49	6¢	50th Anniversary – Air Force	1.00	.26	.17

1958.

❑ C50	5¢	Eagle in Flight (~C48)	1.40	.24	.17
❑ C51	7¢	Jetliner Silhouette, blue	1.00	.24	.17

Scott No.			Line Pair	Unused	Used
1958. Coil Stamp.					
❑ C52	7¢	Jetliner Silhouette (~C51), blue	17.50	2.30	.24

C53

C54

C55

Scott No.			Plate Block	Unused	Used
1959.					
❑ C53	7¢	Alaska Statehood	.95	.26	.18
❑ C54	7¢	Balloon Jupiter	1.46	.32	.18
❑ C55	7¢	Hawaii Statehood	1.00	.26	.18

C56

Scott No.			Plate Block	Unused	Used
❏ C56	10¢	Pan American Games	2.00	.40	.30

C57   **C58**

C59

1959–1961.

❏ C57	10¢	Liberty Bell	6.75	1.40	.90
❏ C58	15¢	Statue of Liberty	2.00	.50	.21
❏ C59	25¢	Abraham Lincoln	3.50	.70	.18

1960.

❏ C60	7¢	Jetliner Silhouette (~C51), carmine	1.00	.26	.17

Scott No.			Line Pair	Unused	Used

Coil Stamp.

❏ C61	7¢	Jetliner Silhouette (~C51), carmine	40.00	4.00	.30

C62   **C63**   **C64**
                                                (C65)

Scott No.			Plate Block	Unused	Used
1961.					
❏ C62	13¢	Liberty Bell	1.80	.42	.18
❏ C63	15¢	Statue of Liberty	1.90	.42	.18

NOTE: No. C58 contains a border extension around the Statue of Liberty; No. C63 does not.

Scott No.					
1962.					
❏ C64	8¢	Jetliner over Capitol	1.25	.32	.17

Scott No.			Line Pair	Unused	Used
Coil Stamp.					
❏ C65	8¢	Jetliner over Capitol (~C64)	7.00	.45	.17

C66   **C67**   **C68**

Scott No.			Plate Block	Unused	Used
1963.					
❏ C66	15¢	Montgomery Blair	3.15	.72	.62
❏ C67	6¢	Eagle Perched on Rock	1.90	.22	.18
❏ C68	8¢	Amelia Earhart	1.50	.30	.18

C69

Scott No.			Plate Block	Unused	Used
1964.					
❏ C69	8¢	Robert Goddard	2.00	.48	.21

C70   **C71**   **C72**
                                    (C73)

Scott No.			Plate Block	Unused	Used
1967.					
❏ C70	8¢	Alaska Purchase	1.50	.30	.19
❏ C71	20¢	Columbia Jays	3.60	1.00	.18
❏ C72	10¢	Runway of Stars	1.50	.25	.18

Scott No.			Line Pair	Unused	Used
1968. Coil Stamp.					
❏ C73	10¢	Runway of Stars (~C72)	2.00	.36	.18

C74

C75

Scott No.			Plate Block	Unused	Used
1968.					
❏ C74	10¢	50th Anniversary of Airmail	2.70	.48	.20
❏ C75	20¢	USA & Jet	2.70	.50	.20

C76

1969.					
❏ C76	10¢	First Man on the Moon	1.70	.37	.20

C77	C78 (C82)	C79 (C83)	C80

1971–1973.					
❏ C77	9¢	Delta Wing	1.35	.30	.24
❏ C78	11¢	Jetliner	1.60	.32	.18
❏ C79	13¢	Winged Letter	1.50	.32	.18
❏ C80	17¢	Statue of Liberty	2.00	.45	.26

C81

Scott No.			Plate Block	Unused	Used
❑ C81	21¢	USA & Jet	2.40	.60	.18

Scott No.			Line Pair	Unused	Used
Coil Stamps.					
❑ C82	11¢	Jetliner (~C78)	1.00	.42	.19
❑ C83	13¢	Winged Letter (~C79)	1.20	.45	.20

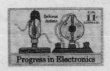

C84	**C85**	**C86**

Scott No.			Plate Block	Unused	Used
1972.					
❑ C84	11¢	City of Refugee	1.55	.32	.21
❑ C85	11¢	Olympics - Skiers	3.50	.34	.18
1973.					
❑ C86	11¢	Progress in Electronics	1.50	.32	.21

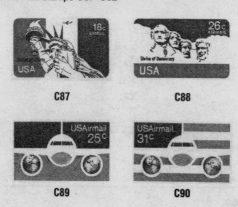

C87   C88

C89   C90

Scott No.			Plate Block	Unused	Used
1974.					
❏ C87	18¢	Statue of Liberty	2.25	.47	.38
❏ C88	26¢	Mount Rushmore	3.10	.70	.20
1976.					
❏ C89	25¢	Jetliner & Globes	3.00	.66	.18
❏ C90	31¢	Jetliner - Stars & Stripes	3.60	.78	.20

C91–92

1979.					
❏ C91	31¢	Wright Bros., large portraits	—	.90	.80
❏ C92	31¢	Wright Bros., small portraits	—	.90	.80
		Pair (C91–C92)	5.00	2.00	.80

C93–94   C95–96   C97

Scott No.			Plate Block	Unused	Used
❏ C93	21¢	Octave Chanute, large portrait	—	.94	.78
❏ C94	21¢	Octave Chanute, small portrait	—	.94	.65
		Pair (C93–C93)	5.00	1.80	.85

1980.

❏ C95	25¢	Wiley Post, large portrait	—	3.00	1.60
❏ C96	25¢	Wiley Post, small portrait	—	3.00	1.60
		Pair (C95–C96)	4.50	1.90	1.60
❏ C97	31¢	Olympics - High Jumper	12.00	.87	.40

C98   C99   C100
(C98A)

1981.

❏ C98	40¢	Philip Mazzei, perf 11	16.00	1.20	.24
❏ C98A	40¢	Philip Mazzei, perf 10½ x 11½	10.50	5.50	2.15
❏ C99	28¢	Blanche Stuart Scott	11.00	.86	.24
❏ C100	35¢	Glenn Curtiss	13.00	.95	.24

C101–104

C105–108

Scott No.			Plate Block	Unused	Used
1983.					
❑ C101	28¢	Olympics - Gymnastics	—	1.30	.32
❑ C102	28¢	Olympics - Hurdles	—	1.30	.32
❑ C103	28¢	Olympics - Basketball	—	1.30	.32
❑ C104	28¢	Olympics - Soccer	—	1.30	.32
		Block of 4 (C101–C104)	6.00	5.50	3.40
❑ C105	40¢	Olympics - Shot Put	—	1.15	.32
❑ C106	40¢	Olympics - Gymnast on Rings	—	1.15	.32
❑ C107	40¢	Olympics - Swimming	—	1.15	.32
❑ C108	40¢	Olympics - Weight Lifting	—	1.15	.32
		Block of 4 (C105–C108)	7.50	6.00	3.60

C109–112

Scott No.			Plate Block	Unused	Used
☐ C109	35¢	Olympics - Fencing	—	1.10	.26
☐ C110	35¢	Olympics - Cycling	—	1.10	.26
☐ C111	35¢	Olympics - Volleyball	—	1.10	.26
☐ C112	35¢	Olympics - Pole Vault	—	1.10	.26
		Block of 4 (C109–C112)	7.75	4.60	2.60

C113

C114

C115

C116

1985.

☐ C113	33¢	Alfred V. Verville	4.25	1.00	.26
☐ C114	39¢	Lawrence & Elmer Sperry	4.75	1.10	.25
☐ C115	44¢	Transatlantic Airmail Clipper	6.50	1.15	.32
☐ C116	44¢	Junipero Serra	9.00	1.35	.50

C117

C118

C119

Scott No.			Plate Block	Unused	Used
1988.					
❏ C117	44¢	New Sweden	9.00	1.45	.74
❏ C118	45¢	Samuel Langley	6.00	1.40	.30
❏ C119	36¢	Igor Sikorsky	5.50	1.10	.38

C120

C121

1989.					
❏ C120	45¢	French Revolution	5.50	1.30	.55
❏ C121	45¢	Carved Figure	6.50	1.30	.40

C122–125

20th Universal Postal Congress

A glimpse at several potential mail delivery methods of the future is the theme of these four stamps issued by the U.S. in commemoration of the convening of the 20th Universal Postal Congress in Washington, D.C. from November 13 through December 14, 1989. The United States, as host nation to the Congress for the first time in ninety-two years, welcomed more than 1,000 delegates from most of the member nations of the Universal Postal Union to the major international event.

©USPS 1989

C126

Scott No.			Plate Block	Unused	Used
❑ C122	45¢	Shuttle in Flight	—	1.32	.34
❑ C123	45¢	Hovercraft	—	1.32	.34
❑ C124	45¢	Moon Rover	—	1.32	.34
❑ C125	45¢	Shuttle Docking	—	1.32	.32
		Block of 4 (C122–C125)	7.75	6.50	4.40
❑ C126	$1.80	Souvenir sheet (~C122–C125)	—	6.00	4.50
❑ C126a-d		Any single stamp, imperforate	—	1.10	.35

C127

Scott No.			Plate Block	Unused	Used
1990.					
❏ C127	45¢	Tropical Beach	8.00	1.50	.46

C128

C129
(C132)

C130

C131

1991.					
❏ C128	50¢	Harriet Quimby	7.10	1.50	.46
❏ C129	40¢	William Piper	6.00	1.20	.45
❏ C130	50¢	Antarctic Treaty	7.00	1.45	.62
❏ C131	50¢	Crossing from Asia	6.50	1.40	.50
❏ C132	40¢	William Piper (~C129)	31.00	2.10	.67

NOTE: On No. C132, the top of Piper's hair touches the top of the stamp; on No. C129, it does not.

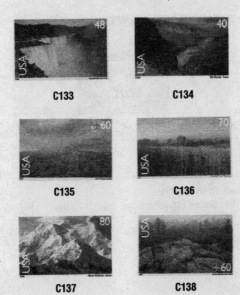

C133

C134

C135

C136

C137

C138

Scott No.			Plate Block	Unused	Used
1993.					
❑ C133	48¢	Niagara Falls	5.00	1.20	.32
❑ C134	40¢	Rio Grande	4.50	1.00	.45
❑ C135	60¢	Grand Canyon	7.00	1.40	.32
❑ C136	70¢	Nine Mile Prairie	8.00	1.60	.46
❑ C137	80¢	Mount McKinley	8.50	1.70	.50
❑ C138	60¢	Acadia National Park	6.00	1.50	.40

AIRMAIL SPECIAL DELIVERY STAMPS

CE1
(CE2)

Scott No.			Plate Block	Unused	Used
❏ CE1	16¢	Great Seal, blue	22.00 (6)	.75	.72
❏ CE2	16¢	Seal (~CE1), red & blue	8.25 (6)	.70	.45

SPECIAL DELIVERY STAMPS

E1

E2
(E3)

E4
(E5)

E6
(E08–E11)

Scott No.			Plate Block	Unused	Used
1885. (NH Add 100%)					
❏ E1	10¢	Blue, inscribed "At Any Special Delivery Office"	—	200.00	26.00
1888. (NH Add 100%)					
❏ E2	10¢	Blue, inscribed "At Any Post Office"	—	180.00	12.00
1893. (NH Add 100%)					
❏ E3	10¢	Orange (~E2)	—	98.00	12.00
1894. (NH Add 100%)					
❏ E4	10¢	Blue, line below "Ten Cents"	—	400.00	22.00
1895. Double Line Watermark. (NH Add 100%)					
❏ E5	10¢	Blue (~E4)	—	130.00	3.00
1902. Double Line Watermark. (NH Add 100%)					
❏ E6	10¢	Bicycle Messenger	—	92.00	3.10

E7	**E12**
(E08–E11)	(E13, E15–E18)

E14
(E19)

Scott No.			Plate Block	Unused	Used

1908. (NH Add 80%)

❏ E7	10¢	Mercury's Helmet	—	46.00	32.00

1911. Perforated 12, Single Line Watermark. (NH Add 80%)

❏ E8	10¢	Bicycle Messenger (~E6)	—	80.00	4.75

1914. Perforated 10, Single Line Watermark. (NH Add 80%)

❏ E9	10¢	Bicycle Messenger (~E6)	—	140.00	6.00

1916. Perforated 10, Unwatermarked. (NH Add 80%)

❏ E10	10¢	Pale Ultramarine (~E6)	—	225.00	25.00

1917. Perforated 11, Unwatermarked. (NH Add 80%)

❏ E11	10¢	Ultramarine (~E6)	155.00 (6)	15.00	1.25

1922–1925. Perforated 11. (NH Add 80%)

❏ E12	10¢	Motorcycle Messenger	300.00 (6)	30.00	.24
❏ E13	10¢	Deep Orange (~E12)	240.00 (6)	22.00	1.35
❏ E14	20¢	Special Delivery Truck	38.00 (6)	2.75	1.20

1927–1951. Perforated 11 x 10½. (NH Add 50%)

❏ E15	10¢	Gray Violet (~E12)	5.50	.80	.16
❏ E16	15¢	Orange (~E12)	5.20	.92	.16
❏ E17	13¢	Blue (~~E12)	4.00	.75	.25
❏ E18	17¢	Yellow (~E12)	21.00	3.20	1.50
❏ E19	20¢	Black (~E14)	8.25	1.45	.20

NOTE: Prices for stamps from 1935 forward are for never-hinged (NH) examples.

E20
(E21)

E22
(E23)

Scott No.			Plate Block	Unused	Used
1954-1971.					
❏ E20	20¢	Letter & Hand, blue	3.75	.74	.15
❏ E21	30¢	Letter & Hand (~E20), maroon	3.50	.80	.20
❏ E22	45¢	Stylized Arrows	6.25	1.60	.32
❏ E23	60¢	Stylized Arrows (~E22)	6.25	1.50	.20

REGISTERED MAIL STAMP

F1

Scott No.			Plate Block	Unused	Used
1911.					
❏ F1	10¢	Eagle	6.00 (6)	48.00	6.25

CERTIFIED MAIL STAMP

FA1

Scott No.			Plate Block	Unused	Used
1955.					
❏ FA1	10¢	Letter Carrier	6.00	.60	.40

POSTAGE DUE STAMPS

NOTE: Prices for unused stamps issued before 1890 are for examples without original gum. Examples with original gum command a premium, which can amount to as much as 50 percent or more. Beware regummed examples. Prices are for sound stamps. Those with faults or defects sell for much less.

J1
(J2–J28)

Scott No.			Unused	Used

1879.

			Unused	Used
❏ J1	1¢	Brown	29.00	4.75
❏ J2	2¢	Brown (~J1)	210.00	6.00
❏ J3	3¢	Brown (~J1)	30.00	4.00
❏ J4	5¢	Brown (~J1)	310.00	24.00
❏ J5	10¢	Brown (~J1)	410.00	16.00
❏ J6	30¢	Brown (~J1)	250.00	26.00
❏ J7	50¢	Brown (~J1)	350.00	29.00

1884–1889.

			Unused	Used
❏ J15	1¢	Red Brown (~J1)	30.00	3.50
❏ J16	2¢	Red Brown (~J1)	36.00	3.25
❏ J17	3¢	Red Brown (~J1)	500.00	92.00
❏ J18	5¢	Red Brown (~J1)	330.00	17.00
❏ J19	10¢	Red Brown (~J1)	300.00	15.00
❏ J20	30¢	Red Brown (~J1)	115.00	30.00
❏ J21	50¢	Red Brown (~J1)	850.00	90.00

1891–1893.

			Unused	Used
❏ J22	1¢	Bright Claret (~J1)	18.00	.80
❏ J23	2¢	Bright Claret (~J1)	18.00	.82
❏ J24	3¢	Bright Claret (~J1)	45.00	4.00
❏ J25	5¢	Bright Claret (~J1)	58.00	5.25
❏ J26	10¢	Bright Claret (~J1)	82.00	12.50
❏ J27	30¢	Bright Claret (~J1)	290.00	86.00
❏ J28	50¢	Bright Claret (~J1)	310.00	94.00

J29
(J30–J68)

Scott No.			Unused	Used
1894. (NH Add 60%)				
❑ J29	1¢	Vermilion	1500.00	370.00
❑ J30	2¢	Vermilion (~J29)	600.00	155.00
❑ J31	1¢	Claret (~J29)	43.00	6.00
❑ J32	2¢	Claret (~J29)	42.00	3.10
❑ J33	3¢	Claret (~J29)	130.00	26.00
❑ J34	5¢	Claret (~J29)	250.00	29.00
❑ J35	10¢	Claret (~J29)	225.00	24.00
❑ J36	30¢	Claret (~J29)	310.00	90.00
❑ J37	50¢	Claret (~J29)	1200.00	290.00
1895. Perforated 12, Double Line Watermark. (NH Add 60%)				
❑ J38	1¢	Claret (~J29)	6.50	.60
❑ J39	2¢	Claret (~J29)	6.50	.60
❑ J40	3¢	Claret (~J29)	47.00	1.80
❑ J41	5¢	Claret (~J29)	45.00	2.00
❑ J42	10¢	Claret (~J29)	66.00	3.50
❑ J43	30¢	Claret (~J29)	450.00	44.00
❑ J44	50¢	Claret (~J29)	310.00	33.00
1910–1912. Perforated 12, Single Line Watermark. (NH Add 60%)				
❑ J45	1¢	Claret (~J29)	30.00	3.00
❑ J46	2¢	Claret (~J29)	32.00	1.00
❑ J47	3¢	Claret (~J29)	460.00	25.00
❑ J48	5¢	Claret (~J29)	75.00	6.50
❑ J49	10¢	Claret (~J29)	94.00	9.00
❑ J50	50¢	Claret (~J29)	800.00	92.00

Scott No.			Unused	Used

1914–1916. Perforated 10, Single Line Watermark. (NH Add 50%)

			Unused	Used
❑ J52	1¢	Carmine (~J29)	45.00	9.50
❑ J53	2¢	Carmine (~J29)	42.00	.70
❑ J54	3¢	Carmine (~J29)	720.00	39.00
❑ J55	5¢	Carmine (~J29)	32.00	2.50
❑ J56	10¢	Carmine (~J29)	46.00	2.00
❑ J57	30¢	Carmine (~J29)	200.00	14.00
❑ J58	50¢	Carmine (~J29)	7000.00	760.00

1916. Perforated 10, Unwatermarked. (NH Add 80%)

			Unused	Used
❑ J59	1¢	Rose (~J29)	2100.00	270.00
❑ J60	2¢	Rose (~J29)	130.00	21.00

Scott No.			Plate Block	Unused	Used

1917–1926. Perforated 11, Unwatermarked. (NH Add 60%)

			Plate Block	Unused	Used
❑ J61	1¢	Carmine Rose (~J29)	35.00 (6)	2.00	.24
❑ J62	2¢	Carmine Rose (~J29)	36.00 (6)	1.75	.35
❑ J63	3¢	Carmine Rose (~J29)	100.00 (6)	10.00	.34
❑ J64	5¢	Carmine Rose (~J29)	90.00 (6)	9.00	.24
❑ J65	10¢	Carmine Rose (~J29)	78.00 (6)	12.00	.45
❑ J66	30¢	Carmine Rose (~J29)	400.00 (6)	67.00	.45
❑ J67	50¢	Carmine Rose (~J29)	660.00 (6)	100.00	.35
❑ J68	½¢	Dull Red (~J29)	12.00 (6)	2.00	.35

J69
(J70–J76, J79–J86)

1930–1931. Perforated 11. (NH Add 60%)

			Plate Block	Unused	Used
❑ J69	½¢	Carmine	40.00 (6)	3.50	1.50
❑ J70	1¢	Carmine (~J69)	36.00 (6)	3.40	.30
❑ J71	2¢	Carmine (~J69)	50.00 (6)	3.75	.35
❑ J72	3¢	Carmine (~J69)	210.00 (6)	24.00	2.40
❑ J73	5¢	Carmine (~J69)	215.00 (6)	18.00	1.90

J77
(J78, J87)

Scott No.			Plate Block	Unused	Used
❏ J74	10¢	Carmine (~J69)	480.00 (6)	37.00	1.00
❏ J75	30¢	Carmine (~J69)	1200.00 (6)	128.00	1.60
❏ J76	50¢	Carmine (~J69)	1200.00 (6)	110.00	1.00
❏ J77	$1	Carmine	210.00 (6)	24.00	1.00
❏ J78	$5	Carmine (~J77)	300.00 (6)	30.00	.21

1931–1956. Perforated 10½ x 11 or 11 x 10½. (NH Add 45%)

❏ J79	½¢	Carmine (~J69)	26.00	1.10	.22
❏ J80	1¢	Carmine (~J69)	2.60	.30	.16
❏ J81	2¢	Carmine (~J69)	2.10	.30	.17
❏ J82	3¢	Carmine (~J69)	3.20	.35	.21
❏ J83	5¢	Carmine (~J69)	4.75	.60	.21
❏ J84	10¢	Carmine (~J69)	10.00	1.30	.21
❏ J85	30¢	Carmine (~J69)	55.00	8.00	.27
❏ J86	50¢	Carmine (~J69)	80.00	16.00	.27
❏ J87	$1	Red (~J77)	240.00	43.00	.30

NOTE: Prices for stamps from this point forward are for never-hinged (NH) examples.

J89
(J88, J90–J104)

Scott No.			Plate Block	Unused	Used
1959.					
❏ J88	½¢	Red & Black (~J89)	200.00	1.50	1.40
❏ J89	1¢	Red & Black	.90	.30	.20

Scott No.			Plate Block	Unused	Used
❏ J90	2¢	Red & Black (~J89)	.55	.25	.18
❏ J91	3¢	Red & Black (~J89)	.65	.23	.16
❏ J92	4¢	Red & Black (~J89)	1.00	.22	.16
❏ J93	5¢	Red & Black (~J89)	.90	.22	.16
❏ J94	6¢	Red & Black (~J89)	1.30	.25	.16
❏ J95	7¢	Red & Black (~J89)	1.80	.30	.16
❏ J96	8¢	Red & Black (~J89)	1.60	.30	.16
❏ J97	10¢	Red & Black (~J89)	1.65	.25	.16
❏ J98	30¢	Red & Black (~J89)	4.50	.90	.20
❏ J99	50¢	Red & Black (~J89)	6.00	1.10	.16
❏ J100	$1	Red & Black (~J89)	11.00	2.30	.16
❏ J101	$5	Red & Black (~J89)	60.00	12.00	.30

1978.

❏ J102	11¢	Red & Black (~J89)	3.80	.60	.50
❏ J103	13¢	Red & Black (~J89)	3.10	.60	.50

1985.

❏ J104	17¢	Red & Black (~J89)	40.00	.65	.50

U.S. OFFICES IN CHINA

K1 Surcharge Style 1   K1 Surcharge Style 2

Scott No.			Plate Block	Unused	Used

1919. New values surcharged (Style 1) on Washington-Franklin Series Stamps. (NH Add 75%)

❑ K1	2¢	On 1¢ green	27.00 (6)	20.00	22.00
❑ K2	4¢	On 2¢ rose	26.00 (6)	20.00	22.00
❑ K3	6¢	On 3¢ violet	54.00 (6)	36.00	50.00
❑ K4	8¢	On 4¢ brown	72.00 (6)	41.00	50.00
❑ K5	10¢	On 5¢ blue	78.00 (6)	47.00	50.00
❑ K6	12¢	On 6¢ orange	88.00 (6)	65.00	60.00
❑ K7	14¢	On 7¢ black	98.00 (6)	62.00	94.00
❑ K8	16¢	On 8¢ olive bistre	85.00 (6)	50.00	62.00
❑ K8a	16¢	On 8¢ olive green	80.00 (6)	52.00	52.00
❑ K9	18¢	On 9¢ orange red	82.00 (6)	52.00	62.00
❑ K10	20¢	On 10¢ yellow orange	76.00 (6)	47.00	54.00
❑ K11	24¢	On 12¢ brown carmine	80.00 (6)	56.00	60.00
❑ K11a	24¢	On 12¢ claret brown	104.00 (6)	66.00	90.00
❑ K12	30¢	On 15¢ gray	100.00 (6)	66.00	95.00
❑ K13	40¢	On 20¢ ultramarine	125.00 (6)	100.00	145.00
❑ K14	60¢	On 30¢ orange red	135.00 (6)	92.00	134.00
❑ K15	$1	On 50¢ violet	650.00 (6)	410.00	48.00
❑ K16	$2	On $1 violet brown	470.00 (6)	340.00	420.00

1922. New Values Surcharged (Style 2) on Washington-Franklin Series Stamps. (NH Add 75%)

❑ K17	2¢	On 1¢ green	110.00 (6)	94.00	85.00
❑ K18	4¢	On 2¢ carmine	110.00 (6)	82.00	80.00

OFFICIAL STAMPS

NOTE: Prices for unused stamps issued before 1890 are for examples without original gum. Examples with original gum command a premium, which can amount to as much as 50 percent or more. Beware regummed examples. Prices are for sound stamps. Those with faults or defects sell for much less.

Official stamps of the nineteenth century (O1–O120) for the various departments utilize the same portraits with each group inscribed for its department. The Post Office Department stamps (O47–O56) are the exception and utilize a different design.

| | | O1 | O2 | O3 | O4 | O5 |
| | | | | | | |

| | | O6 | O7 | O8 | O9 |

Scott No.			Unused	Used

1873. Agriculture Department, Continental Bank Note Co. Printing, Hard Thin Paper.

	Scott No.			Unused	Used
❏	O1	1¢	Yellow	96.00	80.00
❏	O2	2¢	Yellow	65.00	30.00
❏	O3	3¢	Yellow	80.00	12.00
❏	O4	6¢	Yellow	62.00	20.00
❏	O5	10¢	Yellow	100.00	75.00
❏	O6	12¢	Yellow	200.00	115.00
❏	O7	15¢	Yellow	175.00	120.00
❏	O8	24¢	Yellow	180.00	100.00
❏	O9	30¢	Yellow	215.00	120.00

O10 **O15** **O24** **O25**

Scott No.			Unused	Used

1873. Same Portraits as O1–O5, but inscribed Executive Department, Continental Bank Note Co. Printing, Hard Thin Paper.

❑ O10	1¢	Carmine	410.00	210.00
❑ O11	2¢	Carmine	300.00	140.00
❑ O12	3¢	Carmine	310.00	130.00
❑ O13	6¢	Carmine	500.00	340.00
❑ O14	10¢	Carmine	500.00	390.00

1873. Same Portraits as Nos. O1–O7, but inscribed Interior Department, Continental Bank Note Co. Printing, Hard Thin Paper.

❑ O15	1¢	Vermilion (~O1)	27.00	6.00
❑ O16	2¢	Vermilion (~O2)	22.00	7.50
❑ O17	3¢	Vermilion (~O3)	33.00	4.00
❑ O18	6¢	Vermilion (~O4)	27.00	3.40
❑ O19	10¢	Vermilion	27.00	10.00
❑ O20	12¢	Vermilion	40.00	4.75
❑ O21	15¢	Vermilion	56.00	10.00
❑ O22	24¢	Vermilion	45.00	9.00
❑ O23	30¢	Vermilion	60.00	10.00
❑ O24	90¢	Vermilion	132.00	30.00

1873. Same Portraits as Nos. O1–O9, but inscribed Department of Justice, Continental Bank Note Co. Printing, Hard Thin Paper.

❑ O25	1¢	Purple	82.00	58.00
❑ O26	2¢	Purple	135.00	55.00
❑ O27	3¢	Purple	135.00	13.00
❑ O28	6¢	Purple	110.00	22.00
❑ O29	10¢	Purple	160.00	56.00
❑ O30	12¢	Purple	115.00	32.00
❑ O31	15¢	Purple	190.00	100.00
❑ O32	24¢	Purple	575.00	215.00
❑ O33	30¢	Purple	500.00	170.00
❑ O34	90¢	Purple	725.00	350.00

O35   **O47**

Scott No.			Unused	Used

1873. Same Portraits as Nos. O1–O9, but inscribed Navy Department, Continental Bank Note Co. Printing, Hard Thin Paper.

			Unused	Used
❑ O35	1¢	Ultramarine	52.00	27.00
❑ O36	2¢	Ultramarine	48.00	16.00
❑ O37	3¢	Ultramarine	41.00	7.50
❑ O38	6¢	Ultramarine	42.00	11.00
❑ O39	7¢	Ultramarine	270.00	130.00
❑ O40	10¢	Ultramarine	60.00	22.00
❑ O41	12¢	Ultramarine	66.00	26.00
❑ O42	15¢	Ultramarine	120.00	45.00
❑ O43	24¢	Ultramarine	140.00	49.00
❑ O44	30¢	Ultramarine	110.00	25.00
❑ O45	90¢	Ultramarine	450.00	160.00

1873. Post Office Department, Continental Bank Note Co. Printing, Hard Thin Paper.

			Unused	Used
❑ O47	1¢	Black	10.00	6.00
❑ O48	2¢	Black (~O47)	12.00	5.00
❑ O49	3¢	Black (~O47)	3.50	.90
❑ O50	6¢	Black (~O47)	13.00	3.50
❑ O51	10¢	Black (~O47)	48.00	20.00
❑ O52	12¢	Black (~O47)	28.00	5.10
❑ O53	15¢	Black (~O47)	32.00	10.00
❑ O54	24¢	Black (~O47)	38.00	8.00
❑ O55	30¢	Black (~O47)	42.00	11.00
❑ O56	90¢	Black (~O47)	50.00	11.00

057   068   072
(O69–071)

Scott No.			Unused	Used

1873. Same Portraits as Nos. O1–O9, but inscribed State Department, Continental Bank Note Co. Printing, Hard Thin Paper.

❑ 057	1¢	Green	84.00	38.00
❑ 058	2¢	Green	160.00	74.00
❑ 059	3¢	Green	65.00	13.00
❑ 060	6¢	Green	58.00	16.00
❑ 061	7¢	Green	120.00	42.00
❑ 062	10¢	Green	95.00	31.00
❑ 063	12¢	Green	140.00	65.00
❑ 064	15¢	Green	130.00	48.00
❑ 065	24¢	Green	300.00	120.00
❑ 066	30¢	Green	310.00	89.00
❑ 067	90¢	Green	510.00	165.00
❑ 068	$2	Green	620.00	—
❑ 069	$5	Green & Black (~068)	4500.00	2100.00
❑ 070	$10	Green & Black (~068)	2500.00	1500.00
❑ 071	$20	Green & Black (~068)	2200.00	1200.00

1873. Same Portraits as Nos. O1–O9, but inscribed Treasury Department, Continental Bank Note Co. Printing, Hard Thin Paper.

❑ 072	1¢	Brown	30.00	3.60
❑ 073	2¢	Brown	34.00	3.50
❑ 074	3¢	Brown	28.00	7.10
❑ 075	6¢	Brown	32.00	3.10
❑ 076	7¢	Brown	70.00	15.00
❑ 077	10¢	Brown	71.00	9.00
❑ 078	12¢	Brown	70.00	6.00
❑ 079	15¢	Brown	57.00	6.00
❑ 080	24¢	Brown	300.00	47.00

Scott No.			Unused	Used
☐ O81	30¢	Brown	92.00	6.00
☐ O82	90¢	Brown	110.00	7.50

O83

1873. Same Portraits as Nos. O1–O9, but inscribed War Department, Continental Bank Note Co. Printing, Hard Thin Paper.

☐ O83	1¢	Rose	89.00	8.40
☐ O84	2¢	Rose	90.00	7.80
☐ O85	3¢	Rose	95.00	4.00
☐ O86	6¢	Rose	240.00	4.50
☐ O87	7¢	Rose	93.00	40.00
☐ O88	10¢	Rose	36.00	12.00
☐ O89	12¢	Rose	110.00	7.00
☐ O90	15¢	Rose	27.00	9.10
☐ O91	24¢	Rose	28.00	7.00
☐ O92	30¢	Rose	27.00	6.00
☐ O93	90¢	Rose	57.00	25.00

1879. Agriculture Department, American Bank Note Co. Printing, Soft Porous Paper.

☐ O94	1¢	Yellow (~O1)	2300.00	—
☐ O95	3¢	Yellow (~O3)	2100.00	41.00

1879. Same Portraits as Nos. O1–O8, but inscribed Interior Department, American Bank Note Co. Printing, Soft Porous Paper.

☐ O96	1¢	Vermilion	180.00	1200.00
☐ O97	2¢	Vermilion	4.00	.92
☐ O98	3¢	Vermilion	380.00	.86
☐ O99	6¢	Vermilion	600.00	3.10
☐ O100	10¢	Vermilion	57.00	42.00
☐ O101	12¢	Vermilion	92.00	62.00
☐ O102	15¢	Vermilion	210.00	130.00
☐ O103	24¢	Vermilion	2100.00	—

Scott No.			Unused	Used

1879. Same Portraits as Nos. O3 & O4, but inscribed Department of Justice, American Bank Note Co. Printing, Soft Porous Paper.

| ❏ O106 | 3¢ | Purple | 71.00 | 42.00 |
| ❏ O107 | 6¢ | Purple | 180.00 | 100.00 |

1879. Post Office Department, American Bank Note Co. Printing, Soft Porous Paper.

| ❏ O108 | 3¢ | Black (~O47) | 12.00 | 4.00 |

1879. Same Portraits as Nos. O3–O9, but inscribed Treasury Department, American Bank Note Co. Printing, Soft Porous Paper.

❏ O109	3¢	Brown	34.00	3.75
❏ O110	6¢	Brown	60.00	21.00
❏ O111	10¢	Brown	96.00	34.00
❏ O112	30¢	Brown	800.00	170.00
❏ O113	90¢	Brown	1100.00	165.00

1879. Same Portratis as Nos. O1–O9, but inscribed War Department, American Bank Note Co. Printing, Soft Porous Paper.

❏ O114	1¢	Rose	2.60	2.00
❏ O115	2¢	Rose	3.40	1.00
❏ O116	3¢	Rose	3.00	.95
❏ O117	6¢	Rose	3.75	.88
❏ O118	10¢	Rose	27.00	20.00
❏ O119	12¢	Rose	22.00	7.50
❏ O120	30¢	Rose	75.00	47.00

0121
(O122–O126)

0127
(O128–O152)

Scott No.			Unused	Used
1910–1911. Postal Savings Stamps. Double Line Watermark.				
❑ O121	2¢	Black	12.00	1.50
❑ O122	50¢	Dark Green (~121)	122.00	32.00
❑ O123	$1	Ultramarine (~121)	120.00	9.50
Postal Savings Stamps. Single Line Watermark.				
❑ O124	1¢	Dark Violet (~121)	8.50	1.60
❑ O125	2¢	Black (~121)	40.00	6.10
❑ O126	10¢	Carmine (~121)	18.00	2.10

Scott No.			Plate Block	Unused	Used
1983–1985. Engraved.					
❑ O127	1¢	Great Seal	.90	.25	.18
❑ O128	4¢	Great Seal (~O127)	.90	.25	.18
❑ O129	13¢	Great Seal (~O127)	2.20	.50	.45
❑ O130	17¢	Great Seal (~O127)	2.60	.50	.45
❑ O132	$1	Great Seal (~O127)	11.00	3.20	1.10
❑ O133	$5	Great Seal (~O127)	48.00	12.00	7.00

Scott No.			PNC Strip (5)	Unused	Used
Coil Stamps.					
❑ O135	20¢	Great Seal (~O127)	18.00	2.75	.65
❑ O136	22¢	Great Seal (~O127)	12.00	1.50	.92

Scott No.			Plate Block	Unused	Used
1985.					
❑ O138 (14¢)		"D" & Great Seal (~O127)	36.00	4.25	3.65

Scott No.			PNC Strip (5)	Unused	Used
Coil Stamps.					
❏ O138A 15¢	Great Seal (~O127)		—	.65	.55
❏ O138B 20¢	Great Seal (~O127)		—	.68	.55
❏ O139 (22¢)	"D" & Great Seal (~O127)		46.00	4.10	2.70
❏ O140 (25¢)	"E" & Great Seal (~O127)		—	1.20	.80
❏ O141 25¢	Great Seal (~O127)		—	1.10	.62

Scott No.			Plate Block	Unused	Used
1989. Lithographed.					
❏ O143 1¢	Great Seal (~O127)		—	.24	.17

Scott No.			PNC Strip (5)	Unused	Used
Coil Stamps.					
❏ O144 29¢	Great Seal (~O127)		—	1.70	.87
❏ O145 29¢	Great Seal (~O127)		—	1.25	.50

Scott No.			Plate Block	Unused	Used
1991. Lithographed.					
❏ O146 4¢	Great Seal (~O127)		—	.42	.22
❏ O146A 10¢	Great Seal (~O127)		—	.85	.47
❏ O147 19¢	Great Seal (~O127)		—	.86	.60
❏ O148 23¢	Great Seal (~O127)		—	.70	.52
❏ O151 $1	Great Seal (~O127)		—	3.50	2.00

O153
(O154–O157)

Scott No.			PNC Strip (5)	Unused	Used
Coil Stamps.					
❑ O152	(32¢)	"G" & Great Seal (~O127)	—	1.15	.92
❑ O153	32¢	Great Seal	—	1.35	.85

NOTE: No. O153 contains a line of micro-type below the Great Seal.

Scott No.			Plate Block	Unused	Used
1995-2001.					
❑ O154	1¢	Great Seal (~O153)	—	.45	.18
❑ O155	20¢	Great Seal (~O153)	—	.85	.60
❑ O156	23¢	Great Seal (~O153)	—	.92	.65

NOTE: Nos. O154–O156 contain a line of micro-type below the Great Seal.

Scott No.			PNC Strip (5)	Unused	Used
1999-2002. Coil Stamps.					
❑ O157	33¢	Great Seal (~O153)	—	.75	.60
❑ O158	34¢	Great Seal (~O127)	—	.82	.48

NOTE: No. O157 contains a line of micro-type below the Great Seal.

PARCEL POST STAMPS

Q1

Q2

Q3

Q4

Q5

Q6

Q7

Q8

Q9

Q10

Q11

Q12

Scott No.			Plate Block	Unused	Used
1912–1913. (NH Add 85%)					
❑ Q1	1¢	P.O. Clerk	84.00 (6)	3.90	1.15
❑ Q2	2¢	City Carrier	95.00 (6)	3.50	1.00
❑ Q3	3¢	Railway Clerk	170.00 (6)	9.50	4.10
❑ Q4	4¢	Rural Carrier	650.00 (6)	28.00	3.00
❑ Q5	5¢	Mail Train	675.00 (6)	26.00	2.00
❑ Q6	10¢	Steamship	680.00 (6)	40.00	2.40
❑ Q7	15¢	Mail Truck	375.00 (6)	55.00	11.00
❑ Q8	20¢	Airplane	475.00 (6)	110.00	20.00
❑ Q9	25¢	Manufacturing	425.00 (6)	54.00	6.00
❑ Q10	50¢	Dairying	1500.00 (6)	225.00	32.00
❑ Q11	75¢	Harvesting	700.00 (6)	75.00	28.00
❑ Q12	$1	Fruit Growing	1200.00 (6)	265.00	26.00

PARCEL POST POSTAGE DUE STAMPS

JQ1
(JQ2–JQ5)

Scott No.			Plate Block	Unused	Used
1912.	(NH Add 80%)				
❑ JQ1	1¢	Dark Green	360.00 (6)	9.00	4.00
❑ JQ2	2¢	Dark Green (~JQ1)	450.00 (6)	62.00	12.00
❑ JQ3	5¢	Dark Green (~JQ1)	450.00 (6)	15.00	4.50
❑ JQ4	10¢	Dark Green (~JQ1)	1100.00 (6)	135.00	43.00
❑ JQ5	25¢	Dark Green (~JQ1)	725.00 (6)	115.00	4.50

SPECIAL HANDLING STAMPS

QE1
(QE2–QE5)

Scott No.			Plate Block	Unused	Used
1925–1929.	(NH Add 66%)				
❑ QE1	10¢	Yellow Green	28.00 (6)	1.50	1.10
❑ QE2	15¢	Yellow Green (~QE1)	32.00 (6)	2.10	1.10
❑ QE3	20¢	Yellow Green (~QE1)	42.00 (6)	2.40	1.60
❑ QE4	25¢	Yellow Green (~QE1)	200.00 (6)	19.00	7.10
❑ QE4A	25¢	Deep Green (~QE1)	275.00 (6)	25.00	6.50

FEDERAL DUCK STAMPS

Courtesy of Sam Houston Duck Company
P. O. Box 820087, Houston, TX 77282
(Specialized duck catalog
$3.00, refundable with purchase)

JUST WHAT ARE DUCK STAMPS?

The federal duck stamp was created through a wetlands conservation program. President Herbert Hoover signed the Migratory Bird Conservation Act in 1929 to authorize the acquisition and preservation of wetlands as waterfowl habitat.

The law, however, did not provide a permanent source of funds to buy and preserve wetlands. On March 16, 1934, Congress passed, and President Franklin Roosevelt signed, the Migratory Bird Hunting Stamp Act. Popularly known as the Duck Stamp Act, the bill's whole purpose was to generate revenue designated for one specific use: acquiring wetlands for what is now known as the National Refuge System.

It has been proven that sales of duck stamps increase when the public has been informed of how the revenue generated through stamp sales is used.

Jay N. "Ding" Darling, a conservationist and Pulitzer Prize–winning political cartoonist, was appointed the head of the Duck Stamp Program. Darling's pencil sketch of mallards alighting was used on the first duck stamp. The same design was reproduced on Scott 2092, a commemorative marking the 50th anniversary of the Migratory Bird Hunting Stamp Act.

In reality, a "duck stamp" is a permit to hunt, basically a receipt for payment of fees collected. Funds generated are used for the preservation and conservation of wetlands.

The term "duck stamp" is a shortened term for the message "Migratory Bird Hunting and Conservation Stamp," which appears on the federal duck stamp.

In fact, use of the word "duck" is inaccurate, since many migratory waterfowl, including geese, swans, brants, and more, are intended to benefit from the sale of duck stamps.

WHO ISSUES DUCK STAMPS?

Federal duck stamps are now issued by the U.S. Fish and Wildlife Service, Department of Interior United States Government, and have been issued by all states. Currently, 41 states issue duck stamps.

Many foreign countries, including Canada and its provinces, Australia, Russia, Iceland, the United Kingdom, Costa Rica, Hungary, Venezuela, Italy, Argentina, Belgium, Mexico, Ireland, Spain, Israel, Croatia, and New Zealand have issued duck stamps.

The issuing authorities within the various governments that release duck stamps are usually conservation and wildlife departments. These programs must be created by some form of legislation for the resulting stamps to be accepted as a valid governmental issue.

Labels featuring ducks are also issued by various special interest groups, such as Ducks Unlimited, the National Fish and Wildlife Foundation, and the National Wildlife Federation. Their issues are referred to as "society stamps." These items technically are not duck stamps, because the fee structure and disposition of funds are not legislated. However, society stamps are very collectible and often appreciate in value. Funds raised by these organizations are also used for waterfowl and conservation efforts.

Valid organizations and societies of this type perform a major service to conservation by their donations and efforts, and they merit public support.

WHEN ARE DUCK STAMPS ISSUED?

Duck stamps are issued once a year. In most states, hunters are required to purchase both a federal and state stamp before hunting waterfowl.

Waterfowl hunting seasons vary, but most begin in September or October, so naturally, stamps are needed prior to opening day of the hunting season.

Currently, the federal stamp and more than half of the state stamps are issued in July. Some are issued on the first day of the new year, and a few at the last minute in September or early October.

THE COST OF DUCK STAMPS

The annual federal duck stamp had a face value of $1 in 1934, jumped to $2 in 1949, and to $3 in 1959. In 1972 the price increased to $5, then up to $7.50 in 1979, $10 in 1987, $12.50 in 1989, and to $15 beginning in 1991.

For every $15 stamp sold, the federal government retains $14.70 for wetlands acquisition and conservation, so very little gets lost in the system for overhead.

Most state conservation stamps have a face value of $5. South Dakota has the lowest price at $3.00 and Louisiana's non-resident is the highest at $25.00.

Funds generated from state stamps are designated for wetlands restoration and preservation, much like the federal funds, but with a more localized purpose.

Most state agencies sell their stamps at face value. However, some also charge a premium to collectors buying single stamps, to help cover overhead costs. Some states also produce special limited editions for collectors.

FORMAT OF STAMPS

The federal stamp is presently issued in panes of 20 stamps. Originally, the stamps were issued in panes of 28, but because of a change in the printing method (and to make stamps easier to count) the 30-stamp format was adopted in 1959. Then switched to 20 in 2000.

Beginning in 1998, the department of the Interior also issued a single-sheet, self-adhesive Federal stamp to be used in ATM machines and to ease handling in sporting good stores.

Most states and foreign governments follow the federal format. Many states issue a ten-stamp pane for ease of handling and mailing to field offices.

TYPES OF STAMPS

Currently, 41 states issue stamps, of which 12 issue one for collectors and another for hunter use.

Collector stamps are usually in panes of 10 or 30 without tabs. Hunter-type stamps are usually issued in panes of five or 10, many with tabs attached. Hunters use the tabs to list their name, address, age, and other data. Some states use only serial numbers to designate their hunter-type stamp.

State stamps are therefore referred to as either collector stamps or hunter-type stamps. Most dealers will distinguish between these types on their price lists. Separate albums exist for both types and are available from most dealers.

Plate blocks, better described as control number blocks, are designations given to a block of stamps, usually four, with a plate or control number present on the selvage. Such a block is usually located in one or all four corners of a pane. Federal stamps prior to 1959 plus the 1964 issue are collected in blocks of six and must have selvage on two sides.

Governors' Editions have been issued by several state agencies as a means of raising additional income. These stamps are printed in small quantities, most fewer than 1,000. They have a face value of approximately $50, and are imprinted with the name of the state governor.

Governors also hand-sign a limited number of stamps. These are usually available at a premium, generally twice the price of normal singles. Hand-signed or autographed stamps are issued in very small quantities and are scarce to rare.

Governors' Editions are valid for hunting by all issuing states thus far. Obviously none would be used for that purpose, however, as it would destroy the mint condition and lower the value of the stamp.

Artist-Signed Stamps are mint examples of duck stamps autographed by the artist responsible for the artwork on the stamp. Such stamps are rapidly gaining popularity with collectors, and most can be purchased for a small premium over mint examples.

Early federal stamps are particularly valuable and difficult to acquire. Signed stamps by artists now deceased also command a substantial premium.

Printed Text Stamps are another popular collectible. Generally, these preceded the later pictorial issues. The term is applied to stamps required for duck hunting that contain only writing but no waterfowl illustration.

Certain American Indian reservations and tribes also issue waterfowl hunting stamps. The stamps of these sovereign Indian nations allow holders to hunt on that reservation when a federal stamp also is purchased. Reservation stamps are becoming increasingly popular with collectors as more people discover their existence.

ERRORS

With the printing of such a large number of stamps year after year by many different states and printing agencies, errors do occur, but are seldom found. A few federal stamps are known to exist with major errors, but only a few, namely on the 1934, 1946, 1955, 1957, 1959, 1962, 1982, 1986, 1990, 1991, and 1993 issues.

Stamps without perforations, with missing or incorrect color, missing or inverted writing on the reverse are all major errors. Smaller flaws, such as color shifts, misplaced perforations, hickeys (or donuts), and other such anomalies are termed freaks, rather than errors. These, too, are collectible and have value, but they do not command the same attention as major errors. Major errors are extremely rare and exist in small numbers. All errors and freaks on duck stamps are very desirable and add a great deal of interest and value to a collection.

HOW TO COLLECT DUCK STAMPS

The first basic rule is to remember that stamp collecting is very personal. You can make your own rules.

Most collectors prefer to collect mint condition duck stamps. Others prefer collecting stamps on licenses, autographed stamps, plate blocks, stamps signed by hunters, art prints, souvenir cards, first day covers, or a combination. The bottom line, however, is to collect what interests you.

Quality is a very important factor in a stamp collection. This applies not only to duck stamps, but all types. Preserving the mint condition of a stamp is crucial for determining value. A perfectly centered stamp will usually sell for a substantial premium over a stamp with normal centering. Fine to very fine is the norm in stamp collecting, and is the condition priced by Scott.

Care should be taken not to damage a stamp, including the gum. The mint state of a stamp includes the freshness and original gum, so stamp mounts should be utilized when placing a stamp in your album. When a stamp has never been hinged, the abbreviation "NH" is used by dealers.

COLLECTORS ORGANIZATION

The National Duck Stamp Collectors Society exists for the benefit of those who collect duck stamps. Dues are $20 a year and are tax exempt. The NDSCS issues a quarterly newsletter and provides a membership card and lapel pin. Send your $20 directly to the NDSCS, Membership Chairman, P.O. Box 43, Harleysville, PA 19438.

Bob Dumaine is a recognized expert in duck stamps, founder of the National Duck Stamp Collectors Society, writer for *Stamp Collector,* publisher of *The Duck Report,* a past judge in the Federal Duck Stamp Contest, and serves on the expertizing committee of Professional Stamp Experts and recently co-authored an award-winning 208 page book, *The Duck Stamp Story.* Dumaine is the owner of Sam Houston Duck Co., a firm that specializes in duck stamps and related material.

Request your copy of their award-winning Duck Stamp Catalog—80 color illustrated pages jam-packed with information on federal and state duck stamps, artist-signed stamps, prints, conservation issues and much more. Catalog $5.00, refundable with first order.

Sam Houston Duck Company, P.O. Box 820087, Houston, TX 77282; 1-800-231-5926; Fax 1-281-496-1445. Visit our Web site at www. shduck.com.

FEDERAL DUCK STAMP DUCKLINGS

The Junior Duck Stamp Program, a nonprofit organization to promote interest among young people, recently unveiled the design of its first federal junior duck stamp. The program also includes a conservation education curriculum that helps students of all ages. It focuses on wildlife conservation and management, wildlife art, and philately. As an outgrowth, the Junior Duck Stamp Design Competition was developed during 1993.

The resulting stamp, unlike the federal issue, is not valid as a revenue, but emulates the federal program in terms of art selection and the creation of stamps, prints, and other items for sale. All proceeds from the

junior duck stamp go to the United States Fish and Wildlife Foundation to
further its efforts.

The winning design for the first junior duck stamp was submitted
by 16-year-old Jason Parsons of Canton, Ill. His highly realistic colored-
pencil rendition of a male redhead duck was selected from 1,045 entries
in Illinois, then competed nationally. He was honored by a special trip to
Washington, D.C., along with one parent and his art teacher, Scott
Snowman. There Parsons was guest at a special reception where the
second- and third-place winners also were honored.

DUCK STAMP AGENCIES

Courtesy of Sam Houston Duck Co.
(approximate issue month follows state name)

Alabama, (8) Accounting Section, Duck Stamp, Dept. of Conservation &
Natural Resources, 64 N. Union, Montgomery, AL 36130, (334)242-3469.

Alaska, (7) State of Alaska, Dept. of Fish & Game, Licensing Section,
P.O. Box 25525, Juneau, AK 99802-5525, (907)465-2376.

Arizona, (7) Game & Fish Dept., 2222 W. Greenway Rd., Phoenix,
AZ 85023, (602)942-3000.

Arkansas, (7) Game & Fish Commission, Collector Stamps, 2 Natural
Resources Dr., Little Rock, AR 72205, (501)223-6300.

California, (9) Dept. of Fish & Game, License Section, 3211 S. St.,
Sacramento, CA 95816, (916)227-2278.

Colorado, (7) Colorado Wildlife Heritage Foundation, P.O. Box 211512,
Denver, CO 80022, (303)291-7212

Connecticut, (9) Wildlife Division, Dept. of Environmental Protection,
79 Elm St., Hartford, CT 06106, (860)424-3011.

Delaware, (7) Divison of Fish & Wildlife, Box 1401, Dover, DE 19903,
(302)739-5296.

Florida, (7) Game & Fish Comm, Finance, Sect., 620 S. Meridian St.,
Tallahassee, FL 32399-1600, (850)488-5878.

Georgia, (-) Dept. of Natural Resources, 2189 North Lake Pkwy. Bldg.
10 Ste. 108, Tucker, GA 30084, (770)414-3333. (Last stamp issued 1999.)

Hawaii, (9) Division of Forestry & Wildlife, 1151 Punch Bowl St.,
Honolulu, HI 96813, (808)587-4187.

Idaho, (-) Collector Stamps, Idaho Dept. of Fish & Game, Box 25, Boise,
ID 83707, (208)334-3717. (Last stamp issued 1998.)

Illinois, (3) Illinois Dept. of Natural Resources, P.O. Box 19459,
Springfield, IL 62794-9459, (217)785-0972.

Indiana, (12) Indiana Division of Fish & Wildlife, License Section (Stamp). 402 W. Washington Rm. W273, Indianapolis, IN 46204-2267, (317)232-4080.

Iowa, (12) Dept. of Natural Resources, Wallace State Office Building, Des Moines, IA 50319, (515)281-5918.

Kansas, (3) Fish & Game, Pratt Headquarters, 512 SE 25th Ave., Pratt, KS 67124, (316)672-0735.

Kentucky, (9) Dept. of Fish & Wildlife Resources, License Section, Arnold L. Mitchell Bldg., 1 Game Farm Rd., Frankfort, KY 40601, (502)564-7863.

Louisiana, (6) Dept. of Wildlife & Fisheries, P.O. Box 98000, ATTN: Licensing Section, Baton Rouge, LA 70898-9000, (225)765-2347.

Maine, (8) Dept. of Inland Fisheries & Wildlife, 284 State St., State House Station 41, Augusta, ME 04333, (207)287-8000.

Maryland, (8) Dept. of Natural Resources, Licensing & Registration Services, Box 1869, Annapolis, MD 21404, (410)260-8205.

Massachusetts, (12) Division of Fisheries & Game, License Section, 251 Causeway St., Suite 400, Boston, MA 02114-2104, (617)626-1590.

Michigan, (4) Duck Hunters Assn., P.O. Box 200, Midland, MI 48640, (989)631-0151.

Minnesota, (3) Dept. of Natural Resources, License Bureau, 500 Lafayette Rd., St. Paul, MN 55155-4026, (651)296-0701.

Mississippi, (7) Dept. of Wildlife, Fish & Parks, Waterfowl Stamp Coordinator, Box 451, Jackson, MS 39205-0451, (601)432-2400.

Missouri, (-) Dept. of Conservation, Fiscal Section, Box 180, Jefferson, MO 65105, (573)751-4115. (Last stamp issued in 1996.)

Montana, (-) Dept. of Fish, Wildlife & Parks, P.O. Box 200701, Helena, MT 59620-0701, (406)444-2612

Nebraska, (-) Game & Parks Commission, License Section, P.O. Box 30370, Lincoln, NE 68503, (402)471-0641. (Last stamp issued in 1995.)

Nevada, (10) Div. of Wildlife, ATTN: License Office, Stamp Sales, 1100 Valley Rd., Reno, NV 89512, (775)688-1500.

New Hampshire, (8) Fish & Game Dept., License Section, 2 Hazen Dr., Concord, NH 03301, (603)271-6832.

New Jersey, (7) Division of Fish & Wildlife, Waterfowl Stamp, P.O. Box 400, Trenton, NJ 08625-0400, (609)292-2965.

New Mexico, (-) Dept. of Game & Fish, State Capitol, Villagra Bldg., Santa Fe, NM 87503, (505)827-7920. (Last stamp issued in 1994.)

New York, (-) Dept. of Conservation, Division Headquarters, 625 Broadway, Albany, NY 12233-4750, (518)457-4480. (Last stamp issued in 2002.)

North Carolina, (7) Wildlife Resources Commission, Direct Sales Unit, P.O. Box 29565, Raleigh, NC 27626, (919)773-2881.

North Dakota, (7) Game & Fish Dept., Collector Stamps 100 N. Bismark Expressway, Bismark, ND 58501, (701)328-6334.

Ohio, (8) Division of Wildlife, License Section, 1840 Belcher Rd., Columbus, OH 43224-1329, (614)265-6300.

Oklahoma, (8) Dept. of Wildlife Conservation, P.O. Box 53465, Oklahoma City, OK 73152, (405)521-4629.

Oregon, (11) Dept. of Fish & Wildlife, Box 59, Portland, OR 97207, (503)872-5720 ext 5461.

Pennsylvania, (3) Game Commission, License Section, 2001 Elmerton Ave., Harrisburg, PA 17110-9797, (717)787-6286.

Rhode Island, (9) Rhode Island Fish & Wildlife, Division of Fish & Wildlife, 4808 Tower Hill Rd., Wakefield, RI 02879-2207, (401)789-3094.

South Carolina, (7) Dept. of Natural Resources, License Section, P.O. Box 11710, Columbia, SC 29211, (803)734-3833.

South Dakota, (1) Game, Fish & Parks, License Division, 412 W. Missouri, Pierre, SD 57501, (605)773-5527.

Tennessee, (5) Wildlife Resources Agency, ATTN.: Wildlife Stamps, Box 40747, Nashville, TN 37204, (615)781-6501.

Texas, (8) Parks & Wildlife Dept., License Office, 4200 Smith School Rd., Austin, TX 78744, (512)389-4822.

Utah, (-) Division of Wildlife Resources, 1596 W. North Temple, Salt Lake City, UT 84116-3195, (801)538-4841. (Last stamp issued in 1997.)

Vermont, (9) Dept. of Fish & Wildlife, Stamp Order, 103 S. Main St., 10 South, Waterbury, VT 05671-0501, (802)241-3700.

Virginia, (10) c/o VA. Ducks Unlimited, 3318 Derby Lane, Williamsburg, VA 23185, (757)220-3144.

Washington, (7) Dept. of Wildlife, 600 Capitol Way North, Olympia, WA 98501-1091, (360)902-2200.

West Virginia, (-) Dept. of Natural Resources, Waterfowl Stamp Program, Box 67, Elkins, WV 26241, (304)637-0245. (Last stamp issued in 1996.)

Wisconsin, (8) Dept. of Natural Resources, Box 7924, Madison, WI 53707, (608)264-6137.

Wyoming, (1) Game & Fish Dept., ATTN: Alternative Enterprises, 5440 Bishop Blvd., Cheyenne, WY 82006, (307)777-4570.

FEDERAL & INTERNATIONAL AGENCIES

U.S. Dept. of Wildlife, (7) Duck Stamp Office, 4501 North Fairfax Drive, 4th Floor, Arlington, VA 22203, (703)358-2000.

Alberta, (-) R.D. Miner Philatelics, 83 Woodgreen Dr., Calgary, Alberta, Canada T2W 4G6, (403)251-7500.

Argentina, (-) National Art Publishing Corp., 11000 Metro Pkwy. Ste #32, Ft. Myers, FL 33912-1293, (941)939-7518. (Last stamp issued 1996.)

Australia, (-) Jan Sec Fire Stamps, 4/358 Pacific Hwy., Linfield NSW 2070, Australia - P.O. Box 214. (Last stamp issued 1996.)

Canada, (8) Wildlife Habitat Canada, 9 Hinton Ave. North Ste. #200, Ottawa, Ontario, Canada K1Y 4P1.

Croatia, (-) Duck Stamp Fulfillment Center, P.O. Box 17, Sullivan, IL 61951, (217)797-6770. (Last stamp issued 1997.)

Denmark, (-) Duck Stamp Fulfillment Center, 1015 West Jackson, Sullivan, IL 61951, (217)728-8321. (Last stamp issued 1997.)

Ireland, (-) Duck Stamp Fulfillment Center, 1015 West Jackson, Sullivan, IL 61951, (217)728-8321. (Last stamp issued 1998.)

Israel, (-) Fleetwood, #1 Unicover Center, Cheyenne, WY 82008, (307)634-5911. (Last stamp issued 1998.)

Italy, (-) Duck Stamp Fulfillment Center, 1015 West Jackson, Sullivan, IL 61951, (217)728-8321. (Last stamp issued 1998.)

Mexico, (-) Duck Stamp Fulfillment Center, 1015 West Jackson, Sullivan, IL 61951, (217)728-8321. (Last stamp issued 1997.)

New Zealand, (9) Duck Stamp Fulfillment Center, 1015 West Jackson, Sullivan, IL 61951, (217)728-8321. (Last stamp issued 1997.)

Quebec, (4) Rousseau Inc., 230 Rue St., Jacque St., Vieux Montreal, Quebec H2Y1L9, Canada, 1-800-561-9977.

Russia, (4) Fleetwood, #1 Unicover Center, Cheyenne, WY 82008, (307)771-3000.

Spain, (-) National Art Publishing Corp., 11000 Metro Pkwy. Ste. #32, Ft. Myers, FL 33912-1293, (941)939-7518. (Last stamp issued 1996.)

Sweden, (-) Duck Stamp Fulfillment Center, 1015 West Jackson, Sullivan, IL 61951, (217)728-8321. (Last stamp issued 1997.)

United Kingdom, (7) Duck Stamp Fulfillment Center, 1015 West Jackson, Sullivan, IL 61951, (217)728-8321.

Venezuela, (-) National Art Publishing Corp., 11000 Metro Pkwy. Ste. #32, Ft. Myers, FL 33912-129, (941)939-7518. (Last stamp issued 1996.)

All the following have the same contact:

Hines-Proguide, 659 Poplar Grove Rd., Poplar Grove, Nova Scotia B0N 2A0, Canada, (902)757-0153.

British Columbia (10)

Manitoba (10)

New Brunswick (10)

Newfoundland & Labrador (10)

Nunavet Territory (10)

Nova Scotia (10)

Ontario (10)

Prince Edward Island (10)

Saskatchewan (10)

Yukon Territory (10)

FEDERAL MIGRATORY BIRD HUNTING STAMPS

NOTE: The year of issue appears in parentheses. Stamps are inscribed with an expiration date, which is one year later than the issue date, for example, the 1934 stamp reads, "Void After June 30, 1935." Stamps are canceled (used) by the application of the hunter's signature. Unsigned unused stamps (without gum) are considered to be used nevertheless.

PRICING NOTE: Prices are for very fine (VF) never-hinged (NH) examples.

RW1

Scott No.			Plate Block	Unused	Used
❏ RW1	$1	Mallards (1934), blue	1700.00 (6)	950.00	130.00
❏ RW2	$1	Canvasbacks (1935), rose lake	13000.00 (6)	800.00	130.00
❏ RW3	$1	Canada Geese (1936), brown black	3800.00 (6)	370.00	74.00
❏ RW4	$1	Scaups (1937), light green	2700.00 (6)	310.00	50.00
❏ RW5	$1	Pintails (1938), light violet	3200.00 (6)	460.00	58.00
❏ RW6	$1	Green-Winged Teal (1939), chocolate	2100.00 (6)	275.00	45.00
❏ RW7	$1	Black Ducks (1940), sepia	2000.00 (6)	250.00	45.00
❏ RW8	$1	Ruddy Ducks (1941), brown carmine	2100.00 (6)	260.00	45.00
❏ RW9	$1	Widgeon (1942), violet brown	2000.00 (6)	260.00	45.00
❏ RW10	$1	Wood Ducks (1943), deep rose	740.00 (6)	120.00	44.00
❏ RW11	$1	White Fronted Geese (1944), red orange	740.00 (6)	90.00	26.00
❏ RW12	$1	Shovelers (1945), black	450.00 (6)	65.00	17.00

Scott No.			Plate Block	Unused	Used
❑ RW13	$1	Redheads (1946), red brown	340.00 (6)	60.00	14.00
❑ RW14	$1	Snow Geese (1947), black	340.00 (6)	60.00	14.00
❑ RW15	$1	Buffleheads (1948), bright blue	340.00 (6)	60.00	14.00
❑ RW16	$2	Goldeneyes (1949), bright green	400.00 (6)	70.00	14.00
❑ RW17	$2	Trumpeter Swans (1950), violet	610.00 (6)	87.00	9.50
❑ RW18	$2	Gadwalls (1951), gray black	610.00 (6)	87.00	9.50
❑ RW19	$2	Harlequins (1952), ultramarine	610.00 (6)	87.00	9.50
❑ RW20	$2	Blue-winged Teal (1953), dark rose brown	610.00 (6)	87.00	9.50
❑ RW21	$2	Ring-necked Ducks (1954), black	610.00 (6)	87.00	9.50
❑ RW22	$2	Blue Geese (1955), dark blue	610.00 (6)	87.00	9.50
❑ RW23	$2	Mergansers (1956), black	610.00 (6)	87.00	9.50
❑ RW24	$2	American Eider (1957), emerald	610.00 (6)	87.00	9.50
❑ RW25	$2	Canada Geese (1958), black	610.00 (6)	87.00	9.50
❑ RW26	$3	Labrador (1959) multicolored	610.00	110.00	9.50
❑ RW27	$3	Redheads (1960), multicolored	450.00	85.00	12.50
❑ RW28	$3	Mallards (1961), multicolored	460.00	85.00	12.50
❑ RW29	$3	Pintails (1962), multicolored	620.00	115.00	12.50
❑ RW30	$3	American Brant (1963), multicolored	600.00	85.00	12.50
❑ RW31	$3	Nene Geese (1964), multicolored	2200.00	110.00	12.50

RW32

Scott No.			Plate Block	Unused	Used
❑ RW32	$3	Canvasbacks (1965), multicolored	600.00	110.00	11.00
❑ RW33	$3	Whistling Swans (1966), multicolored	600.00	110.00	11.00
❑ RW34	$3	Oldsquaws (1967), multicolored	610.00	120.00	11.00
❑ RW35	$3	Mergansers (1968), multicolored	300.00	67.00	8.50
❑ RW36	$3	White-winged Scoters (1969), multicolored	315.00	67.00	8.50
❑ RW37	$3	Ross' Geese (1970), multicolored	315.00	67.00	8.50
❑ RW38	$3	Cinnamon Teal (1971), multicolored	225.00	55.00	8.50
❑ RW39	$5	Emperor Geese (1972), multicolored	90.00	22.00	8.50
❑ RW40	$5	Steller's Eiders (1973), multicolored	77.00	16.00	8.50
❑ RW41	$5	Wood Ducks (1974), multicolored	77.00	16.00	8.50
❑ RW42	$5	Decoy/Canvasbacks (1975), multicolored	72.00	16.00	8.50
❑ RW43	$5	Canada Geese (1976), emerald & black	72.00	16.00	8.50
❑ RW44	$5	Ross' Geese (1977), multicolored	72.00	16.00	8.50
❑ RW45	$5	Mergansers (1978), multicolored	72.00	16.00	8.50
❑ RW46	$7.50	Green-winged Teal (1979), multicolored	72.00	16.00	8.00

Scott No.			Plate Block	Unused	Used
❑ RW47	$7.50	Mallards (1980), multicolored	76.00	19.00	8.50
❑ RW48	$7.50	Ruddy Ducks (1981), multicolored	76.00	19.00	8.50
❑ RW49	$7.50	Canvasbacks (1982), multicolored	76.00	19.00	11.00
❑ RW50	$7.50	Pintails (1983), multicolored	76.00	19.00	11.00
❑ RW51	$7.50	Widgeons (1984), multicolored	76.00	19.00	11.00
❑ RW52	$7.50	Cinnamon Teal (1985), multicolored	76.00	19.00	11.00
❑ RW53	$7.50	Fulvous Whistling Duck (1986), multicolored	76.00	19.00	11.00
❑ RW54	$10	Redheads (1987), multicolored	100.00	25.00	11.00
❑ RW55	$10	Snow Goose (1988), multicolored	100.00	25.00	12.00
❑ RW56	$12.50	Lesser Scaup (1989), multicolored	100.00	25.00	12.00
❑ RW57	$12.50	Black-bellied Whistling Duck (1990), multicolored	100.00	25.00	12.00
❑ RW58	$15	King Eider (1991), multicolored	100.00	26.00	15.00
❑ RW59	$15	Spectacled Eiders (1992), multicolored	115.00	26.00	15.00
❑ RW60	$15	Canvasbacks (1993), multicolored	115.00	26.00	15.00
❑ RW61	$15	Red-breasted Mergansers (1994), multicolored	115.00	26.00	15.00
❑ RW62	$15	Mallards (1995), multicolored	115.00	26.00	15.00
❑ RW63	$15	Sun Scoter (1996), multicolored	115.00	26.00	15.00

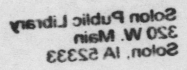

RW64

Scott No.			Plate Block	Unused	Used
❏ RW64	$15	Canada Goose (1997), multicolored	115.00	26.00	15.00
❏ RW65	$15	Barrow Golden Eyes (1998), multicolored	115.00	26.00	15.00
❏ RW65		PSA Type (1998)	—	22.00	12.50
❏ RW66	$15	Greater Scaup (1999), multicolored	115.00	26.00	14.00
❏ RW66		PSA Type (1999)	—	22.00	12.50
❏ RW67	$15	Mottled duck (2000), multicolored	115.00	26.00	14.00
❏ RW67		PSA Type (2000)	—	22.00	12.50
❏ RW68	$15	Pintail (2001), multicolored	115.00	26.00	14.00
❏ RW68		PSA Type (2001)	—	22.00	12.50
❏ RW69	$15	Black Scoter (2002), multicolored	115.00	26.00	14.00
❏ RW69		PSA Type (2002)	—	22.00	12.50
❏ RW70	$15	Snow Goose (2003), multicolored	115.00	26.00	14.00
❏ RW70		PSA Type (2003)	—	22.00	12.50
❏ RW71	$15	Red Heads (2004), multicolored	115.00	26.00	14.00
❏ RW71		PSA Type (2004)	—	22.00	12.50

MINT SHEETS

❏ 643	2¢	Vermont	280.00	❏ 724	3¢	Penn	70.00
❏ 644	2¢	Burgoyne	280.00	❏ 725	3¢	Webster	84.00
❏ 645	2¢	Valley Forge	187.00	❏ 726	3¢	Oglethorpe	72.00
❏ 646	2¢	Molly Pitcher	200.00	❏ 727	3¢	Newburgh	28.00
❏ 647	2¢	Hawaii	850.00	❏ 728	1¢	Chicago	26.00
❏ 648	5¢	Hawaii	2100.00	❏ 729	3¢	Chicago	30.00
❏ 649	2¢	Aeronautics	98.00	❏ 732	3¢	N.R.A.	24.00
❏ 650	5¢	Aeronautics	435.00	❏ 733	3¢	Byrd	55.00
❏ 651	2¢	George R. Clark	70.00	❏ 734	5¢	Kosciuszko	130.00
❏ 653	½¢	Hale	23.00	❏ 736	3¢	Maryland	36.00
❏ 654	2¢	Edison-Flat	160.00	❏ 737	3¢	Mother's Day Rotary	16.00
❏ 655	2¢	Edison-Rotary	1340.00	❏ 738	3¢	Mother's Day Flat	22.00
❏ 657	2¢	Sullivan	150.00	❏ 739	3¢	Wisconsin	20.00
❏ 680	2¢	Fallen Timbers	149.00	❏ 740	1¢	Nat'l. Parks	11.00
❏ 681	2¢	Ohio Canal	140.00	❏ 741	2¢	Nat'l. Parks	13.00
❏ 682	2¢	Mass. Bay	115.00	❏ 742	3¢	Nat'l. Parks	14.00
❏ 683	2¢	Carolina-Charleston	185.00	❏ 743	4¢	Nat'l. Parks	39.00
❏ 684	1½¢	Harding	46.00	❏ 744	5¢	Nat'l. Parks	62.00
❏ 685	4¢	Taft	130.00	❏ 745	6¢	Nat'l. Parks	101.00
❏ 688	2¢	Braddock	160.00	❏ 746	7¢	Nat'l. Parks	64.00
❏ 689	2¢	Von Steuben	96.00	❏ 747	8¢	Nat'l. Parks	150.00
❏ 690	2¢	Pulaski	50.00	❏ 748	9¢	Nat'l. Parks	140.00
❏ 702	2¢	Red Cross	25.00	❏ 749	10¢	Nat'l. Parks	250.00
❏ 703	2¢	Yorktown	26.00	❏ 752	3¢	Newburg	410.00
❏ 704	½¢	Wash. Bicent'l	20.00	❏ 753	3¢	Byrd	575.00
❏ 705	1¢	Wash. Bicent'l	24.00	❏ 754	3¢	Mother's Day	180.00
❏ 706	1½¢	Wash. Bicent'l	76.00	❏ 755	3¢	Wisconsin	175.00
❏ 707	2¢	Wash. Bicent'l	21.00	❏ 756	1¢	Park	58.00
❏ 708	3¢	Wash. Bicent'l	95.00	❏ 757	2¢	Park	72.00
❏ 709	4¢	Wash. Bicent'l	50.00	❏ 758	3¢	Park	156.00
❏ 710	5¢	Wash. Bicent'l	260.00	❏ 759	4¢	Park	280.00
❏ 711	6¢	Wash. Bicent'l	520.00	❏ 760	5¢	Park	480.00
❏ 712	7¢	Wash. Bicent'l	58.00	❏ 761	6¢	Park	610.00
❏ 713	8¢	Wash. Bicent'l	500.00	❏ 762	7¢	Park	490.00
❏ 714	9¢	Wash. Bicent'l	400.00	❏ 763	8¢	Park	570.00
❏ 715	10¢	Wash. Bicent'l	1650.00	❏ 764	9¢	Park	620.00
❏ 716	2¢	Lake Placid	74.00	❏ 765	10¢	Park	950.00
❏ 717	2¢	Arbor Day	35.00	❏ 766a	1¢	Chicago	370.00
❏ 718	2¢	Olympics	215.00	❏ 767a	3¢	Chicago	380.00
❏ 719	5¢	Olympics	345.00	❏ 768a	3¢	Byrd	550.00
❏ 720	3¢	Washington	30.00	❏ 769	1¢	Park	260.00

❑ 770	3¢	Park	700.00		❑ 862	5¢	Alcott	40.00
❑ 771	16¢	Air Spec. Deal	800.00		❑ 863	10¢	Clemens	192.00
❑ 772	3¢	Connecticut	16.00		❑ 864	1¢	Longfellow	27.00
❑ 773	3¢	San Diego	12.00		❑ 865	2¢	Whittier	15.50
❑ 774	3¢	Boulder Dam	12.00		❑ 866	3¢	Lowell	18.00
❑ 775	3¢	Michigan	15.00		❑ 867	5¢	Whitman	50.00
❑ 776	3¢	Texas	14.00		❑ 868	10¢	Riley	225.00
❑ 777	3¢	Rhode Island	25.00		❑ 869	1¢	Mann	13.00
❑ 782	3¢	Arkansas	22.00		❑ 870	2¢	Hopkins	12.50
❑ 783	3¢	Oregon	14.00		❑ 871	3¢	Elliot	19.00
❑ 784	3¢	Susan B. Anthony	21.00		❑ 872	5¢	Willard	50.00
❑ 785	1¢	Army	14.00		❑ 873	10¢	B.T. Washington	205.00
❑ 786	2¢	Army	13.00		❑ 874	1¢	Audubon	16.00
❑ 787	3¢	Army	20.00		❑ 875	2¢	Long	15.00
❑ 788	4¢	Army	36.00		❑ 876	3¢	Burbank	20.00
❑ 789	5¢	Army	50.00		❑ 877	5¢	Reed	32.00
❑ 790	1¢	Navy	7.00		❑ 878	10¢	Addams	121.00
❑ 791	2¢	Navy	13.00		❑ 879	1¢	Fosters	19.00
❑ 792	3¢	Navy	18.00		❑ 880	2¢	Sousa	14.00
❑ 793	4¢	Navy	41.00		❑ 881	3¢	Herbert	17.00
❑ 794	5¢	Navy	50.00		❑ 882	5¢	MacDowell	46.00
❑ 795	3¢	N.W. Territory	17.00		❑ 883	10¢	Nevin	340.00
❑ 796	5¢	Virginia Dare	23.00		❑ 884	1¢	Sturat	20.00
❑ 798	3¢	Constitution	30.00		❑ 885	2¢	Whistler	13.00
❑ 799	3¢	Hawaii	15.00		❑ 886	3¢	St. Gaudens	21.00
❑ 800	3¢	Alaska	15.00		❑ 887	5¢	French	50.00
❑ 801	3¢	Puerto Rico	15.00		❑ 888	10¢	Remington	185.00
❑ 802	3¢	Virgin Islands	13.00		❑ 889	1¢	Whitney	22.00
❑ 835	3¢	Ratification	28.00		❑ 890	2¢	Morse	16.00
❑ 836	3¢	Swede-Finn	15.00		❑ 891	3¢	McCormick	28.00
❑ 837	3¢	N.W. Territory	32.00		❑ 892	5¢	Howe	105.00
❑ 838	3¢	Iowa	22.00		❑ 893	10¢	Bell	1100.00
❑ 852	3¢	Golden Gate	13.00		❑ 894	3¢	Pony Express	25.00
❑ 853	3¢	N.Y. Fair	16.00		❑ 895	3¢	Pan America	21.00
❑ 854	3¢	Inauguration	46.00		❑ 896	3¢	Idaho	14.00
❑ 855	3¢	Baseball	120.00		❑ 897	3¢	Wyoming	15.00
❑ 856	3¢	Canal Zone	23.00		❑ 898	3¢	Coronado	15.00
❑ 857	3¢	Printing	12.00		❑ 899	1¢	Defense	15.00
❑ 858	3¢	Four States	12.00		❑ 900	2¢	Defense	15.00
❑ 859	1¢	Irving	15.00		❑ 901	3¢	Defense	18.00
❑ 860	2¢	Cooper	18.00		❑ 902	3¢	Emancipation	21.00
❑ 861	3¢	Emerson	15.00		❑ 903	3¢	Vermont	21.00

☐ 904	3¢ Kentucky	16.00	
☐ 905	3¢ Win the War	20.00	
☐ 906	5¢ China	75.00	
☐ 907	2¢ Allied Nations	11.00	
☐ 908	1¢ Four Freedoms	11.00	
☐ 909	5¢ Poland	14.00	
☐ 910	5¢ Czechoslovakia	15.00	
☐ 911	5¢ Norway	11.00	
☐ 912	5¢ Luxembourg	11.50	
☐ 913	5¢ Netherlands	11.50	
☐ 914	5¢ Belgium	11.50	
☐ 915	5¢ France	11.00	
☐ 916	5¢ Greece	38.00	
☐ 917	5¢ Yugoslavia	25.00	
☐ 918	5¢ Albania	26.00	
☐ 919	5¢ Austria	20.00	
☐ 920	5¢ Denmark	25.00	
☐ 921	5¢ Korea	16.00	
☐ 909–21	Set of 13	240.00	
☐ 922	3¢ Railroad	16.00	
☐ 923	3¢ Steamship	21.00	
☐ 924	3¢ Telegraph	13.00	
☐ 925	3¢ Corregidor	12.00	
☐ 926	3¢ Motion Pictures	13.00	
☐ 927	3¢ Florida	12.00	
☐ 928	5¢ United Nations	12.00	
☐ 929	3¢ Iwo Jima	21.00	
☐ 930	1¢ Roosevelt	6.00	
☐ 931	2¢ Roosevelt	6.00	
☐ 932	3¢ Roosevelt	8.00	
☐ 933	5¢ Roosevelt	12.50	
☐ 934	3¢ Army	12.00	
☐ 935	3¢ Navy	13.00	
☐ 936	3¢ Coast Guard	12.50	
☐ 937	3¢ Alfred E. Smith	20.00	
☐ 938	3¢ Texas	14.00	
☐ 939	3¢ Merchant Marine	10.00	
☐ 940	3¢ Discharge Emblem	20.00	
☐ 941	3¢ Tennessee	16.00	
☐ 942	3¢ Iowa	13.00	
☐ 943	3¢ Smithsonian	9.00	
☐ 944	3¢ Kearny	9.00	
☐ 945	3¢ Edison	19.00	
☐ 946	3¢ Pulitzer	12.00	
☐ 947	3¢ CIPEX	10.00	
☐ 949	3¢ Doctors	9.00	
☐ 950	3¢ Utah	8.50	
☐ 951	3¢ Constitution	9.00	
☐ 952	3¢ Everglades	12.00	
☐ 953	3¢ Carver	16.00	
☐ 954	3¢ Gold Rush	13.00	
☐ 955	3¢ Mississippi	11.00	
☐ 956	3¢ Chaplains	12.00	
☐ 957	3¢ Wisconsin	10.00	
☐ 958	5¢ Swedish Pioneer	10.00	
☐ 959	3¢ Women	11.00	
☐ 960	3¢ White	12.00	
☐ 961	3¢ U.S. Canada	9.00	
☐ 962	3¢ Key	12.50	
☐ 963	3¢ Youth	9.50	
☐ 964	3¢ Oregon	9.00	
☐ 965	3¢ Stone	13.00	
☐ 966	3¢ Palomar	13.00	
☐ 967	3¢ Barton	10.00	
☐ 968	3¢ Poultry	13.00	
☐ 969	3¢ Gold Star	7.00	
☐ 970	3¢ Fort Kearny	10.00	
☐ 971	3¢ Firemen	14.00	
☐ 972	3¢ Indian Centennial	10.00	
☐ 973	3¢ Rough Riders	10.00	
☐ 974	3¢ Juliette Low	15.00	
☐ 975	3¢ Will Rogers	16.00	
☐ 976	3¢ Fort Bliss	15.00	
☐ 977	3¢ Moina Michael	12.50	
☐ 978	3¢ Gettysburg	15.00	
☐ 979	3¢ Turners	13.00	
☐ 980	3¢ Harris	19.00	
☐ 981	3¢ Minnesota	8.00	
☐ 982	3¢ Washington & Lee	10.00	
☐ 983	3¢ Puerto Rico	8.00	
☐ 984	3¢ Annapolis	10.50	
☐ 985	3¢ G.A.R.	11.00	
☐ 986	3¢ Poe	20.00	
☐ 987	3¢ Bankers	17.00	

☐ 988	3¢	Gompers	10.00	☐ 1030	½¢	Franklin	9.00
☐ 989	3¢	Capitol Statue	7.50	☐ 1031	1¢	Washington	7.00
☐ 990	3¢	White House	10.00	☐ 1031A	1¼¢	Palace of Governors	7.00
☐ 991	3¢	Supreme Court	11.00	☐ 1032	1½¢	Mount Vernon	25.00
☐ 992	3¢	Capitol Building	10.00	☐ 1033	2¢	Jefferson	12.00
☐ 993	3¢	Casey Jones	15.00	☐ 1034	2½¢	Bunker Hill	21.00
☐ 994	3¢	Kansas City	16.00	☐ 1035	3¢	Liberty	12.00
☐ 995	3¢	Boy Scouts	12.00	☐ 1036	4¢	Lincoln	25.00
☐ 996	3¢	Indiana	15.00	☐ 1037	4½¢	Hermitage	25.00
☐ 997	3¢	California	11.00	☐ 1038	5¢	Monroe	26.00
☐ 998	3¢	Confederate	14.00	☐ 1039	6¢	Roosevelt	42.00
☐ 999	3¢	Nevada	8.00	☐ 1040	7¢	Wilson	30.00
☐ 1000	3¢	Cadillac at Detroit	10.00	☐ 1041	8¢	Liberty	32.00
☐ 1001	3¢	Colorado	9.50	☐ 1042	8¢	Liberty (re-engraved)	31.00
☐ 1002	3¢	Chemical	14.00	☐ 1042A	8¢	Pershing	31.00
☐ 1003	3¢	Battle of Brooklyn	11.00	☐ 1043	9¢	Alamo	46.00
☐ 1004	3¢	Betsy Ross	12.00	☐ 1044	10¢	Independence Hall	45.00
☐ 1005	3¢	4-H Clubs	17.00	☐ 1044A	11¢	Liberty	41.00
☐ 1006	3¢	B&O Railroad	12.00	☐ 1045	12¢	Harrison	54.00
☐ 1007	3¢	A.A.A.	12.50	☐ 1046	15¢	Jay	95.00
☐ 1008	3¢	NATO	15.00	☐ 1047	20¢	Monticello	75.00
☐ 1009	3¢	Grand Coulee Dam	9.00	☐ 1048	25¢	Revere	170.00
☐ 1010	3¢	Lafayette	16.00	☐ 1049	30¢	Lee	175.00
☐ 1011	3¢	Rushmore	9.00	☐ 1050	40¢	Marshall	280.00
☐ 1012	3¢	Engineers	13.00	☐ 1051	50¢	Stone	215.00
☐ 1013	3¢	Armed Forces Women	9.00	☐ 1052	$1	Henry	575.00
☐ 1014	3¢	Gutenberg	8.00	☐ 1053	$5	Hamilton	810.00
☐ 1015	3¢	Newspaper Boys	8.00	☐ 1060	3¢	Nebraska	7.50
☐ 1016	3¢	Red Cross	9.00	☐ 1061	3¢	Kansas	8.00
☐ 1017	3¢	National Guard	7.00	☐ 1062	3¢	George Eastman	13.00
☐ 1018	3¢	Ohio	22.00	☐ 1063	3¢	Lewis & Clark	14.00
☐ 1019	3¢	Washington	8.50	☐ 1064	3¢	Penn Academy	15.00
☐ 1020	3¢	Louisiana	14.00	☐ 1065	3¢	Colleges	13.00
☐ 1021	5¢	Opening of Japan	15.00	☐ 1066	8¢	Rotary	16.00
☐ 1022	3¢	Bar Association	13.00	☐ 1067	3¢	Reserves	8.00
☐ 1023	3¢	Sagamore Hill	10.00	☐ 1068	3¢	Vermont	15.00
☐ 1024	3¢	Future Farmers	10.00	☐ 1069	3¢	Great Lakes	11.00
☐ 1025	3¢	Trucking	10.00	☐ 1070	3¢	Atoms for Peace	11.00
☐ 1026	3¢	Patton	10.00	☐ 1071	3¢	Ft. Ticonderoga	12.50
☐ 1027	3¢	New York City	10.00	☐ 1072	3¢	Andrew Mellon	22.00
☐ 1028	3¢	Gadsden Purchase	10.00	☐ 1073	3¢	Benj. Franklin	12.00
☐ 1029	3¢	Columbia U.	11.00	☐ 1074	3¢	B. T. Washington	11.00

❑ 1076	3¢	FIPEX	8.00	❑ 1121	4¢	Webster	15.00
❑ 1077	3¢	Wild Turkey	7.00	❑ 1122	4¢	Forest Conserv.	8.00
❑ 1078	3¢	Antelope	7.00	❑ 1123	4¢	Ft. Duquesne	14.00
❑ 1079	3¢	King Salmon	11.00	❑ 1124	4¢	Oregon	7.50
❑ 1080	3¢	Pure Food & Drug	10.00	❑ 1125	4¢	San Martin	10.50
❑ 1081	3¢	Wheatland	11.00	❑ 1126	8¢	San Martin	16.00
❑ 1082	3¢	Labor Day	12.00	❑ 1127	4¢	NATO	12.00
❑ 1083	3¢	Nassau Hall	12.50	❑ 1128	4¢	Arctic Exploration	12.50
❑ 1084	3¢	Devils Tower	7.00	❑ 1129	8¢	World Peace	14.00
❑ 1085	3¢	Children	8.00	❑ 1130	4¢	Silver Centennial	9.00
❑ 1086	3¢	Hamilton	7.50	❑ 1131	4¢	Seaway	11.00
❑ 1087	3¢	Polio	7.50	❑ 1132	4¢	49-Star Flag	7.50
❑ 1088	3¢	Geodetic	7.10	❑ 1133	4¢	Soil Conserv.	7.50
❑ 1089	3¢	Architects	7.40	❑ 1134	4¢	Petroleum	13.00
❑ 1090	3¢	Steel Industry	7.75	❑ 1135	4¢	Dental Health	11.00
❑ 1091	3¢	Naval Review	7.10	❑ 1136	4¢	Reuter	12.00
❑ 1092	3¢	Oklahoma	7.25	❑ 1137	8¢	Reuter	16.00
❑ 1093	3¢	Teachers	10.00	❑ 1138	4¢	McDowell	17.00
❑ 1094	4¢	48-Star Flag	8.00	❑ 1139	4¢	Credo – Washington	10.50
❑ 1095	3¢	Shipbuilding	15.00	❑ 1140	4¢	Credo – Franklin	11.00
❑ 1096	8¢	Magsaysay	11.00	❑ 1141	4¢	Credo – Jefferson	12.00
❑ 1097	3¢	Lafayette	15.00	❑ 1142	4¢	Credo – Key	13.00
❑ 1098	3¢	Whooping Cranes	11.00	❑ 1143	4¢	Credo – Lincoln	11.00
❑ 1099	3¢	Religious Freedom	8.00	❑ 1144	4¢	Credo – Henry	10.50
❑ 1100	3¢	Horticulture	8.00	❑ 1145	4¢	Boy Scouts	15.00
❑ 1104	3¢	Brussels Exhib.	8.00	❑ 1146	4¢	Winter Olympics	8.00
❑ 1105	3¢	James Monroe	12.00	❑ 1147	4¢	Masaryk	12.00
❑ 1106	3¢	Minnesota	8.00	❑ 1148	8¢	Masaryk	15.00
❑ 1107	3¢	Geophysical Year	7.25	❑ 1149	4¢	Refugee Year	7.50
❑ 1108	3¢	Gunston Hall	7.25	❑ 1150	4¢	Water Conserv.	7.75
❑ 1109	3¢	Mackinac Bridge	7.25	❑ 1151	4¢	SEATO	10.00
❑ 1110	4¢	Bolivar	11.00	❑ 1152	4¢	Women	7.00
❑ 1111	8¢	Bolivar	15.00	❑ 1153	4¢	50-Star Flag	7.50
❑ 1112	4¢	Atlantic Cable	7.50	❑ 1154	4¢	Pony Express	14.00
❑ 1113	1¢	Lincoln	3.00	❑ 1155	4¢	Handicapped	7.00
❑ 1114	3¢	Lincoln	12.50	❑ 1156	4¢	Forestry	7.00
❑ 1115	4¢	Lincoln-Douglas	15.00	❑ 1157	4¢	Mexican Ind.	7.00
❑ 1116	4¢	Lincoln	13.00	❑ 1158	4¢	U.S.-Japan	7.00
❑ 1117	4¢	Kossuth	10.50	❑ 1159	4¢	Paderewski	11.50
❑ 1118	8¢	Kossuth	18.00	❑ 1160	8¢	Paderewski	19.00
❑ 1119	4¢	Free Press	7.50	❑ 1161	4¢	Robert Taft	21.00
❑ 1120	4¢	Overland Mail	13.00	❑ 1162	4¢	Wheels of Freedom	7.50

❑ 1163	4¢	Boys' Clubs	12.00
❑ 1164	4¢	Automated P.O.	17.00
❑ 1165	4¢	Mannerheim	11.00
❑ 1166	8¢	Mannerheim	17.00
❑ 1167	4¢	Campfire Girls	14.00
❑ 1168	4¢	Garibaldi	11.00
❑ 1169	8¢	Garibaldi	12.00
❑ 1170	4¢	George	16.00
❑ 1171	4¢	Carnegie	21.00
❑ 1172	4¢	Dulles	16.00
❑ 1173	4¢	Echo I	15.00
❑ 1174	4¢	Gandhi	11.00
❑ 1175	8¢	Gandhi	17.00
❑ 1176	4¢	Range Conserv.	8.00
❑ 1177	4¢	Greeley	20.00
❑ 1178	4¢	Ft. Sumter	25.00
❑ 1179	4¢	Shiloh	15.00
❑ 1180	5¢	Gettysburg	21.00
❑ 1181	5¢	Wilderness	18.00
❑ 1182	5¢	Appomattox	31.00
❑ 1183	4¢	Kansas	10.00
❑ 1184	4¢	Norris	15.00
❑ 1185	4¢	Naval Aviation	8.00
❑ 1186	4¢	Workmen's Comp.	7.50
❑ 1187	4¢	Remington	9.50
❑ 1188	4¢	China	13.00
❑ 1189	4¢	Basketball	15.00
❑ 1190	4¢	Nursing	16.00
❑ 1191	4¢	New Mexico	7.50
❑ 1192	4¢	Arizona	7.50
❑ 1193	4¢	Project Mercury	12.00
❑ 1194	4¢	Malaria	7.75
❑ 1195	4¢	Hughes	7.80
❑ 1196	4¢	Seattle Fair	7.25
❑ 1197	4¢	Louisiana	16.00
❑ 1198	4¢	Homestead	7.00
❑ 1199	4¢	Girl Scouts	7.00
❑ 1200	4¢	McMahon	12.50
❑ 1201	4¢	Apprenticeship	7.10
❑ 1202	4¢	Rayburn	10.00
❑ 1203	4¢	Hammarskjold	7.00
❑ 1204	4¢	Hammarskjold invert	10.00
❑ 1205	4¢	Christmas Wreath	14.00
❑ 1206	4¢	Education	7.50
❑ 1207	4¢	Winslow Homer	12.50
❑ 1208	5¢	U.S. Flag	16.00
❑ 1209	1¢	Jackson	8.00
❑ 1213	5¢	Washington	17.00
❑ 1230	5¢	Carolina	16.00
❑ 1231	5¢	Food for Peace	8.00
❑ 1232	5¢	West Virginia	10.00
❑ 1233	5¢	Emancipation	10.00
❑ 1234	5¢	Alliance for Progress	8.00
❑ 1235	5¢	Hull	15.00
❑ 1236	5¢	E. Roosevelt	13.00
❑ 1237	5¢	Sciences	8.00
❑ 1238	5¢	City Mail	7.50
❑ 1239	5¢	Red Cross	7.25
❑ 1240	5¢	Christmas Tree	20.00
❑ 1241	5¢	Audubon	14.00
❑ 1242	5¢	Sam Houston	12.00
❑ 1243	5¢	Russell	16.00
❑ 1244	5¢	World's Fair	12.50
❑ 1245	5¢	John Muir	7.00
❑ 1246	5¢	J. F.K.	24.00
❑ 1247	5¢	New Jersey	15.00
❑ 1248	5¢	Nevada	11.00
❑ 1249	5¢	Register & Vote	7.00
❑ 1250	5¢	Shakespeare	7.00
❑ 1251	5¢	Doctors Mayo	13.00
❑ 1252	5¢	Music	7.50
❑ 1253	5¢	Homemakers	7.50
❑ 1254–57	5¢	Christmas	34.00
❑ 1258	5¢	Verrazano Bridge	13.00
❑ 1259	5¢	Modern Art	7.50
❑ 1260	5¢	Amateur Radio	15.00
❑ 1261	5¢	New Orleans	20.00
❑ 1262	5¢	Physical Fitness	7.50
❑ 1263	5¢	Fight Cancer	7.25
❑ 1264	5¢	Churchill	12.00
❑ 1265	5¢	Magna Carta	8.00
❑ 1266	5¢	Cooperation Year	8.00
❑ 1267	5¢	Salvation Army	8.00
❑ 1268	5¢	Dante Alighieri	8.00

❑ 1269	5¢	Herbert Hoover	13.00	❑ 1321	5¢	Christmas	12.00
❑ 1270	5¢	Robert Fulton	7.40	❑ 1322	5¢	Cassatt	7.50
❑ 1271	5¢	Florida	12.00	❑ 1323	5¢	Grange	11.00
❑ 1272	5¢	Traffic Safety	8.00	❑ 1324	5¢	Canada	7.50
❑ 1273	5¢	John S. Copley	13.00	❑ 1325	5¢	Erie Canal	14.00
❑ 1274	11¢	I.T.U.	26.00	❑ 1326	5¢	Peace	12.50
❑ 1275	5¢	Stevenson	7.50	❑ 1327	5¢	Thoreau	15.00
❑ 1276	5¢	Christmas	14.00	❑ 1328	5¢	Nebraska	14.50
❑ 1278	1¢	Jefferson	6.75	❑ 1329	5¢	Voice of America	8.00
❑ 1279	1¼¢	Gallatin	18.00	❑ 1330	5¢	Davy Crockett	15.00
❑ 1280	2¢	Wright	7.50	❑ 1331–32	5¢	Space Twins	50.00
❑ 1281	3¢	Parkman	10.00	❑ 1333	5¢	Urban Planning	8.00
❑ 1282	4¢	Lincoln	30.00	❑ 1334	5¢	Finland	7.50
❑ 1283	5¢	Washington	18.00	❑ 1335	5¢	Eakins	13.00
❑ 1283B	5¢	Washington	14.00	❑ 1336	5¢	Christmas	7.50
❑ 1284	6¢	Roosevelt	23.00	❑ 1337	5¢	Mississippi	16.00
❑ 1285	8¢	Einstein	35.00	❑ 1338	6¢	Flag	16.00
❑ 1286	10¢	Jackson	41.00	❑ 1338D	6¢	Flag	17.50
❑ 1286A	12¢	Ford	34.00	❑ 1338F	8¢	Flag	21.00
❑ 1287	13¢	Kennedy	51.00	❑ 1339	6¢	Illinois	17.00
❑ 1288	15¢	Holmes (type I)	41.00	❑ 1340	6¢	Hemisfair '68	8.00
❑ 1288A	15¢	Holmes (type II)	80.00	❑ 1341	$1	Airlift	145.00
❑ 1289	20¢	Marshall	70.00	❑ 1342	6¢	Youth	7.50
❑ 1290	25¢	Douglass	98.00	❑ 1343	6¢	Law & Order	15.00
❑ 1291	30¢	Dewey	115.00	❑ 1344	6¢	Register & Vote	8.00
❑ 1292	40¢	Paine	120.00	❑ 1345–54	6¢	Flags	20.00
❑ 1293	50¢	Stone	140.00	❑ 1355	6¢	Disney	42.00
❑ 1294	$1	O'Neill	310.00	❑ 1356	6¢	Marquette	16.00
❑ 1306	5¢	Migratory Bird	8.00	❑ 1357	6¢	Daniel Boone	15.00
❑ 1307	5¢	Humane Treatment	7.50	❑ 1358	6¢	Arkansas River	15.00
❑ 1308	5¢	Indiana	15.00	❑ 1359	6¢	Leif Erikson	12.00
❑ 1309	5¢	Clown	12.50	❑ 1360	6¢	Cherokee Strip	13.00
❑ 1310	5¢	SIPEX	8.00	❑ 1361	6¢	Trumball	18.00
❑ 1312	5¢	Bill of Rights	8.00	❑ 1362	6¢	Waterfowl	13.00
❑ 1313	5¢	Poland	8.00	❑ 1363	6¢	Christmas	10.00
❑ 1314	5¢	Park Service	10.00	❑ 1364	6¢	Chief Joseph	15.00
❑ 1315	5¢	Marine Reserve	8.00	❑ 1365–68	6¢	Beautification	25.00
❑ 1316	5¢	Women's Clubs	8.00	❑ 1369	6¢	American Legion	8.00
❑ 1317	5¢	J. Appleseed	12.00	❑ 1370	6¢	Grandma Moses	8.00
❑ 1318	5¢	Beautification	7.50	❑ 1371	6¢	Apollo 8	15.00
❑ 1319	5¢	Great River Road	15.00	❑ 1372	6¢	W. C. Handy	16.00
❑ 1320	5¢	Servicemen	7.50	❑ 1373	6¢	California	11.00

❑ 1374	6¢	Powell	15.00	❑ 1433	8¢	John Sloan	12.00
❑ 1375	6¢	Alabama	16.00	❑ 1434–35	8¢	Space Achiev.	12.50
❑ 1376–79	6¢	Botanical	30.00	❑ 1436	8¢	Dickinson	15.00
❑ 1380	6¢	Webster	14.00	❑ 1437	8¢	Puerto Rico	12.00
❑ 1381	6¢	Baseball	46.00	❑ 1438	8¢	Drug Abuse	11.00
❑ 1382	6¢	Football	26.00	❑ 1439	8¢	CARE	12.00
❑ 1383	6¢	Eisenhower	5.00	❑ 1440	8¢	Landmarks	10.00
❑ 1384	6¢	Christmas	11.00	❑ 1444	8¢	Christmas	10.00
❑ 1385	6¢	Hope	9.00	❑ 1445	8¢	Partridge	10.00
❑ 1386	6¢	Harnett	5.00	❑ 1446	8¢	Lanier	17.00
❑ 1387–90	6¢	Conservation	8.50	❑ 1447	8¢	Peace Corps	12.00
❑ 1391	6¢	Maine	12.50	❑ 1448–51	2¢	Cape Hatteras	11.00
❑ 1392	6¢	Bison	13.00	❑ 1452	6¢	Wolf Trap	13.00
❑ 1393	6¢	Eisenhower	16.50	❑ 1453	8¢	Old Faithful	8.00
❑ 1393D	7¢	Franklin	26.00	❑ 1454	15¢	Mt. McKinley	21.00
❑ 1394	8¢	Eisenhower	23.00	❑ 1455	8¢	Family Planning	12.50
❑ 1395	8¢	Eisenhower	20.00	❑ 1456–59	8¢	Craftsmen	13.00
❑ 1396	8¢	U.S.P.S. Logo	21.00	❑ 1460	6¢	Cycling	9.00
❑ 1397	14¢	LaGuardia	34.00	❑ 1461	8¢	Bobsledding	10.00
❑ 1398	16¢	Pyle	50.00	❑ 1462	15¢	Running	20.00
❑ 1399	18¢	Blackwell	51.00	❑ 1463	8¢	P.T.A.	15.00
❑ 1400	21¢	Giannini	62.00	❑ 1464	8¢	Wildlife	11.00
❑ 1405	6¢	Masters	15.00	❑ 1468	8¢	Mail Order	15.00
❑ 1406	6¢	Suffrage	11.00	❑ 1469	8¢	Osteopath	19.00
❑ 1407	6¢	South Carolina	16.00	❑ 1470	8¢	Tom Sawyer	15.00
❑ 1408	6¢	Stone Mountain	15.00	❑ 1471	8¢	Christmas	10.50
❑ 1409	6¢	Fort Snelling	10.00	❑ 1472	8¢	Santa	13.00
❑ 1410–13	6¢	Conservation	17.00	❑ 1473	8¢	Pharmacy	20.00
❑ 1414	6¢	Christmas	8.00	❑ 1474	8¢	Stamp Collecting	10.00
❑ 1414a	6¢	Precanceled	12.00	❑ 1475	8¢	LOVE	12.00
❑ 1415–18	6¢	Toys	24.00	❑ 1476	8¢	Printing Press	11.00
❑ 1415a–18a	6¢	Toys precancel	35.00	❑ 1477	8¢	Broadside	11.00
❑ 1419	6¢	U.N.	9.00	❑ 1478	8¢	Post Rider	12.00
❑ 1420	6¢	Pilgrims	9.00	❑ 1479	8¢	Drummer	12.00
❑ 1421–22	6¢	Veterans	10.00	❑ 1480–83	8¢	Tea Party	14.00
❑ 1423	6¢	Wool	9.00	❑ 1484	8¢	Gershwin	11.00
❑ 1424	6¢	MacArthur	16.00	❑ 1485	8¢	Jeffers	10.00
❑ 1425	6¢	Give Blood	8.00	❑ 1486	6¢	Tanner	11.00
❑ 1426	8¢	Missouri	12.00	❑ 1487	8¢	Cather	12.00
❑ 1427–30	8¢	Wildlife	9.00	❑ 1488	8¢	Copernicus	12.00
❑ 1431	8¢	Antarctic	11.00	❑ 1489–98	8¢	Postal People	15.00
❑ 1432	8¢	Bicentennial	13.00	❑ 1499	8¢	Truman	13.00

❏ 1500	6¢	Electronics	11.00
❏ 1501	8¢	Electroncs	13.00
❏ 1502	15¢	Electronics	22.00
❏ 1503	8¢	L.B. J.	10.00
❏ 1504	8¢	Angus Cattle	11.00
❏ 1505	10¢	Chautauqua	14.00
❏ 1506	10¢	Winter Wheat	14.00
❏ 1507	8¢	Christmas	12.00
❏ 1508	8¢	Christmas Tree	13.00
❏ 1509	10¢	Crossed Flags	27.00
❏ 1510	10¢	Jeff. Memorial	30.00
❏ 1511	10¢	ZIP Code	29.00
❏ 1525	10¢	V.F.W.	13.00
❏ 1526	10¢	Robert Frost	23.00
❏ 1527	10¢	Expo '74	11.00
❏ 1528	10¢	Horse Racing	22.00
❏ 1529	10¢	Skylab	14.00
❏ 1530–37	10¢	UPU	11.00
❏ 1538–41	10¢	Minerals	14.50
❏ 1542	10¢	Ft. Harrod	17.00
❏ 1543–46	10¢	Independence	16.00
❏ 1547	10¢	Energy	13.00
❏ 1548	10¢	Sleepy Hollow	14.00
❏ 1549	10¢	Retarded Children	13.00
❏ 1550	10¢	Christmas	13.00
❏ 1551	10¢	Currier & Ives	13.00
❏ 1552	10¢	Weather Vane	16.00
❏ 1553	10¢	West	21.00
❏ 1554	10¢	Dunbar	21.00
❏ 1555	10¢	Griffith	20.00
❏ 1556	10¢	Pioneer 10	15.50
❏ 1557	10¢	Mariner 10	15.50
❏ 1558	10¢	Bargaining	14.00
❏ 1559	8¢	Ludington	11.00
❏ 1560	10¢	Poor	14.00
❏ 1561	10¢	Salomon	16.00
❏ 1562	18¢	Francisco	22.00
❏ 1563	10¢	Lexington-Concord	14.00
❏ 1564	10¢	Bunker Hill	13.00
❏ 1565–68	10¢	Armed Forces	16.00
❏ 1569–70	10¢	Apollo-Soyuz	7.50
❏ 1571	10¢	Women's Year	12.00
❏ 1572–75	10¢	Transportation	15.00
❏ 1576	10¢	Peace Thru Law	15.50
❏ 1577–78	10¢	Banking/Commerce	14.50
❏ 1579	10¢	Christmas	15.00
❏ 1580	10¢	Prang	17.00
❏ 1580B	10¢	Prang	42.00
❏ 1581	1¢	Inkwell	6.00
❏ 1582	2¢	Lectern	7.00
❏ 1584	3¢	Ballot Box	12.00
❏ 1585	4¢	Books	12.00
❏ 1591	9¢	Capitol Dome	25.00
❏ 1592	10¢	Justice	28.00
❏ 1593	11¢	Printing Press	32.00
❏ 1594	12¢	Torch	32.00
❏ 1596	13¢	Eagle	36.00
❏ 1597	15¢	U.S. Flag	46.00
❏ 1599	16¢	Liberty	50.00
❏ 1603	24¢	North Church	65.00
❏ 1604	28¢	Ft. Nisqually	74.00
❏ 1605	29¢	Lighthouse	90.00
❏ 1606	30¢	School House	90.00
❏ 1608	50¢	Lamp	140.00
❏ 1610	$1	Lamp	300.00
❏ 1611	$2	Lamp	540.00
❏ 1612	$5	Lantern	1350.00
❏ 1622	13¢	Flag & Hall	36.00
❏ 1622C	13¢	Flag & Hall	180.00
❏ 1629–31	13¢	Fife & Drum	24.00
❏ 1632	13¢	Interphil	17.00
❏ 1633–82	13¢	State Flags	30.00
❏ 1683	13¢	Telephone	20.00
❏ 1684	13¢	Aviation	19.00
❏ 1685	13¢	Chemistry	24.00
❏ 1691–94	13¢	Signers	36.00
❏ 1695–98	13¢	Olympics	23.00
❏ 1699	13¢	Maass	21.00
❏ 1700	13¢	Ochs	16.00
❏ 1701	13¢	Christmas	17.00
❏ 1702	13¢	Winter Pastime	21.00
❏ 1703	13¢	Winter Pastime	22.00
❏ 1704	13¢	Princeton	18.00
❏ 1705	13¢	Recording	23.00

❑ 1706–09	13¢	Pottery	15.00		❑ 1789	15¢	Jones, 11x12	21.00
❑ 1710	13¢	Spirit of St. Louis	18.00		❑ 1789A	15¢	Jones, 11	36.00
❑ 1711	13¢	Colorado	20.00		❑ 1789B	15¢	Jones, 12	—
❑ 1712–15	13¢	Butterflies	19.00		❑ 1790	10¢	Olympics	15.00
❑ 1716	13¢	Lafayette	20.00		❑ 1791–94	15¢	Olympics	25.00
❑ 1717–20	13¢	Craftsmen	19.00		❑ 1795–98	15¢	Olympics	26.00
❑ 1721	13¢	Peace Bridge	22.00		❑ 1799	15¢	Madonna	42.00
❑ 1722	13¢	Oriskany	17.00		❑ 1800	15¢	Santa	42.00
❑ 1723–24	13¢	Energy	16.00		❑ 1801	15¢	Rogers	21.00
❑ 1725	13¢	Alta	20.00		❑ 1802	15¢	Vietnam Vets	26.00
❑ 1726	13¢	Confederation	22.00		❑ 1803	15¢	W. C. Fields	21.00
❑ 1727	13¢	Talking Pictures	20.00		❑ 1804	15¢	Banneker	35.00
❑ 1728	13¢	Saratoga	15.00		❑ 1805–10	15¢	Letters	34.00
❑ 1729	13¢	Valley Forge	35.00		❑ 1818	(18¢)	"B" Stamp	54.00
❑ 1730	13¢	Mailbox	37.00		❑ 1821	15¢	Perkins	22.00
❑ 1731	13¢	Sandburg	25.00		❑ 1822	15¢	Madison	72.00
❑ 1732–33	13¢	Cook	24.00		❑ 1823	15¢	Bissell	29.00
❑ 1734	13¢	Indian	55.00		❑ 1824	15¢	Keller	31.00
❑ 1735	(15¢)	"A" Stamp	43.00		❑ 1825	15¢	V.A.	23.00
❑ 1744	13¢	Tubman	26.00		❑ 1826	15¢	Galvez	28.00
❑ 1745–48	13¢	Quilts	20.00		❑ 1827–30	15¢	Coral	22.00
❑ 1753	13¢	French Alliance	15.00		❑ 1831	15¢	Labor	22.00
❑ 1754	13¢	Pap Test	24.00		❑ 1832	15¢	Wharton	24.00
❑ 1755	13¢	Rodgers	29.00		❑ 1833	15¢	Learning	27.00
❑ 1756	15¢	Cohan	31.00		❑ 1834–37	15¢	Masks	27.00
❑ 1757	13¢	CAPEX	19.00		❑ 1838–41	15¢	Architecture	26.00
❑ 1758	15¢	Photography	17.00		❑ 1842	15¢	Madonna	22.00
❑ 1759	15¢	Viking	22.00		❑ 1843	15¢	Drum & Wreath	22.00
❑ 1760–63	15¢	Owls	22.00		❑ 1844	1¢	Dix	10.00
❑ 1764–67	15¢	Trees	19.00		❑ 1845	2¢	Stravinsky	9.00
❑ 1768	15¢	Madonna	42.00		❑ 1846	3¢	Clay	11.00
❑ 1769	15¢	Rocking Horse	43.00		❑ 1847	4¢	Schurz	12.00
❑ 1770	15¢	R. F. Kennedy	25.00		❑ 1848	5¢	Buck	15.00
❑ 1771	15¢	M.L. King.	31.00		❑ 1849	6¢	Lippmann	19.00
❑ 1772	15¢	Year of Child	24.00		❑ 1850	7¢	Baldwin	29.00
❑ 1773	15¢	Steinbeck	24.00		❑ 1851	8¢	Knox	25.00
❑ 1774	15¢	Einstein	31.00		❑ 1852	9¢	Thayer	33.00
❑ 1775–78	15¢	Toleware	19.00		❑ 1853	10¢	Russell	38.00
❑ 1779–82	15¢	Architecture	25.00		❑ 1854	11¢	Partridge	46.00
❑ 1783–86	15¢	Flowers	25.00		❑ 1855	13¢	Horse	44.00
❑ 1787	15¢	Seeing for Me	29.00		❑ 1856	14¢	Lewis	42.00
❑ 1788	15¢	Spec. Olympics	25.00		❑ 1857	17¢	Carson	49.00

❏ 1858	18¢	Mason	46.00		❏ 2003	20¢	Netherlands	35.00
❏ 1859	19¢	Sequoyah	60.00		❏ 2004	20¢	Library of Congress	28.00
❏ 1860	20¢	Bunche	66.00		❏ 2006–09	20¢	Energy	37.00
❏ 1861	20¢	Gallaudet	70.00		❏ 2010	20¢	Alger	28.00
❏ 1862	20¢	Truman	64.00		❏ 2011	20¢	Aging	28.00
❏ 1863	22¢	Audubon	73.00		❏ 2012	20¢	Barrymores	28.00
❏ 1864	30¢	Laubach	85.00		❏ 2013	20¢	Walker	30.00
❏ 1865	35¢	Drew	115.00		❏ 2014	20¢	Peace Garden	31.00
❏ 1866	37¢	Millikan	108.00		❏ 2015	20¢	Libraries	28.00
❏ 1867	39¢	Clark	110.00		❏ 2016	20¢	Robinson	110.00
❏ 1868	40¢	Gilbreth	110.00		❏ 2017	20¢	Touro	50.00
❏ 1869	50¢	Nimitz	117.00		❏ 2018	20¢	Wolf Trap	28.00
❏ 1874	15¢	Dirksen	24.00		❏ 2019	20¢	Architecture	34.00
❏ 1875	15¢	Young	25.00		❏ 2023	20¢	Francis of Assisi	30.00
❏ 1876–79	18¢	Flowers	29.00		❏ 2024	20¢	de Léon	39.00
❏ 1890	18¢	Flag-Grain	54.00		❏ 2025	13¢	Kitten & Puppy	23.00
❏ 1894	20¢	Flag-Court	96.00		❏ 2026	20¢	Madonna	31.00
❏ 1910	18¢	Red Cross	28.00		❏ 2027	20¢	Christmas	42.00
❏ 1911	18¢	Savings & Loan	26.00		❏ 2031	20¢	Science/Industry	28.00
❏ 1912–19	18¢	Space	34.00		❏ 2032–35	20¢	Ballooning	27.00
❏ 1920	18¢	Management	26.00		❏ 2036	20¢	Sweden	27.00
❏ 1921–24	18¢	Habitats	30.00		❏ 2037	20¢	C.C.C.	28.00
❏ 1925	18¢	Disabled	26.00		❏ 2038	20¢	Priestley	31.00
❏ 1926	18¢	Millay	27.00		❏ 2039	20¢	Volunteer	30.00
❏ 1927	18¢	Alcoholism	57.00		❏ 2040	20¢	German Immigr.	28.00
❏ 1928–31	18¢	Architecture	36.00		❏ 2041	20¢	Brooklyn Bridge	27.00
❏ 1932	18¢	Zaharias	35.00		❏ 2042	20¢	T.V.A.	32.00
❏ 1933	18¢	Jones	66.00		❏ 2043	20¢	Fitness	31.00
❏ 1934	18¢	Remington	27.00		❏ 2044	20¢	Joplin	33.00
❏ 1935	18¢	Hoban	26.00		❏ 2045	20¢	Medal of Honor	32.00
❏ 1936	20¢	Hoban	28.00		❏ 2046	20¢	Babe Ruth	115.00
❏ 1937–38	18¢	Yorktown Map	29.00		❏ 2047	20¢	Hawthorne	33.00
❏ 1939	(20¢)	Madonna	53.00		❏ 2048	13¢	Olympics	32.00
❏ 1940	(20¢)	Teddy Bear	27.00		❏ 2052	20¢	Treaty of Paris	25.00
❏ 1941	20¢	Hanson	32.00		❏ 2053	20¢	Civil Service	32.00
❏ 1942–45	20¢	Cactus	30.00		❏ 2054	20¢	The Met	33.00
❏ 1946	(20¢)	"C" Stamp	56.00		❏ 2055–58	20¢	Inventors	41.00
❏ 1950	20¢	F.D.R.	28.00		❏ 2059–62	20¢	Streetcars	40.00
❏ 1951	20¢	Love	31.00		❏ 2063	20¢	Madonna	28.00
❏ 1952	20¢	Washington	30.00		❏ 2064	20¢	Santa Claus	34.00
❏ 1953–02	20¢	State Birds	42.00		❏ 2065	20¢	Martin Luther	28.00
❏ 1953A–02A	20¢	State Birds	50.00		❏ 2066	20¢	Alaska	28.00

☐ 2067–70	20¢	Olympics	41.00
☐ 2071	20¢	FDIC	28.00
☐ 2072	20¢	Love	30.00
☐ 2073	20¢	Woodson	31.00
☐ 2074	20¢	Conservation	28.00
☐ 2075	20¢	Credit Union	29.00
☐ 2076–79	20¢	Orchids	30.00
☐ 2080	20¢	Hawaii	31.00
☐ 2081	20¢	Archives	30.00
☐ 2082–85	20¢	Olympics	47.00
☐ 2086	20¢	Louisiana Expo	37.00
☐ 2087	20¢	Health Research	33.00
☐ 2088	20¢	Fairbanks	36.00
☐ 2089	20¢	Thorpe	39.00
☐ 2090	20¢	McCormack	28.00
☐ 2091	20¢	Seaway	29.00
☐ 2092	20¢	Wetlands	43.00
☐ 2093	20¢	Roanoke	37.00
☐ 2094	20¢	Melville	28.00
☐ 2095	20¢	Moses	44.00
☐ 2096	20¢	Smokey	36.00
☐ 2097	20¢	Clemente	130.00
☐ 2098–01	20¢	Dogs	30.00
☐ 2102	20¢	Anti-Crime	28.00
☐ 2103	20¢	Hispanic	22.00
☐ 2104	20¢	Family Unity	41.00
☐ 2105	20¢	E. Roosevelt	28.00
☐ 2106	20¢	Readers	34.00
☐ 2107	20¢	Madonna	27.00
☐ 2108	20¢	Santa Claus	28.00
☐ 2109	20¢	Vietnam Memorial	36.00
☐ 2110	22¢	Kern	33.00
☐ 2111	(22¢)	"D" Stamp	105.00
☐ 2114	22¢	Flag	60.00
☐ 2137	22¢	Bethune	46.00
☐ 2138–41	22¢	Decoys	100.00
☐ 2142	22¢	Special Olympics	27.00
☐ 2143	22¢	Love	35.00
☐ 2144	22¢	Electrification	54.00
☐ 2145	22¢	AMERIPEX	28.00
☐ 2146	22¢	Adams	29.00
☐ 2147	22¢	Bartholdi	28.00

☐ 2152	22¢	Korea Veterans	43.00
☐ 2153	22¢	Social Security	30.00
☐ 2154	22¢	WW I Veterans	40.00
☐ 2155–58	22¢	Horses	125.00
☐ 2159	22¢	Education	68.00
☐ 2160–63	22¢	Youth Year	60.00
☐ 2164	22¢	Hunger	32.00
☐ 2165	22¢	Madonna	31.00
☐ 2166	22¢	Poinsettia	30.00
☐ 2167	22¢	Arkansas	57.00
☐ 2168	1¢	Mitchell	11.00
☐ 2169	2¢	Lyon	9.00
☐ 2170	3¢	White	12.00
☐ 2171	4¢	Flanagan	14.00
☐ 2172	5¢	Black	36.00
☐ 2173	5¢	Marin	19.00
☐ 2175	10¢	Red Cloud	41.00
☐ 2176	14¢	Howe	43.00
☐ 2177	15¢	Cody	78.00
☐ 2178	17¢	Lockwood	55.00
☐ 2179	20¢	Apgar	54.00
☐ 2180	21¢	Carlson	61.00
☐ 2181	23¢	Cassatt	60.00
☐ 2182	25¢	London	67.00
☐ 2183	28¢	Sitting Bull	87.00
☐ 2184	29¢	Warren	87.00
☐ 2185	29¢	Jefferson	87.00
☐ 2186	35¢	Chavez	100.00
☐ 2187	40¢	Chenault	110.00
☐ 2188	45¢	Cushing	130.00
☐ 2189	52¢	Humphrey	170.00
☐ 2190	56¢	Harvard	165.00
☐ 2191	65¢	Arnold	175.00
☐ 2192	75¢	Wilkie	200.00
☐ 2193	$1	Revel	380.00
☐ 2194	$1	Hopkins	62.00
☐ 2195	$2	Bryan	525.00
☐ 2196	$5	Harte	260.00
☐ 2202	22¢	Love	34.00
☐ 2203	22¢	Truth	42.00
☐ 2204	22¢	Texas	34.00
☐ 2210	22¢	Hospitals	36.00

❑ 2211	22¢	Ellington	32.00	❑ 2376	22¢	Rockne	45.00
❑ 2220–23	22¢	Explorers	70.00	❑ 2377	25¢	Ouimet	53.00
❑ 2224	22¢	Liberty	37.00	❑ 2378	25¢	Love	70.00
❑ 2235–38	22¢	Navajo Carpets	50.00	❑ 2379	45¢	Love	66.00
❑ 2239	22¢	Eliot	40.00	❑ 2380	25¢	Gymnast	42.00
❑ 2240–43	22¢	Carvings	45.00	❑ 2386–89	25¢	Explorers	60.00
❑ 2244	22¢	Madonna	60.00	❑ 2390–93	25¢	Carousel	62.00
❑ 2245	22¢	Village Scene	62.00	❑ 2394	$8.75	Express Mail	525.00
❑ 2246	22¢	Michigan	29.00	❑ 2399	25¢	Madonna	33.00
❑ 2247	22¢	Pan Am Games	30.00	❑ 2400	25¢	Winter Scene	32.00
❑ 2248	22¢	Love	60.00	❑ 2401	25¢	Montana	35.00
❑ 2249	22¢	du Sable	32.00	❑ 2402	25¢	Randolph	37.00
❑ 2250	22¢	Caruso	30.00	❑ 2403	25¢	North Dakota	38.00
❑ 2251	22¢	Girl Scouts	30.00	❑ 2404	25¢	Washington	36.00
❑ 2275	22¢	United Way	28.00	❑ 2410	25¢	Stamp Expo '89	37.00
❑ 2277	(25¢)	"E" Stamp	82.00	❑ 2411	25¢	Toscanini	36.00
❑ 2278	25¢	Flag	70.00	❑ 2412	25¢	House of Reps.	44.00
❑ 2286–35	22¢	Wildlife	72.00	❑ 2413	25¢	Senate	47.00
❑ 2336	22¢	Delaware	42.00	❑ 2414	25¢	Executive Br.	44.00
❑ 2337	22¢	Pennsylvania	46.00	❑ 2415	25¢	Supreme Court	42.00
❑ 2338	22¢	New Jersey	46.00	❑ 2416	25¢	South Dakota	42.00
❑ 2339	22¢	Georgia	42.00	❑ 2417	25¢	Gehrig	60.00
❑ 2340	22¢	Connecticut	46.00	❑ 2418	25¢	Hemingway	41.00
❑ 2341	22¢	Massachusetts	46.00	❑ 2419	$2.40	Moon Landing	160.00
❑ 2342	22¢	Maryland	51.00	❑ 2420	25¢	Letter Carriers	25.00
❑ 2343	22¢	South Carolina	50.00	❑ 2421	25¢	Bill of Rights	46.00
❑ 2344	22¢	New Hampshire	50.00	❑ 2422–25	25¢	Dinosaurs	56.00
❑ 2345	22¢	Virginia	49.00	❑ 2426	25¢	Southwest	33.00
❑ 2346	22¢	New York	47.00	❑ 2427	25¢	Madonna	34.00
❑ 2347	22¢	North Carolina	47.00	❑ 2428	25¢	Sleigh	33.00
❑ 2348	22¢	Rhode Island	55.00	❑ 2434	25¢	UPU	45.00
❑ 2349	22¢	Morocco	30.00	❑ 2439	25¢	Idaho	32.00
❑ 2350	22¢	Faulkner	48.00	❑ 2440	25¢	Love	31.00
❑ 2351–54	22¢	Lace	37.00	❑ 2442	25¢	Wells	44.00
❑ 2360	22¢	Constitution	48.00	❑ 2444	25¢	Wyoming	35.00
❑ 2361	22¢	CPAs	170.00	❑ 2445–49	25¢	Films	78.00
❑ 2367	22¢	Madonna	60.00	❑ 2449	25¢	Moore	31.00
❑ 2368	22¢	Ornament	62.00	❑ 2476	1¢	Kestrel	7.00
❑ 2369	22¢	Skier	36.00	❑ 2477	1¢	Kestrel	7.50
❑ 2370	22¢	Australial	25.00	❑ 2478	3¢	Bluebird	10.00
❑ 2371	22¢	Johnson	33.00	❑ 2479	19¢	Fawn	51.00
❑ 2372–75	22¢	Cats	42.00	❑ 2480	30¢	Cardinal	74.00

❑ 2481	45¢	Sunfish	100.00	
❑ 2482	$2	Bobcat	94.00	
❑ 2496	25¢	Olympians	41.00	
❑ 2506–07	25¢	Micronesia	42.00	
❑ 2508–11	25¢	Sea Mammals	41.00	
❑ 2512	25¢	Grand Canyon	40.00	
❑ 2513	25¢	Eisenhower	42.00	
❑ 2514	25¢	Madonna	36.00	
❑ 2515	25¢	Christmas Tree	36.00	
❑ 2517	(29¢)	"F" Stamp	80.00	
❑ 2521	(4¢)	Make Up Rate	12.00	
❑ 2524	29¢	Tulip	76.00	
❑ 2524A	29¢	Tulip	90.00	
❑ 2531	29¢	Flags	100.00	
❑ 2531A	29¢	Torch	78.00	
❑ 2532	50¢	Switzerland	62.00	
❑ 2533	29¢	Vermont	60.00	
❑ 2534	29¢	Savings Bonds	40.00	
❑ 2535	29¢	Love	40.00	
❑ 2535A	29¢	Love	50.00	
❑ 2537	52¢	Love Birds	76.00	
❑ 2538	29¢	Saroyan	40.00	
❑ 2539	$1	Olympic Rings	56.00	
❑ 2540	$2.90	Eagle	180.00	
❑ 2541	$9.95	Express Mail	500.00	
❑ 2542	$14	Express Mail	700.00	
❑ 2543	$2.90	Spacecraft	300.00	
❑ 2544	$3	Space Shuttle	140.00	
❑ 254A	$10.75	Space Shuttle	600.00	
❑ 2550	29¢	Porter	46.00	
❑ 2551	29¢	Desert Storm	46.00	
❑ 2553–57	29¢	Olympics	42.00	
❑ 2558	29¢	Numismatics	50.00	
❑ 2559	29¢	WWar II, 1941	22.00	
❑ 2560	29¢	Basketball	47.00	
❑ 2561	29¢	D.C.	37.00	
❑ 2567	29¢	Matzeliger	40.00	
❑ 2579	(29¢)	Santa	37.00	
❑ 2587	32¢	Polk	86.00	
❑ 2590	$1	Burgoyne	54.00	
❑ 2592	$5	Washington/Jackson	270.00	
❑ 2611–15	29¢	Olympics	36.00	
❑ 2616	29¢	Stamp Expo	36.00	
❑ 2617	29¢	DuBois	46.00	
❑ 2618	29¢	Love	39.00	
❑ 2619	29¢	Baseball	62.00	
❑ 2620–23	29¢	Columbus	40.00	
❑ 2630	29¢	Stock Exchange	31.00	
❑ 2631–24	29¢	Space	52.00	
❑ 2635	29¢	Alaska Hiway	38.00	
❑ 2636	29¢	Kentucky	38.00	
❑ 2637–41	29¢	Olympics	34.00	
❑ 2647–96	29¢	Wildflowers	50.00	
❑ 2697	29¢	WW II, 1942	24.00	
❑ 2698	29¢	Parker	41.00	
❑ 2699	29¢	von Kármán	38.00	
❑ 2700	29¢	Minerals	41.00	
❑ 2704	29¢	Cabrillo	41.00	
❑ 2711–14	29¢	Christmas	46.00	
❑ 2720	29¢	Rooster	21.00	
❑ 2721	29¢	Elvis	38.00	
❑ 2722	29¢	Oklahoma!	32.00	
❑ 2723	29¢	Williams	40.00	
❑ 2723A	29¢	Williams	950.00	
❑ 2724–30	29¢	Singers	50.00	
❑ 2746	29¢	Julian	42.00	
❑ 2747	29¢	Oregon Trail	41.00	
❑ 2748	29¢	Univ. Games	40.00	
❑ 2749	29¢	Grace Kelly	38.00	
❑ 2750–53	29¢	Circus	48.00	
❑ 2754	29¢	Cherokee Strip	17.00	
❑ 2755	29¢	Acheson	38.00	
❑ 2756–59	29¢	Horse Racing	40.00	
❑ 2765	29¢	WWar II, 1943	23.00	
❑ 2766	29¢	Louis	51.00	
❑ 2771–74	29¢	Singers	24.00	
❑ 2779–82	29¢	Postal Museum	23.00	
❑ 2783–84	29¢	Deafness	19.00	
❑ 2785–88	29¢	Literature	44.00	
❑ 2789	29¢	Madonna	36.00	
❑ 2791–94	29¢	Christmas	46.00	
❑ 2804	29¢	Mariana Is.	17.00	
❑ 2805	29¢	Columbus	40.00	
❑ 2806	29¢	AIDS	40.00	

❏ 2807–11	29¢	Olympics	21.00
❏ 2812	29¢	Murrow	36.00
❏ 2814C	29¢	Love	51.00
❏ 2815	52¢	Love	75.00
❏ 2816	29¢	Davis	18.00
❏ 2817	29¢	Year of Dog	30.00
❏ 2818	29¢	Buffalo Soldiers	18.00
❏ 2819–28	29¢	Film Stars	37.00
❏ 2834	29¢	Soccer	18.00
❏ 2835	40¢	Soccer	21.00
❏ 2836	50¢	Soccer	30.00
❏ 2838	29¢	WW II, 1944	23.00
❏ 2839	29¢	Rockwell	43.00
❏ 2842	29¢	Moon	560.00
❏ 2848	29¢	Meany	38.00
❏ 2849–53	29¢	Singers	26.00
❏ 2854–61	29¢	Singers	45.00
❏ 2862	29¢	Thurber	40.00
❏ 2863–66	29¢	Sea Wonders	32.00
❏ 2867–68	29¢	Cranes	20.00
❏ 2869	29¢	Legends	19.00
❏ 2870	29¢	Legends	175.00
❏ 2871	29¢	Madonna	40.00
❏ 2872	29¢	Stocking	37.00
❏ 2876	29¢	Year of Boar	19.00
❏ 2877	(4¢)	Make-up Rate	9.00
❏ 2878	(4¢)	Make-up Rate	11.00
❏ 2879	(20¢)	"G" Stamp	65.00
❏ 2880	(20¢)	"G" Stamp	67.00
❏ 2881	(32¢)	"G" Stamp	240.00
❏ 2882	(32¢)	"G" Stamp	90.00
❏ 2897	32¢	Flag	96.00
❏ 2933	32¢	Hershey	80.00
❏ 2934	32¢	Farley	81.00
❏ 2935	32¢	Luce	16.00
❏ 2936	32¢	Wallace	16.00
❏ 2938	46¢	Benedict	124.00
❏ 2940	55¢	Hamilton	130.00
❏ 2941	55¢	Morrill	27.00
❏ 2942	77¢	Breckinridge	36.00
❏ 2943	78¢	Paul	200.00
❏ 2948	(32¢)	Love	41.00
❏ 2950	32¢	Florida	24.00
❏ 2951–54	32¢	Environment	16.00
❏ 2955	32¢	Nixon	41.00
❏ 2956	32¢	Coleman	40.00
❏ 2957	32¢	Love	41.00
❏ 2958	55¢	Love	75.00
❏ 2961–65	32¢	Sports	21.00
❏ 2966	32¢	POW - MIA	16.00
❏ 2967	32¢	Marilyn	27.00
❏ 2968	32¢	Texas	21.00
❏ 2974	32¢	U.N.	16.00
❏ 2975	32¢	Civil War	14.00
❏ 2976–79	32¢	Carousel	24.00
❏ 2980	32¢	Suffrage	32.00
❏ 2981	32¢	WW II, 1945	26.00
❏ 2982	32¢	Armstrong	22.00
❏ 2983–92	32¢	Singers	28.00
❏ 2998	60¢	Rickenbacker	86.00
❏ 2999	32¢	Palau	40.00
❏ 3000	32¢	Comics	17.00
❏ 3001	32¢	Annapolis	18.00
❏ 3002	32¢	Williams	21.00
❏ 3003	32¢	Christmas	40.00
❏ 3004–07	32¢	Christmas	45.00
❏ 3019–23	32¢	Autos	24.00
❏ 3024	32¢	Utah	40.00
❏ 3031	1¢	Kestrel	6.00
❏ 3031A	1¢	Kestrel	6.00
❏ 3032	2¢	Woodpecker	8.00
❏ 3033	3¢	Blue Bird	11.00
❏ 3036	$1	Red Fox	50.00
❏ 3058	32¢	Just	19.00
❏ 3059	32¢	Smithsonian	19.00
❏ 3060	32¢	Year of Rat	22.00
❏ 3061–64	32¢	Scientists	20.00
❏ 3065	32¢	Scholarships	51.00
❏ 3066	50¢	Cochran	65.00
❏ 3067	32¢	Marathon	17.00
❏ 3068	32¢	Olympics	15.00
❏ 3069	32¢	O'Keeffe	17.00
❏ 3070	32¢	Tennessee	40.00
❏ 3072–76	32¢	Dance	20.00

❏ 3077–80	32¢	Prehistoric	20.00
❏ 3081	32¢	Breast Cancer	24.00
❏ 3082	32¢	Dean	20.00
❏ 3083–86	32¢	Folk Heroes	20.00
❏ 3087	32¢	Olympics	21.00
❏ 3088	32¢	Iowa	41.00
❏ 3090	32¢	RFD	16.00
❏ 3091–95	32¢	Riverboats	21.00
❏ 3096–99	32¢	Musicians	22.00
❏ 3100–03	32¢	Composers	21.00
❏ 3104	23¢	Fitzgerald	35.00
❏ 3105	32¢	Endangered	16.00
❏ 3106	32¢	Computers	30.00
❏ 3107	32¢	Madonna	38.00
❏ 3108–11	32¢	Christmas	52.00
❏ 3118	32¢	Hanukkah	16.00
❏ 3120	32¢	Year of Ox	19.00
❏ 3121	32¢	Davis	20.00
❏ 3125	32¢	Learning	20.00
❏ 3130–31	32¢	Pacific 97	17.00
❏ 3134	32¢	Wilder	16.00
❏ 3135	32¢	Wallenberg	16.00
❏ 3136	32¢	Dinosaurs	10.00
❏ 3139	50¢	Pacific 97	11.00
❏ 3140	60¢	Pacific 97	16.00
❏ 3141	32¢	Marshall Plan	16.00
❏ 3142	32¢	Aircraft	16.00
❏ 3147	32¢	Lombardi	21.00
❏ 3148	32¢	Bryant	18.00
❏ 3149	32¢	Warner	18.00
❏ 3150	32¢	Halas	18.00
❏ 3151	32¢	Dolls	11.00
❏ 3152	32¢	Bogart	18.00
❏ 3153	32¢	Stars & Strips	38.00
❏ 3154–57	32¢	Opera	24.00
❏ 3158–65	32¢	Composers	22.00
❏ 3166	32¢	Varela	17.00
❏ 3167	32¢	Air Force	16.00
❏ 3168–72	32¢	Monsters	21.00
❏ 3173	32¢	Flight	16.00
❏ 3174	32¢	Military Women	17.00
❏ 3175	32¢	Kwanzaa	40.00
❏ 3179	32¢	Year of Tiger	17.00
❏ 3180	32¢	Skiing	19.00
❏ 3181	32¢	Walker	19.00
❏ 3182	32¢	1900s	12.00
❏ 3183	32¢	1910s	12.00
❏ 3184	32¢	1920s	12.00
❏ 3185	32¢	1930s	11.00
❏ 3186	33¢	1940s	12.00
❏ 3187	33¢	1950s	12.00
❏ 3188	33¢	1960s	12.00
❏ 3189	33¢	1970s	11.00
❏ 3190	33¢	1980s	11.00
❏ 3191	33¢	1990s	11.00
❏ 3192	32¢	The Maine	19.00
❏ 3193–87	32¢	Flowers	16.00
❏ 3198–02	32¢	Calder	18.00
❏ 3203	32¢	Cinco de Mayo	17.00
❏ 3209	1¢–$2	Trans-Mississippi	12.00
❏ 3210	$1	Cattle in Storm	22.00
❏ 3211	32¢	Airlift	16.00
❏ 3212–19	32¢	Singers	20.00
❏ 3220	32¢	Spanish Settlement	18.00
❏ 3221	32¢	Benét	18.50
❏ 3226	32¢	Hitchcock	16.00
❏ 3227	32¢	Organ Donors	16.00
❏ 3230–34	32¢	Bright Eyes	22.00
❏ 3235	32¢	Klondike	17.00
❏ 3236	32¢	Art	16.00
❏ 3237	32¢	Ballet	17.00
❏ 3238–42	32¢	Future Space	16.00
❏ 3243	32¢	Giving	16.00
❏ 3249–52	32¢	Wreaths	17.00
❏ 3257	(1¢)	Weather Vane	4.00
❏ 3258	(1¢)	Weather Vane	4.00
❏ 3259	22¢	Uncle Sam	10.00
❏ 3260	(33¢)	Hat	35.00
❏ 3261	$3.20	Space Shuttle	170.00
❏ 3262	$11.75	Space Shuttle	600.00
❏ 3272	33¢	Year of Rabbit	16.00
❏ 3273	33¢	Malcolm X	21.00
❏ 3276	33¢	Hospice	15.00
❏ 3277	33¢	Flag	80.00

❑ 3286	33¢	Irish	16.00
❑ 3287	33¢	Lunt & Fontanne	16.00
❑ 3288–92	33¢	Arctic Animals	16.00
❑ 3293	33¢	Desert	10.00
❑ 3308	33¢	Rand	14.00
❑ 3309	33¢	Cinco de Mayo	15.00
❑ 3314	33¢	Bartram	15.00
❑ 3315	33¢	Prostate Cancer	14.00
❑ 3316	33¢	Gold Rush	15.00
❑ 3317–20	33¢	Fish	15.00
❑ 3321–24	33¢	Extreme Sports	15.00
❑ 3325	33¢	Glass	14.00
❑ 3329	33¢	Cagney	16.00
❑ 3330	33¢	Mitchell	25.00
❑ 3331	33¢	Who Served	18.00
❑ 3332	45¢	U.P.U.	18.00
❑ 3333–37	33¢	Trains	20.00
❑ 3338	33¢	Olmsted	16.00
❑ 3339–44	33¢	Composers	16.00
❑ 3345–50	33¢	Composers	18.00
❑ 3351	33¢	Insects	15.00
❑ 3352	33¢	Hanukkah	16.00
❑ 3354	33¢	NATO	16.00
❑ 3356–59	33¢	Stag	15.00
❑ 3369	33¢	New Year	16.00
❑ 3370	33¢	Year of Dragon	16.00
❑ 3371	33¢	Harris	14.00
❑ 3372	33¢	Submarine	14.00
❑ 3378	33¢	Rain Forest	10.00
❑ 3379–83	33¢	Nevelson	16.00
❑ 3385–88	33¢	Hubble	16.00
❑ 3389	33¢	Samoa	15.00
❑ 3390	33¢	Library of Cong.	16.00
❑ 3393	33¢	War Heroes	16.00
❑ 3397	33¢	Runners	16.00
❑ 3398	33¢	Adoption	16.00
❑ 3399–02	33¢	Sports	15.00
❑ 3403	33¢	Flags	15.00
❑ 3408	33¢	Baseball	15.00
❑ 3414–17	33¢	Drawings	15.00
❑ 3420	10¢	Stillwell	9.00
❑ 3426	33¢	Pepper	15.00
❑ 3431	76¢	Caraway	31.00
❑ 3632	37¢	Ferber	25.00
❑ 3438	33¢	California	15.00
❑ 3439–43	33¢	Fish	15.00
❑ 3444	33¢	Wolfe	14.00
❑ 3445	33¢	White House	14.00
❑ 3446	33¢	Robinson	14.00
❑ 3448	(34¢)	Flag	16.00
❑ 3449	(34¢)	Flag	21.00
❑ 3467	21¢	Buffalo	52.00
❑ 3468	21¢	Buffalo	10.00
❑ 3468A	23¢	Washington	13.00
❑ 3469	34¢	Flag	12.00
❑ 3470	34¢	Flag	15.00
❑ 3471	55¢	Eagle	23.00
❑ 3471A	57¢	Eagle	24.00
❑ 3472	$3.50	Capitol Dome	17.00
❑ 3473	$12.25	Wash. Monument	600.00
❑ 3499	55¢	Love	22.00
❑ 3500	34¢	Year of Snake	16.00
❑ 3501	34¢	Wilkins	15.00
❑ 3502	34¢	Illustrators	15.00
❑ 3503	34¢	Diabetes	14.00
❑ 3504	34¢	Nobel Prize	16.00
❑ 3505		Inverts	9.00
❑ 3506	34¢	Prairie	9.00
❑ 3507	34¢	Snoopy	20.00
❑ 3508	34¢	Veterans	16.00
❑ 3509	34¢	Kahlo	14.50
❑ 3510–19	34¢	Stadiums	14.50
❑ 3521	34¢	Bernstein	14.00
❑ 3523	34¢	Ball	14.00
❑ 3524–27	34¢	Quilts	14.00
❑ 3528–31	34¢	Carniverous	14.00
❑ 3532	34¢	Eid	14.00
❑ 3533	34¢	Fermi	14.00
❑ 3537–40	34¢	Christmas	14.00
❑ 3545	34¢	Monroe	15.00
❑ 3546	34¢	Thanks	15.00
❑ 3547	34¢	Hanukkah	15.00
❑ 3548	34¢	Kwanzaa	15.00
❑ 3551	57¢	Love	22.00

❏ 3552–55	34¢	Olympics	15.00	❏ 3672	37¢	Hanukkah SA	14.75
❏ 3556	34¢	Mentoring	15.00	❏ 3673	37¢	Kwanzaa SA	14.75
❏ 3557	34¢	Hughes	15.00	❏ 3674	37¢	Islamic Festival	14.75
❏ 3558	34¢	Birthday	15.00	❏ 3675	37¢	Madonna (pane of 20)	14.75
❏ 3559	34¢	Year of Horse	15.00	❏ 3676–79	37¢	Snowman	14.75
❏ 3560	34¢	West Point	15.00	❏ 3692	37¢	Cary Grant	14.75
❏ 3561–10	34¢	Greetings	32.00	❏ 3695	37¢	Happy Birthday	14.75
❏ 3611	34¢	Pine Forest	8.00	❏ 3746	37¢	Thurgood Marshall SA	14.75
❏ 3613	3¢	Star	7.00	❏ 3747	37¢	Year of the Ram SA	14.75
❏ 3614	3¢	Star	6.00	❏ 3748	37¢	Zora Neale Hurston	
❏ 3646	60¢	Eagle	24.00			SA	14.75
❏ 3647	$3.85	Jefferson Memorial	160.00	❏ 3751	10¢	U.S. Clock	4.50
❏ 3648	$13.65	Capitol Dome	550.00	❏ 3757	1¢	Tiffany Lamp	38.75
❏ 3649	37¢	Photography	14.00	❏ 3771	80¢	Special Olympics	30.00
❏ 3650	37¢	Audubon	15.00	❏ 3773	37¢	Ohio Statehood	14.75
❏ 3651	37¢	Houdini	15.00	❏ 3774	37¢	Pelican Island	14.75
❏ 3652	37¢	Andy Warhol	14.75	❏ 3781	37¢	Cesar Chavez SA	14.75
❏ 3653–56	37¢	Teddy Bears	14.75	❏ 3782	37¢	Louisiana Purchase SA	14.75
❏ 3657	37¢	Love Pane of 20	24.00	❏ 3784	37¢	Purple Heart	14.75
❏ 3659	37¢	Ogden Nash SA	14.75	❏ 3785	37¢	Sea Coast	14.75
❏ 3660	37¢	Duke Kahanamoku	14.75	❏ 3786	37¢	Audrey Hepburn	14.75
❏ 3661–64	37¢	American Bats	14.75	❏ 3787–91	37¢	Cape Henry	
❏ 3665–68	37¢	Nellie Bly	14.75			Lighthouse	14.75
❏ 3669	37¢	Irving Berlin	14.75	❏ 3803	37¢	Korean War	14.75
❏ 3670–71	37¢	Neuter and Spay	14.75	❏ 3812	37¢	Roy Acuff	14.75

SEMIPOSTAL STAMPS

❏ B1	(32¢+8¢)	Breast Cancer	21.00	❏ B2	(34¢+11¢)	Heroes of 2001	17.00

AIRMAIL

❏ C25	6¢	Transport	10.00	❏ C38	5¢	New York	23.00
❏ C26	8¢	Transport	12.00	❏ C39	6¢	DC-4	19.00
❏ C27	10¢	Transport	74.00	❏ C40	6¢	Alexandria	12.00
❏ C28	15¢	Transport	160.00	❏ C42	10¢	UPU	16.00
❏ C29	20¢	Transport	120.00	❏ C43	15¢	UPUI	22.00
❏ C30	30¢	Transport	150.00	❏ C44	25¢	UPUI	37.00
❏ C31	50¢	Transport	760.00	❏ C45	6¢	Wright Bros.	13.00
❏ C32	5¢	DC-4, large	9.00	❏ C46	80¢	Diamond Head	330.00
❏ C33	5¢	DC-4, small	16.00	❏ C47	6¢	Flight	10.00
❏ C34	10¢	Building	15.00	❏ C48	4¢	Eagle	16.00
❏ C35	15¢	N.Y. Skyline	23.00	❏ C49	6¢	Air Force	10.00
❏ C36	25¢	Golden Gate	56.00	❏ C50	5¢	Eagle	16.00

❑ C51	7¢	Jetliner, blue	17.00
❑ C53	7¢	Alaska	12.00
❑ C54	7¢	Balloon Jupiter	15.00
❑ C55	7¢	Hawaii	12.00
❑ C56	10¢	Pan Am Games	13.00
❑ C57	10¢	Liberty Bell	74.00
❑ C58	15¢	Statue of Liberty	22.00
❑ C59	25¢	Abraham Lincoln	34.00
❑ C60	7¢	Jetliner, carmine	22.00
❑ C62	13¢	Liberty Bell	22.00
❑ C63	15¢	Statue of Liberty	22.00
❑ C64	8¢	Jetliner-Capitol	23.00
❑ C66	15¢	Blair	31.00
❑ C67	6¢	Eagle	18.00
❑ C68	8¢	Amelia Earhart	16.00
❑ C69	8¢	Robert Goddard	21.00
❑ C70	8¢	Alaska Purchase	15.00
❑ C71	20¢	Columbia Jays	44.00
❑ C72	10¢	Runway of Stars	30.00
❑ C74	10¢	Biplane	16.00
❑ C75	20¢	USA & Jet	25.00
❑ C76	10¢	Moon Landing	12.00
❑ C77	9¢	Delta Wing	26.00
❑ C78	11¢	Jetliner	32.00
❑ C79	13¢	Winged Letter	37.00
❑ C80	17¢	Statue of Liberty	24.00
❑ C81	21¢	USA & Jet	28.00
❑ C84	11¢	City of Refugee	17.00
❑ C85	11¢	Skiers	16.00
❑ C86	11¢	Electronics	17.00
❑ C87	18¢	Statue of Liberty	24.00
❑ C88	26¢	Mt. Rushmore	36.00
❑ C89	25¢	Jetliner & Globes	35.00
❑ C90	31¢	Jetliner	45.00

❑ C91–92	31¢	Wright Bros.	84.00
❑ C93–94	21¢	Chanute	90.00
❑ C95–96	25¢	Post	165.00
❑ C97	31¢	High Jumper	42.00
❑ C98	40¢	Mazzei, perf 11	62.00
❑ C98A	40¢	Mazzei, perf 10½ x11½	47.00
❑ C99	28¢	Scott	41.00
❑ C100	35¢	Curtiss	47.00
❑ C101–4	28¢	Olympics	64.00
❑ C105–8	40¢	Olympics	62.00
❑ C109–12	35¢	Olympics	68.00
❑ C113	33¢	Verville	45.00
❑ C114	39¢	Sperry	55.00
❑ C115	44¢	Clipper	58.00
❑ C116	44¢	Serra	68.00
❑ C117	44¢	New Sweden	74.00
❑ C118	45¢	Langley	65.00
❑ C119	36¢	Sikorsky	55.00
❑ C120	45¢	French Revolution	36.00
❑ C121	45¢	Carved Figure	66.00
❑ C122–5	45¢	Space Travel	66.00
❑ C127	45¢	Tropical Beach	75.00
❑ C128	50¢	Quimby	68.00
❑ C129	40¢	Piper	60.00
❑ C130	50¢	Antarctic	67.00
❑ C131	50¢	Asia Crossing	67.00
❑ C132	40¢	Piper	91.00
❑ C133	48¢	Niagara Falls	22.00
❑ C134	40¢	Rio Grande	17.00
❑ C135	60¢	Grand Canyon	26.00
❑ C136	70¢	Nine Mile Prairie	28.00
❑ C137	80¢	Mount McKinley	31.00
❑ C138	60¢	Acadia National Park	22.00

SPECIAL DELIVERY

❑ E20	20¢	Letter, blue	32.00
❑ E21	30¢	Letter, maroon	38.00

❑ E22	45¢	Arrows	67.00
❑ E23	60¢	Arrows	72.00

CERTIFIED MAIL

❑ FA1	10¢	Letter Carrier	25.00

POSTAGE DUE

☐ J88	½¢	Red & Black	385.00	☐ J97	10¢	Red & Black	27.00
☐ J89	1¢	Red & Black	6.50	☐ J98	30¢	Red & Black	72.00
☐ J90	2¢	Red & Black	8.00	☐ J99	50¢	Red & Black	126.00
☐ J91	3¢	Red & Black	10.00	☐ J100	$1	Red & Black	280.00
☐ J92	4¢	Red & Black	17.00	☐ J101	$5	Red & Black	910.00
☐ J93	5¢	Red & Black	15.00	☐ J102	11¢	Red & Black	32.00
☐ J94	6¢	Red & Black	18.00	☐ J103	13¢	Red & Black	34.00
☐ J95	7¢	Red & Black	23.00	☐ J104	17¢	Red & Black	100.00
☐ J96	8¢	Red & Black	24.00				

OFFICIAL STAMPS

☐ O127	1¢	Great Seal	9.00	☐ O146	4¢	Great Seal	14.00
☐ O128	4¢	Great Seal	11.00	☐ O146A	10¢	Great Seal	24.00
☐ O129	13¢	Great Seal	44.00	☐ O147	19¢	Great Seal	54.00
☐ O130	17¢	Great Seal	47.00	☐ O148	23¢	Great Seal	62.00
☐ O132	$1	Great Seal	260.00	☐ O151	$1	Great Seal	435.00
☐ O133	$5	Great Seal	980.00	☐ O154	1¢	Great Seal	10.00
☐ O138	(14¢)	"D"	440.00	☐ O155	20¢	Great Seal	58.00
☐ O143	1¢	Great Seal	10.00	☐ O156	23¢	Great Seal	63.00

AMERICAN FIRST DAY COVERS
THE AMERICAN FIRST DAY COVER SOCIETY

The FIRST and ONLY not-for-profit, non-commercial, International Society devoted exclusively to First Day Covers and First Day Cover collecting.

FIRST DAYS IS THE AWARD-WINNING OFFICIAL PUBLICATION OF THE AMERICAN FIRST DAY COVER SOCIETY. FDC collecting is a hands-on hobby of personal involvement—much more than simple collecting. It encourages the individual collector to fully develop his range of interests so that his collection is a reflection of his personal tastes. FDCs will encourage your creativity to reach full expression by adapting cachets or cancellations or using combinations (related stamps). In this hobby uniqueness is the rule, not the exception.

BUT . . . *FIRST DAYS* IS AVAILABLE ONLY TO MEMBERS OF THE AFDCS. It's just ONE of the many benefits of membership. Whether you are interested in topical areas of collecting, working on serious research, or just learning more about the hobby in general, this is the organization for you.

AMERICAN FIRST DAY COVER SOCIETY

CHAPTERS

A complete list of all of the chapters of the American First Day Cover Society, along with names of the chapter representatives, is included in The Official Blackbook Price Guide to United States Postage Stamps. This list is found after this introduction to First Day Covers collecting and before the Glossary of First Day Cover Terms. If you see a chapter that meets in your area, or one that features the type of cover you collect, do not hesitate to contact the chapter representative for more information.

American First Day Cover Society chapters can be reached through the contact person listed, or you can contact the AFDCS chapter coordinator, Foster E. Miller, III, P.O. Box 44, Annapolis, MD 20701, e-mail: fmiller@pobox.net.

#1. Queen City Stamp & Cover Club: James Demos, 69 Liberty Corner Rd., Warren, NJ 07059

#2. Baltimore Philatelic Society, Inc.: Alice M. L. Robinson, 1224 N. Calvert St., Baltimore, MD 21202

#3. Motor City Stamp & Cover Club: Robert Quintero, 22608 Poplar Ct., Hazel Park, MI 48030

#4. ChicagoLand FDC Society: Randall Sherman, 1101 W. Columbia Ave. #212, Chicago, IL 60626

#5. W. Suburban Stamp Club of Plymouth: Editor, Newsletter, P.O. Box 700049, Plymouth, MI 48170

#6. Harford County Stamp Club: Kenneth Rapple, P.O. Box 163, Bel Air, MD 21014

#7. Carroll County Philatelic Assoc.: Blair H. Law, 4510 Willow View St., Hampstead, MD 21074

#8. Robert C Graebner Chapter of AFDCS: Rollin Beiser, 13000 Evans, Ford Ct., Clifton, VA 20124

#9. Metropolitan FDC Society: Benjamin Green, 66-15 Thornton Pl, Rego Park, NY 11374

#10. FDC Collectors Club: Stephen Neulander, 951 Brookside Lane, Deerfield, IL 60015

#11. Coryell's Ferry Stamp Club: Mrs. Frank Davis, P.O. Box 52, Penns Park, PA 18943

#12. Ft. Findlay Stamp Club: Tom Foust, 5578 State Rt. 186, McComb, OH 45858

#13. Hazlet Stamp Club: Oscar Strandberg, 54 Crestview Dr, Middletown, NJ 07748

#14. Columbus Philatelic Club: Paul Gault, P.O. Box 20711, Columbus, OH 43220

#15. Autograph Chapter of AFDCS: George Haggas, P.O. Box 1463, Merchantville, NJ 08109

#17. Columbia Philatelic Society: Harold T. Babb, 341 Tram Rd., Columbia, SC 29210

#18. FDC Unit of Clifton Stamp Society: Andrew Boyajian, P.O. Box 229, Hasbrouck Heights, NJ 07604

#19. George Washington Masonic Stamp Club: Stan Longenecker, 930 Wood St., Mount Joy, PA 17552

#20. Hamilton Township Philatelic Society: John Ranto, 10 Cranbrook Rd., Hamilton, NJ 08690

#21. Joplin Stamp Club: Fred Roesel, 4225 East 25th St., Joplin, MO 64801

#22. Gulf Coast FDC Group: Monte Eiserman, 14359 Chadbourne, Houston, TX 77079

#23. Claude C. Ries Chapter of AFDCS: Rick Whyte, 2870 N. Town Ave., Apt. 137, Pomona, CA 91767

#24. The 7/1/71 Affair: Roy E. Mooney, P.O. Box 2539, Cleveland, GA 30528

#25. Central NY FDC Society: Rick Kase, P.O. Box 10833, Rochester, NY 14610

#26. Journalists, Authors and Poets on Stamps (JAPOS): Clete Delvaux, 1600 Rushwoods Ct., Green Bay, WI 59301

#27. Louisville FDC Society: Arthur S. Buchter, 5410 Cannonwood Ct., Louisville, KY 40229

#28. North Texas Chapter of AFDCS: Paul Benson, 201 Willow Creek Circle, Allen, TX 77079

#29. Long Island Cover and Autograph Society: Secretary LIC&AS, Box 2095, Port Washington, NY 11050

#30. American Ceremony Program Society: Monte Eiserman, 14359 Chadbourne, Houston, TX 77079

#31. Florida Chapter of AFDCS: George Athens, 3295 Datura Rd., Venice, FL 34293

#32. Ohio Cachetmakers Assoc.: Chris & Denise Lazaroff, 2967 Aylesbury St. NW, N. Canton, OH 44720

#33. Gateway to the West Chpt. of AFDCS: Art Rosenberg, 8686 Delmar Blvd., #2W, St. Louis, MO 63124

#35. Society of Philatelists & Numismatists: Joe R. Ramos, 1929 Millis St., Montebello, CA 90640

#36. Cachet Makers Assoc.: Chris Lazarolt, 2467 Aylesbury St., NW, N. Canton, OH 44720

#37. Maximum Card Study Unit: Gary Denis, P.O. Box 766, Patuxent River, MD 20670

#38. Rochester Philatelic Assoc.: Joe Doles, 105 Lawson Rd., Rochester, NY 14616

#39. Tucson Stamp Club: Alex Lutgendorf, P.O. Box 50603, Tucson, AZ 85703

#40. North Carolina Chapter of AFDCS: Eric Wile, 2202 Jane St., Greensboro, NC 27407

#41. Gay and Lesbian History on Stamps: Ed Centeno, P.O. Box 140942, Dallas, TX 75214

#42. Hand-Painted Cover Chapter of AFDCS: Alan Freedman, 48 Kent Rd., Hillsdale, NJ 07642

#43. Multnomah Children's Covers: Tommy Lee, 4572 Catalpa St., Los Angeles, CA 90032

#44. American Indian Philatelic Society: Dean Lilly, 5460 Margie Lane, Oak Forest, IL 60542

#45. Harry C. Ioor Chapter of AFDCS: Patrick Tudor, 920 N. Bolton Ave., Indianapolis, IN 46219

#46. Molly Pitcher Stamp Club: Gary Dubnik, 74 Cumberland Ave., Verona, NJ 07044

#47. National Duck Stamp Collectors Society: Secretary, P.O. Box 43, Harleysville, PA 19438

#48. Art Cover Exchange (ACE): Joseph Doles, 105 Lawson Rd., Rochester, NY 14616

#49. Waterbury Stamp Club: Laurent Corriveau, P.O. Box 581, Waterbury, CT 06720

#52. Dayton Stamp Club: Frank Shivly, 415 Far Hills Ave., Dayton, OH 45409

#53. Virtual Stamp Club: Lloyd de Vries, Box 561, Paramus, NJ 07653, e-mail: stamps@pobox.com

#54. Norwalk Stamp Club: Richard Hoffman, Box 267, Norwalk, CT 06856

#55. Junior Philatelists of America: Erik Thompsen, 25301 Emperial Drive, Eagle River, AK 99577

#56. American Society of Philatelic Pages and Panels: Gerald Blankenship, P.O. Box 475, Crosby, TX 77532

#57. Stamp Collector Club of Toledo: Frank Ellis, 1436 Abbott, Toledo, OH 43604

#58. U.S. Presidential Inaugural Philatelic Society: Ed Krohn, P.O. Box 357309, Gainesville, FL 32655

#59. Australian Society: Noei Almeida, P.O. Box 768, Dandenong 3173 Australia

#60. Ebony Society of Philatelic Events Reflection (ESPER): Eugene Robinson, 112–45 175th St., Jamaica, NY 11433

A GLOSSARY OF
FIRST DAY COVER TERMS

Compiled by FIRST DAYS Staff

Add-on—A cachet design added to a cover which was originally uncacheted. An add-on cachet should be identified by maker and date so that it is clear that it is not contemporary with the cover. Unfortunately, many add-ons are not so identified.

Aerogramme—Postal stationery characterized by a single sheet which may be folded into an envelope, sealed, and then sent at a rate less than the airmail letter rate. Postage is usually but not always imprinted. Also known as aerogram.

AFDCS—American First Day Cover Society.

All-over cachet—A cachet design that covers most of or the entire face (front) of the envelope, as compared to one that occupies just the left side.

All-purpose cachet—A cachet with a general design that can be used for any stamp subject. It has no specific theme. Also, General Purpose.

Alternate cancel—Any First Day cancellation from the official First Day city, other than the official First Day of Issue postmarks supplied by the USPS. (These are sometimes referred to as semi-officials, or by the specific name of the cancel, such as plug, slogan, show, or ship cancels, etc.)

AMF—Air Mail Field. Found in many postmarks of postal facilities located in airports.

Autographed—An autographed envelope bears one or more signatures of individuals who are usually associated with the stamp. The autograph relationships may be the stamp subject, the designer, the local postmaster, dignitaries present at the dedication ceremony, etc. Authenticity and possible mechanical application of an autograph are significant considerations.

Auxiliary markings—Postal markings which are occasionally found on First Day Covers such as "Registered," "Insured," "Return to Sender," "Postage Due ——¢," etc.

B/4—Block of four stamps. Also B4.

Back stamp—The arrival mark of the destination city which usually appears on the reverse of the cover. Most registered covers are back-stamped on arrival.

Booklet pane—A sheetlet of stamps removed from a stamp booklet which may have one or more such panes. On FDC it is desirable to include the tab which is used to bind the pane into the booklet. This may not be possible with some modern issues.

Bullseye—also, bull's-eye. 1) The dial or circular portion of a postmark used by itself as a cancel. 2) Any circular postmark struck directly on the center of a stamp. (See Socked-on-the-nose.)

Cachet—Any textual or graphic design which has been applied to a cover usually, but not always, on the left side of the envelope. A cachet may be produced by any means—printed, rubber stamped, hand drawn, etc. A First Day cachet should be related specifically to the stamp on the cover.

Cachetmaker—One who designs and/or produces cacheted envelopes. Cachets may be identified by the artist's name, brand name, or manufacturing firm.

Cancel—The portion of a postmark which defaces or "kills" the stamp. Often loosely used interchangeably with "postmark."

CDS—Circular date stamp, ie. the dial or circular portion of the postmark.

Ceremony program—The printed program usually distributed by the Post Office or sponsoring organization at the First Day dedication of a new stamp. These are usually collected with the new stamp affixed and cancelled on the First Day.

Classic—The period prior to 1930 during which few First Day Covers were serviced and cachets were not common.

Coil—Stamps produced in rolls for use in vending machines. They are characterized by two opposite edges being straight or imperforate. A horizontal coil stamp is imperforate top and bottom and a vertical coil is straight-edged at the left and right sides.

Combo—One or more thematically related stamps affixed to a FDC. Also, combination cover.

Commemorative—A stamp, usually of large format, which is issued to salute or honor a person, event, state, organization, place, etc. Typically issued on an anniversary in a multiple of 10, 50, 100 years, etc. and produced in limited quantities. Contrasted with "definitive."

Commercial FDCs—FDCs sponsored by an individual, company, or organization used for promoting a service, product or as a gesture of goodwill.

Contract station—A sub-unit of a larger post office which is contracted to a private individual. Most contract stations are located in private business establishments.

Corner card—The imprint at the upper left corner of a cover which may be the return address or other identification of the sender.

Counterfeit—A stamp, postmark, or cachet created in direct imitation of a genuine item and intended to deceive. It is a Federal offense to counterfeit any postal marking or postal issue.

Cover—An envelope that has seen postal service or has a cancelled stamp on it, usually one with philatelic interest. May exemplify some segment of postal history or simply be a souvenir of an event or a place.

Crash cover—Any cover or FDC salvaged from the crash of a plane or vehicle in which it was carried. Usually bears postal markings explaining its damaged condition.

CXL—Abbreviation for "cancel." Also, cxl.

Definitive—Stamp issued for an indefinite period in an indefinite quantity to meet an ordinary postal rate. Designs do not usually honor a specific time dated event or person; most frequently in small format. Contrasted with "commemorative." Also known as "regular issue."

Designated First Day—The date officially announced by the Post Office for the sale of a new postal issue. Many issues prior to 1922 had no designated First Day. Covers cancelled prior to the designated dates are predates.

Dial—Circular portion of a postmark, usually containing the city, date and time. See bullseye.

Dual cancel—Two related or unrelated cancellations on a cover, each cancelling a stamp. One or both cancels may be for a First Day.

Duplex cancel—A metal handstamp containing both cancel and postmark in a single unit. Often found on FDCs before the mid-1930s.

EDC—Earliest documented cover. The earliest known postmark on a postal issue which had no designated First Day. Used interchangeably with EKU.

EFO—Errors, Freaks, and Oddities, i.e., stamps, cachets, cancellations, etc. that contain unintended mistakes or design faults.

EKU—Earliest known use. A designation for the earliest identified postmark on a stamp for which a first day of issue was not designated.

Electric eye (EE)—An electronic device which guides the perforating equipment during stamp manufacture. This is accomplished by heavy ink dashes in the selvage, which are used for detection and alignment. FDCs of EE stamps must have the selvage with dashes attached to the stamps.

Embossing—The process of impressing a design in relief into the paper of an envelope.

Engraved—A method of printing in which the lines of the design are cut into metal, which are recessed to retain the ink. The paper is forced under pressure into these lines to pick up the ink. Hence engraved cachets appear to have the design raised above the paper surface.

Error—A consistent abnormal variety created by a mistake in the production of a stamp or postmark. For example, the name of a city may be misspelled in the First Day cancel. Used in contrast to "freak."

Esoterica—Any item, other than a cover or envelope, that has been First Day cancelled that doesn't fit any of the regular collecting categories.

Event cover—A cacheted cover, not a FDC, prepared as a souvenir of a specific event or an anniversary of an event.

Event program—A list of events or speakers in any program related to the stamp release, such as a stamp show, any function at which a stamp is released, or any event honoring the same event as the stamp.

Fancy cancel—A cancellation which is or includes a design. The term is normally used for 19th-century cancels which were created by local postal officials according to personal whim. Also, see pictorial.

Favor cancel—Any postal marking supplied as a favor or accommodation for a stamp collector.

FD—First Day.

FDC—First Day Cover. (FDCs—plural)

FDOI—First Day Of Issue. The slogan found in most First Day cancellations since Sc. 795, released in 1937.

FFC—First flight cover, ie. a cover flown on the inaugural flight of a new air route.

Filler—A stiff piece of paper, cardboard, or plastic found inside a First Day Cover. It provides necessary stiffness for a clearer cancellation. It also protects the cover from bending when it travels through the mail stream. Fillers, also termed stuffers, occasionally are imprinted with an advertising message or information pertaining to the stamp or cachet on the cover.

First cachet—The initial cachet commercially produced by a cachetmaker.

First Day—The day on which a stamp for the first time is officially sold by the Post Office.

First Day cover—Cover with a new stamp(s) or postal indicia, cancelled on the First Day.

Flag cancel—A cancellation used during the early 20th century incorporating a flag design. The stripes of the flag are the killer bars. Also, any more recent cancel with a similar design.

Flocked—A cachet production method in which powdered cloth is adhered to the envelope in the desired design.

Forgery—A fraudulently produced or altered philatelic item intended to deceive the collector.

Frank—A stamp, mark, or signature that shows payment of postage on a piece of mail. (A signature, with no stamp or paid marking, is called a Free Frank. Free as available to Congress and the President.)

Freak—An abnormal variety created by an unusual circumstance and not repeated with regularity. For example, a FDC may bear only a portion of a postmark because the cover was misfed into the cancelling machine. Used in contrast to "error."

General purpose (GP)—A cachet with a general design that is non-specific and may be used with any stamp subject. Also, All-purpose.

Hand cancel (HC)—A canceller which is applied to stamps individually and by hand. May be manufactured of plastic, rubber, or steel and is similar to a rubber stamp.

Hand-drawn (H/D)—A cachet applied to a cover by hand with pen, pencil, brush, chalk, or other art media. Each cachet is made individually and is an original.

Handmade (H/M)—A cachet applied to a cover by hand by adding seals, pasteups, collage, or similar materials. Each cachet is made individually and is an original.

Hand-painted (H/P) or Hand-colored (H/C)—A printed, hand-drawn or handmade cachet to which hand painting or hand coloring has been added.

HC, H/C, H/D, H/M, H/P—See preceding definitions.

HPO—Highway Post Office. The Post Office sorted mail on special motor vehicles in transit between cities. This system was in use from the late 1930s through the mid-1970s. FDCs were occasionally cancelled with HPO markings.

IA—Ink addressed. Refers to the method of addressing a cover.

Inaugural cover—A cover cancelled on the day that a president is sworn into office. Since 1957 the words INAUGURATION DAY have been incorporated into the cancel. The site was usually Washington, D.C., although other locations, like the President's city of birth, are now being designated. (In 1957 and 1985 the inauguration date fell on a Sunday. In both cases, covers of January 20, the private swearing-in ceremony, and January 21, the date of the public ceremony, both exist, and both are considered collectible.)

Indicia—An imprint on postal stationery indicating prepayment of postage. The plural is also "indicia."

Joint issue—Two or more stamps issued by different countries to commemorate the same event, topic, place, or person. Officially sanctioned joint issues are intentionally issued with the cooperation of the postal services of the countries involved.

Killer bars—The horizontal lines of a postmark which cancel the stamp. Since 1937 the FIRST DAY OF ISSUE slogan has appeared between the bars of most First Day cancels.

LA—Label addressed. Refers to the addressing method on a cover.

LSASE—A legal-sized, stamped, self-addressed envelope. See SASE.

Last Day—The final day of a postal rate, post office operation, or similar occurrence. A cover cancelled on this day is referred to as a last day cover.

Lithography, or litho—A common method of printing stamps and cachets in which the design is transferred from a smooth plate by selective inks which wet only the design portion of the printing plate.

LL—Lower left. Refers to the plate number or marginal marking position on a sheet of stamps.

LR—Lower right. Refers to the marginal marking position.

Luminescent—The condition of a stamp or postal stationery which has been treated with chemicals which are sensitive to and glow under ultraviolet (UV) light. This permits automatic cancelling equipment to detect the position of the postage on the cover and to orient it for rapid mechanical cancelling.

Machine cancel (MC)—A cancellation applied by an automatic cancelling device or machine.

Maximum card—A picture (post)card with a reproduction of the stamp or related subject from which the stamp was derived. Maximum card specialists prefer that the card and the stamp be as directly related as possible, but not be reproduced. The attempt is to achieve maximum agreement or concordance between the stamp subject and postcard. The stamp and cancel are usually placed on the illustrated side. This may be cancelled on the First Day of the stamp. See "Souvenir card."

Mellone catalog—A series of cachet catalogs for various time periods. They feature cachet illustrations with assigned code numbers for identification.

Mylar—Dupont's trademark for a durable plastic (polyester) film often recommended for storing stamps or covers because of its excellent chemical stability and the protection offered.

Nondenominated—Stamp or postal stationery without denomination or value in the design. These were created by the Post Office in anticipation of postal rate change when the exact rates could not be determined in advance.

Obliterator—Another term for the cancel portion of a postmark which defaces or obliterates the stamp.

OE—An abbreviation which indicates that a cover has been opened at the end or side.

Official—1) Of or related to the Federal government. USPS postmarks are official markings. 2) Stamps or stationery issued for use by government departments in the course of official business.

Official cachet—1) A cachet produced and applied by or for postal administrations. Official cachets are rare on U.S. FDCs but are common for many other countries. 2) Loosely used to refer to cachets authorized or sponsored by an organization closely associated with the issuance of a stamp, more properly called a sponsored cachet. The word "official" is abused by some cachetmakers.

Official FDC—Any First Day Cover with an official government postmark. This term is often misused for covers with sponsored cachets.

Offset—A printing method in which the design is transferred by ink from the image to another surface and then applied to the paper.

OT—An abbreviation indicating that a cover has been opened at the top.

PA—Pencil addressed. Refers to the method of cover addressing.

Patriotic or patriotic cachet—Design with patriotic or nationalistic theme, most often used to bolster public spirit during periods of war or national stress.

PB—Plate block. A group of stamps with the plate number in the selvage. May contain four or more stamps depending on the configuration of the printed numbers.

Peelable label—A self-stick label that can be easily removed from a cover without leaving adhesive or blemish. Used for addressing covers—later removed to create unaddressed covers.

Philatelic center—A post office window or station where most currently available stamps may be purchased by collectors. Created for the convenience of stamp collectors. Also postique.

Photocachet—A cachet consisting in part or entirely of a photograph.

Pictorial—A cancellation incorporating a pictorial design. Pictorial First Day cancels were used by the United States from 1958 to 1962 and are becoming more widespread on FDC issues of the 1980s and '90s. Many postiques each have a unique pictorial cancel. Many non-FD pictorial cancels are available nationwide, and are used for a limited time at special public or philatelic events.

Planty Catalogue—Catalog of U.S. cachets, for various year periods in individual volumes, assembled by Prof. Earl Planty. Planty identification designations are referred to as Planty Numbers.

Plug cancel—Colloquial name for a round, double circle marking, officially known as a validator stamp. The plug is chiefly used on postal receipts and registered envelopes. Also called a registry cancel or round-dater.

PNC—1) Plate Number Coil, ie. a coil stamp with a plate number thereon. 2) Philatelic-numismatic cover, ie. a cover with a cancelled stamp and a visible coin on the front, both thematically related. May be a FDC for the stamp.

POD—Post Office Department, the predecessor of the USPS. Also USPOD.

Polysleeve—Any of a variety of generally clear plastic sleeves, usually closed on two or three sides, to contain covers so they may be handled without soiling or damage.

Postage due—Stamps issued to indicate a penalty for insufficient postage. Postage due stamps are not used to pay postage, yet some issues are known on FDCs. These FDCs were cancelled inadvertently or by favor.

Postal card—A government produced postcard with an indicia indicating prepayment of postage.

Postal stationery—Postal cards, aerogrammes, and envelopes on which postage has been imprinted. Created as a convenience for the public so postage need not be applied.

Post-cancelled (post-dated, back-dated)—A cover which has been cancelled on a date later than that indicated on the postmark.

Postcard—A privately produced card usually bearing an illustration on one side and spaces for message, address, and postage on the other.

Postique—A special station or location at a post office where collectors may obtain currently available stamps. Each office usually has its own pictorial cancellation.

Postmark—A postal marking which indicates the time and point of origin of the mail to which it is applied. Often loosely used interchangeably with "Cancel."

Precancel—Stamps or stationery issued by the Post Office with words or lines printed thereon which prevent further use of the stamp. Precancelled stamps need not be cancelled again during mail handling. The standard First Day postmarks, however, are applied to FDCs of precancels.

Predate—A cover with a stamp cancelled earlier than the officially designated First Day of sale. Predates usually are created when stamps are sold prior to the official release date, contrary to postal regulations. Predates can exist only for issues with a designated First Day date.

Presentation album—Album containing a pane of a new stamp which is distributed to each dignitary at a First Day dedication ceremony. The album may have the recipient's name engraved on it. The first album is always for the President of the United States.

Presidentials—The 1938 series of definitive stamps featuring the Presidents of the United States.

Prexy—An information alternative term to designate the Presidential series of definitives.

PR—Pair of stamps.

Printed cachets—A cachet design type that is produced by printing, using any one of many methods.

Program—See Ceremony program.

Rag content—Pertains to the use of cotton fiber rather than wood pulp in the manufacture of envelopes. High rag content or 100 percent rag envelopes resist the ravages of time much better than do wood fiber covers, which contain processing chemicals that eventually discolor the paper and make the envelope more brittle.

Regular issue—Stamp issued for an indefinite period and quantity for ordinary postal use. See definitive.

RPO—Railway post office. A system once used by the POD to process mail in railroad cars enroute between cities. A distinctive cancel was used and FDCs exist with RPO postmarks.

Registry cancel—See plug.

RSA—Rubber-stamp addressed. A cover addressing method.

RSC—Rubber-stamp cachet.

Rubber stamps (R/S) cachet—A cachet applied to a cover using a rubber stamp. This method or device was very popular in the 1930s.

SASE—Self-addressed stamped envelope or SAE—self-addressed envelope. See also "LSASE."

Scott—Philatelic Publishing Company which produces Scott catalogs. A Scott (Sc.) number refers to a Scott catalog number to identify a stamp—a widely accepted practice.

Second-Day cover—A cover postmarked on the day following the First Day Of Issue. These were popular in the 1940s when the stamps were available at the Philatelic Agency in Washington, DC, on the second day.

Self-adhesive—A pre-gummed postage stamp on a peelable backing which requires no moisture for affixing to an envelope.

Selvage—The edges of a stamp pane beyond the perforations—including the portions that contain marginal markings as plate numbers, copyright notice, and other symbols/text. The plain selvage is usually removed from stamps when preparing FDCs, except for plate numbers and other collectible markings. Also spelled "selvedge."

Service—The act of affixing a stamp to and having it cancelled on a cover.

Servicer—One who performs the act of servicing. Frequently a person who does so on a commercial and large volume basis.

SGL—Single stamp. Also "sgl."

Ship cancel—A cancellation applied aboard a vessel—most frequently U.S. Navy although there are others. Ship cancels are fairly common but such strikes on FDCs are considered unusual because they represent a special effort in order to be obtained.

Show cancel—Special Post Office cancellation designed for and applied at a philatelic show or exhibition station.

Silk cachet—A cachet type with a pictorial design printed on a piece of fabric with a silky finish.

Slogan cancel—A cancellation with a message incorporated, such as— "Mail Early Before Christmas" or "Fight Tuberculosis."

Socked-on-the-nose (SOTN)—Designation for a stamp where the circle of the postmark falls exactly on the center. Another designation for "bullseye."

Souvenir card—A commemorative card, usually with reproductions of previously issued stamps and an inscription, issued by postal authorities in conjunction with a special philatelic event. The card or stamp units cannot be used for postal purposes but are often enhanced by collectors with an actual stamp and cancel.

Souvenir program—See ceremony program.

Sponsor (cachet)—Individual or organization that has commissioned an established cachetmaker to prepare a special design in addition to the regular cachet for a particular issue. The term is sometimes used interchangeably with "cachetmaker."

Sponsored cachet—A cachet authorized or sponsored by an organization closely associated with the issuance of a stamp. See also "Official cachet," No. 2.

Station cancel—A cancellation applied at a temporary postal station established for a convention, exhibition, or other special event.

Stuffer—See filler.

Tagged—Stamp or postal stationery which has had the postage area treated with a material sensitive to ultraviolet (UV) light, so that the cover can be mechanically oriented for canceling. Also luminescent.

Thermography—A printing method for producing raised designs by use of a special powder and heat. Often called, "poor man's embossing."

Tied—The cancellation overlaps the stamp, falling on both the postage and the cover thus affirming that the stamp was affixed prior to the postmarking. Also may be applied to non-postal labels or adhesives to show contemporaneous usage.

Toning—A deleterious condition of a cover resembling darkening or discoloration caused by excess gum at the edge of the stamp or a stain from the gum of the envelope flap. May also result from chemicals used in the production of inexpensive envelopes.

Trade name—A name or identification assigned to a cachet line by the producer. Example: Washington Press produces Artcraft Cachets.

UA—Unaddressed. A cover which does not have an address.

UL—Upper left. Refers to the position of stamp marginal markings.

Unaddressed (UA)—A cover which has no address.

Uncacheted—A cover which has no cachet design.

Unofficial cancel—A private, non-postal marking, usually resembling an official postmark, applied to a stamp or cover.

Unofficial FDC (UO)—A FDC cancelled with other than the official FIRST DAY OF ISSUE slogan cancel or official First Day pictorial cancelled supplied by the USPS for the First Day. For FDCs before the initial use of the FDOI slogan, this term refers to any city other than that which was officially designated. (There is much controversy among specialists and purists about this definition. Some dislike the use of the word "unofficial" as all postmarks are official cancellations of the USPS. Some would like to make a further distinction between stamps purchased in the official FD city, versus stamps sold in error on or before the FD in cities other than the FD city. Both of these are points well taken, but basically UOs are any FDC serviced in the city of issue or another location with any cancel other than the official FD cancel supplied by the USPS. A UO FDC must have the correct First Day date.)

UO—Unofficial First Day cover.

UR—Upper right. Refers to the position of the marginal markings on stamp selvage.

USPS—United States Postal Service, established in 1971.

Validator—See plug.

FIRST DAY COVERS

NOTE: "D.C." indicates Washington, D.C., as the official city and date of issue. Other cities with significantly different values are also listed. When no city is indicated, the number of cities in which the stamps were issued is indicated.

Scott No.			Single	Block of 4
Uncacheted.				
❏ 551	½¢	Hale (D.C. & New Haven, CT, 4/4/25)	20.00	24.00
❏ 552	1¢	Franklin (D.C., 1/17/23)	22.50	42.00
❏ 552	1¢	Franklin (Philadelphia, PA)	47.00	55.00
❏ 553	1½¢	Harding (D.C., 3/19/25)	26.00	32.00
❏ 554	2¢	Washington (D.C., 1/15/23)	38.00	48.00
❏ 555	3¢	Lincoln (D.C., 2/12/23)	37.00	50.00
❏ 555	3¢	Lincoln (Hodgenville, KY)	210.00	325.00
❏ 556	4¢	Martha Washington (D.C., 1/15/23)	65.00	82.00
❏ 557	5¢	Roosevelt (D.C., 10/27/22)	120.00	175.00
❏ 557	5¢	Roosevelt (New York, NY)	260.00	410.00
❏ 557	5¢	Roosevelt (Oyster Bay, NY)	1900.00	—
❏ 558	6¢	Garfield (D.C., 11/20/22)	200.00	270.00
❏ 559	7¢	McKinley (D.C., 5/1/23)	160.00	175.00
❏ 559	7¢	McKinley (Niles, OH)	200.00	—
❏ 560	8¢	Grant (D.C., 5/1/23)	175.00	210.00
❏ 561	9¢	Jefferson (D.C., 1/15/23)	165.00	210.00
❏ 562	10¢	Monroe (D.C., 1/15/23)	170.00	210.00
❏ 563	11¢	Hayes (D.C., 10/4/22)	1000.00	3750.00
❏ 563	11¢	Hayes (Fremont, OH)	2700.00	—
❏ 564	12¢	Cleveland (D.C., Boston, MA, Caldwell, NJ, 3/20/23)	200.00	330.00
❏ 565	14¢	Indian (D.C., 5/1/23)	360.00	450.00
❏ 565	14¢	Indian (Muskogee, OK)	2100.00	5800.00
❏ 566	15¢	Statue of Liberty (D.C., 11/11/22)	525.00	850.00
❏ 567	20¢	Golden Gate (5/1/23)	600.00	950.00
❏ 567	20¢	Golden Gate (San Francisco)	3600.00	—
❏ 568	25¢	Niagara Falls (D.C., 11/11/22)	650.00	900.00
❏ 569	30¢	Bison (D.C., 3/20/23)	810.00	1200.00
❏ 570	50¢	Arlington (D.C., 11/11/22)	1525.00	—
❏ 571	$1	Lincoln Memorial (D.C., Springfield, IL 2/12/23)	6800.00	18,000.00
❏ 572	$2	U.S. Capitol (D.C., 3/20/23)	19,000.00	—

Scott No.			Single	Block of 4
❑ 573	$5	America (D.C., 3/20/23)	34,000.00	—
❑ 576	1½¢	Harding (D.C., 4/4/25)	46.00	60.00
❑ 581	1¢	Franklin (D.C., 10/17/23)	710.00	—
❑ 582	1½¢	Harding (D.C., 3/19/25)	42.00	50.00
❑ 583a	2¢	Washington (booklet pane, D.C., 8/27/26)	1250.00	—
❑ 584	3¢	Lincoln (D.C., 8/1/25)	52.00	80.00
❑ 585	4¢	Martha Washington (D.C., 4/4/25)	52.00	80.00
❑ 586	5¢	Roosevelt (D.C., 4/4/25)	52.00	80.00
❑ 587	6¢	Garfield (D.C., 4/4/25)	52.00	80.00
❑ 588	7¢	McKinley (D.C., 5/29/26)	70.00	80.00
❑ 589	8¢	Grant (D.C., 5/29/26)	72.00	93.00
❑ 590	9¢	Jefferson (D.C., 5/29/26)	72.00	93.00
❑ 591	10¢	Monroe (D.C., 6/8/25)	85.00	125.00
❑ 597	1¢	Franklin (coil, D.C., 7/18/23)	710.00	—
❑ 598	1½¢	Harding (coil, D.C., 3/19/25)	450.00	—
❑ 599	2¢	Washington (coil, D.C., 1/15/23)	2700.00	—
❑ 600	3¢	Lincoln (coil, D.C., 5/10/24)	120.00	—
❑ 602	5¢	Roosevelt (coil, D.C., 3/5/24)	110.00	—
❑ 603	10¢	Monroe (coil, D.C., 2/1/24)	120.00	—
❑ 604	1¢	Franklin (coil, D.C., 7/19/24)	95.00	—
❑ 605	1½¢	Harding (coil, D.C., 5/9/25)	75.00	—
❑ 606	2¢	Washington (coil, D.C., 12/31/23)	140.00	—
❑ 610	2¢	Harding (D.C., Marion, OH 9/1/25)	25.00	42.00
❑ 611	2¢	Harding (imperf., D.C., 11/15/23)	90.00	110.00
❑ 612	2¢	Harding (perf. 10, D.C., 9/12/23)	100.00	115.00
❑ 614	1¢	Huguenot-Walloon (5/1/24)	38.00	55.00
❑ 615	2¢	Huguenot-Walloon (5/1/24)	48.00	67.00
❑ 616	5¢	Huguenot-Walloon (5/1/24)	75.00	90.00
❑ 614–616		Huguenot-Walloon, set on one cover (5/1/24),from any of the following cities: Albany, NY, Allentown, PA, Charleston, SC, Jacksonville, FL, Lancaster, PA, Mayport, FL, New Rochelle, NY, New York, NY, Philadelphia, PA, Reading, PA, and Washington, D.C.	140.00	—
❑ 617	1¢	Lexington-Concord (4/4/25)	25.00	40.00
❑ 618	2¢	Lexington-Concord (4/4/25)	25.00	40.00
❑ 619	5¢	Lexington-Concord (4/4/25)	70.00	100.00

Scott No.			Single	Block of 4
❏ 617–619		Lexington-Concord, set on one cover (4/4/25), from any of the following cities: Boston, MA, Cambridge, MA, Concord, MA, Lexington, MA, or Washington, D.C. Concord, MA sells for 25% more.	140.00	—
❏ 620	2¢	Norse-American (5/18/25)	18.00	37.00
❏ 621	5¢	Norse-American (5/18/25)	30.00	42.00
❏ 620–621		Norse-American, set on one cover (5/18/25) from any of the following cities: Angola, IN, Benson, MN, Decoran, IA, Minneapolis, MN, Northfield, MN, St. Paul, MN, or Washington, D.C.	58.00	90.00
❏ 622	13¢	Harrison	18.00	30.00
❏ 622	13¢	Harrison (Indianapolis, IN, 1/11/26)	20.00	50.00
❏ 622	13¢	Harrison (North Bend, OH, 1/11/26)	140.00	280.00
❏ 623	17¢	Wilson (New York, NY, Princeton, NJ, Staunton, VA, Washington, D.C., 12/28/25)	20.00	32.00
❏ 627	2¢	Sesquicentennial (Boston, MA, Philadelphia,PA, D.C., 5/10/26)	10.00	15.00
❏ 628	5¢	Erikson (Chicago, IL, Minneapolis, MN, New York, NY, D.C. 5/29/26)	20.00	25.00
❏ 629	2¢	White Plains (White Plains, NY, New York, NY, Philadelphia, PA Expo 10/18/26)	7.50	11.00
❏ 630	2¢	White Plains (complete sheet, 10/18/26)	1400.00	—
❏ 631	1½¢	Harding (D.C., 8/27/26)	45.00	50.00
❏ 632	1¢	Franklin (D.C., 6/10/27)	45.00	50.00
❏ 632a	1¢	Franklin booklet of 6 (D.C. 11/2/27)	3600.00	
❏ 633	1½¢	Harding (D.C., 5/17/27)	42.00	65.00
❏ 634	2¢	Washington (D.C., 12/10/26)	46.00	52.00
❏ 635	3¢	Lincoln (D.C., 2/3/27)	40.00	50.00
❏ 635a	3¢	Bright Violet (D.C., 2/7/34)	28.00	40.00
❏ 636	4¢	Martha Washington (D.C., 5/17/27)	40.00	65.00
❏ 637	5¢	Roosevelt (D.C., 3/24/27)	35.00	40.00
❏ 638	6¢	Garfield (D.C., 7/27/27)	42.00	50.00

Scott No.			Single	Block of 4
❏ 639	7¢	McKinley (D.C., 3/24/27)	44.00	50.00
❏ 640	8¢	Grant (D.C., 6/10/27)	50.00	60.00
❏ 641	9¢	Jefferson (D.C., 5/17/27)	60.00	50.00
❏ 642	10¢	Monroe (D.C., 2/3/27)	50.00	90.00
❏ 643	2¢	Vermont (Burlington, VT, D.C., 8/3/27)	7.00	8.00
❏ 644	2¢	Burgoyne (Albany, NY, Rome, NY, Syracuse, NY, Utica, NY, and D.C., 8/3/27)	9.00	10.00
❏ 645	2¢	Valley Forge (Cleveland Phil Sta., OH, Lancaster, PA, Norriston, PA, Philadelphia, PA, Valley Forge, PA, West Chester, PA, and D.C., 5/26/28)	3.00	4.00
❏ 646	2¢	Molly Pitcher (Freehold, NJ, Red Bank, NJ, D.C., 10/20/18)	6.00	14.00
❏ 647	2¢	Hawaii (Honolulu, HI, D.C., 8/13/28)	19.00	20.00
❏ 648	5¢	Hawaii (Honolulu, HI, D.C., 8/13/28)	20.00	—
❏ 647–648		Hawaii set on one cover (8/13/28)	36.00	65.00
❏ 649	2¢	Aero Conf. (D.C., 12/12/28)	7.00	9.00
❏ 650	5¢	Aero Conf. (D.C., 12/12/28)	8.00	10.00
❏ 649–650		Areo Conf. set on one cover (12/12/18)	12.00	20.00
❏ 651	2¢	Clark (Vincennes, IN, 2/25/29)	5.00	8.00
❏ 653	½¢	Hale (D.C., 5/25/29)	—	20.00
❏ 654	2¢	Electric Light (Menlopark, NJ, 6/5/29)	7.50	10.00
❏ 655	2¢	Electric Light (D.C., 6/11/29)	70.00	80.00
❏ 656	2¢	Electric Light (coil, 6/11/29)	120.00	—
❏ 657	2¢	Sullivan (16 different New York cities and D.C., 6/17/29)	3.00	6.00
❏ 658	1¢	Kansas (D.C., 5/1/29)	25.00	30.00
❏ 659	1½¢	Kansas (D.C., 5/1/29)	26.00	30.00
❏ 660	2¢	Kansas (D.C., 5/1/29)	26.00	30.00
❏ 661	3¢	Kansas (D.C., 5/1/29)	26.00	30.00
❏ 662	4¢	Kansas (D.C., 5/1/29)	60.00	80.00
❏ 663	5¢	Kansas (D.C., 5/1/29)	60.00	80.00
❏ 664	6¢	Kansas (D.C., 5/1/29)	150.00	100.00
❏ 665	7¢	Kansas (D.C., 5/1/29)	90.00	100.00
❏ 666	8¢	Kansas (D.C., 5/1/29)	90.00	100.00
❏ 667	9¢	Kansas (D.C., 5/1/29)	90.00	100.00
❏ 668	10¢	Kansas (D.C., 5/1/29)	90.00	100.00
❏ 658–668		Kansas set on one cover (D.C., 5/1/29)	1000.00	—

Scott No.			Single	Block of 4
❑ 669	1¢	Nebraska (D.C., 5/1/29)	40.00	50.00
❑ 670	1½¢	Nebraska (D.C., 5/1/29)	40.00	50.00
❑ 671	2¢	Nebraska (D.C., 5/1/29)	40.00	50.00
❑ 672	3¢	Nebraska (D.C., 5/1/29)	40.00	50.00
❑ 673	4¢	Nebraska (D.C., 5/1/29)	50.00	60.00
❑ 674	5¢	Nebraska (D.C., 5/1/29)	60.00	65.00
❑ 675	6¢	Nebraska (D.C., 5/1/29)	65.00	80.00
❑ 676	7¢	Nebraska (D.C., 5/1/29)	65.00	80.00
❑ 677	8¢	Nebraska (D.C., 5/1/29)	65.00	80.00
❑ 678	9¢	Nebraska (D.C., 5/1/29)	65.00	80.00
❑ 679	10¢	Nebraska (D.C., 5/1/29)	75.00	—
❑ 659–669		Nebraska set on one cover (D.C., 5/1/29)	1200.00	—
❑ 680	2¢	Fallen Timbers (5 cities 9/14/29)	3.50	6.50
❑ 681	2¢	Ohio River (7 cities 10/19/29)	3.50	6.50
❑ 682	2¢	Massachusetts Bay Colony (2 cities 4/8/30)	3.50	6.50
❑ 683	2¢	Carolina-Charleston (4/10/30)	3.50	6.50
❑ 684	1½¢	Harding Marion, OH(12/1/30)	4.00	5.00
❑ 685	4¢	Taft Cinncinnati, OH (6/4/30)	4.00	5.00
❑ 686	1½¢	Harding Marion, OH (coil, 12/1/30)	4.00	5.00
❑ 687	4¢	Taft (coil, D.C., 9/18/30)	30.00	—
❑ 688	2¢	Braddock (7/9/30)	4.00	6.00
❑ 689	2¢	Von Steuben	4.00	6.00
❑ 690	2¢	Pulaski (12 cities, 1/16/31)	4.50	6.00
❑ 692	11¢	Hayes (D.C., 9/4/31)	95.00	120.00
❑ 693	12¢	Cleveland (D.C., 8/25/31)	95.00	120.00
❑ 694	13¢	Harrison (D.C., 9/4/31)	95.00	120.00
❑ 695	14¢	Indian (D.C., 9/8/31)	95.00	120.00
❑ 696	15¢	Liberty (D.C., 8/27/31)	95.00	120.00
❑ 697	17¢	Wilson (D.C., 7/27/31)	120.00	135.00
❑ 698	20¢	Golden Gate (D.C., 9/8/31)	120.00	135.00
❑ 699	25¢	Niagara Falls (D.C., 7/27/31)	175.00	135.00
❑ 700	30¢	Bison (D.C., 9/8/31)	160.00	135.00
❑ 701	50¢	Arlington (D.C., 9/4/31)	250.00	300.00
❑ 702	2¢	Red Cross (2 cities 5/21/31)	3.25	4.50
❑ 703	2¢	Yorktown (2 cities, 10/19/31)	3.25	5.00
❑ 704	½¢	Olive Brown (D.C., 1/1/32)	—	3.50
❑ 705	1¢	Green (D.C., 1/1/32)	3.25	4.00

Scott No.			Single	Block of 4
❑ 706	1½¢	Brown (D.C., 1/1/32)	3.00	4.25
❑ 707	2¢	Carmine Rose (D.C., 1/1/32)	3.00	4.25
❑ 708	3¢	Deep Violet (D.C., 1/1/32)	3.00	4.25
❑ 709	4¢	Light Brown (D.C., 1/1/32)	3.00	4.25
❑ 710	5¢	Blue (D.C., 1/1/32)	3.00	4.25
❑ 711	6¢	Red Orange (D.C., 1/1/32)	3.00	4.25
❑ 712	7¢	Black (D.C., 1/1/32)	3.00	4.25
❑ 713	8¢	Olive Bistre (D.C., 1/1/32)	3.00	4.25
❑ 714	9¢	Pale Red (D.C., 1/1/32)	3.00	4.25
❑ 715	10¢	Orange Yellow (D.C., 1/1/32)	3.00	4.25
❑ 704–715		set on one cover	40.00	—
❑ 716	2¢	Olympic Winter Games (1/25/32)	3.00	4.00
❑ 717	2¢	Arbor Day (4/22/32)	3.40	4.10
❑ 718	3¢	Olympic Summer Games (6/15/32)	3.00	4.00
❑ 719	5¢	Olympic Summer Games (6/15/32)	4.00	5.00
❑ 718–719		Olympic Summer Games set on one cover	4.50	6.00
❑ 720	3¢	Washington (D.C., 6/16/32)	3.50	5.00
❑ 720b	3¢	Washington (booklet of 6, D.C., 7/25/32)	45.00	—
❑ 721	3¢	Washington (coil, D.C., 6/24/32)	4.75	—
❑ 722	3¢	Washington (coil, D.C., 10/12/32)	4.75	—
❑ 723	6¢	Garfield (coil, 8/18/32)	4.75	—
❑ 724	3¢	William Penn (3 cities, 10/24/32)	3.75	4.50
❑ 725	3¢	Daniel Webster (3 cities, 10/24/32)	3.75	4.50
❑ 726	3¢	Gen. Oglethorpe (2/12/32)	3.75	4.50
❑ 727	3¢	Peace Proclamation (4/19/32)	3.75	4.50
❑ 728	1¢	Century of Progress (5/25/32)	2.40	3.60
❑ 729	3¢	Century of Progress (5/25/32)	2.40	4.00
❑ 728–729		Century of Progress set on one cover	3.50	5.00
❑ 730	1¢	American Philatelic Society (full sheet)	70.00	—
❑ 730a	1¢	American Philatelic Society (8/25/33)	3.00	4.00
❑ 731	3¢	American Philatelic Society (full sheet)	75.00	—
❑ 731a	3¢	American Philatelic Society (8/25/33)	2.75	4.20
❑ 732	3¢	National Recovery Administration (D.C., 8/15/33)	2.75	4.20
❑ 733	3¢	Byrd Antarctic (D.C., 10/9/33)	4.00	6.25
❑ 734	5¢	Kosciuszko (6 cities, 10/13/33)	4.00	6.25
❑ 734	5¢	Kosciuszko (Pittsburg, PA)	4.00	6.00
❑ 735	3¢	National Exhibition (full sheet)	4.00	—

Scott No.			Single	Block of 4
❏ 735a	3¢	National Exhibition (2/10/34)	4.50	6.00
❏ 736	3¢	Maryland Tercentenary (3/23/34)	2.75	4.00
❏ 737	3¢	Mothers of America (D.C., 5/2/34)	2.75	4.00
❏ 738	3¢	Mothers of America (D.C., 5/2/34)	3.25	4.00
❏ 739	3¢	Wisconsin (7/9/34)	3.00	3.50
❏ 740	1¢	Parks, Yosemite (2 cities, 7/16/34)	3.00	4.00
❏ 741	2¢	Parks, Grand Canyon (2 cities, 7/24/34)	3.00	4.00
❏ 742	3¢	Parks, Mt. Rainier (2 cities, 8/3/34)	3.00	4.00
❏ 743	4¢	Parks, Mesa Verde (2 cities, 9/25/34)	3.00	4.00
❏ 744	5¢	Parks, Yellowstone (2 cities, 7/30/34)	3.00	4.00
❏ 745	6¢	Parks, Crater Lake (2 cities, 9/5/34)	3.00	4.00
❏ 746	7¢	Parks, Acadia (2 cities, 10/2/34)	3.00	4.00
❏ 747	8¢	Parks, Zion (2 cities, 9/18/34)	4.50	5.00
❏ 748	9¢	Parks, Glacier Park (2 cities, 8/27/34)	4.50	5.00
❏ 749	10¢	Parks, Smoky Mountains (2 cities, 10/8/34)	4.50	5.00
❏ 750	3¢	American Philatelic Society (full sheet)	36.00	—
❏ 750a	3¢	American Philatelic Society (8/28/34)	4.00	—
❏ 751	1¢	Trans-Mississippi Philatelic Expo, (full sheet)	25.00	—
❏ 751a	1¢	Trans-Mississippi Philatelic Expo. (10/10/34)	3.00	—
❏ 752	3¢	Peace Commemoration (D.C., 3/15/35)	5.50	6.00
❏ 753	3¢	Byrd (D.C., 3/15/35)	5.00	6.00
❏ 754	3¢	Mothers of America (D.C., 3/15/35)	5.00	6.00
❏ 755	3¢	Wisconsin (D.C., 3/15/35)	5.00	6.00
❏ 756	1¢	Parks, Yosemite (D.C., 3/15/35)	5.00	6.00
❏ 757	2¢	Parks, Grand Canyon (D.C., 3/15/35)	5.00	6.00
❏ 758	3¢	Parks, Mount Ranier (D.C., 3/15/35)	5.00	6.00
❏ 759	4¢	Parks, Mesa Verde (D.C., 3/15/35)	5.00	6.00
❏ 760	5¢	Parks, Yellowstone (D.C., 3/15/35)	5.00	6.00
❏ 761	6¢	Parks, Crater Lake (D.C., 3/15/35)	6.00	9.00
❏ 762	7¢	Parks, Acadia (D.C., 3/15/35)	6.00	9.00
❏ 763	8¢	Parks, Zion (D.C., 3/15/35)	6.00	9.00
❏ 764	9¢	Parks, Glacier Park (D.C., 3/15/35)	6.00	9.00
❏ 765	10¢	Parks, Smoky Mountains (D.C., 3/15/35)	6.00	9.00
❏ 766a	1¢	Century of Progress (D.C., 3/15/35)	6.00	8.00
❏ 767a	3¢	Century of Progress (D.C., 3/15/35)	6.00	8.00
❏ 768a	3¢	Byrd (D.C., 3/15/35)	6.00	8.00
❏ 769a	1¢	Parks, Yosemite (D.C., 3/15/35)	5.00	8.00

Scott No.			Single	Block of 4
❏ 770a	3¢	Parks, Mount Ranier (D.C., 3/15/35)	6.00	6.50
❏ 771	16¢	Airmail, special delivery (D.C., 3/15/35)	6.00	6.50

Cacheted Covers.

NOTE: For dates of issue, see **Uncacheted Covers** above.

❏ 610	2¢	Harding	700.00	—
❏ 617	1¢	Lexington-Concord	100.00	—
❏ 618	2¢	Lexington-Concord	100.00	—
❏ 619	5¢	Lexington-Concord	200.00	—
❏ 620–621		Norse American set on one cover	170.00	
❏ 623	17¢	Wilson	278.00	—
❏ 627	2¢	Sesquicentennial	74.00	—
❏ 628	5¢	Erikson	400.00	—
❏ 629	2¢	White Plains	65.00	—
❏ 630	2¢	White Plains (souvenir sheet) single	62.00	—
❏ 635a	3¢	Bright Violet	45.00	—
❏ 643	2¢	Vermont	45.00	90.00
❏ 644	2¢	Burgoyne	53.00	80.00
❏ 645	2¢	Valley Forge	50.00	70.00
❏ 646	2¢	Molly Pitcher	90.00	—
❏ 647	2¢	Hawaii	65.00	82.00
❏ 648	5¢	Hawaii	75.00	90.00
❏ 647–648		Hawaii set on one cover	110.00	—
❏ 649	2¢	Aero Conf.	50.00	64.00
❏ 650	5¢	Aero Conf.	52.00	60.00
❏ 649–650		Aero Conf. set on one cover	62.00	—
❏ 651	2¢	Clark	30.00	40.00
❏ 654	2¢	Electric Light	30.00	40.00
❏ 655	2¢	Electric Light	120.00	—
❏ 656	2¢	Electric Light (coil)	240.00	—
❏ 657	2¢	Sullivan, Auburn N.Y.	26.00	40.00
❏ 680	2¢	Fallen Timbers	26.00	40.00
❏ 681	2¢	Ohio River	26.00	40.00
❏ 682	2¢	Massachusetts Bay Colony	26.00	40.00
❏ 683	2¢	California-Charleston	26.00	40.00
❏ 684	1½¢	Harding	26.00	40.00
❏ 685	4¢	Taft	50.00	60.00
❏ 686	1½¢	Harding (coil)	50.00	60.00
❏ 687	4¢	Taft (coil)	82.00	90.00

Scott No.			Single	Block of 4
❑ 688	2¢	Braddock	30.00	40.00
❑ 689	2¢	Von Steuben	30.00	40.00
❑ 690	2¢	Pulaski	30.00	40.00
❑ 702	2¢	Red Cross	30.00	40.00
❑ 703	2¢	Yorktown	40.00	50.00
❑ 704	½¢	Olive Brown	15.00	20.00
❑ 705	1¢	Green	15.00	20.00
❑ 706	1½¢	Brown	15.00	20.00
❑ 707	2¢	Carmine Rose	15.00	20.00
❑ 708	3¢	Deep Violet	15.00	20.00
❑ 709	4¢	Light Brown	15.00	20.00
❑ 710	5¢	Blue	15.00	20.00
❑ 711	6¢	Red Orange	15.00	20.00
❑ 712	7¢	Black	15.00	20.00
❑ 713	8¢	Olive Bistre	16.00	25.00
❑ 714	9¢	Pale Red	16.00	25.00
❑ 715	10¢	Orange Yellow	20.00	25.00
❑ 704–715		Set on one cover	165.00	—
❑ 716	2¢	Olympic Winter Games	18.00	34.00
❑ 717	2¢	Arbor Day	17.00	30.00
❑ 718	3¢	Olympic Summer Games	20.00	36.00
❑ 719	5¢	Olympic Summer Games	20.00	36.00
❑ 718–719		Set on one cover	30.00	40.00
❑ 720	3¢	Washington	34.00	40.00
❑ 720b	3¢	Booklet pane of 6	180.00	—
❑ 721	3¢	Washington (coil)	40.00	—
❑ 722	3¢	Washington (coil)	40.00	—
❑ 723	6¢	Garfield (coil)	48.00	—
❑ 724	3¢	William Penn	18.00	22.00
❑ 725	3¢	Daniel Webster	18.00	22.00
❑ 726	3¢	Gen. Oglethorpe	18.00	22.00
❑ 727	3¢	Peace Proclamation	18.00	22.00
❑ 728	1¢	Century of Progress	18.00	22.00
❑ 729	3¢	Century of Progress	16.00	22.00
❑ 730	1¢	American Philatelic Society (full sheet)	150.00	—
❑ 730a	1¢	American Philatelic Society (single)	17.00	27.00
❑ 731	3¢	American Philatelic Society (full sheet)	160.00	—
❑ 731a	3¢	American Philatelic Society (single)	16.00	20.00
❑ 732	3¢	National Recovery Administration	14.00	24.00
❑ 733	3¢	Byrd Antarctic	26.00	32.00

Scott No.			Single	Block of 4
❑ 734	5¢	Kosciuszko	16.00	22.00
❑ 734b	5¢	Kosciuszko (Pittsburgh, PA)	40.00	60.00
❑ 735	3¢	National Exhibition (full sheet)	40.00	—
❑ 735a	3¢	National Exhibition (single)	16.00	—
❑ 736	3¢	Maryland Tercentenary	15.00	20.00
❑ 737	3¢	Mothers of America	14.00	20.00
❑ 738	3¢	Mothers of America	14.00	20.00
❑ 739	2¢	Wisconsin	14.00	20.00
❑ 740	1¢	Parks, Yosemite	14.00	20.00
❑ 741	2¢	Parks, Grand Canyon	14.00	20.00
❑ 742	3¢	Parks, Mt. Ranier	14.00	20.00
❑ 743	4¢	Parks, Mesa Verde	14.00	20.00
❑ 744	5¢	Parks, Yellowstone	14.00	20.00
❑ 745	6¢	Parks, Crater Lake	11.00	16.00
❑ 746	7¢	Parks, Acadia	11.00	16.00
❑ 747	8¢	Parks, Zion	11.00	16.00
❑ 748	9¢	Parks, Glacier Park	11.00	16.00
❑ 749	10¢	Parks, Smoky Mountains	11.00	16.00
❑ 750	3¢	American Philatelic Society (full sheet)	50.00	—
❑ 750a	3¢	American Philatelic Society (single)	15.00	20.00
❑ 751	1¢	Trans-Mississippi Expo. (full sheet)	40.00	—
❑ 751a	1¢	Trans-Mississippi Expo. (single)	12.00	16.00
❑ 752	3¢	Peace Commemoration	35.00	42.00
❑ 753	3¢	Byrd	30.00	36.00
❑ 754	3¢	Mothers of America	30.00	36.00
❑ 755	3¢	Wisconsin Tercentenary	30.00	36.00
❑ 756	1¢	Parks, Yosemite	25.00	35.00
❑ 757	2¢	Parks, Grand Canyon	25.00	35.00
❑ 758	3¢	Parks, Mount Rainier	25.00	35.00
❑ 759	4¢	Parks, Mesa Verde	25.00	35.00
❑ 760	5¢	Parks, Yellowstone	25.00	35.00
❑ 761	6¢	Parks, Crater Lake	25.00	35.00
❑ 762	7¢	Parks, Acadia	25.00	35.00
❑ 763	8¢	Parks, Zion	25.00	35.00
❑ 764	9¢	Parks, Glacier Park	25.00	35.00
❑ 765	10¢	Parks, Smoky Mountains	25.00	35.00
❑ 766a	1¢	Century of Progress	35.00	50.00
❑ 767a	3¢	Century of Progress	35.00	50.00
❑ 768a	3¢	Byrd	35.00	50.00
❑ 769a	1¢	Parks, Yosemite	35.00	50.00

Scott No.			Single	Block of 4
❑ 770a	3¢	Parks, Mount Rainier	40.00	50.00
❑ 771	16¢	Airmail, special delivery	40.00	50.00

Scott No.			Single	Block	Plate Block
❑ 772	3¢	Connecticut Tercentenary	8.00	10.00	17.50
❑ 773	3¢	California Exposition	8.00	10.00	17.50
❑ 774	3¢	Boulder Dam	9.00	11.00	18.00
❑ 775	3¢	Michigan Centenary	9.00	11.00	18.00
❑ 776	3¢	Texas Centennial	10.00	12.00	20.00
❑ 777	3¢	Rhode Island Tercentenary	8.00	10.00	19.00
❑ 778	3¢	TIPEX	5.00	12.00	—
❑ 782	3¢	Arkansas Centennial	8.00	11.00	16.00
❑ 783	3¢	Oregon Territory	8.00	11.00	16.00
❑ 784	3¢	Susan B. Anthony	8.00	11.00	16.00
❑ 785	1¢	Army	5.00	6.00	15.00
❑ 786	2¢	Army	7.00	7.50	15.00
❑ 787	3¢	Army	7.00	7.50	15.00
❑ 788	4¢	Army	7.00	7.50	15.00
❑ 789	5¢	Army	7.00	7.50	15.00
❑ 790	1¢	Navy	5.00	7.50	15.00
❑ 791	2¢	Navy	6.00	7.50	15.00
❑ 792	3¢	Navy	6.00	7.50	15.00
❑ 793	4¢	Navy	6.00	7.50	15.00
❑ 794	5¢	Navy	6.00	7.50	15.00
❑ 795	3¢	Ordinance of 1787	7.50	7.50	13.00
❑ 796	5¢	Virginia Dare	7.50	7.50	13.00
❑ 797	10¢	Souvenir Sheet	8.00	—	—
❑ 798	3¢	Constitution	8.00	10.00	12.00
❑ 799	3¢	Hawaii	8.00	10.00	12.00
❑ 800	3¢	Alaska	8.00	10.00	12.00
❑ 801	3¢	Puerto Rico	8.00	10.00	12.00
❑ 802	3¢	Virgin Islands	8.00	10.00	12.00
❑ 803	½¢	Franklin	4.50	5.00	10.00
❑ 804	1¢	Washington	4.50	5.00	10.00
❑ 805	1½¢	Martha Washington	4.50	5.00	10.00
❑ 806	2¢	Adams	4.50	5.00	10.00
❑ 807	3¢	Jefferson	4.00	5.00	10.00

NOTE: Beginning with No. 795, first day covers bear the slogan cancellation "First Day Issue."

Scott No.			Single	Block	Plate Block
❑ 808	4¢	Madison	3.50	5.00	7.50
❑ 809	4½¢	White House	3.50	5.00	7.50
❑ 810	5¢	Monroe	3.50	5.00	7.50
❑ 811	6¢	Adams	3.50	5.00	7.50
❑ 812	7¢	Jackson	3.50	5.00	7.50
❑ 813	8¢	VanBuren	3.50	5.00	7.50
❑ 814	9¢	Harrison	3.50	6.00	7.50
❑ 815	10¢	Tyler	3.50	6.00	11.00
❑ 816	11¢	Polk	4.00	6.50	11.00
❑ 817	12¢	Taylor	4.00	6.50	11.00
❑ 818	13¢	Fillmore	4.00	6.50	11.00
❑ 819	14¢	Pierce	4.00	6.50	11.00
❑ 820	15¢	Buchanan	4.00	6.50	11.00
❑ 821	16¢	Lincoln	4.50	6.50	11.00
❑ 822	17¢	Johnson	4.50	6.00	8.00
❑ 823	18¢	Grant	4.50	6.00	8.00
❑ 824	19¢	Hayes	4.50	6.00	8.00
❑ 825	20¢	Garfield	5.00	6.00	8.00
❑ 826	21¢	Arthur	5.00	6.50	8.00
❑ 827	22¢	Cleveland	5.00	6.50	8.00
❑ 828	24¢	Harrison	5.00	6.50	8.00
❑ 829	25¢	McKinley	5.00	6.50	11.00
❑ 830	30¢	Roosevelt	6.00	10.00	12.00
❑ 831	50¢	Taft	12.00	16.00	21.00
❑ 832	$1	Wilson	36.00	60.00	90.00
❑ 832c	$1	Wilson	20.00	28.00	50.00
❑ 833	$2	Harding	110.00	150.00	200.00
❑ 834	$5	Coolidge	210.00	280.00	450.00
❑ 835	3¢	Constitution	6.50	10.00	13.00
❑ 836	3¢	Swedes and Finns	6.50	10.00	13.00
❑ 837	3¢	Northwest Sesquicentennial	6.50	10.00	13.00
❑ 838	3¢	Iowa	6.50	10.00	13.00
❑ 852	3¢	Golden Gate Expo	6.50	10.00	13.00
❑ 853	3¢	N.Y. World's Fair	6.50	10.00	13.00
❑ 854	3¢	Washington Inauguration	6.50	10.00	13.00
❑ 855	3¢	Baseball Centennial	20.00	30.00	40.00
❑ 856	3¢	Panama Canal	6.00	10.00	12.00
❑ 857	3¢	Printing Tercentenary	6.00	10.00	12.00
❑ 858	3¢	50th Statehood Anniversary	6.00	8.00	12.00
❑ 859	1¢	Washington Irving	2.50	5.00	7.00

Scott No.			Single	Block	Plate Block
❑ 860	2¢	James Fenimore Cooper	3.00	5.00	7.00
❑ 861	3¢	Ralph Waldo Emerson	3.00	5.00	8.00
❑ 862	5¢	Louisa May Alcott	4.00	6.00	9.00
❑ 863	10¢	Samuel L. Clemens	7.00	9.00	22.00
❑ 864	1¢	Henry W. Longfellow	3.50	4.50	8.50
❑ 865	2¢	John Greenleaf Whittier	3.50	4.50	8.50
❑ 866	3¢	James Russell Lowell	3.50	4.50	8.50
❑ 867	5¢	Walt Whitman	3.75	6.00	10.00
❑ 868	10¢	James Whitcomb Riley	6.00	6.00	20.00
❑ 869	1¢	Horace Mann	4.00	6.00	7.00
❑ 870	2¢	Mark Hopkins	4.00	6.00	7.00
❑ 871	3¢	Charles W. Eliot	4.00	6.00	7.00
❑ 872	5¢	Frances E. Willard	4.00	7.50	12.00
❑ 873	10¢	Booker T. Washington	7.50	12.00	24.00
❑ 874	1¢	John James Audubon	4.00	4.50	9.00
❑ 875	2¢	Dr. Crawford W. Long	4.00	4.50	9.00
❑ 876	3¢	Luther Burbank	4.00	4.50	9.00
❑ 877	5¢	Dr. Walter Reed	4.00	6.00	9.00
❑ 878	10¢	Jane Addams	5.00	8.50	20.00
❑ 879	1¢	Stephen Collins Foster	4.00	5.00	7.50
❑ 880	2¢	John Philip Sousa	4.00	5.00	7.50
❑ 881	3¢	Victor Herbert	4.00	5.00	7.50
❑ 882	5¢	Edward A. MacDowell	4.00	6.00	9.00
❑ 883	10¢	Ethelbert Nevin	7.00	9.00	20.00
❑ 884	1¢	Gilbert Charles Stuart	3.50	4.00	6.00
❑ 885	2¢	James A. McNeill Whistler	3.50	4.00	6.00
❑ 886	3¢	Augustus Saint-Gaudens	3.50	4.00	6.00
❑ 887	5¢	Daniel Chester French	4.00	5.00	12.00
❑ 888	10¢	Frederic Remington	6.00	7.50	21.00
❑ 889	1¢	Eli Whitney	4.10	6.00	9.00
❑ 890	2¢	Samuel F.B. Morse	4.10	6.00	9.00
❑ 891	3¢	Cyrus Hall McCormick	4.10	6.00	9.00
❑ 892	5¢	Elias Howe	3.75	8.00	20.00
❑ 893	10¢	Alexander Graham Bell	6.50	9.00	30.00
❑ 894	3¢	Pony Express	6.50	8.00	11.00
❑ 895	3¢	Pan American Union	6.00	8.00	12.00
❑ 896	3¢	Idaho Statehood	6.00	8.00	12.00
❑ 897	3¢	Wyoming Statehood	6.00	8.00	12.00
❑ 898	3¢	Coronado Expedition	6.00	8.00	12.00
❑ 899	1¢	Defense	6.00	8.00	12.00

Scott No.			Single	Block	Plate Block
❑ 900	2¢	Defense	5.50	8.00	12.00
❑ 901	3¢	Defense	5.50	8.00	12.00
❑ 899-901		Defense set on one cover	7.00	9.00	—
❑ 902	3¢	Thirteenth Amendment	7.00	9.00	12.00
❑ 903	3¢	Vermont Statehood	7.00	9.00	12.00
❑ 904	3¢	Kentucky Statehood	4.00	6.00	9.00
❑ 905	3¢	"Win the War"	4.00	8.00	11.00
❑ 906	5¢	Chinese Commemorative	7.50	10.00	14.00
❑ 907	2¢	United Nations	3.75	6.50	9.00
❑ 908	1¢	Four Freedoms	4.50	7.00	10.00
❑ 909	5¢	Poland	4.50	7.00	11.00
❑ 910	5¢	Czechoslovakia	4.50	7.00	9.00
❑ 911	5¢	Norway	4.50	7.00	9.00
❑ 912	5¢	Luxembourg	4.50	7.00	9.00
❑ 913	5¢	Netherlands	4.50	7.00	9.00
❑ 914	5¢	Belgium	4.50	7.00	9.00
❑ 915	5¢	France	4.50	7.00	9.00
❑ 916	5¢	Greece	4.50	7.00	9.00
❑ 917	5¢	Yugoslavia	4.50	7.00	9.00
❑ 918	5¢	Albania	4.50	7.00	9.00
❑ 919	5¢	Austria	4.50	7.00	9.00
❑ 920	5¢	Denmark	4.50	7.00	9.00
❑ 921	5¢	Korea	4.50	7.00	9.00
❑ 922	3¢	Railroad	5.00	7.50	9.50
❑ 923	3¢	Steamship	4.25	5.50	9.00
❑ 924	3¢	Telegraph	5.00	6.00	9.00
❑ 925	3¢	Philippines	5.00	7.00	8.00
❑ 926	3¢	Motion Picture	5.00	7.00	8.00
❑ 927	3¢	Florida	5.00	7.00	8.00
❑ 928	5¢	United Nations Conference	5.00	7.00	8.00
❑ 929	3¢	Iwo Jima	11.00	13.00	16.00
❑ 929, 934–936		Set on one cover	9.00	—	—
❑ 930	1¢	Roosevelt	3.50	6.00	7.50
❑ 931	2¢	Roosevelt	3.50	6.00	7.50
❑ 932	3¢	Roosevelt	3.50	6.00	7.50
❑ 933	5¢	Roosevelt	3.50	6.00	7.50
❑ 930–933		Roosevelt set on one cover	9.00	—	—
❑ 934	3¢	Army	4.50	6.00	7.50
❑ 935	3¢	Navy	4.50	6.00	7.00
❑ 936	3¢	Coast Guard	4.50	6.00	7.25

Scott No.			Single	Block	Plate Block
❑ 937	3¢	Alfred E. Smith	3.50	4.50	7.00
❑ 938	3¢	Texas	4.75	6.00	8.00
❑ 939	3¢	Merchant Marine	4.75	6.00	8.00
❑ 940	3¢	Honorable Discharge	4.75	6.00	8.00
❑ 941	3¢	Tennessee	3.50	5.00	7.50
❑ 942	3¢	Iowa	3.50	5.00	7.50
❑ 943	3¢	Smithsonian	3.50	5.00	7.50
❑ 944	3¢	Santa Fe	3.50	5.00	7.50
❑ 945	3¢	Thomas A. Edison	3.50	5.00	7.50
❑ 946	3¢	Joseph Pulitzer	3.50	5.00	7.50
❑ 947	3¢	Stamp Centenary	3.50	5.00	7.50
❑ 948	5¢,10¢	Centenary Exhibition Sheet	3.75	—	—
❑ 949	3¢	Doctors	4.00	5.00	7.50
❑ 950	3¢	Utah	3.00	5.00	7.50
❑ 951	3¢	"Constitution"	3.50	5.00	7.50
❑ 952	3¢	Everglades Park	3.50	5.00	7.50
❑ 953	3¢	Carver	3.50	5.00	7.50
❑ 954	3¢	California Gold	3.00	4.50	6.00
❑ 955	3¢	Mississippi Territory	3.00	4.50	6.00
❑ 956	3¢	Four Chaplains	3.00	4.50	6.00
❑ 957	3¢	Wisconsin Centennial	3.00	4.50	6.00
❑ 958	5¢	Swedish Pioneers	3.00	4.50	6.00
❑ 959	3¢	Women's Progress	3.00	4.50	6.00
❑ 960	3¢	William Allen White	3.00	4.50	6.00
❑ 961	3¢	U.S.-Canada Friendship	3.00	4.50	6.00
❑ 962	3¢	Francis Scott Key	3.00	4.50	6.00
❑ 963	3¢	Salute to Youth	3.00	4.50	6.00
❑ 964	3¢	Oregon Territory	3.00	4.50	6.00
❑ 965	3¢	Harlan Fiske Stone	3.00	4.50	6.00
❑ 966	3¢	Palomar Observatory	3.00	4.50	6.00
❑ 967	3¢	Clara Barton	3.00	4.50	6.00
❑ 968	3¢	Poultry Industry	3.00	4.50	6.00
❑ 969	3¢	Gold Star Mothers	3.00	4.50	6.00
❑ 970	3¢	Volunteer Fireman	4.00	6.00	7.50
❑ 971	3¢	Ft. Kearney, Nebraska	3.25	4.50	6.00
❑ 972	3¢	Indian Centennial	3.25	4.50	6.00
❑ 973	3¢	Rough Riders	3.25	4.50	6.00
❑ 974	3¢	Juliette Low	3.25	4.50	7.50
❑ 975	3¢	Will Rogers	3.25	4.50	6.00
❑ 976	3¢	Fort Bliss	3.25	4.60	6.50

Scott No.			Single	Block	Plate Block
❏ 977	3¢	Moina Michael	3.00	4.50	6.50
❏ 978	3¢	Gettysburg Address	3.00	7.00	7.50
❏ 979	3¢	American Turners Society	3.00	4.50	6.25
❏ 980	3¢	Joel Chandler Harris	3.00	4.50	6.25
❏ 981	3¢	Minnesota Territory	3.00	4.50	6.25
❏ 982	3¢	Washington and Lee University	3.00	4.50	6.25
❏ 983	3¢	Puerto Rico Election	3.00	4.50	6.25
❏ 984	3¢	Annapolis, Md.	3.00	4.50	6.25
❏ 985	3¢	G.A.R.	3.00	4.50	6.25
❏ 986	3¢	Edgar Allan Poe	3.00	4.50	6.50
❏ 987	3¢	American Bankers Association	3.00	4.50	6.75
❏ 988	3¢	Samuel Gompers	3.00	4.50	6.75
❏ 989	3¢	Freedom Statue	3.00	4.50	6.75
❏ 990	3¢	Executive	3.00	4.50	6.75
❏ 991	3¢	Judicial	3.00	4.50	6.75
❏ 992	3¢	Legislative	2.75	4.50	6.75
❏ 989–992		Capital set on one cover	4.00	—	—
❏ 993	3¢	Railroad Engineers	2.75	4.50	6.75
❏ 994	3¢	Kansas City Centenary	2.75	4.50	6.75
❏ 995	3¢	Boy Scout	3.75	7.50	8.00
❏ 996	3¢	Indiana Ter. Sesquicentennial	2.25	4.50	5.00
❏ 997	3¢	California Statehood	2.25	4.50	5.00
❏ 998	3¢	United Confederate Veterans	2.25	4.50	6.00
❏ 999	3¢	Nevada Centennial	2.25	4.50	6.00
❏ 1000	3¢	Landing of Cadillac	2.25	4.50	6.00
❏ 1001	3¢	Colorado Statehood	2.25	4.50	6.00
❏ 1002	3¢	American Chemical Society	2.25	4.50	6.00
❏ 1003	3¢	Battle of Brooklyn	2.25	4.50	6.00
❏ 1004	3¢	Betsy Ross	2.25	4.50	6.00
❏ 1005	3¢	4-H Clubs	2.25	4.50	6.00
❏ 1006	3¢	B & O Railroad	2.25	4.50	6.00
❏ 1007	3¢	American Automobile Assoc.	2.25	4.50	6.00
❏ 1008	3¢	NATO	2.25	4.50	6.00
❏ 1009	3¢	Grand Coulee Dam	2.25	4.50	6.00
❏ 1010	3¢	Lafayette	2.25	4.50	6.00
❏ 1011	3¢	Mt. Rushmore Memorial	2.25	4.50	6.00
❏ 1012	3¢	Civil Engineers	2.25	4.50	6.00
❏ 1013	3¢	Service Women	2.25	4.50	6.00
❏ 1014	3¢	Gutenberg Bible	2.25	4.50	6.00
❏ 1015	3¢	Newspaper Boys	2.25	4.50	6.00

Scott No.			Single	Block	Plate Block
❏ 1016	3¢	Red Cross	2.25	4.50	6.00
❏ 1017	3¢	National Guard	2.25	4.50	6.00
❏ 1018	3¢	Ohio Sesquicentennial	2.25	4.50	6.00
❏ 1019	3¢	Washington Territory	2.25	4.50	6.00
❏ 1020	3¢	Louisiana Purchase	2.25	4.50	6.00
❏ 1021	5¢	Opening of Japan	2.25	4.50	6.00
❏ 1022	3¢	American Bar Association	2.25	4.50	6.00
❏ 1023	3¢	Sagamore Hill	2.25	4.50	6.00
❏ 1024	3¢	Future Farmers	2.25	4.50	6.00
❏ 1025	3¢	Trucking Industry	2.25	4.50	6.00
❏ 1026	3¢	Gen. George S. Patton, Jr.	2.25	4.50	6.00
❏ 1027	3¢	New York City	2.25	4.50	6.00
❏ 1028	3¢	Gadsden Purchase	2.25	4.50	6.00
❏ 1029	3¢	Columbia University	2.25	4.50	6.00
❏ 1030	½¢	Franklin	—	2.25	3.75
❏ 1031	1¢	Washington	—	2.25	3.75
❏ 1031a	1¼¢	Palace of Governors	—	2.25	3.75
❏ 1032	1½¢	Mount Vernon	—	2.25	3.75
❏ 1033	2¢	Jefferson	—	2.25	3.75
❏ 1034	2½¢	Bunker Hill	—	2.25	3.75
❏ 1035	3¢	Statue of Liberty	2.10	4.00	5.50
❏ 1036	4¢	Lincoln	2.10	4.00	5.50
❏ 1037	4½¢	Hermitage	2.10	4.25	5.50
❏ 1038	5¢	Monroe	2.10	4.25	5.50
❏ 1039	6¢	Roosevelt	2.10	4.25	5.50
❏ 1040	7¢	Wilson	2.10	4.25	5.50
❏ 1041	8¢	Statue of Liberty	2.10	4.25	5.50
❏ 1042	8¢	Statue of Liberty	2.10	4.25	5.50
❏ 1042a	8¢	Pershing	2.50	4.75	7.00
❏ 1043	9¢	The Alamo	2.10	4.50	6.00
❏ 1044	10¢	Independence Hall	2.10	4.50	6.00
❏ 1045	12¢	Harrison	2.10	4.50	6.00
❏ 1046	15¢	John Jay	2.10	4.50	6.00
❏ 1047	20¢	Monticello	2.10	4.50	6.00
❏ 1048	25¢	Paul Revere	2.10	4.50	6.00
❏ 1049	30¢	Robert E. Lee	4.10	5.75	7.00
❏ 1050	40¢	John Marshall	4.50	7.00	8.50
❏ 1051	50¢	Susan Anthony	5.50	10.00	16.00
❏ 1052	$1	Patrick Henry	9.50	15.00	20.00
❏ 1053	$5	Alexander Hamilton	45.00	80.00	100.00

Scott No.			Single	Block	Plate Block
❑ 1054	1¢	Washington (coil)	2.10	—	—
❑ 1055	2¢	Jefferson (coil)	2.10	—	—
❑ 1056	2½¢	Bunker Hill (coil)	2.10	—	—
❑ 1057	3¢	Statue of Liberty (coil)	2.10	—	—
❑ 1058	4¢	Lincoln (coil)	2.10	—	—
❑ 1059	4½¢	The Hermitage (coil)	2.10	—	—
❑ 1059a	25¢	Paul Revere (coil)	2.25	—	—
❑ 1060	3¢	Nebraska Territory	2.15	4.25	5.00
❑ 1061	3¢	Kansas Territory	2.15	4.25	5.00
❑ 1062	3¢	George Eastman	2.15	4.25	5.00
❑ 1063	3¢	Lewis & Clark	2.15	4.25	5.00
❑ 1064	3¢	Pennsylvania Academy	2.15	4.25	5.00
❑ 1065	3¢	Land Grant Colleges	2.50	4.50	6.50
❑ 1066	8¢	Rotary International	3.00	4.50	6.50
❑ 1067	3¢	Armed Forces Reserve	2.25	4.50	6.50
❑ 1068	3¢	New Hampshire	2.25	5.00	6.00
❑ 1069	3¢	Soo Locks	2.25	5.00	6.00
❑ 1070	3¢	Atoms for Peace	2.25	5.00	6.00
❑ 1071	3¢	Fort Ticonderoga	2.25	5.00	6.00
❑ 1072	3¢	Andrew W. Mellon	2.25	5.00	6.00
❑ 1073	3¢	Benjamin Franklin	2.25	5.00	6.00
❑ 1074	3¢	Booker T. Washington	2.25	5.00	6.00
❑ 1075	3¢, 8¢	FIPEX Souvenir Sheet	6.00	—	—
❑ 1076	3¢	FIPEX	2.65	3.75	5.00
❑ 1077	3¢	Wildlife (Turkey)	2.25	3.75	5.00
❑ 1078	3¢	Wildlife (Antelope)	2.25	3.75	5.00
❑ 1079	3¢	Wildlife (Salmon)	2.25	3.75	5.00
❑ 1080	3¢	Pure Food and Drug Laws	2.25	3.75	5.00
❑ 1081	3¢	Wheatland	2.25	3.75	5.00
❑ 1082	3¢	Labor Day	2.25	3.75	5.00
❑ 1083	3¢	Nassau Hall	2.25	3.75	5.00
❑ 1084	3¢	Devil's Tower	2.25	3.75	5.00
❑ 1085	3¢	Children	2.25	3.75	5.00
❑ 1086	3¢	Alexander Hamilton	2.25	3.75	5.00
❑ 1087	3¢	Polio	2.25	4.00	6.50
❑ 1088	3¢	Coast & Geodetic Survey	2.00	3.50	5.50
❑ 1089	3¢	Architects	2.00	3.50	5.50
❑ 1090	3¢	Steel Industry	2.00	3.50	5.50
❑ 1091	3¢	Naval Review	2.00	3.50	5.50
❑ 1092	3¢	Oklahoma Statehood	2.00	3.50	5.50

Scott No.			Single	Block	Plate Block
❑ 1093	3¢	School Teachers	2.50	3.75	6.00
❑ 1094	4¢	Flag	2.50	3.75	6.00
❑ 1095	3¢	Shipbuilding	2.50	3.75	6.00
❑ 1096	8¢	Ramon Magsaysay	2.50	3.75	6.00
❑ 1097	3¢	Lafayette Bicentenary	2.50	3.75	6.00
❑ 1098	3¢	Wildlife (Whooping Crane)	2.50	3.75	6.00
❑ 1099	3¢	Religious Freedom	2.50	3.75	6.00
❑ 1100	3¢	Gardening Horticulture	2.50	3.75	6.00
❑ 1104	3¢	Brussels Exhibition	2.50	3.75	6.00
❑ 1105	3¢	James Monroe	2.50	3.75	6.00
❑ 1106	3¢	Minnesota Statehood	2.50	3.75	6.00
❑ 1107	3¢	International Geophysical Year	2.50	3.75	6.00
❑ 1108	3¢	Gunston Hall	2.50	3.75	6.00
❑ 1109	3¢	Mackinac Bridge	2.50	3.75	6.00
❑ 1110	4¢	Simon Bolivar	2.50	3.75	6.00
❑ 1111	8¢	Simon Bolivar	2.50	3.75	6.00
❑ 1110–1111		Bolivar set on one cover	3.75	4.50	6.00
❑ 1112	4¢	Atlantic Cable	2.00	3.75	6.00
❑ 1113	1¢	Lincoln Sesquicentennial	2.00	3.75	6.00
❑ 1114	3¢	Lincoln Sesquicentennial	2.00	3.75	6.00
❑ 1115	4¢	Lincoln-Douglas Debates	1.75	3.75	5.00
❑ 1116	4¢	Lincoln Sesquicentennial	1.75	3.75	5.00
❑ 1113–1116		Lincoln set on one cover	8.00	3.75	—
❑ 1117	4¢	Lajos Kossuth	1.75	3.75	5.00
❑ 1118	8¢	Lajos Kossuth	1.75	3.75	6.00
❑ 1117–1118		Kossuth set on one cover	2.50	—	—
❑ 1119	4¢	Freedom of Press	2.00	3.50	4.50
❑ 1120	4¢	Overland Mail	2.00	3.50	4.50
❑ 1121	4¢	Noah Webster	2.00	3.50	4.50
❑ 1122	4¢	Forest Conservation	2.00	3.50	4.50
❑ 1123	4¢	Fort Duquesne	2.00	3.50	4.50
❑ 1124	4¢	Oregon Statehood	2.00	3.50	4.50
❑ 1125	4¢	San Martin	2.00	3.50	4.50
❑ 1126	8¢	San Martin	2.00	3.50	4.50
❑ 1125–1126		San Martin set on one cover	2.50	—	—
❑ 1127	4¢	NATO	2.00	3.50	4.50
❑ 1128	4¢	Arctic Explorations	2.00	3.50	4.50
❑ 1129	8¢	World Trade	2.00	3.50	4.50
❑ 1130	4¢	Silver Centennial	2.00	3.50	4.50
❑ 1131	4¢	St. Lawrence Seaway	2.00	3.50	4.50

Scott No.			Single	Block	Plate Block
❑ 1132	4¢	Flag	2.00	3.25	4.50
❑ 1133	4¢	Soil Conservation	2.00	3.25	4.50
❑ 1134	4¢	Petroleum Industry	2.50	3.75	4.75
❑ 1135	4¢	Dental Health	2.50	3.75	4.75
❑ 1136	4¢	Reuter	2.50	3.75	4.60
❑ 1137	8¢	Reuter	2.50	3.75	4.60
❑ 1136–1137		Reuter set on one cover	2.75	—	—
❑ 1138	4¢	Dr. Ephraim McDowell	2.10	3.75	4.60
❑ 1139	4¢	Washington "Credo"	2.10	3.75	4.60
❑ 1140	4¢	Franklin "Credo"	2.10	3.75	4.60
❑ 1141	4¢	Jefferson "Credo"	2.10	3.75	5.00
❑ 1142	4¢	Francis Scott Key "Credo"	2.10	3.75	4.60
❑ 1143	4¢	Lincoln "Credo"	2.10	3.75	5.00
❑ 1144	4¢	Patrick Henry "Credo"	2.10	3.75	4.60
❑ 1145	4¢	Boy Scouts	2.50	3.75	5.00
❑ 1146	4¢	Olympic Winter Games	2.00	3.75	4.50
❑ 1147	4¢	Masaryk	2.00	3.75	4.25
❑ 1148	8¢	Masaryk	2.00	3.75	4.25
❑ 1147–1148		Masaryk set on one cover	2.75	3.75	—
❑ 1149	4¢	World Refugee Year	2.00	3.75	5.00
❑ 1150	4¢	Water Conservation	2.00	3.75	5.00
❑ 1151	4¢	SEATO	2.00	3.75	5.00
❑ 1152	4¢	American Woman	2.00	3.75	5.00
❑ 1153	4¢	50-Star Flag	2.00	3.75	4.25
❑ 1154	4¢	Pony Express Centennial	2.10	3.75	5.00
❑ 1155	4¢	Employ the Handicapped	2.00	3.75	5.00
❑ 1156	4¢	World Forestry Congress	2.00	3.75	5.00
❑ 1157	4¢	Mexican Independence	2.00	3.75	5.00
❑ 1158	4¢	U.S. Japan Treaty	2.00	3.75	5.00
❑ 1159	4¢	Paderewski	2.00	3.75	5.00
❑ 1160	8¢	Paderewski	2.00	3.75	5.00
❑ 1159–1160		Paderewski set on one cover	2.75	3.75	—
❑ 1161	4¢	Robert A. Taft	2.00	3.75	5.00
❑ 1162	4¢	Wheels of Freedom	2.00	3.75	5.00
❑ 1163	4¢	Boys' Clubs	2.00	3.75	5.00
❑ 1164	4¢	Automated P.O.	2.00	3.75	5.00
❑ 1165	4¢	Mannerheim	2.00	3.75	5.00
❑ 1166	8¢	Mannerheim	2.00	3.75	5.00
❑ 1165–1166		Mannerheim set on one cover	2.75	3.75	—
❑ 1167	4¢	Camp Fire Girls	2.00	3.75	5.00

Scott No.			Single	Block	Plate Block
❑ 1168	4¢	Garibaldi	2.00	3.50	5.00
❑ 1169	8¢	Garibaldi	2.00	3.50	5.00
❑ 1168–1169		Garibaldi set on one cover	2.75	—	—
❑ 1170	4¢	Senator George	2.00	3.50	5.00
❑ 1171	4¢	Andrew Carnegie	2.00	3.50	5.00
❑ 1172	4¢	John Foster Dulles	2.00	3.50	5.00
❑ 1173	4¢	Echo I	2.00	3.50	5.00
❑ 1174	4¢	Gandhi	2.00	3.50	5.00
❑ 1175	8¢	Gandhi	2.00	3.50	5.00
❑ 1174–1175		Gandhi set on one cover	2.75	—	—
❑ 1176	4¢	Range Conservation	2.00	3.00	5.00
❑ 1177	4¢	Horace Greeley	2.00	3.00	5.00
❑ 1178	4¢	Fort Sumter	3.00	4.50	5.00
❑ 1179	4¢	Battle of Shiloh	3.00	4.50	5.00
❑ 1180	5¢	Battle of Gettysburg	3.00	4.50	5.00
❑ 1181	5¢	Battle of Wilderness	3.00	4.50	5.00
❑ 1182	5¢	Appomattox	3.00	4.50	5.00
❑ 1179–1182		Set on one cover	10.00	—	—
❑ 1183	4¢	Kansas Statehood	2.50	4.00	5.00
❑ 1184	4¢	Senator Norris	2.00	3.50	5.00
❑ 1185	4¢	Naval Aviation	2.00	3.00	5.00
❑ 1186	4¢	Workmen's Compensation	2.00	3.00	5.00
❑ 1187	4¢	Frederic Remington	2.10	3.00	5.20
❑ 1188	4¢	China Republic	4.00	5.50	6.50
❑ 1189	4¢	Naismith	7.00	8.00	9.00
❑ 1190	4¢	Nursing	8.00	11.00	15.00
❑ 1191	4¢	New Mexico Statehood	1.80	2.75	4.00
❑ 1192	4¢	Arizona Statehood	1.80	2.75	4.00
❑ 1193	4¢	Project Mercury	3.10	5.00	7.00
❑ 1194	4¢	Malaria Eradication	2.00	3.00	4.50
❑ 1195	4¢	Charles Evans Hughes	2.00	3.00	4.50
❑ 1196	4¢	Seattle World's Fair	2.00	3.00	4.50
❑ 1197	4¢	Louisiana Statehood	2.00	3.00	4.50
❑ 1198	4¢	Homestead Act	2.00	3.00	4.50
❑ 1199	4¢	Girl Scouts	3.00	4.75	6.00
❑ 1200	4¢	Brien McMahon	2.00	3.00	4.25
❑ 1201	4¢	Apprenticeship	2.00	3.00	4.25
❑ 1202	4¢	Sam Rayburn	2.00	3.00	4.25
❑ 1203	4¢	Dag Hammarskjold	2.00	3.00	4.25
❑ 1204	4¢	Hammarskjold "Error"	4.50	7.00	9.00

Scott No.			Single	Block	Plate Block
❑ 1205	4¢	Christmas	1.75	3.00	4.75
❑ 1206	4¢	Higher Education	1.75	3.00	4.75
❑ 1207	4¢	Winslow Homer	1.75	3.00	4.75
❑ 1208	4¢	Flag	1.75	3.00	4.75
❑ 1209	1¢	Jackson	1.75	3.00	4.75
❑ 1213	5¢	Washington	1.75	3.00	4.75
❑ 1225	1¢	Jackson (coil)	1.75	—	—
❑ 1229	5¢	Washington (coil)	1.75	—	—
❑ 1230	5¢	Carolina Charter	1.75	3.00	4.50
❑ 1231	5¢	Food for Peace	1.75	3.00	4.50
❑ 1232	5¢	West Virginia Statehood	1.75	3.00	4.50
❑ 1233	5¢	Emancipation Proclamation	1.75	3.00	4.50
❑ 1234	5¢	Alliance for Progress	1.75	3.00	4.50
❑ 1235	5¢	Cordell Hull	1.75	3.00	4.50
❑ 1236	5¢	Eleanor Roosevelt	1.75	3.00	4.50
❑ 1237	5¢	Science	1.75	3.00	4.50
❑ 1238	5¢	City Mail Delivery	1.75	3.00	4.50
❑ 1239	5¢	Red Cross	1.75	3.00	4.50
❑ 1240	5¢	Christmas	1.75	3.00	4.50
❑ 1241	5¢	Audubon	1.75	3.00	4.50
❑ 1242	5¢	Sam Houston	1.75	3.00	4.50
❑ 1243	5¢	Charles Russell	1.75	3.00	5.00
❑ 1244	5¢	N.Y. World's Fair	1.75	3.00	4.50
❑ 1245	5¢	John Muir	1.75	3.00	4.50
❑ 1246	5¢	John F. Kennedy	2.75	3.50	5.00
❑ 1247	5¢	New Jersey Tercentenary	1.75	3.00	4.50
❑ 1248	5¢	Nevada Statehood	1.75	3.00	4.50
❑ 1249	5¢	Register & Vote	1.75	3.00	4.50
❑ 1250	5¢	Shakespeare	1.75	3.50	4.50
❑ 1251	5¢	Drs. Mayo	4.00	5.00	7.00
❑ 1252	5¢	American Music	2.75	3.50	5.50
❑ 1253	5¢	Homemakers	1.80	3.00	4.10
❑ 1254–57	5¢	Christmas	1.80	4.50	8.00
❑ 1258	5¢	Verrazano Narrows Bridge	1.80	3.50	4.20
❑ 1259	5¢	Fine Arts	1.80	3.50	4.20
❑ 1260	5¢	Amateur Radio	2.60	3.50	4.20
❑ 1261	5¢	Battle of New Orleans	1.80	3.50	4.20
❑ 1262	5¢	Physical Fitness	1.80	3.50	4.20
❑ 1263	5¢	Cancer Crusade	1.80	3.50	6.00
❑ 1264	5¢	Churchill	1.80	3.15	4.25

Scott No.			Single	Block	Plate Block
❏ 1265	5¢	Magna Carta	2.00	3.50	4.50
❏ 1266	5¢	Int'l. Cooperation Year	2.00	3.50	4.50
❏ 1267	5¢	Salvation Army	2.00	3.50	4.50
❏ 1268	5¢	Dante	2.00	3.50	4.50
❏ 1269	5¢	Herbert Hoover	2.00	3.50	4.50
❏ 1270	5¢	Robert Fulton	2.00	3.50	4.50
❏ 1271	5¢	Florida Settlement	2.00	3.50	4.50
❏ 1272	5¢	Traffic Safety	2.00	3.50	4.50
❏ 1273	5¢	Copley	2.00	3.50	4.50
❏ 1274	11¢	Int'l. Telecommunication Union	1.80	2.50	5.00
❏ 1275	5¢	Adlai Stevenson	1.80	2.50	5.00
❏ 1276	5¢	Christmas	1.80	2.50	5.00
❏ 1278	1¢	Jefferson	1.80	2.50	5.00
❏ 1279	1¼¢	Gallatin	1.80	2.50	5.00
❏ 1280	2¢	Wright	1.80	2.50	5.00
❏ 1281	3¢	Parkman	1.80	2.50	5.00
❏ 1282	4¢	Lincoln	1.80	2.50	5.00
❏ 1283	5¢	Washington	1.80	2.50	5.00
❏ 1283b	5¢	Washington	1.80	2.50	5.00
❏ 1284	6¢	Roosevelt	1.80	2.50	5.00
❏ 1285	8¢	Einstein	2.00	2.50	5.00
❏ 1286	10¢	Jackson	1.75	3.50	5.00
❏ 1286a	12¢	Ford	1.75	3.50	5.00
❏ 1287	13¢	Kennedy	2.10	4.50	7.00
❏ 1288	15¢	Holmes	1.80	3.50	4.50
❏ 1289	20¢	Marshall	1.80	3.00	6.00
❏ 1290	25¢	Douglas	1.80	3.00	6.00
❏ 1291	30¢	Dewey	2.50	4.00	6.00
❏ 1292	40¢	Paine	3.25	5.00	7.50
❏ 1293	50¢	Stone	3.50	8.00	10.00
❏ 1294	$1	O'Neill	4.00	8.00	12.00
❏ 1295	$5	Moore	46.00	70.00	120.00
❏ 1304	5¢	Washington (coil)	—	1.60 (pr)	3.25 (lp)
❏ 1305	6¢	Roosevelt (coil)	—	1.60 (pr)	3.25 (lp)
❏ 1305c	$1	O'Neill (coil)	—	1.60 (pr)	3.25 (lp)
❏ 1306	5¢	Migratory Bird Treaty	2.75	4.10	5.50
❏ 1307	5¢	Humane Treatment of Animals	2.25	4.00	5.00
❏ 1308	5¢	Indiana Statehood	1.80	3.50	5.00
❏ 1309	5¢	Circus	3.00	4.00	5.50
❏ 1310	5¢	SIPEX	1.80	3.00	4.10

Scott No.			Single	Block	Plate Block
❑ 1311	5¢	SIPEX (sheet)	2.00	3.25	4.20
❑ 1312	5¢	Bill of Rights	2.00	3.25	4.20
❑ 1313	5¢	Polish Millennium	2.00	3.25	4.20
❑ 1314	5¢	National Park Service	2.00	3.25	4.20
❑ 1315	5¢	Marine Corps Reserve	2.00	3.25	5.00
❑ 1316	5¢	Gen'l. Fed. of Women's Clubs	2.00	3.25	5.50
❑ 1317	5¢	Johnny Appleseed	1.80	3.00	4.50
❑ 1318	5¢	Beautification of America	1.80	3.00	4.50
❑ 1319	5¢	Great River Road	1.80	2.50	4.25
❑ 1320	5¢	Savings Bonds	1.80	2.50	4.25
❑ 1321	5¢	Christmas	1.80	2.50	4.25
❑ 1322	5¢	Mary Cassatt	1.80	2.50	4.25
❑ 1323	5¢	National Grange	1.80	2.50	4.25
❑ 1324	5¢	Canada Centenary	1.80	2.50	4.25
❑ 1325	5¢	Erie Canal	1.80	2.50	4.25
❑ 1326	5¢	Search for Peace	1.80	2.50	4.25
❑ 1327	5¢	Thoreau	1.80	2.50	4.25
❑ 1328	5¢	Nebraska Statehood	1.80	2.50	4.25
❑ 1329	5¢	Voice of America	1.80	2.50	4.25
❑ 1330	5¢	Davy Crockett	1.80	2.50	4.25
❑ 1331–32	5¢	Space Accomplishments	10.00	20.00 (pr)	24.00
❑ 1333	5¢	Urban Planning	1.80	2.50	4.50
❑ 1334	5¢	Finland Independence	1.80	2.50	4.50
❑ 1335	5¢	Thomas Eakins	1.80	2.50	4.50
❑ 1336	5¢	Christmas	1.80	2.50	4.50
❑ 1337	5¢	Mississippi Statehood	1.80	2.50	4.50
❑ 1338	6¢	Flag	1.80	2.50	4.50
❑ 1339	6¢	Illinois Statehood	1.80	2.50	4.50
❑ 1340	6¢	Hemis Fair '68	1.80	2.50	4.50
❑ 1341	$1	Airlift	7.00	12.00	17.00
❑ 1342	6¢	Youth-Elks	1.80	2.10	4.25
❑ 1343	6¢	Law and Order	3.10	4.50	7.50
❑ 1344	6¢	Register and Vote	2.50	2.10	4.25
❑ 1345–54	6¢	Historic Flags (on one cover)	8.00	—	14.00
❑ 1345–54		Set on 10 covers	30.00	—	—
❑ 1355	6¢	Disney	10.00	12.00	21.00
❑ 1356	6¢	Marquette	1.80	2.50	4.50
❑ 1357	6¢	Daniel Boone	1.80	2.50	4.50
❑ 1358	6¢	Arkansas River	1.80	2.50	4.50

Scott No.			Single	Block	Plate Block
❑ 1359	6¢	Leif Erikson	1.80	2.75	4.50
❑ 1360	6¢	Cherokee Strip	1.80	2.75	4.50
❑ 1361	6¢	John Trumbull	1.80	2.75	4.50
❑ 1362	6¢	Waterfowl Conservation	2.00	4.00	4.50
❑ 1363	6¢	Christmas	2.00	4.00	4.50
❑ 1364	6¢	American Indian	1.80	3.00	4.75
❑ 1365–68	6¢	Beautification of America	2.00	7.00	10.00
❑ 1369	6¢	American Legion	1.80	4.00	5.00
❑ 1370	6¢	Grandma Moses	2.00	4.00	5.00
❑ 1371	6¢	Apollo 8	2.75	6.00	8.00

NOTE: From No. 1372 to date, most first day covers have a value of $1.80 to $2.00 for single stamps, $2.75 to $4.00 for blocks of four and $4.00 to $5.00 for plate blocks of four.

STAMP COLLECTORS' TERMINOLOGY

Adhesives—A term given to stamps that have gummed backs and are intended to be pasted on articles and items that are to be mailed.

Aerophilately—The collecting of airmail or any form of stamps related to mail carried by air.

Airmail—Any mail carried by air.

Albino—An uncolored embossed impression of a stamp generally found on envelopes.

Approvals—Stamps sent to collectors. They are examined by the collector, who selects stamps to purchase and returns balance with payment for the stamps he retained.

Arrow Block—An arrow-like mark found on blocks of stamps in the selvage. This mark is used as a guide for cutting or perforating stamps.

As-is—A term used when selling a stamp. It means no representation is given as to its condition or authenticity. Buyers should beware.

Backprint—Any printing that may appear on reverse of stamp.

Backstamp—The postmark on the back of a letter indicating what time or date the letter arrived at the post office.

Bantams—A miniature stamp given to a war economy issue of stamps from South Africa.

Batonne—Watermarked paper used in printing stamps.

Bicolored—A two-color printed stamp.

Bisect—A stamp that could be used by cutting in half and at half the face value.

Block—A term used for a series of four or more stamps attached at least two high and two across.

Bourse—A meeting or convention of stamp collectors and dealers where stamps are bought, sold, and traded.

Cachet—A design printed on the face of an envelope, generally celebrating the commemoration of a new postage stamp issue. Generally called a first-day cover.

Cancellation—A marking placed on the face of a stamp to show that it has been used.

Cancelled to Order—A stamp cancelled by the government without being used. Generally remainder stamps or special issues. Common practice of Russian nations.

Centering—The manner in which the design of a stamp is printed and centered upon the stamp blank. A perfectly centered stamp would have equal margins on all sides.

Classic—A popular, unique, highly desired, or very artistic stamp. Not necessarily a rare stamp, but one sought after by the collector. Generally used only for nineteenth-century issues.

Coils—Stamps sold in rolls for use in vending machines.

Commemorative—A stamp issued to commemorate or celebrate a special event.

Crease—A fold or wrinkle in a stamp.

Cut Square—An embossed staple removed from the envelope by cutting.

Dead Country—A country no longer issuing stamps.

Demonetized—A stamp no longer valid for use.

Error—A stamp printed or produced with a major design or color defect.

Essay—Preliminary design for a postage stamp.

Face Value—The value of a stamp indicated on the face or surface of the stamp.

Frank—A marking on the face of an envelope indicating the free and legal use of postage. Generally for government use.

Fugitive Inks—A special ink used to print stamps, which can be rubbed or washed off easily, to eliminate erasures and forgeries.

General Collector—One who collects all kinds of issues and all types of stamps from different countries.

Granite Paper—A type of paper containing colored fibers to prevent forgery.

Gum—The adhesive coating on the back of a stamp.

Handstamped—A stamp that has been handcancelled.

Hinge—A specially gummed piece of glassine paper used to attach a stamp to the album page.

Imperforate—A stamp without perforations.

Inverted—Where one portion of a stamp's design is inverted or upside down from the remainder of the design.

Local Stamps—Stamps that are only valid in a limited area.

Margin—The unprinted area around a stamp.

Miniature Sheet—A smaller-than-usual sheet of stamps.

Mint Condition—A stamp in original condition as it left the postal printing office.

Mirror Print—A stamp error printed in reverse as though looking at a regular stamp reflected in a mirror.

Multicolored—A stamp printed in three or more colors.

Never Hinged—A stamp in original mint condition never hinged in an album.

Off Paper—A used stamp that has been removed from the envelope to which it was attached.

On Paper—A used stamp still attached to the envelope.

Original Gum—A stamp with the same or original adhesive that was applied in the manufacturing process.

Pair—Two stamps unseparated.

Pen Cancellation—A stamp cancelled by pen or pencil.

Perforation Gauge—A printed chart containing various sizes of perforation holes used in determining the type or size of perforation of a stamp.

Perforations—Holes punched along stamp designs allowing stamps to be easily separated.

Philatelist—One who collects stamps.

Pictorial Stamps—Stamps that bear large pictures of animals, birds, flowers, etc.

Plate Block Number—The printing plate number used to identify a block of four or more stamps taken from a sheet of stamps.

Postally Used—A stamp that has been properly used and cancelled.

Precancels—A stamp that has been cancelled in advance. Generally used on bulk mail.

Reissue—A new printing of an old stamp that has been out of circulation.

Revenue Stamp—A label or stamp affixed to an item as evidence of tax payment.

Seals—An adhesive label that looks like a stamp, used for various fund-raising campaigns.

Se-tenant—Two or more stamps joined together, each having a different design or value.

Sheet—A page of stamps as they are printed, usually separated before distribution to post offices.

Soaking—Removing used stamps from paper to which they are attached by soaking in water. (NOTE: Colored cancels may cause staining to other stamps.)

Souvenir Sheet—One or more specially designed stamps printed by the government in celebration of a special stamp.

Splice—The splice made between rolls of paper in the printing operation. Stamps printed on this splice are generally discarded.

Tete-Beche—A pair of stamps printed together so that the images point in opposite vertical directions.

Transit Mark—A mark made by an intermediate post office between the originating and final destination post office.

Typeset Stamp—A stamp printed with regular printer's type, as opposed to engraved, lithographed, etc.

Ungummed—Stamps printed without an adhesive back.

Unhinged—A stamp that has never been mounted with the use of a hinge.

Unperforated—A stamp produced without perforations.

Vignette—The central design portion of a stamp.

Want List—A list of stamps a collector needs to fill gaps in his collection.

Watermark—A mark put into paper by the manufacturer, not readily seen by the naked eye.

Wrapper—A strip of paper with adhesive on one end, used for wrapping bundles of mail. Especially in Great Britain, it refers to any bit of paper to which a used stamp is still attached.

EQUIPMENT

To collect stamps properly a collector will need some "tools of the trade." These need not be expensive and need not all be bought at the very outset. That might, in fact, be the worst thing to do. Many a beginning collector has spent his budget on equipment, only to have little or nothing left for stamps and then loses interest in the hobby.

It may be economical in the long run to buy the finest quality accessories, but few collectors, just starting out, have a clear idea of what they will and will not be needing. It is just as easy to make impulse purchases of accessories as of stamps and just as unwise. Equipment must be purchased on the basis of what sort of collection is being built now, rather than on what the collection may be in the future. There is no shame in working up from an elementary album.

Starter Kits. Starter or beginner outfits are sold in just about every variety shop, drugstore, etc. These come in attractive boxes and contain a juvenile or beginner's album; some stamps, which may be on paper and in need of removal; a packet of gummed hinges; tongs; a pocket stockbook or file; and often other items such as a perforation gauge, booklet on stamp collecting, magnifier, and watermark detector. These kits are specially suited to young collectors and can provide a good philatelic education.

Albums. When the hobby began, more than a century ago, collectors mounted their stamps in whatever albums were at hand. Scrapbooks, school exercise tablets, and diaries all were used, as well as homemade albums. Today a number of firms specialize in printing albums of all kinds for philatelists, ranging from softbounds for the cautious type to huge multi-volume sets that cost hundreds of dollars. There are general worldwide albums, country albums, U.N. albums, and albums for mint sheets, covers, and every other conceivable variety of philatelic material. Choose your album according to the specialty you intend to pursue. It is not necessary, however, to buy a printed album at all. Many collectors feel there is not enough room for creativity in a printed album and prefer to use a binder with unprinted sheets. This allows items to be arranged at will on the page, rather than following the publisher's format, and for a personal write-up to be added. Rod-type binders will prove more durable and satisfactory than ring binders for heavy collections. The pages of an album should not be too thin, unless only one side is used. The presence of tiny crisscrossing lines (quadrilled sheets) is intended as an aid to correct alignment. Once items have been mounted and written up, these lines are scarcely visible and do not interfere with the attractiveness of the page.

Hinges. These are small rectangular pieces of lightweight paper, usually clear or semiopaque, gummed and folded. One side is moistened and affixed to the back of the stamp and the other to the album page. Hinges are sold in packets of 1,000 and are very inexpensive. Though they are by far the most popular device for mounting stamps, the hobbyist has his choice of a number of other products if hinges are not satisfactory to him. These include cello mounts, which encase the stamp in clear sheeting and have a black background to provide a kind of frame. These are self-sticking. Their cost is much higher than hinges. The chief advantage of cello mounts is that they prevent injuries to the stamp and eliminate the moistening necessary in using hinges; however, they add considerably to the weight of each page, making flipping through an album less convenient, and become detached from the page more readily than hinges.

Glassine Interleaving. These are sheets made of thin semitransparent glassine paper, the same used to make envelopes in which stamps are stored. They come punched to fit albums of standard size and are designed to be placed between each set of sheets, to prevent stamps on one page from becoming entangled with those on the facing page. Glassine interleaving is not necessary if cello mounts are used, but any collection mounted with conventional hinges should be interleaved. The cost is small. Glassine interleaving is sold in packets of 100 sheets.

Magnifier. A magnifier is a necessary tool for most stamp collectors, excepting those who specialize in first-day covers or other items that would not likely require study by magnification. There are numerous types and grades on the market, ranging in price from about $1 to more than $20. The quality of magnifier to buy should be governed by the extent to which it is likely to be used, and the collector's dependence upon it for identification and study. A collector of plate varieties ought to have the best magnifier he can afford and carry it whenever visiting dealers, shows, or anywhere that he may wish to examine specimens. A good magnifier is also necessary for a specialist in grilled stamps and for collectors of Civil War and other nineteenth-century covers. Those with built-in illumination are best in these circumstances.

Tongs. Beginners have a habit of picking up stamps with their fingers, which can cause injuries, smudges, and grease stains. Efficient handling of tongs is not difficult to learn, and the sooner the better. Do not resort to ordinary tweezers, but get a pair of philatelic tongs which are specially shaped and of sufficiently large size to be easily manipulated.

Perforation Gauge. A very necessary, inexpensive article, as the identification of many stamps depends upon a correct measuring of their perforations.

TEN LOW-COST WAYS TO START COLLECTING STAMPS

Courtesy of the
American Philatelic Society.

If you have recently started collecting stamps, or are thinking about starting, you may be wondering if the hobby is expensive. Can you enjoy it with limited financial resources? What if you have no money at all for the hobby?

One of the biggest questions any stamp collector faces is where to find stamps inexpensively. If you intend to save stamps of the United States or the world and want to save used as well as unused stamps, the opportunities are really great. Not all collections consist mainly of unused stamps that you buy in the post office. Used stamps are worth saving, have value, and they may cost you nothing.

Many stamp collectors save only used stamps. Others save both used and unused ones. Others save stamps only from one country or one part of the world. Some collectors save stamps by "topic," for example, stamps that depict horses or trains or birds. There are any number of different types of collections.

1. All postally used stamps started out being received in someone's mailbox, at no cost to the person receiving them. The first place to search for stamps, then, is your own mailbox. Don't be discouraged when you notice that many senders use postage meters or the imprint "Bulk Rate Postage Paid" on their envelopes to enjoy a better postal rate or to keep from affixing stamps. Also, when people do use real stamps, they often use the same common small ones.

You can begin to change this by asking people who write to you to use commemorative stamps on their mail. These are normally the larger stamps issued to honor famous people, places, or events. These stamps are printed in lesser quantities than the common smaller (definitive) stamps and usually are of much more interest to collectors. Many people will remember to ask for commemorative stamps at the post office when mailing letters to you or your family if you let them know you are a stamp collector. Also, if you write away for offers that require postage or a self-addressed, stamped envelope, you can put commemoratives on your return envelope, knowing that they will come back to you later.

2. Neighbors, friends, and relatives are another good source of stamps. The majority of people just throw away stamps when they receive them on mail and are only too happy to save them for someone who appreciates them. You may even know someone who gets letters from other countries who can save these stamps, too. Always be on the lookout for potentially good stamp contacts, and don't be afraid to ask them to go through their mail for you before they throw away all the envelopes.

3. Office mail may be even better. You may know someone who works in an office that gets a lot of mail. Out of 100 letters a day, there may be ten or twenty good stamps that are being thrown away. Many businesses get a lot of foreign mail and regularly throw away stamps that have interest and/or value to a collector.

4. Ask friends and coworkers to save envelopes with stamps for you. Youngsters can parents if they have any old letters, which may have stamps on the envelopes. When taking stamps off envelopes, always tear off the corner so that there is paper all around the stamp, and the stamp and all its perforations are undamaged. Anyone who is saving stamps for you should be told that this is the way to do it; otherwise, he/she may try to peel the stamp off the envelope. This will cause thin spots or tears, both of which ruin a stamp's appearance and lessen its value to collectors. If you run across envelopes that are very old or have postal markings that may be of particular interest, it is best to save the entire envelope until you can find out if the stamp is worth more attached to the cover.

Now that you have stamps on paper, what do you do with them? The most common way to get stamps off paper is to soak them in cool water, then dry them on paper. To understand more about soaking stamps, it is best to find a handbook on stamp collecting at the library.

There is a lot to learn about stamps as you get more and more of them. For example, different shades of color may exist on stamps with the same design, or they may have different perforation measurements (number of holes per side). Major varieties of stamps and "catalog values" are listed in stamp catalogs, which are available in most libraries. The most common one, the Scott Standard Postage Stamp Catalogue, has a very good section in front that explains how stamps are made and how to tell varieties apart, as well as how to use the catalog. Having access to a catalog in a nearby library is very useful until you decide if you want one of your own.

5. Longtime collectors may be another source of stamps. Usually a person who has been a collector for a number of years has developed many sources for stamps. The collector may have thousands of duplicates, some of which may be very inexpensive while others may have more value. Often older collectors are willing to help new philatelists get started by giving them stamps, or at least providing packets of stamps much more cheaply than can be purchased in stores or by mail.

6. Many stamp companies advertise free stamps. However, these ads must be read carefully before you send away for anything. Usually these ads offer "approvals," which means they will send you the free stamps advertised, plus an assortment of other stamps which you may either buy or return. By sending for the free stamps, you have already agreed that you will return the other stamps within a reasonable period of time if you do not buy anything. Usually you must pay the return postage. This is a convenient way to buy stamps from your own home.

7. Stamp clubs are another place to get stamps. A club may offer stamps as prizes, or have inexpensive stamps you can afford to buy.

Some stamp clubs sponsor junior clubs that meet at schools or the local YMCA or community center. If you are fortunate enough to have one of these in your area, it can be a great source of both stamps and advice.

8. One way to increase your sources for stamps and also have a lot of fun is to help start a local club, if one does not already exist. All it takes are four or five other stamp collectors who are interested in getting together to learn about and trade stamps and ideas.

9. Obtaining a pen pal in another country is a very good way to get stamps from that country. His or her extra stamps may seem really common in that country, but over here they are much scarcer. Your own stamps may look fairly common to you, but he or she is sure to appreciate them.

10. Trading off your duplicate stamps can be a lot of fun. Even if you don't know many collectors where you live, stamps are so lightweight that they can easily be traded by mail. Check out the stamp newspapers and magazines available at your local library for classified ads that list stamp trades. You may find, for example, that another collector will send you 100 large foreign stamps if you send 100 U.S. commemoratives. Usually schools do not subscribe to any of the periodical stamp publications, so you will have to go to your public library. (Many stamp publications also offer to send one free sample issue if you request it, because they are always looking for potential new subscribers.)

Collecting stamps need not be an expensive hobby. Thousands of stamps are issued every year, and while some of them cost many dollars, others cost just a few cents each. Nobody expects you to try to save every stamp that exists, and the key to enjoying philately is to save whatever you enjoy the most! With free stamps and a few inexpensive accessories, such as a small album and a package of stamp hinges, even collectors with little money can have a great time. Don't forget to mention stamps, stamp albums, and hinges before your birthday or Christmas! Also remember that a great many inexpensive stamps in the past have turned into more valuable stamps over the years.

THREE TIPS FOR STAMP COLLECTORS:

Soaking Stamps,
Choosing an Album, and Using Tongs.

Courtesy of the American Philatelic Society.

• TIP 1: SOAKING STAMPS

BEFORE SOAKING

Set aside any stamps on colored paper, or on paper with a colored backing. Pick out any stamps with colored cancellations, especially with red or purple ink.

Set aside any dark-colored stamps, stamps on poor-quality paper, or with strange-looking inks that might dissolve in the water and stain other stamps being soaked, etc. Any "problem" stamps must be handled carefully later, one at a time.

Trim the envelope paper close to the stamp, being careful not to cut the perforated edges or otherwise damage the stamp.

SOAKING THE STAMPS

Use a shallow bowl and fill it with several inches of cool-to-lukewarm water. (Never use hot water.) Float the stamps with the picture side up. Make sure the stamps have room to float and do not stick to one another. Don't soak too many at one time.

Let the stamps float until the glue dissolves and the stamps slide easily off the paper. Paper is very weak when it is wet and it's easy to tear a wet stamp if you handle it roughly. Be patient, and let the water do its work!

Rinse the back of the stamp gently in fresh water to make sure all the glue is off. Change the water in the soaking bowl often to make sure it is clean.

Place the stamps to dry on paper towels or old newspapers. (Don't use the Sunday comics! The colored inks might stick to the wet stamps.) It's a good idea to use your stamp tongs (see p. 574) to lift the wet stamps, instead of using your fingers. Lay the stamps in a single layer, and so they are not touching one another.

Let the stamps dry on their own. They may curl a little or look wrinkled, but don't worry about that. When they are completely dry, lift them with your tongs and put them in a phone book or a dictionary or some other book. (Special "stamp drying books" also can be purchased.) It's important not to put the stamps in a book until they are completely dry. After a few days, they should be nice and flat, and you can put them in your collection.

STAMPS ON COLORED PAPER OR WITH COLORED-INK CANCELS

Cut away all the excess envelope paper without harming the edges of the stamp.

Fill a shallow dish with cool water (cooler than you would usually use for soaking) and float the stamp face up. If the water becomes stained before the stamp is free from the paper, empty it out and use clean water, to prevent the stamp from being stained.

Dry as before.

DIRTY OR STAINED STAMPS

These can be soaked carefully in a small amount of undiluted liquid dishwashing detergent (not dishwasher detergent), then rinsed in clean cool water.

Very badly stained stamps can be washed gently in a weak solution of water and a bit of enzyme laundry detergent. Careful! This can work too well and remove the printing ink!

SELF-ADHESIVE STAMPS

Some self-adhesive stamps have a special, water-soluble backing, and they can be soaked off envelopes. You just need extra patience, as they may have to soak for an hour or more before they will separate from the backing paper. In general, U.S. self-adhesive stamps from about 1990 and later can be soaked with water; earlier ones cannot. If you don't want to try soaking, just trim the paper closely around a self-adhesive stamp on cover, and then mount it in your collection with a stamp mount.

• TIP 2: CHOOSING AN ALBUM

You've raided the mailbox, rummaged in the wastebasket in the post office lobby, and pestered your friends to save their envelopes. Now that you have all these philatelic goodies, where will you put them?

True, an ordinary shoebox gives storage space, but you should want a nicer home for your treasures—a place to display your material, not just store it. And, on the practical side, stamps and covers (envelopes with stamps on them, used in the mail) kept in a shoebox or paper folder risk damage from dirt or creases, losing value as well as beauty.

Since the first known commercial stamp album was published in 1862, the stamp hobby has grown tremendously, and many types of albums have become available.

When buying a home for your collection, here are some things to think about:

It may be your first album, but it probably will not be your last or only one. Your first album may be a kind of experiment, unless you already have seen someone else's album and think that kind would be right for you too. You also may have tried homemade pages and got some ideas of what you would want in a standard album.

If you are buying an album in person, rather than by mail, listen to the seller's advice, but don't be fully convinced by claims that one or another album is "the best." An album may be by a famous maker, and expensive, but that doesn't make it "the best" one for you. Be a careful shopper; consider all the factors—appearance, price, format—and make the best choice. Good beginners' albums are available that are not too expensive, are fully illustrated to show which stamp goes where, and may even contain extra information, such as maps and facts about the countries.

Certain styles of albums can present problems. For example, if an album is designed for stamps to be mounted on the front and back of each page, when the book is closed, the stamps can become tangled with one another on the facing pages. Opening the book may tear the mounted stamps apart. If you are looking at an album with this page format and don't like that aspect, but do like other things about the album, buy some good-quality plastic sheets to insert between the pages, and prevent the tangles.

You may choose not to buy a top-of-the-line album because of cost, but do be willing to pay for some quality. An album with pages of flimsy paper will not stand up to the stress of increasing numbers of stamps as you fill the album. An album with torn, falling-out pages is not much better than the old shoebox.

Homemade pages can be experimented with before album-shopping or may even become your permanent storage choice. Some options include a notebook or looseleaf binder of plain paper, though longtime, safest storage of your stamps should be on acid-free paper. If you have an unusual specialty, or enjoy unique arrangements, no standard album may ever suit your needs, and homemade will be best.

Blank, acid-free album pages punched for three-hole binders are widely available. It is easy to assemble a safe, stable home for your personalized collection, if you don't need or want the kind of structured format that standard albums provide. Makers of custom pages and albums advertise regularly in the philatelic press.

Buying an album is not so different from buying anything else: Think before and during the purchase; buy as wisely as you can and not over your budget; and don't be too discouraged if your first acquisition turns out to be less than perfect. You will always need places for temporary storage as you continue in the hobby. Old albums never go to waste!

• TIP 3: USING TONGS

Philatelic tongs (not to be confused with the tweezers in the medicine cabinet) are must-have items for every stamp collector. Get into the habit early of using your tongs every time you work with your stamps. They will act as clean extensions of your fingers and keep dirt, skin oil, and other harmful things from getting on your philatelic paper.

It's important to use tongs correctly and carefully. As with knives, scissors, and other helpful tools, tongs used carelessly are harmful rather than helpful. Cut some plain paper into stamp-sized pieces and practice using your tongs, watching what happens as you change the angle, pressure, and method of using them.

Grip a bit of paper strongly with the pointy-end style of tongs and watch what happens. If that were a favorite stamp, would you have wanted that hole poked in the middle of it? Keep experimenting, and you will find that it's not difficult to hold a stamp firmly but gently with tongs.

There are several common styles of tongs, to suit your preference and for special purposes.

Some have very pointed ends; they touch only a tiny part of the stamp, but there is the risk of poking holes through it. Working with extra-long tongs (five or six inches) with small pointed tips requires a lot of dexterity, and while experts may prefer them, they may not be comfortable or necessary for "everyday" stamp work.

The rounded, spatula-type style known as the "spade" are good, general-purpose tongs. A squared-off version of the spade also is commonly available, though the rather sharp corners present the same kind of risk as the thin, pointy tongs. One handy style is angled, with a bend near the tips that makes it easier to remove stamps from watermark or soaking trays, or to insert and remove stamps from stockbooks or mounts.

Tongs cost anywhere from a couple of dollars to quite a few for some of the imported, high-quality models. A special gift for a philatelist would be some gold-plated tongs, which are not hard to find, believe it or not! Tongs can be found anywhere stamp supplies are sold; check under "Accessories" in the philatelic press ads.

Tongs are among the least expensive and most essential stamp-hobby needs. You may even want to have several different kinds on hand— instead of your hands! Your stamps will appreciate it.

BUYING STAMPS

There are many ways to buy stamps: packets, poundage mixtures, approvals, new issue services, auctions, and a number of others. To buy wisely, a collector must get to know the language of philately and the techniques used by dealers and auctioneers in selling stamps.

Packets of all different worldwide stamps are sold in graduated sizes from 1,000 up to 50,000. True to their word, they contain no duplicates. The stamps come from all parts of the world and date from the 1800s to the present. Both mint and used are included. When you buy larger quantities of most things, a discount is offered; with stamp packets, it works in reverse. The larger the packet, the higher its price per stamp. This is because the smaller packets are filled almost exclusively with low-grade material.

Packets are suitable only as a collection base. A collector should never count on them to build his entire collection. The contents of one worldwide packet are much like that of another. Country jackets are sold in smaller sizes, but there are certain drawbacks with packets.

1. Most packets contain some cancelled-to-order stamps, which are not very desirable for a collection. These are stamps released with postmarks already on them, and are classified as used but have never gone through the mail. Eastern Europe and Russia are responsible for many C.T.O.s.

2. The advertised value of packets bears little relation to the actual value. Packet makers call attention to the catalog values of their stamps, based on prices listed in standard reference works. The lowest sum at which a stamp can be listed in these books is 2¢, therefore, a packet of 1,000 automatically has a minimum catalog value of $20. If the retail price is $3 this seems like a terrific buy when, in fact, most of those thousand stamps are so common they are almost worthless.

Poundage mixtures are very different than packets. Here the stamps are all postally used (no C.T.O.s) and still attached to small fragments of envelopes or parcel wrappings. Rather than sold by count, poundage mixtures are priced by the pound or ounce and quite often by kilos. Price varies depending on the grade, and the grade depends on where the mixture was assembled. Bank mixtures are considered the best, as banks receive a steady flow of foreign registered mail. Mission mixtures are also highly rated. Of course, the mixture should be sealed and unpicked. Unless a mixture is advertised as unpicked, the high values have been removed. The best poundage mixtures are sold only by mail. Those available in shops are of medium or low quality. Whatever the grade, poundage mixtures can be counted on to contain duplicates.

If you want to collect the stamps of a certain country, you can leave a standing order for its new releases with a new-issue service. Whenever that government puts out stamps, they will be sent to the collector along with a bill. Usually the service will supply only mint copies. The price charged is not the face value, but the face value with a surcharge added to meet the costs of importing, handling, and the like. New issue services are satisfactory only if the collector is positive he wants all the country's stamps, no matter what. Remember that its issues could include semi-postals, long and maybe expensive sets, and extra high values.

By far the most popular way to buy stamps is via approvals. There is nothing new about approvals, as they go back to the Victorian era. Not all services are alike, though. Some offer sets, while others sell penny approvals. Then there are remainder approvals, advanced approvals, and seconds on approval. Penny approvals are really a thing of the past, though the term is still used. Before inflation, dealers would send a stockbook containing several thousand stamps, all priced at a penny each. If all the stamps were kept, the collector got a discount plus the book! Today the same sort of service can be found, but instead of 1¢ per stamp, the price is anywhere from 3¢ to 10¢. Remainder approvals are made up from collection remainders. Rather than dismount and sort stamps from incoming collections, the approval merchant saves himself time by sending them out right on the album pages. The collector receives leaves from someone else's collection with stamps mounted just as he arranged them. Seconds on approval are slightly defective specimens of scarce stamps, which would cost more if perfect. Advanced approvals are designed for specialized collectors who know exactly what they want and have a fairly substantial stamp budget.

In choosing an approval service you should know the ground rules of approval buying and not be unduly influenced by promotional offers. Most approval merchants allow the selections to be kept for ten days to two weeks. The unbought stamps are then returned along with payment for those kept. As soon as the selection is received back, another is mailed. This will go on, regardless of how much or how little is bought, until the company is notified to refrain from sending further selections. The reputable services will always stop when told.

Approval ads range from splashy full-pagers in the stamp publications to small three-line classified announcements in magazines and newspapers. Most firms catering to beginners offer loss leaders, or stamps on which they take a loss for the sake of getting new customers. If an approval dealer offers 100 pictorials for a dime, it is obvious he is losing money on that transaction, as 10¢ will not even pay the postage. It is very tempting to order these premiums. Remember that when ordering approvals. What sort of service is it? Will it offer the kind of stamps desired? Will prices be high to pay for the loss leaders? Be careful of confusing advertisements. Sometimes the premium offers seem to promise more than they actually do. A rare, early stamp may be pictured. Of course you do not receive the stamp, but merely a modern commemorative picturing it.

Auction Sales. Stamp auctions are held all over the country and account for millions of dollars in sales annually. Buying at auction is exciting and can be economical. Many sleepers turn up—stamps that can be bought at less than their actual value. To be a good auction buyer, the philatelist must know stamps and their prices pretty well, and know the ropes of auctions. An obvious drawback of auctions is that purchases are not returnable. A dealer will take back a stamp that proves not to a collector's liking, but an auctioneer will not. Also, auctioneers require immediate payment while a dealer may extend credit.

Stamps sold at auction come from private collections and the stocks of dealers; not necessarily defunct dealers, but those who want to get shelf space. Because they were brought together from a variety of sources, the nature and condition will vary. In catalog descriptions the full book value will be given for each stamp, but of course defective stamps will sell for much less than these figures. A bidder must calculate how much less. Other lots which can be difficult for the bidder to evaluate are those containing more than one stamp. Sometimes a superb specimen will be lotted along with a defective one. Then there are bulk lots which contain odds and ends from collections and such. It is usual in auctioning a collection for the better stamps to be removed and sold separately. The remainder is then offered in a single lot, which may consist of thousands or even tens of thousands of stamps. By all means examine lots before bidding. A period of inspection is always allowed before each sale, usually for several days. There may or may not be an inspection on sale day. If the bidder is not able to make a personal examination but must bid on strength of the catalog description, he should scale his bids for bulk lots much lower than for single stamp lots. He might bid $50 on a single stamp lot with a catalog value of $100, if the condition is listed as top-notch, but to bid one-half catalog value on a bulk lot would not be very wise. These lots are not scrutinized very carefully by the auctioneers and some stamps are bound to be disappointing. There may be some heavily canceled, creased, torn, etc. Also, there will very likely be duplication. A bid of one-fifth the catalog value on a bulk lot is considered high. Often a one-tenth bid is successful.

The mechanics of stamp auctions may strike the beginner as complicated. They are run no differently than other auctions. All material to be sold is lotted by the auctioneer; that is, broken down into lots or units and bidding is by lot. Everything in the lot must be bid on, even if just one of the stamps is desired. The motive of bulk lotting is to save time and give each lot a fair sales value.

Before the sale a catalog is published listing all the lots, describing the contents and sometimes picturing the better items. Catalogs are in the mail about 30 days before the sale date. If a bid is to be mailed, it must be sent early. Bids that arrive after the sale are disqualified, even if they would have been successful.

When the bid is received it is entered into a bidbook, along with the bidder's name and address. On sale day each lot opens on the floor at one level above the second-highest mail bid. Say the two highest mail bids are $30 and $20. The floor bidding would begin at $25. If the two highest bids are $100 and $500, the opening bid would probably be $150. The larger the amounts involved, the bigger will be the advances. The auctioneer will not accept an advance of $5 on a $500 lot; but on low-value lots even dollar advances are sometimes made. Then it becomes a contest of floor versus book. The auctioneer acts as an agent, bidding for the absentee until his limit is reached. If the floor tops him, he has lost. If the floor does not get as high as his bid, he wins the lot at one advance over the highest floor bid.

When a collector buys stamps by mail from a dealer, he should choose one who belongs to the American Stamp Dealers' Association or A.S.D.A. The emblem is carried in their ads.

HOW TO ORDER STAMPS "TOLL-FREE" FROM THE USPS

You can now order stamps, toll-free, from the USPS by calling the Philatelic Fulfillment Service Center located in Kansas City, Missouri, 1-800-782-6724. Listening to a computerized voice, you can choose from six options using a touch-tone phone: 1) ordering stamps, 2) catalog requests, subscription programs information, 3) customer assistance, 4) personalized envelopes, post offices and official mail agencies. This is a very useful service. It is recommended that you first order one of the catalogs, "Stamps, Etc." or "Not Just Stamps" in order to correctly place your order for stamps.

SELLING STAMPS

Almost every collector becomes a stamp seller sooner or later. Duplicates are inevitably accumulated, no matter how careful one may be in avoiding them. Then there are the G and VG stamps that have been replaced with F and VF specimens, and have become duplicates by intent. In addition to duplicates, a more advanced collector is likely to have stamps that are not duplicates but for which he has no further use. These will be odds and ends, sometimes quite valuable ones, that once suited the nature of his collection but are now out of place. Collectors' tastes change. The result is a stockpile of stamps that can be converted back to cash.

The alternative to selling the stamps you no longer need or want is trading them with a collector who does want them, and taking his unwanted stamps in return. All stamp clubs hold trading sessions. Larger national stamp societies operate trade-by-mail services for their members. The APS (American Philatelic Society) keeps $8,000,000 worth of stamps constantly circulating in its trading books or "circuit" books. Trading can be an excellent way of disposing of surplus stamps. In most cases it takes a bit longer than selling. Another potential drawback, especially if you are not a club member, is finding the right person with the right stamps.

The nature and value of the material involved may help in deciding whether to sell outright or trade. Also, there are your own personal considerations. If you're not going to continue in the stamp hobby, or need cash for some purpose other than stamp buying, trading is hardly suitable. Likewise, if you have developed an interest in some very exotic group of stamps or other philatelic items it may be impossible to find someone to trade with.

Once you have decided to sell, if indeed you do make that decision, the matter revolves upon how. To a stamp shop? To another collector? Through an auction house? Possibly by running your own advertisements and issuing price lists, if you have enough stamps and spare time to make this worthwhile?

While some individuals have an absolute horror at the prospect of selling anything, stamp collectors tend to enjoy selling. It is difficult to say why. Some enjoy it so much they keep right on selling stamps, as a business, long after their original objective is achieved. Nearly all professional stamp dealers were collectors before entering the trade.

Selling your stamps outright to a dealer, especially a local dealer whom you can personally visit, is not necessarily the most financially rewarding but it is quick and very problem-free. Of course it helps if the dealer knows you and it's even better if he knows some of your stamps. Dealers have no objection to repurchasing stamps they've sold to you. You will find that the dealers encourage their customers to sell to them just as much as they encourage them to buy. The dealers are really anxious to get your stamps if you have good salable material from popular countries. In fact most dealers would prefer buying from the public rather than any other source.

The collector selling stamps to a dealer has to be reasonable in his expectations. A dealer may not be able to use all the stamps you have. It is simply not smart business for a dealer to invest money in something he may not be able to sell. So, if you have esoteric or highly specialized items for sale, it might be necessary to find a specialist who deals in those particular areas rather than selling to a neighborhood stamp shop.

The local stamp shop will almost certainly want to buy anything you can offer in the way of medium-to-better-grade U.S. stamps of all kinds, including the so-called "back of the book" items. He may not want plate blocks or full sheets of commemoratives issued within the past 20 years. Most dealers are well supplied with material of this nature and have opportunities to buy more of it every day. The same is true of first-day covers, with a few exceptions, issued from the 1960s to the present. The dealers either have these items abundantly or can get them from a wholesaler at rock-bottom prices. They would rather buy stamps that are a bit harder to get from the wholesalers, or for which the wholesalers charge higher prices. On the whole you will meet with a favorable reception when offering U.S. stamps to a local dealer. With foreign stamps it becomes another matter: what do you have and how flexible are you in price? Nearly all the stamp shops in this country do stock foreign stamps to one extent or another. They do not, as a rule, attempt to carry comprehensive or specialized stocks of them. In the average shop you will discover that the selection of general foreign consists of a combination of modern mint sets, topicals, souvenir sheets, packets which come from the wholesaler, and a small sprinkling of older material, usually pre-1900. The price range of this older material will be $5 to $50. Non-specialist collectors of foreign stamps buy this type of item and that is essentially who the local shop caters to. When a local dealer buys rare foreign stamps or a large foreign collection, it is not for himself. He buys with the intent of passing them along to another dealer who has the right customers lined up. He acts only as a middleman or go-between. Therefore the price you receive for better-grade foreign stamps tends to be lower than for better-grade U.S., which the dealer buys for his own use.

What is a fair price to get for your stamps? This is always difficult to say, as many variable factors are involved. Consider their condition. Think in terms of what the dealer could reasonably hope to charge for them at retail and stand a good chance of selling them. Some of your stamps may have to be discounted because of no gum, poor centering, bent perfs, hinge remnants, repairs, or other problems. But even if your stamps are primarily F or VF, a dealer cannot pay book values for them. If you check his selling prices on his specimens of those same stamps, you can usually count on receiving from 40 to 50 percent of those prices. Considering the discount made from book values by the dealer in pricing his stock, your payment may work out to about 25 percent of book values. For rare U.S. stamps in top condition you can do better than 25 percent, but on most stamps sold to a dealer this is considered a fair offer. Keep in mind that the difference between a dealer's buying and selling prices is not just "profit margin." Most of the markup goes toward operating costs, for without this markup, there would be no stamp dealers.

WHAT IS AN ERROR, FREAK, OR ODDITY?

In an attempt to answer the questions above, an article, "Listing of Existing EFO Variations According to Group," by Mr. John M. Hotchner, was published originally in the June 1982 issue of *The EFO Collector,* the quarterly journal of the Errors, Freaks, Oddities Collectors Club. Resulting correspondence and experience in the EFO field, plus selected portions of Mr. Hotchner's article, are contained herein to attempt to provide some guidance as to what constitutes an error, freak, or oddity.

Nothing makes a philatelist's head turn so fast as an obvious error in an issued stamp. Many of philately's true blue-chip errors are from the early days. The United States 1869 inverts on the fifteen-cent, twenty-four-cent and thirty-cent values, Spain's 1851 two-real value in a six-real blue sheet, New South Wales stamps of the 1850s and '60s with the wrong watermark, etc.

Why? Most stamps of this era had relatively small printings compared to today's. In addition, they were used with little thought given to looking for or saving errors or misprints of lesser significance. Most of the varieties that have been found were used, and exist in very small quantities. Incidentally, this is a very good reason for one to keep one's eye open, for there remains a possibility that classic errors can still be found in old albums or accumulations.

In the early days of philately, collectors gathered EFOs (errors, freaks, oddities) to dress up their country or topical collections. Many modern collectors continue to collect EFOs in that fashion. There has, however, been a recent increase in collecting and studying EFOs as a specialty area.

Modern-day specialization has been fostered by the greatly increased awareness of and search for EFO material. This is a search which is often rewarded because of the increasing complexity of modern production equipment and the continuing pressure to reduce cost.

The lack of commonly accepted definitions of EFO terms has been an impediment to the growth of EFO philately. In the absence of a clear sense of what EFOs include, philatelists, in large numbers, have found the area complex and difficult. It has been hard to understand how values developed, so collectors merely kept what they came across, but rarely sought out EFO material unless it was listed in a catalog.

Catalog listing is, of course, reserved for errors. Catalog-listed errors get space in albums. Thus, recognized errors tend to have an increased value because collectors search for them because they like to fill their empty album spaces. Without a catalog listing, the remainder of EFO material tended to wallow in a valley of conflicting and confusing opinion and wildly varying prices. Also, if an item lacks catalog recognition, one might call the item a "freak," "oddity," or "variety."

The answer to an often-asked question regarding EFOs—"Aren't they expensive?"—is that while some EFOs are valued in the thousands of dollars, others cost no more than a regular used stamp. In fact, it is quite possible for one to find a spectacular EFO item in one's own mailbox. You have probably heard of collectors who bought stamps or postal stationery at their local post office only to find something wrong with the purchase. Think of some of the people who used their find before they realized they had an EFO item. Knowledge is the key to recognizing EFO material when you find it.

The best possible source of information and education can be obtained by becoming a member of a philatelic organization such as the American Philatelic Society (APS), The American Topical Association (ATA), etc.; by joining specialty groups such as the Bureau Issues Association (BIA), The Errors, Freaks, Oddities Collectors Club (EFOCC), etc.; by subscribing to publications such as Linn's, Meekels, *Stamp Collector,* etc.; by joining libraries such as the Cardinal Spellman Museum, the Western Philatelic Library, etc. Through these organizations and publications, one will obtain knowledge so that one can differentiate between what a postal entity designs and what is the produced product.

The following is the best tool, to date, to attempt to type EFO material that is at variance from the intended design.

ERRORS

To be classed as such, an item must be completely missing a production step, i.e. the item must be completely missing a color, completely missing required perforations, contain an inverted design step, etc. Other examples might be:

- Perforations entirely missing between stamps—one or more sides.
- Perforations fully doubled or tripled.
- Perforations of wrong gauge applied.
- Items unintentionally printed on paper watermarked for another issue, or not watermarked at all.

FREAKS

To be classed as such, an item might have a lesser degree of production problem, or problems that are partial and not repeatable. Examples might be:

- Perforations shifted into the design portion of an issue.
- Overinking, underinking, smeared inking.
- Foldovers, foldunders, creases creating crazy perforations.
- Printer's waste (by definition, "Unlawfully Salvaged"). This category would include rejection markings that indicate material that should have been destroyed.
- Gutter snipes (less than a full stamp on one side).

ODDITIES

"Oddities" or, as European collectors seem to favor, "Varieties" include unusual issuances. Examples might be:

- Stamps printed on backs of stamps.
- Usages (bisects).
- Essays, proofs, specimens.
- Cancel/meter varieties.
- Unusual local overprints.
- Double transfers, layout lines, position dots.
- Pre–first-day-of-issue cancels.

The bottom line is any item, be it freak, error, oddity, or variety, can be collected as a specialty, or a collector can try to obtain an example of each. Some collectors will restrict their collecting to one country, or even one major issue within a country. Others simply accumulate and enjoy anything they come across with no particular rhyme-or-reasoned order.

The Errors, Freaks, Oddities Collectors Club has an international membership, quarterly publication and mail auction, heir's assistance program, study groups, etc. Annual dues are $16 USD North America, Europe $30 USD. Sample copy of The EFO Collector is $3 USD, or mint postage. EFOCC, P.O. Box 1126, Kingsland, GA 31548-1126; (912) 729-1573; FAX: (912) 729-1585; e-mail—cwouscg@aol.com.

PUBLICATIONS—
LINN'S STAMP NEWS

Linn's Stamp News is a tabloid-size newspaper for stamp collectors. It has been published continuously as a weekly since 1928. Both in terms of page count and circulation, Linn's is the largest publication in the stamp hobby. Each issue of Linn's contains a vast quantity of words and pictures designed to appeal to stamp collectors at every level of interest.

As the dominant publication in the stamp hobby, each weekly issue of Linn's is crammed with news and other information stamp collectors need to know, including details on how to order first-day covers directly from the U.S. Postal Service and information on how to order new-issue stamps at face value directly from overseas post offices. Lavishly illustrated features discuss virtually every aspect of the world's most popular collecting hobby, in terms that beginners and newcomers can easily understand. "Trends of Stamp Values" monitors prices (and price changes) for more than 100,000 stamps from every nation of the world. "Linn's U.S. Stamp Market Index" is the stamp equivalent of the Dow Jones Industrial Average. "U.S. Stamp Facts" provides weekly information about classic U.S. stamps in a compact and highly visual format. "Stamp Collecting Made Easy" explains complexities of stamp collecting in an illustrated how-to feature. "Focus on Forgeries" provides visual clues to identify common fake stamps.

One of the most interesting features of Linn's is its advertising. Each issue contains fifty or more pages of ads from dealers seeking to buy or sell stamps. Linn's classified advertising section consists of fifteen or more pages of small ads from dealers and collectors, all arranged by classification, to help busy collectors locate just what they need.

The publication isn't cheap (current subscription price is $45.95 a year), but stamp collectors say they can't do without it. You can see for yourself, because the publishers of Linn's will send a free sample copy to Blackbook readers. Write to Linn's Blackbook Offer, P.O. Box 29, Sidney, OH 45365.

Linn's also maintains a Web site for Internet users. Linn's Web site at www.linns.com features highlights of the weekly *Linn's Stamp News* as well as "Linn's U.S. Stamp Program," new-issue listings, and an archive of reference material and information on stamp-collecting basics.

Linn's also operates an online retail database, "Linn's Zillions of Stamps," that allows collectors the convenience to shop at one online address for the stamps, covers, and supplies they need anytime, night or day. And Linn's Stampsites.com searchable database has indexed the entire content of more than 20,000 stamp-collecting Web pages worldwide.

THE NATIONAL POSTAL MUSEUM

On July 30, 1993, the National Postal Museum opened its doors to the public, marking the creation of a new Smithsonian Institution museum, and making way for the nation's first major museum devoted to postal history and philately.

In what is a sophisticated and highly interactive museum, the National Postal Museum in Washington, D.C., features exhibitions that tell the history of the nation's mail service, from the Colonial era and the Pony Express to the art of letters and the beauty and lore of stamps.

"The theme of the museum is 'America's history is in the mail.' We are presenting American history from a new perspective," says James H. Bruns, former director of the National Postal Museum. "The museum is intended to inspire appreciation for a system that affects our lives every day. The history of America's mail service is the history of our success as a nation. The museum tells an upbeat and endearing story of American ingenuity and remarkable progress."

The Postal Museum is located at First Street and Massachusetts Avenue N.E. on the lower level of the former Washington City Post Office Building, which is on Capitol Hill next to Union Station. The museum houses and displays the nation's stamp and postal history collection, the largest and most comprehensive of its kind in the world.

"Not only is America's history in the mail, its future is in the mail, too," says William J. Henderson, former Chief Executive Officer and Postmaster General of the U.S. Postal Service. "We want people to understand the role the Postal Service has played for more than two centuries in helping our nation grow and prosper, and the important social and economic role the mail continues to play for the United States."

The museum occupies approximately 75,000 square feet, with more than 25,000 square feet devoted to exhibit space. It also features a Library Research Center, a Discovery Room for educational programs, a museum shop, and a philatelic sales center. The Library Research Center, available to the public by appointment, is among the largest postal history and philatelic research centers in the world, with more than 40,000 volumes and manuscripts. The museum also houses collections, conservation facilities, and curatorial and administrative offices.

HISTORY

The National Postal Museum was made possible by an agreement between the Smithsonian and the United States Postal Service. The museum was established after lengthy negotiations about relocating the Smithsonian's vast postal history and philatelic collection of more than 16 million stamps, covers, and artifacts. Previously housed on the third and fourth floors of the National Museum of American History, the collection lacked adequate exhibit, storage, and research space in that location.

On November 6, 1990, the Smithsonian Institution and the U.S. Postal Service signed an agreement in which the Postal Service would provide the site and approximately $15.4 million for start-up and construction costs and the Smithsonian would administer the museum and its staff.

The National Postal Museum is funded by both the Postal Service and the Smithsonian, as well as by money raised from endowments and ongoing fund-raising campaigns. The Smithsonian contribution to the new museum has been the same as that spent on the collection when it was at the Museum of American History. The more than $3 million raised from private organizations through March 1993 went toward the installation of the new and expanding exhibits. Private funds continue to be used to develop and expand exhibits.

THE COLLECTION

The National Philatelic Collection was established at the Smithsonian in 1886 with the donation of a sheet of 10-cent Confederate postage stamps. Generous gifts from individuals and foreign governments, transfers from government agencies and purchases have increased the collection to today's total of more than 16 million items.

From 1908 until 1963, the collection was housed in the Smithsonian's Arts and Industries Building on the National Mall. In 1964, the collection was moved to the National Museum of American History where it was expanded to include postal history and stamp production. In addition to the stamp collection, the museum has postal stationery covers, postal history material that predates stamps, vehicles used to transport the mail, mailboxes, meters, greeting cards, and letters.

EXHIBITIONS

More than 50,000 stamps and objects, and 400 graphics are on display throughout the museum's five major exhibit galleries that explore different facets of mail communication and history. The galleries include:

MOVING THE MAIL

Faced with the challenge of moving the mail quickly, the postal service looked to trains, automobiles, airplanes, and buses to deliver the mail, all of which are the focus of the museum's 90-foot-high Atrium gallery. After the Civil War, postal officials began to take advantage of railway trains for moving and sorting the mail. Sorting the mail while it was being carried between towns was a revolutionary approach to mail delivery, involving generations of devoted postal employees who worked as railway mail clerks.

Airmail service was established between New York, Philadelphia, and Washington, D.C., in 1918 with the remarkable pioneering flights of pilots Torrey Webb, James Edgerton, H. Paul Culver, and George Boyle. Airmail service was the base from which America's commercial aviation industry developed.

Some of the most ambitious movers of the mail were not aviators, railway mail clerks, or even postal employees. They are the star route contractors, who have delivered mail with everything from mules to motorcycles, including the 1850s Concord-style stagecoach on display in the museum.

THE ART OF CARDS AND LETTERS

While other galleries focus on systems of mail service, this gallery emphasizes letters. A cherished art form, letters are windows into history, used throughout museum displays to relate personal stories of survival, success, and tragedy. Through an array of wartime correspondence from World War I to Desert Storm, as well as objects and a video, one section highlights the struggle of soldiers and their loved ones to maintain ties during war. Changing exhibits in this gallery concentrate on the important stories letters tell of families and friends bound by these missives over land and across time.

BINDING THE NATION

The museum's first gallery provides an overview of the events in America from colonial times through the 19th century, stressing the importance of written communication in the young nation. As early as 1673, regular mail was carried between New York and Boston following Indian trails. That route, once known as the King's Best Highway, is now U.S. Route 1.

Benjamin Franklin, a colonial postmaster for the British government, played a key role in establishing mail service in the colonies, as well as in forging a strong link between colonial publishers and the postal service. Many newspapers that relied heavily on information carried in the mail customarily adopted the word "Post" into their title. Newspapers were so important to the dissemination of information to the people that they were granted cheaper postage rates.

By 1800, mail was carried over more than 9,000 miles of postal roads. The challenge of developing mail service over long distances is the central theme of "The Expanding Nation," which features the famed Pony Express. At an interactive video station, visitors can create their own postal route.

CUSTOMERS AND COMMUNITIES

By the turn of the 20th century, nearly 10,000 letter carriers worked in over 400 cities. The nation's population was expanding at top speed, and with it, the nation's mail volume and the need for personal mail delivery. This gallery focuses on the modern changes in mail service introduced at the turn of the century.

Crowded cities inspired postal officials to experiment with a variety of mail delivery systems, such as the impressive but ultimately impractical underground pneumatic tubes. Home delivery of mail began in the cities during the Civil War, when postal officials decided it was inhumane to require soldiers' families to receive death notices at post office windows.

As rural Americans watched city residents receive free home delivery, they began to demand equal treatment. This was the start of Rural Free Delivery. Facets of Rural Free Delivery and its important and often heartwarming role in the fabric of the nation is explored with photographs, mail vehicles, and a variety of rural mailboxes.

The history of the vast direct mail industry is the subject of a special interactive gallery. Through the use of sophisticated technology, the exhibition "What's in the Mail for You!" uses touch screen panels, three-dimensional projections, video workstations, holograms, and computer interactives to tell the story of the mailing industry and its function as a major means of commerce in America. This hands-on exhibit allows visitors to create a mailer and "target" customers; related exhibit topics look at different mail marketing techniques, the key to a successful mail campaign, and the success stories of well-known mail order entrepreneurs like L.L. Bean.

STAMPS AND STORIES

Among some 20 million stamp collectors in the United States, many are casual collectors, while others work at the hobby with a devotion to detail and scholarship unmatched by other pastimes. This gallery is for all collectors, as well as for those who know little about the renowned hobby of philately. The history of the stamp begins in 1840, when Great Britain issued the first gummed postage stamp. Since then stamps of every subject, shape, and design have been produced for consumer use or as collectibles.

Serving not only as proof of postage, stamps are also miniature works of art, keepsakes, and rare treasures—as well as the workhorses of the automated postal system. Some stamps tell stories, while others contain secrets and hidden meanings.

Some of the highlights of the gallery are priceless rarities from the museum's vast collection, including inverted stamps and scarce covers. Videos address questions of how and why stamps were invented, and how they are printed. A selection of more than 55,000 stamps is on display, and will be rotated every six months.

Within the exhibit galleries are more than 30 interactive areas, including, for example, video games that invite visitors to choose the best mail route between various cities in the 1800s, or deliver mail in a DeHavilland biplane. The museum features 17 video presentations, with topics ranging from America's railway mail clerks, the star route contractors, early letter carriers, and transportation technology, to stories about mail-train wrecks and robberies, and postal workers.

THE JEANETTE CANTRELL RUDY GALLERY

In this 800-square-foot gallery, a major exhibition devoted to federal duck stamps, entitled "Artistic License: The Duck Stamp Story," opened in Spring 1996. Made possible by a generous donation from Jeanette Cantrell Rudy of Nashville, TN., the exhibition explores the history of duck stamps, their contribution to the conservation of America's waterways, and the extraordinary craftsmanship that goes into their creation. A selection of rare duck stamps is on display, drawn from the collections of Mrs. Rudy and from the National Postal Museum.

TOURS

One-hour highlights tours are offered daily at 11 a.m. and 1 p.m. The National Postal Museum's Education Office will arrange guided tours for school and camp groups from September through May. Group leaders should call (202) 357-2991 (Voice) or (202) 633-9849 (TTY) for more information.

MUSEUM DESIGNED SPECIFICALLY TO HOUSE UNIQUE COLLECTION

The National Postal Museum was designed by the firm of Florance Eichbaum Esocoff King Architects. Chief among the objectives for designing the museum was the desire to create a maximum-security facility to protect the Smithsonian's priceless stamp collection, while at the same time creating an aesthetically rich setting that will attract visitors and encourage exploration of the museum's themes of postal history and philately.

The new museum's centerpiece is a 90-foot-high atrium that projects through the center of the quadrangle-shaped City Post Office Building.

Three airmail planes hang from steel girders inside the atrium, which has a glass ceiling 1.5 inches thick. The entire atrium area houses mail transportation vehicles and related displays; however, enough space on the atrium's marble floor remains for visitors to observe the intricate envelope and stamp design within the floor's tiles.

The museum is equipped with an array of sophisticated surveillance and safety equipment. The museum's research facilities, including the 6,000-square-foot Library Research Center, are meant to enhance the work and study of visiting researchers and scholars. The library features a specimen study room, an audio-visual viewing room, and a separate library of rare books.

HISTORIC BUILDING ENHANCES MUSEUM'S MESSAGE

The Washington City Post Office Building was built between 1911 and 1914 to serve as the District's central post office facility. Designed by architect Daniel Burnham, architect of Union Station, the City Post Office Building was built next door to the elegant train station in order to expedite the distribution of incoming mail to the nation's capital.

Completely renovated and restored to its original appearance, the City Post Office Building houses the National Postal Museum as well as a full-service post office and several federal agencies. The museum is located in what was once the building's mail processing and distribution center. An impressively ornate historic marble lobby, formerly the main service area of the City Post Office Building, will now serve as the foyer to the National Postal Museum. The Beaux Arts–style building is eligible for listing in the National Register of Historic Places.

EDUCATION PROGRAMS AND CHANGING EXHIBITIONS

The National Postal Museum offers a series of educational outreach activities. Through scheduled events in the museum's Discovery Center, individuals from preschool age to adult are invited to participate in events that aim to enhance the information presented in exhibits. Activities range from learning more about the art of stamps, postal transportation, automation, and mail delivery to letter writing and the analysis of historic letters. The museum also engages in school and community collaborative projects.

LIBRARY RESEARCH CENTER

With its more than 40,000 volumes and manuscripts, the museum's Library Research Center is among the world's largest philatelic and postal history research facilities. The 6,000-square-foot library features a rare-book reading room, an audiovisual room, research cubbies, and a workroom for viewing items from the collection. The library also offers current philatelic and postal magazines and newsletters as well as U.S.

Postal Service publications and annual reports. The center is operated by the Smithsonian Institution Libraries. It is open to the public by appointment from 10 a.m. to 4 p.m., Monday through Friday. For more information, call (202) 633-9370.

PUBLICATIONS

The official newsletter of the National Postal Museum is a quarterly, titled *EnRoute,* and is available by becoming a member of the National Postal Museum for $25.00 annually. A six-month calendar of events and membership information is offered by request by calling (202) 633-9385.

STAFF

The museum staff includes fifty-two full-time professional positions.

THE JUNIOR PHILATELISTS
OF AMERICA

ABOUT THE JPA

There are many stamp organizations in North America today—national, state, and local. The major societies are naturally operated by and for adult collectors. Young people may be allowed to join, but usually are not given an active role.

In the JPA, the situation is different. It is a group run by and for young people, age eighteen and under. Junior members operate services, write for the publication, serve on study groups and committees, and elect their own officers.

The JPA is a dynamic organization; the Officers and Board of the JPA are willing to listen to each and every idea of the membership. Please tell us what you want to see in the JPA. After all, as a member, it is your organization.

Open to Collectors of All Ages—Beginners or Advanced. There's no minimum age for JPA membership. We welcome the youngest and newest collector as well as the advanced philatelist. Everyone can benefit from JPA services and publications!

BENEFITS OF MEMBERSHIP

- You'll be part of an exciting organization that is bringing change and excitement to stamp collecting.

- The opportunity to participate in all of the JPA's activities and our bimonthly magazine, *The Philatelic Observer.*

- Access to the JPA's services, including Pen Pals, Stamp Identification, American Philatelic Research Library access, and periodic stamp auctions.

- The JPA Study Groups are a great way to meet up with other members interested in the same types of stamps as you are interested in.

- As soon as you join you will receive a "Goodie Packet" filled with stamps, a membership card, more information on JPA services, and other great free stuff that varies from month to month.

- Every two months all members receive a copy of *The Philatelic Observer,* which is filled with interesting articles from JPA members as well as prominent stamp collectors.

SERVICES AVAILABLE TO MEMBERS OF THE JPA

Awards Committee

Contact Central Office to request awards for your stamp show/ exhibition (JPA, P.O Box 2625, Albany, OR 97321). For more information, contact Central Office.

Educational Projects

Teachers and Stamp Club Leaders, we have stamps and stamp collecting information available for use in clubs and classrooms.

Library Services

The American Philatelic Research Library is open to JPA members. Others may browse the library to find books that can be checked out at their local library. Look in the latest Philatelic Observer for the person to contact to access the library.

MEMBERSHIP APPLICATION AND DUES

JPA dues are quite reasonable, set with a young person's budget in mind. For more information on dues and membership contact the JPA.

Junior Philatelists of America
P.O. Box 2625
Albany, OR 97321
Website: jpastamps.org.

Pen Pals Service

Looking for a Pen Pal somewhere in the world? Send your name, JPA No., and what type of Pen Pal you are looking for to the Pen Pal Chairman, Todd Richard.

Recruiting Committee

Help recruit more members to keep the JPA growing! You could even earn next year's dues free! Contact Central Office for Membership Applications and share the JPA's Web site with your friends.

Public Relations

Do you have a Hobbies or Collectibles section in your local paper? Find out how to get the word out about the JPA. Contact Sharolyn Chicoine.

The Philatelic Observer

The JPA's very own award-winning newsletter is sent to all members every two months! It's filled with information, games, and stories from and about other members! For a sample copy of *The Philatelic Observer*, send $1.

Pamphlets

JPA pamphlets are available free of charge from JPA Central Office, P.O. Box 2625, Albany, OR 97321 for members and nonmembers alike. Please send an SASE.

Stamp Identification

Simply send a photocopy of any stamp you can't identify along with an SASE to the address in the front of the Observer.

Welcoming Committee

Do you need help on writing "Welcome Letters" to new JPA members? Look in the front of your Observer to see who to contact.

Member E-mail Address Directory

Keep up-to-date with Collin Rickman. Contact him with your JPA No. and e-mail address to be added or removed. Members' e-mail addresses are not included unless they have asked to be included.

Stamp Clusters

Welcome to the Junior Philatelists of America's Stamp Clusters Program! We are glad you've decided to learn more about the program. This handbook has been developed to give you a guided tour into the fun and excitement of participating in one or more JPA study groups. Stamp Clusters are actually a means to learn more about your collecting interests and possible ways to increase your collection through stamp trading and auctions. There is no actual studying required, just an interest in sharing your knowledge, or a desire to learn more about the stamps you collect, and more fun adventures with your collection. There are no special requirements to join any Stamp Clusters other than being a JPA member. It does not matter how long you have been a member, your age, or your knowledge about a particular subject. Even foreign members can join Stamp Clusters. There are no additional dues required to participate in any Stamp Clusters and you need no special equipment. All you need is an interest in learning more about the stamps you collect. You may even join more than one Cluster. You will be able to explore and participate in such activities as

- Contests and games
- Auctions
- Columnist for *The Philatelic Observer*
- Pen pals
- Adult mentors
- Chairing a Stamp Cluster
- Creating new Stamp Clusters
- Exhibiting your stamps

Many fun opportunities await you when you join a Stamp Cluster. You find that members are excited about the stamps they collect and want to share their enthusiasm and knowledge with other JPA members.

What Stamp Clusters Are Currently Available?

- Asia Stamp Cluster—Sara Reis

Do you have an interest in the Orient? How about the East Indies? Or the Himalayas? Then join the Asian Stamp Cluster! Our purpose is to try and learn what little bits we can of the world's largest land mass, from the Ural Mountains to the Pacific Ocean. It's an open forum about Asia, where we all can talk about the countries, topics, and other things that we want to talk about.

- Canadian Stamp Cluster—Tyson Evensen

The Canadian Stamp Cluster is finally out of the grave and back in full motion. If you want to join this fun and informational group, please send me a request! Expect articles, information, and a contest or two. If anyone signing up could write an article on Canadian stamps, that would be great. Look in the Observer for Tyson's address.

- European Stamp Cluster—Todd Richard

Do you collect European stamps and would like to join a free group that gives you the opportunity to participate in contests, quizzes, and write articles for The Philatelic Observer? If your answer is yes and you are a JPA member, the European Stamp Cluster is for you.

- First Day Cover Stamp Cluster—Erik Tomsen

If you're a member of the JPA, then why not join the FDCSC?

The FDCSC (First Day Cover Stamp Cluster) specializes in the study of First Day Covers. Even if you don't collect FDCs, they're a lot of fun to learn about—why not give it a shot? Who knows . . . you may even learn so much about FDCs that you'll want to start collecting them, too!

• Historical Stamp Cluster—Paul Daugherty

Learn about the history of the world in a fun way, the Historical Stamp Cluster! Going back in time by the method of philately, we can see the World War (etc.) all over again, by games, puzzles, a newsletter, and much, much, more! Do you want to join? Or do you have a question or a comment?

• Topical Stamp Cluster—Tyne Rice-Narusch

If you are a JPA member and enjoy any topic of stamps, then this is the Stamp Cluster for you! In our bimonthly newsletter, the Variety, we have a certain topic that the members help decide! There are also contests, prizes, etc., and this is all free!

• U.S. Stamp Cluster—Julie Daly

Join the U.S. Stamp Cluster, and see what all the fuss is about! Keep up-to-date on U.S. stamp news with the full-color newsletter The American Essence. Participate in group discussions, quizzes, contests. Build your collection with the trading circuit and classified ads, plus take part in activities and earn prizes.

• Women on Stamps Cluster—Emily Veysey

Do you collect famous women on stamps—or is this a subject that interests you? Join this Stamp Cluster and the fun is just beginning! Learn more about the famous women found on stamps all over the world while having fun with all sorts of games and quizzes.

How Long Can I Stay in a Stamp Cluster?

All questions, comments, or concerns concerning the JPA Cluster Program should be directed to Alison Turtledove (alcyone175@aol.com), Second V.P.

Participation in any given Stamp Cluster is solely up to the individual JPA member. Not all members will be interested in participating in a Stamp Cluster. There are no time constraints on any member of the JPA. We hope that you'll enjoy the activities provided in the Stamp Cluster program so much that you will participate indefinitely.

How Do I Get More Information about Joining a Study Cluster?

The Philatelic Observer contains a listing of current Stamp Clusters along with the name and address of the Chairperson. Simply contact the Chairperson for the Stamp Cluster you are interested in joining. For general information about the Stamp Clusters, contact the JPA Second Vice President.

How Do Stamp Clusters Correspond?

The Stamp Cluster Chair can provide you with a list of names and addresses of the members in your Stamp Cluster. Correspondence is usually carried on directly between members of that particular Stamp

Cluster or through articles and columns in the Observer. Your Stamp Cluster Chair's address can be found on the inside front cover of the *Observer*. (Please include a #10 SASE.)

How to Start a New Stamp Cluster

While the current Stamp Cluster program covers many popular areas of stamp collecting, there are undoubtedly JPA members who collect stamps that don't fit into any one of the established groups. Any active member may emerge as the leader of the proposed Stamp Cluster. This member should have significant contact with other interested JPA members. A formal request is sent to the President and Second Vice President (Coordinator of the Stamp Clusters) by postal mail. This request should include the proposed name of the cluster; proposed Chairperson's name, age, address, and JPA No.; and the names, addresses, and JPA Nos. of other interested members. A brief statement on how this Stamp Cluster will benefit JPA should be included in your submission. Upon approval for the new Cluster and the appointment of the Chair by the President, a new Cluster can be formed.

What Activities Are Offered in the Observer?

Most of the activities of a Stamp Cluster center around the concepts of education, encouragement, and the fellowship of stamp collecting.

The Philatelic Observer—Allows Stamp Cluster members and Adult Supporting Mentors the opportunity to submit articles and columns relating to their Stamp Cluster topic. Through these columns and articles you will be able to participate in such activities as

- Auctions
- Contests
- Educational articles
- Games
- Stamp Cluster quizzes

Columnist for the Observer—Ideas for columns and articles may be submitted to the Stamp Cluster Chair or the editor of the *Observer*. You should furnish both the Chair and the editor a copy of your article or column. It is not mandatory to write for the newsletter, but if you have an interesting subject to share, why not give it a try? The Stamp Cluster Chairperson can provide you with information for resources relating to your Stamp Cluster topic when participating as a columnist for the *Observer*.

Stamp Cluster Quizzes—Generally follow an article or column pertaining to an individual Stamp Cluster. These quizzes may be submitted to the Stamp Cluster Chairperson either by the writer of an article or by any member of a group. Directions for participation are always included, and usually a philatelic prize is offered to the winner. (Winners of such quizzes and contests are usually listed in Recent Winners.)

Contests—Related to a particular area of study may take any form such as an essay, stamp design, cacheted covers, etc. Ideas for contests may be submitted by members of a Stamp Cluster to the Chairperson. These contests may also be sponsored by a member of the Advisory Council, the Educational Director, an Adult Advisor, or another philatelic society.

Games—Featured on the "Fun Page," may be submitted to the editor of the *Observer* or to the Stamp Cluster Chair. Word search and crossword puzzles, logic problems, cryptograms, and matching games are very popular with many of the readers.

Auctions—Relating to specific Stamp Cluster interests usually take the form of a mini lot auction. These auctions generally contain ten or less items. Auction lots usually consist of donated materials and are generally sponsored by the Educational Director or by an adult advisor to a particular Stamp Cluster. All junior members of JPA may bid on lots featured. The instructions for any type of auction will appear in the *Observer* preceding the auction lots. Money received from the successful bidders of these auctions is used to support and improve the JPA programs.

Newsletters—Many Stamp Clusters have their own newsletters. These newsletters may be circulated by the Stamp Cluster Chair.

What Other Activities Are Offered?

Recruit new members to any Stamp Cluster by writing a welcome letter to new members. Often new members will list their collecting interests, which will give you an opportunity to include them in your Stamp Cluster. If you need more information about recruiting new members to your Stamp Cluster, contact your Stamp Cluster Chairperson.

Pen Pals—Matching your collecting interests may be available through the Pen Pals Service. The coordinator of the Pen Pals Service often receives inquiries from youth groups in other countries requesting pen pals for their youth. To find out more information about JPA's Pen Pal Service, write to the coordinator listed in the Departments and Services Directory.

Contests sponsored by other philatelic societies or periodicals may occasionally appear in *The Philatelic Observer*. These contests may take the form of essays, mini exhibits, or quizzes. All JPA members are encouraged to participate in these contests.

The Stamp Cluster Chair can provide you with a list of names and addresses of the other members of the Stamp Cluster if you wish to establish a pen pal just within the Stamp Cluster you belong to.

Is There Assistance for a Stamp Cluster?

Write to the Second Vice President for assistance with all aspects of your Stamp Cluster. Assistance available to your Cluster and/or individual members can include, but is not limited to, the following:

- Sample letters
- Adult supporting member mentors
- Auctions, contests, and quizzes
- Pen pal service
- Library services, including research support for columnists
- Information about foreign postal administrations
- Information about other societies specializing in your Cluster's interests
- Adult mentors for exhibiting

Additional assistance can be obtained from the Board of Directors and JPA Officers. Their addresses can be found in the Departments and Services Directory located in the *Observer*.

How Do You Become a Stamp Cluster Chair?

The Chairperson of a Stamp Cluster is appointed by the JPA President and works directly with the Second Vice President, who is the coordinator of the Stamp Clusters. Vacancies are announced in the *Observer*. Since JPA members live all over the United States and in other countries, the majority of Stamp Cluster contact will be made through the *Observer* and through letter writing. A candidate for a Chairperson position should have good communication and organizational skills. The Chairperson of each Stamp Cluster is the leader and coordinator of the activities of the Cluster. They are responsible for Clusters' activity updates, recruiting new members, trading programs, and establishing relationships with adult supporting member mentors.

Chairperson Stamp Cluster Kit—Currently in the works for and will be available exclusively to a Stamp Cluster Chair. The kit is a user-friendly tool to help organize and guide Chairs with their responsibilities and Cluster's activities. Each Chair will be responsible for the care and updating of this resource kit.

How Can I Get Exhibiting Help from a Stamp Cluster?

A Stamp Cluster is a great place to start when you are interested in exhibiting. The Stamp Cluster Chair can match you with an adult supporting member mentor who can advise you on the exhibiting process, inform you about the entry process, and even critique your exhibit.

How Can Adult Supporting Members Get Involved with JPA Stamp Clusters?

Adult supporting members are the most valuable resource to any Stamp Cluster. Many adults have many years of expertise and knowledge about philately. They may participate by

- Answering questions of individuals or Stamp Cluster Chairs
- Assisting a Stamp Cluster Chair with mailing lists and updating the Chair's resource kit
- Submitting articles or columns for publication
- Assisting with contests
- Developing and/or coordinating auctions with the Stamp Cluster Chairperson or the Educational Director
- Designing games or puzzles
- Facilitating trading or exchange programs
- Mentoring individual members with an exhibiting project

The best way to support youth in philately is to get involved. The Stamp Cluster Mentorship allows you to actively participate in youth philately within your own boundaries and sharing your expertise in a particular area of philately.

Any adult supporting member interested in getting involved and nurturing future philatelists should contact the Membership Services Department, which coordinates adult supporting member mentorships with the Second Vice President. Their names and addresses can be found in the Departments and Services Directory located in the *Observer*.

THE AMERICAN
PHILATELIC SOCIETY

The American Philatelic Society is an internationally recognized association of both stamp experts and enthusiasts that offers a number of services and educational opportunities for stamp collectors. The APS is the national representative to the International Federation of Philately (FIP) and is affiliated more than 650 local stamp clubs (APS chapters) and nearly 200 "specialty groups" (APS affiliates).

Anyone may browse the 200,000+ items currently offered for sale at www.stampstore.org, the Society's online sales site, but buying and/or selling is a privilege of membership. The online site features some rarities and more expensive stamps, in addition to many modestly priced items.

The services that are available with an APS membership include a monthly subscription to *The American Philatelist*, one of the premier stamp magazines in the world, as well as numerous other brochures and publications that are available at a discount to members. The APS Sales Division provides an opportunity for collectors to buy or sell stamps through the mail. Members may request "circuits" of stamps or covers in more than 160 categories of countries and topics. The items are priced by the submitting members, and most range from under $1 to $20.

The APS also provides an insurance program for members living in the United States, Canada, the United Kingdom, and many other countries. The insurance policy does not require a detailed inventory, only a general description of a collection and a value estimate, and may be applied for along with APS membership.

In addition to the APS, the American Philatelic Center also houses the American Philatelic Research Library, with a wide range of resource material encompassing thousands of books, journals, auction catalogs, and other material that are loaned or photocopied and available to members by mail for a nominal fee. The APRL publishes the *Philatelic Literature Review*, a quarterly journal covering literature of interest to collectors. The magazine is available by separate subscription.

The APS offers a weeklong Summer Seminar on Philately that features hands-on instruction by prominent experts. In addition, the APS Education Department produces many brochures and other materials and answers inquiries from beginner and intermediate collectors on various "how-to" aspects of the hobby.

Other APS services include authentication of members' stamps by the APEX expertizing service, estate advice, a translation service for international trading, and an annual convention-exhibition stamp show.

THE AMERICAN PHILATELIST

The Society's monthly magazine, which is included in the membership fee, features regular columns on U.S. stamps, stamp clubs, exhibitions, topical collecting, and more; articles by experienced philatelists; how-to columns on using the Society's Sales Division; and detailed listings of all new stamps and postal stationery issued by the U.S. Postal Service.

MEMBERSHIP INFORMATION

The APS offers a variety of memberships including special rates for other family members, foreign members, and lifetime memberships. The Society operates on a calendar year. Initial membership fees are pro-rated on a quarterly basis and include a $3 admission fee. The current schedule of membership fees is listed below.

Application received by	Membership Fee		
APS National Headquarters	U.S.	Canada	Other Countries
October, November, December	$38.00	$41.00	$48.00
January, February, March	29.25	31.50	36.75
April, May, June	20.50	22.00	25.50
July, August, September	11.25	12.50	14.25

For more information, call or write the American Philatelic Society at:

APS

100 Match Factory Place
Belleforte, PA 16823
(814) 933-3803, FAX (814) 933-6128
E-mail: apsinfo@stamps.org

For those with access to the Internet, the APS maintains a Web site at http://www.stamps.org. The site contains current APS news, such as minutes of recent official meetings and upcoming events; access to the American Philatelic Research Library; descriptions of member services;

online StampStore, listings of books and other items for sale by the APS; educational courses; youth activities; free beginning stamp course; and an online membership application form. The page also has links to many other philatelic sites on the Internet.

Members also may sign up for online correspondence courses on different aspects of the hobby.

LOCAL STAMP CLUBS

Numerous local stamp clubs exist all across the country, far too many to mention individually. Most hold regular meetings, often featuring presentations or slide programs by established collectors, and many permit trading sessions, an activity enjoyed by all. Newcomers, especially, find local stamp clubs useful in enriching their understanding and appreciation of the hobby. Some, either individually or in concert with other local clubs, sponsor annual stamp shows that feature exhibits as well as a dealer bourse.

Many local clubs are chapters of the American Philatelic Society. The APS Chapter Activities Committee serves as a focal point for services available to local stamp clubs. The committee publishes a quarterly newsletter, sponsors a publications contest, and conducts other programs for local clubs. APS chapters may schedule APS Sales Division circuits and philatelic slide programs produced by the Society exclusively for use by chapters for their meetings. Information about local APS chapters can be obtained from the APS, 100 Match Factory Place, Belleforte, PA 16823; (814) 933-3803; or on the APS Web site www.stamps.org.

Information about local clubs that are not APS chapters often can be obtained by checking with a local stamp dealer or clerk in the nearest Postal Service philatelic center.

HOUSE OF COLLECTIBLES SERIES

Title	ISBN	Price	Author
The Official® Price Guides to			
America's State Quarters	0609807706	$6.99	Ganz
American Arts & Crafts, 3rd ed.	060980989X	$21.95	Rago
American Patriotic Memorabilia	0609810146	$16.95	Pollack
Classic Video Games	0375720383	$16.95	Ellis
Clocks	0609809733	$19.95	Korz
Collecting Books, 4th ed.	0609807692	$18.00	Tedford/Goudey
Collector Knives, 14th ed.	1400048346	$17.95	Price
Collector Plates, 7th ed.	0676601545	$19.95	Rinker Ent.
Costume Jewelry, 3rd ed.	0609806688	$17.95	Miller
Dinnerware of the 20th Century	0676600859	$29.95	Rinker
Glassware, 3rd ed.	067660188X	$17.00	Pickvet
Hake's Character Toys, 4th ed.	0609808222	$35.00	Hake
Hislop's International Fine Art	0609808745	$20.00	Hislop
Indian Arrowheads, 8th ed.	0609810537	$26.00	Overstreet
Kiss Collectibles	1400050294	$18.00	Floren
Military Collectibles, 6th ed.	0676600522	$20.00	Austin
Mint Errors, 6th ed.	0609808559	$15.00	Herbert
Movie Autographs and Memorabilia	1400047315	$20.00	Cohen
Native American Art	0609809660	$24.00	Reno
Overstreet Comic Book Grading Guide	0609810529	$24.00	Overstreet/Blumberg
Overstreet Comic Books, 34th ed.	1400046696	$25.00	Overstreet
Overstreet Indian Arrowheads, 7th ed.	0609808699	$24.00	Overstreet
Pottery & Porcelain, 8th ed.	0876378939	$18.95	Duke
Quilts, 2nd ed.	1400047978	$16.00	Barach
Records, 16th ed.	0609809083	$25.95	Osborne
Vintage Fashion and Fabrics	0609808133	$17.00	Smith
The Official® Guides to			
Coin Grading and Counterfeit Detection, 2nd ed.	0375720502	$19.95	PCGS
Flea Market Prices, 2nd ed.	1400048893	$14.95	Rinker
How to Make Money in Coins Right Now, 2nd ed.	0609807463	$14.95	Travers
Directory to U.S. Flea Markets, 8th ed.	0609809229	$14.00	Werner
One-Minute Coin Expert, 4th ed.	0609807471	$7.99	Travers
Stamp Collector's Bible	0609808842	$22.00	Datz
The Official® Beckett Sports Cards Price Guides to			
Baseball Cards 2005, 25th ed.	0375721002	$7.99	Beckett
Basketball Cards 2006, 14th ed.	0375721045	$7.99	Beckett
Football Cards 2006, 24th ed.	0375721029	$7.99	Beckett
The Official® Blackbook Price Guides to			
U.S. Coins 2006, 44th ed.	1400048443	$7.99	Hudgeons
U.S. Paper Money 2006, 38th ed.	1400048451	$6.99	Hudgeons
U.S. Postage Stamps 2006, 28th ed.	140004846X	$8.99	Hudgeons
World Coins 2006, 9th ed.	1400048478	$7.99	Hudgeons
Instant Expert			
Collecting Oriental Rugs	0375720448	$12.95	Ware
Collecting Teapots	0375720456	$12.95	Rousmaniere
Collecting Art Deco	0375720421	$12.95	Fusco
Collecting Books	0375720545	$12.95	Budman

The Blackbooks!

| 1-4000-4844-3 | 1-4000-4845-1 | 1-4000-4847-8 | 1-4000-4846-X |
| $7.99 (Canada: $11.99) | $6.99 (Canada: $10.99) | $7.99 (Canada: $11.99) | $8.99 (Canada: $12.99) |

The leading authorities on U.S. coins, U.S. postage stamps, and world coins!

All national bestsellers, these dynamic books are the *proven* annual guides for collectors in these fields!

● **Coins**—Every U.S. coin evaluated . . . features the American Numismatic Association Official Grading System
● **Paper Money**—Every government-issued note covered
● **World Coins**—Features the most popular and collectible foreign coins from forty-eight countries around the world
● **Postage Stamps**—Brings the current value of each U.S. postage stamp along with its illustration on every page

BUY IT ● USE IT ● BECOME AN EXPERT™

Available from House of Collectibles in bookstores everywhere!